American Literature

Other titles in *The Essential Glossary* series

FRENCH CULTURE AND SOCIETY   Michael Kelly
SPANISH CULTURE AND SOCIETY   Barry Jordan
GERMAN CULTURE AND SOCIETY   Holger Briel
FRANCOPHONE STUDIES   Margaret Majumdar

Forthcoming

POST-COLONIAL STUDIES   John Thieme
IRISH STUDIES   John Goodby
ROMANTICISM   John Strachan
SEXUALITY   Jo Eadie

American Literature
The Essential Glossary

Stephen Matterson
School of English, Trinity College, University of Dublin

A member of the Hodder Headline Group
LONDON
Distributed in the United States of America by
Oxford University Press Inc., New York

First published in Great Britain in 2003 by
Arnold, a member of the Hodder Headline Group,
338 Euston Road, London NW1 3BH

http://www.arnoldpublishers.com

Distributed in the United States of America by
Oxford University Press Inc.,
198 Madison Avenue, New York, NY10016

The advice and information in this book are believed to be true and
accurate at the date of going to press, but neither the authors nor the publisher
can accept any legal responsibility or liability for any errors or omissions.

British Library Cataloguing in Publication Data
A catalogue record for this book is available from the British Library

Library of Congress Cataloging-in-Publication Data
A catalog record for this book is available from the Library of Congress

ISBN 0 340 80703 2 (hb)
ISVN 0 340 80704 0 (pb)

1 2 3 4 5 6 7 8 9 10

Typeset in 10/12pt Minion by Phoenix Photosetting, Chatham, Kent
Printed and bound in Great Britain by MPG Books Ltd, Bodmin, Cornwall

What do you think about this book? Or any other Arnold title?
Please send your comments to feedback.arnold@hodder.co.uk

The dichotomy is not between realists and artists. There must be few pure realists and few pure artists. We are hybrids absorbed in hybrid literature.

Wallace Stevens

It has been our fate as a nation not to have ideologies, but to be one.

Richard Hofstadter

I asked the captain what his name was
And how come he didn't drive a truck:
He said his name was Columbus;
I just said 'Good luck.'

Bob Dylan

Contents

Introduction   ix
Acknowledgements   xi

Glossary   1

Bibliography   247

Index of writers and works   287

Introduction

The aims of this Glossary are reasonably modest, and it is intended to be of use to students of American literature at all levels. It is intended also to be useful for anyone studying American history or American studies who needs an awareness of American literature and a reliable reference guide. I hope that it will have a place alongside other reference books, and that as well as being accurate and concise when consulted for reference, it will also be a point of departure for further study. Its relative shortness should make it obvious that it makes no pretence at being an exhaustively inclusive reference work. It might be as well to point out a few of the other things that the book is not and which it doesn't do: it isn't a glossary of writers and literary works; it isn't a bibliography of American literature; it doesn't provide plot summaries of literary works, and it is not a narrative account of American literature. Certainly, there are entries on influential writers and on some important works of American literature, and many of the entries include brief suggestions for further reading. This Glossary mostly consists of more than four hundred entries on literary styles, traditions, movements, subjects and historical events that feature significantly in American literature. The entries have been chosen simply by trying to determine what would be useful for anyone studying American literature to know, or to be able to check quickly.

Accordingly, this book can be used in several ways. It can be used as a ready reference book, to check, for example, when Horatio Alger died, who was president in 1843, who were the members of the Violet Quill, and in what order the Leatherstocking novels were published. It can also be used for finding information on historical events that are frequently referred to by American writers, and, usually, entries on events such as the Salem witch trials, the Kennedy assassination and Nat Turner's Revolt will identify literary works in which the event is examined. In this way the Glossary should be a starting point for further reading, or for anyone doing research in a particular area, and it is in this spirit that many of the entries indicate three or four references to what I have found to be useful secondary material.

Because (unusually) this Glossary has an Index of Writers and Works, it can also be used for reference to the many writers and works mentioned in the Glossary that have no separate entry. If you need to find something, try the main entries first, but if that's no help, then use the index. Thus, if you need to check who wrote *The House on Mango Street* and when it was published, or the full title of Mary Rowlandson's narrative, then you can do that via the index. The index can also be used to follow through a range of references to writers and works, whether or not they also have individual entries. You can find out a reasonable amount concerning, say, John Greenleaf Whittier or *Pudd'nhead Wilson* by tracing the indexed references to various entries in which they appear. Within each entry, cross-references to other entries are indicated by small capital letters for the entry heading or related words. Also within each entry author dates are given for each author mentioned who does not have an individual entry.

I should say that I have very much enjoyed the eighteen months that I have spent preparing this book. I've reread (and read for the first time) many texts with great pleasure, I've entered areas that were not previously well-known to me, and I've revisited much American writing with the same sense of excitement and freshness that I had when I was an undergraduate. Throughout, it has been brought home to me again and again what an extraordinarily rich and varied literature the United States has. (To the horror of family, friends and colleagues, it has also given me ideas for about eighteen more books.) Writing this Glossary has been a challenge, and it has certainly entailed far more study and time than may seem evident from these relatively brief entries. But it has invariably been an enjoyable project and I hope that the pleasure I've had in working for and writing this book will be conveyed to those who are going to use it.

Stephen Matterson

Acknowledgements

I should like to thank the library staff at Trinity College, University of Dublin, for their friendliness and efficiency during the preparation of this Glossary, the library staff at the University of Louisiana in Baton Rouge for their assistance during my visit there in December 2001, and Trinity College for the research maintenance grant which made that visit possible. Even in my increasingly costive prose, 'Acknowledgements' would be the longest entry in this Glossary if I were to specify everyone who has helped in its preparation. I'm grateful to all who have listened, understood, cajoled. You know who I mean; thank you for enriching this book. I should like specifically to acknowledge Elena Seymenliyska, the original commissioning editor at Arnold, and the teachers who first guided me in my understanding of American literature: John Coggrave and the late Harold Sykes.

Abolitionism   The most extreme of the various movements dedicated to the abolition of American SLAVERY. Since colonial times there had been opposition to slavery, particularly from the QUAKERS, and there had been small anti-slavery movements since the 1780s, but it was in the early 19ᵗʰ century with the threat of the expansion of slavery into the Western territories that concerted resistance began. In 1831 William Lloyd Garrison (1805–79) began publishing the abolitionist newspaper *The Liberator* and founded the New England Anti-Slavery Society. This was followed in 1833 by the founding of the American Anti-Slavery Society, in which Garrison was also involved. Anti-slavery movements were never entirely united in their aims or their methods. While the abolitionists advocated immediate abolition without compensation, others had a gradualist approach, and others were opposed primarily to the introduction of slavery into the territories. 'Abolitionist' was a term of abuse in the South, but abolitionism was not widely accepted even in the North; many viewed the movement as extreme and dangerous, and there were many instances of violent attacks on abolitionists and their property. Some of this opposition was rooted in racism, and some arose from the fears of Northern workers over the possible flooding of the labour market if the slaves were freed. Others opposed abolitionism on the grounds that it threatened the existence of the Union by sectionalizing the United States over one issue, possibly leading to SECESSION, and that the CONSTITUTION permitted individual states to decide whether to allow slavery.

Garrison was a Christian militant, a PURITAN who defined abolitionism in terms of a holy mission, part of a moral crusade that was termed the 'Second Great Awakening'. (He called the South 'one great Sodom'.) As a pacifist, Garrison was reluctant to involve the abolition movement in violence, or even in politics, but as opposition to slavery deepened during the 1840s and 1850s, more extreme abolitionists emerged, who were keen to take direct action; JOHN BROWN'S RAID in 1859 was a potent example of such extremism. Eventually the abolitionist involvement in politics became inevitable, and the FREE SOIL PARTY and later the Republican Party arose from variants of abolitionism. Although the EMANCIPATION PROCLAMATION and the THIRTEENTH AMENDMENT ended slavery, many members of abolitionist movements were involved in other reform endeavours, such as pacifism, TEMPERANCE and the early FEMINIST MOVEMENT, which continued after the CIVIL WAR.

Creative writing was both stimulated by the anti-slavery cause and helped in the definition and furthering of that cause. Before the development of abolitionism, individual writers had attacked slavery, including Samuel Sewall (1652–1730); John Woolman (1720–72) in two essays, 'Some Considerations on the Keeping of Negroes'

1

(1754, 1762); Benjamin FRANKLIN in his 1790 satire 'On the Slave Trade', and J. Hector St John de Crèvecoeur (1735–1813) in his depiction of Charlestown in *Letters from an American Farmer* (1782). It was in the 1820s and 1830s, though, that the mass of anti-slavery pamphlets, speeches, poems, novels and narratives was published. Significantly, one aspect of abolitionism was in sponsoring publication of the SLAVE NARRATIVE, the testimony of ex-slaves. Such sponsorship could be problematic in that the narratives were shaped to the needs of the abolitionists rather than to the subjective self-expression of the individual (comparable to the way in which ex-slaves were exhibited at abolitionist meetings). Nevertheless the abolitionist cause provided a hitherto virtually non-existent means of publication to African American writers, and works by David Walker (1785–1830), Sojourner Truth (1797–1883), William Wells Brown (?1814–84), Frances E. W. Harper (1825–1911), Harriet Wilson (?1828–?63), Frederick DOUGLASS and Harriet JACOBS were widely disseminated and helped define the first phase of AFRICAN AMERICAN LITERATURE. Douglass founded his own abolitionist newspaper, *North Star*, in 1847.

The work of Harriet Beecher STOWE, which includes *Uncle Tom's Cabin* (1852), *A Key to Uncle Tom's Cabin* (1853) and *Dred: A Tale of the Great Dismal Swamp* (1856, based on NAT TURNER'S REVOLT), was almost certainly the most influential of all abolitionist writing. *Uncle Tom's Cabin* was especially important, a best-selling novel that was often dramatized and that supposedly led Abraham Lincoln to say to Stowe, in 1862, that she was 'the little woman who started this great war'. Other significant anti-slavery writers include Lydia Maria Child (1802–80), John Greenleaf Whittier (1807–92), Sarah Moore Grimké (1792–1873) and Angelina Emily Grimké Weld (1805–79).

Accounts of the abolitionists and anti-slavery movements include *The Abolitionist Legacy* by James M. McPherson (1975), *Anti-Slavery Reconsidered* (1979), edited by Lewis Perry and Michael Fellman, and *The Abolitionist Sisterhood* (1994) by Jean Fagan Yellin.

Abortion Abortion, which had long been practised by a variety of methods, was criminalized throughout the United States by 1900 through laws passed by individual states. These were enacted for several reasons, but they largely resulted from the American Medical Association's attempt to regulate unqualified medical practitioners. Abortion was still practised, and several groups were formed to assist women obtain abortions; the most famous was the Jane group, which operated in Chicago in the early 1970s. After the development of various women's movements demanding decriminalization in the 1960s, abortion became a contentious issue, often reflected in literature of the period. In their landmark 1973 judgment Roe v. Wade the SUPREME COURT declared state anti-abortion laws unconstitutional, since they invalidated constitutional guarantees of privacy. The judgment effectively decriminalized abortion within certain limits. Abortion has remained an often bitterly divisive social issue.

Literary depictions of abortion and examinations of it as a political, personal and legal issue appear in a wide range of poems, stories and novels, by writers including William FAULKNER, Ernest HEMINGWAY, Mary McCarthy (1912–89), Gwendolyn BROOKS, John Barth (b. 1930), John Updike (b. 1932), Joan Didion (b. 1934), Alice WALKER and Gloria Naylor (b. 1950).

Further reading

From Abortion to Reproductive Freedom (1990), edited by Marlene Gerber Fried; Contested Lives (1998) by Faye D. Ginsburg, and Abortion, Choice and Contemporary Fiction (1990) by Judith Wilt.

Abstract expressionism   Label applied to several linked movements in American painting that originated in New York during the 1940s and were highly influential from the late 1950s onwards. In varying degrees abstract expressionists shared a commitment to non-referential art and reacted against the conventions of REALISM. Some, notably Jackson Pollock (1912–56), developed a style that activated intuition and instinct. Some chose to ground their work in primitivism, some made use of surrealism, while some, notably Mark Rothko (1903–70), used large blocks of colour in what was termed 'colour field' painting. As well as Pollock and Rothko, prominent abstract expressionists include Willem De Kooning (1904–97), Clyfford Still (1904–80), Franz Kline (1910–62), Robert Motherwell (1915–91) and Helen Frankenthaler (b. 1928).

Absurd   Style of writing developed since 1945 in which the futility of human actions is emphasized, often through ludicrous or comic situations. The absurd is rooted in the philosophy of existentialism, and has been especially favoured by dramatists. Albert Camus, Eugène Ionesco and Samuel Beckett made the absurd especially influential in Europe; it has been less prominent in the United States. The plays of Edward Albee (b. 1928) and Arthur Kopit (b. 1937) use absurd elements, but the absurd has been most evident in fiction since the 1960s, notably in works by Joseph Heller (1923–99), Kurt Vonnegut (b. 1922), John Barth (b. 1930), Donald Barthelme (1931–89), Robert Coover (b. 1932) and Thomas PYNCHON. Prior to the development of the modern concept of the absurd, American writers often used absurdity, for instance comically in the TALL TALE tradition, or for satirical purposes, as in *Pudd'nhead Wilson* (1894) by Mark TWAIN and in the fiction of Nathanael West (1903–40).

Further reading

The Absurd Hero in American Fiction (1981) by David Galloway and A Cheerful Nihilism (1971) by Richard Hauck.

Adamic tradition   A theme much developed in American writing, especially by men. In this tradition, referring to the biblical Book of Genesis, the American hero is represented as a new Adam in the Garden of Eden. Both the essential innocence of the archetypal American hero and the sense of America as a fresh beginning are thereby emphasized. Many critics refer to this tradition, notably D. H. Lawrence in his *Studies in Classic American Literature* (1923), and it received its most influential examination in *The American Adam* (1955) by R. W. B. Lewis. Lewis focused on what he considered the beginnings of the Adamic myth in literature of the period 1820–60. He wrote of the insistence on 'the authentic American as a figure of heroic innocence and vast potentialities, poised at the start of a new history'. To this was added the task God assigned to Adam, of naming the new landscape and its objects. American poets, notably Walt WHITMAN, have taken very seriously this need to find a language appropriate to the 'new world'.

The Adamic tradition is a significant presence in the works of many diverse writers, including James Fenimore COOPER, Ralph Waldo EMERSON, Henry David THOREAU, Whitman, Henry JAMES, William Carlos WILLIAMS, Wallace STEVENS, F. Scott FITZGERALD, Ernest HEMINGWAY and J. D. Salinger (b. 1919). Some writers, notably Nathaniel HAWTHORNE, Herman MELVILLE and William FAULKNER, have developed the tradition to explore the tragic end of innocence.

The Adventures of Huckleberry Finn   Mark TWAIN's novel is one of the most influential and important works of American literature. First published in England in 1884 (American publication was delayed because an illustration of Uncle Silas had been rendered obscene by the addition of a penis), the novel is ostensibly a sequel to *The Adventures of Tom Sawyer* (1876), although it is fundamentally different in terms of language, character and point of view. Set in the Mississippi Valley of the 1840s, the story is told by the 12-year-old Huck and involves his escape from Widow Douglas, who has adopted him, the growth of his friendship with the runaway slave Jim and their adventures on the Mississippi as they journey south. Huck's moral development is the novel's major theme, and this development is evident in his decision to assist Jim in his quest for freedom. The adventures culminate in Huck being reunited with Tom Sawyer in Arkansas, an elaborate plan to free Jim, and the revelation that Jim had already been freed in the will of his owner Miss Watson, and that Tom knew this. The story ends with Huck disgusted at 'sivilization' and planning to renounce society and 'light out for the territory' alone.

The novel masterfully combines satire, ROMANCE, PASTORAL, comedy, BURLESQUE and tragedy. It has typically been regarded as a mythic novel for Americans, since Huck embodies characteristics of the American hero: openness, innocence, ingenuity, individuality, desire for freedom and a moral integrity that originates from within. The novel's influence derives also from Twain's use of the American vernacular for serious rather than for comic purposes. The river has also played a significant role in mythic readings of the novel. However, the work has always been controversial. Originally it was considered unsuitable for children because of its coarse language, violence and immorality. More recently it has been open to censure in the belief that it perpetuates racial stereotypes and racist language (in 1957 the NAACP declared it 'racially offensive'), and because of the narrow representation of women as domesticating and oppressive.

Further reading

Huckleberry Finn as Idol and Target (1997) by Jonathan Arac; *The Critical Response to Mark Twain's 'Huckleberry Finn'* (1991), edited by Laurie Champion, and *Satire or Evasion? Black Perspectives on 'Huckleberry Finn'* (1992), edited by James S. Leonard, Thomas A. Tenney and Thadious M. Davis.

African American literature   The history of African American literature may usefully be divided into five periods, and in each of these the prominent literature is both shaped by and helps to shape the social situation of blacks at the time. These periods are: the time of SLAVERY, 1746–1865; RECONSTRUCTION and after, 1865–1919; the HARLEM RENAISSANCE and MODERNISM, 1919–60; the BLACK ARTS MOVEMENT, 1960–70; and writing after 1970.

Until 1865 writing by African Americans is dominated by the fact of slavery. The first known writing by an African in the American colonies is a poem by Lucy Terry (?1730–1821) published in 1746. Like Olaudah Equiano (?1745–97) and Phillis WHEATLEY, Terry was born in Africa and brought to the colonies as a slave. Wheatley, a poet, was the first African American to publish a book (1773). Equiano wrote an important account of his life, published in 1789. This account prefigured the SLAVE NARRATIVE, which was to become the dominant genre in the first period of African American writing. Given the racist beliefs of the time, the very act of writing by an African American was important in demonstrating a capacity for higher thought and therefore as evidence of full humanity. The fugitive slave narrative flourished during the 1850s until emancipation. It typifies much later African American writing in aiming to alter the consciousness of its readership in an attempt to improve or draw attention to the social conditions of blacks. This sense of mission or purpose has often been considered a distinguishing feature of African American writing and it was especially evident between 1865 and 1919. In this period, prose literature and the essay are dominant, while poetry and drama are less in evidence. The essay form was an important weapon in fighting for social justice, and also for reflecting on the dilemmas facing the recently freed blacks. The great tradition of African American essay writing has its roots in this period, notably in the work of W. E. B. DU BOIS, and is linked to traditions of preaching and oratory. Influential prose writers include Charles W. Chesnutt (1858–1932) and James Weldon Johnson (1871–1938). Paul Laurence Dunbar (1872–1906) is an important poet, among the first to use black vernacular in poetry.

It is with the Harlem Renaissance that African American writing starts to thrive in all genres, with the poets Claude McKay (1889–1948), Sterling A. Brown (1901–89), Langston Hughes (1902–67) and Countee Cullen (1903–46) and the novelists Zora Neale HURSTON, Nella Larsen (1893–1964) and Jean Toomer (1894–1967). The renaissance was very much a northern urban movement, associated with modernism. It reflected the new confidence of urban blacks, yet even with this confidence there were still dilemmas to be confronted. In his 1926 essay 'The Negro Artist and the Racial Mountain' Langston Hughes criticized those writers who worked in what he considered white forms, condemning 'this urge within the race towards whiteness'. But the question of how to maintain a black identity in writing was an important one for the African American writer. For those like Hughes, the poet's use of black vernacular and black musical expression was an important positive statement of racial identity, but for others, such as Countee Cullen, this use of 'low' forms meant that the black artist would be marginalized from the mainstream of valued 'high' art.

This problem receded over time as the distinction between so-called 'high' and 'low' art became less pronounced, and as later African American poets, notably Gwendolyn Brooks, moved freely between Euro-American forms such as the sonnet and poetic forms based on African American vernacular. The period 1940–60, after the Harlem Renaissance and before the Black Arts Movement, was a time of great consolidation and developing diversity of African American writing. Several major writers emerged; in addition to Brooks there were the novelists and essayists Richard Wright, Ralph Ellison and James Baldwin and the dramatist Lorraine Hansberry (1930–65), whose *A Raisin in the Sun* (1959) was the first play by a black woman to be produced on Broadway. As ever, social concerns were necessarily evident, exacerbated by an increased expression of black anger and frustration, seen in works such as Wright's *Native Son* (1940). An intense debate developed between Wright, Ellison and Baldwin over the aesthetic status of the protest novel and the function of the aesthetic for the black writer.

It was the Black Arts Movement, however, which sought a fusion between aesthetics and social protest; as one of its leaders, Imamu Amiri Baraka, wrote in 1969, 'We want "poems that kill"'. The new black writing was strongly linked to new forms of militant social protest by blacks, more extreme than those evident in the CIVIL RIGHTS MOVEMENT. It was also expressive of a new pride in blackness and a renewed interest in the African origins of black Americans. As well as Baraka, key writers of the period include the poets Etheridge Knight (1931–85), Sonia Sanchez (b. 1934) and Nikki Giovanni (b. 1943), the novelist Alex Haley (1921–92), whose *Roots* (1976) became an influential best-seller, and the essayist Eldridge Cleaver (b. 1935). Black drama achieved a special prominence in this period, with Baraka being an important influence, and this period also saw the early work of August Wilson.

African American writing since 1970 has become more diverse than ever before, and it has notably seen the emergence of two major women writers, Toni Morrison (first African American to be awarded the NOBEL PRIZE FOR LITERATURE) and Alice Walker. Important poets include June Jordan (1936–2002), Michael S. Harper (b. 1938) and Rita Dove (b. 1952), while John Edgar Wideman (b. 1941), Jamaica Kincaid (b. 1949) and Gloria Naylor (b. 1950) are significant novelists. The essay tradition has continued, with important essays by Morrison, Walker, Jordan, Audre Lorde (1934–92), Ishmael Reed (b. 1938) and bell hooks (b. 1952). August Wilson has developed into a major American dramatist, his 1985 play *Fences* being a significant critical and popular success. In spite of the rich diversity of contemporary African American writing, many writers are united by an intensive interrogation into American history and share an awareness of the heritage of black writing. Where it was once considered marginal and of minority interest, African American literature has come to be a defining force in American writing.

For critical accounts of African American literature, see: *Blues, Ideology and African American Literature* by Houston A. Baker (1984); *The Signifying Monkey* (1988) by Henry Louis Gates, Jr; *African American Theatre* (1994) by Samuel A. Hay; *Liberating Voices* (1991) by Gayl Jones; *Doers of the Word* (1995) by Carla L. Peterson, and *The Black Columbiad* (1994), edited by Werner Sollors and Maria Deidrich. Two important recent anthologies are *The Norton Anthology of African American Literature* (1997), edited by Henry Louis Gates, Jr, and Nellie Y. McKay, and *Call and Response: The Riverside Anthology of the African American Literary Tradition* (1998), edited by Patricia Liggins Hill.

Agrarians   Group of Southern intellectuals formed in Tennessee in 1930, dedicated to the identification of the South as a distinct region. The group was formed partly in reaction to ridicule of the 'backward' South after the 1925 SCOPES TRIAL. The Agrarians fostered a conservative ideal of hierarchical pre-CIVIL WAR non-industrial Southern society, in reaction to what they saw as the dehumanizing scientific industrialism of the North. They were made up of historians and social scientists as well as critics and creative writers, and their first publication was a collection of essays (by 'Twelve Southerners') entitled *I'll Take My Stand* (1930), the title deriving from the Civil War song 'Dixie'.

Although the Agrarians were not exclusively literary, they had a significant impact on the development of Southern REGIONALISM and the SOUTHERN RENAISSANCE. Some of its key members, notably John Crowe Ransom (1888–1974), Allen Tate (1899–1979) and Robert Penn Warren (1905–89), had been members of the FUGITIVES, and after Agrarianism ended at the end of the 1930s were later to be significant in the development of NEW CRITICISM. Others associated with the group included John Gould Fletcher (1886–1950), Donald Davidson (1893–1968) and Cleanth Brooks (1906–94).

Further reading

The Southern Agrarians (1988) by Paul K. Conkin and A Band of Prophets (1982), edited by William C. Harvard and Walter Sullivan.

Alcoholism   Alcoholism has been a significant topic in American literature, and many American writers have been alcoholics. Literary representations of the alcoholic have varied considerably over time, and have generally reflected prevailing ideas about whether alcoholism is a voluntarily chosen behaviour, a physiological disease, a condition that has psychological origins, or whether it has a genetic cause. Depictions have ranged from demonization in 19th century TEMPERANCE literature to sophisticated examinations of alcoholism in the 20th century. Drinking has been especially associated with manliness. There has also been a large number of AUTOBIOGRAPHICAL works dealing with the experience of alcoholism; these include *John Barleycorn* (1913) by Jack London (1876–1916), F. Scott FITZGERALD's *The Crack-Up* (1945) and *A Drinking Life* (1994) by Pete Hammill (b. 1935). While alcoholism features prominently in many works, notably Ernest HEMINGWAY's *The Sun Also Rises* (1926), Fitzgerald's *Tender is the Night* (1934), and Eugene O'NEILL's LONG DAY'S JOURNEY INTO NIGHT (1956), it is dealt with directly in various texts, including *Ten Nights in a Barroom and What I Saw There* (1854) by Timothy Shay Arthur (1809–85), *The Lost Weekend* (1944) by Charles Jackson (1903–68), and the autobiographical novel *Recovery* (1973) by John Berryman (1914–72), which is concerned with the treatment administered under the programme of Alcoholics Anonymous, founded in 1935.

Writers who were alcoholics include O. Henry (1862–1910), London, O'Neill, Djuna Barnes (1892–1982), Fitzgerald, William FAULKNER, Hemingway, Raymond CHANDLER, Dorothy Parker (1893–1967), John Steinbeck (1902–68), John O'Hara (1905–70), John Cheever (1912–82), Jean Stafford (1915–79), Berryman, Hayden Carruth (b. 1921), Truman Capote (1924–84) and Raymond CARVER. In the 1990s it was estimated that there were up to 5.5 million alcoholics in the United States, or 4.2 per cent of the adult population. Of these, over 4.5 million were men and almost one million were women.

Further reading

The White Logic (1994) by John W. Crowley; *The Thirsty Muse* (1989) by Tom Dardis, and *Equivocal Spirits* (1987) by Thomas B. Gilmore.

Alger, Horatio Phenomenally successful writer of CHILDREN'S LITERATURE. With total sales of over 20 million copies, Alger has been one of the most widely read of all American authors. He was born in 1832 in Chelsea, Massachusetts, and after attending Harvard he was ordained a UNITARIAN minister in 1864. A scandal resulted in his leaving the ministry in 1866, and he published his first novel, *Ragged Dick; or, Street Life in New York with the Bootblacks*, in 1868. About 130 novels followed, in which the formula of *Ragged Dick* was much repeated. Alger died in 1899 in Natick, Massachusetts.

Typical of most of Alger's work, *Ragged Dick* tells of an orphaned shoeshine boy, Dick Hunter, who lives on the streets of Manhattan but eventually achieves a respectable position through determination, hard work, thrift and the ability to seize good fortune when it appears. The style is simple and the moral clear. Alger's emphasis is on the possibility of self-improvement for those who desire and deserve it and the focus is entirely on the individual (he never, for instance, criticizes the social conditions that lead to orphans living on the streets). Alger's narratives appealed primarily because they were such straightforward representations of the American ideal of self-achievement.

Later writers made sometimes sophisticated use of the Alger narrative, notably F. Scott FITZGERALD in THE GREAT GATSBY and in the 1924 short story 'Absolution', Nathanael West (1903–40) in *A Cool Million* (1934) and Ralph ELLISON in INVISIBLE MAN.

Further reading

The Fictional Republic (1994) by Carol Nackenoff and *The Lost Life of Horatio Alger* (1985) by Gary Scharnhorst and Jack Bales.

Allotment   The distribution of Native American reservation lands began officially with the assimilationist Dawes General Allotment Act of 1887. Under it, an agreed acreage of reservation land would become the property of individual Native Americans or families, with the expectation that it would be cultivated. Individuals were entitled to an allotment of 80 acres, families to 160, and allotment holders were entitled to become United States citizens. The act nullified original treaties that had specifically guaranteed reservation land as communal. Furthermore, it permitted any non-allotted land to be sold to non-Indians. The act had serious consequences for Native Americans. Few adjusted to farming the land, families were dispersed, many Indians became landless, and land purchase by non-Indians considerably reduced the areas of reservations. It has been estimated that by 1932 whites owned two-thirds of the 138 million acres the Indians had held before the act. In 1934 reforms passed with the Indian Reorganization Act prevented further sales to whites and attempted to restore land to communal ownership.

America   The name 'America' first appeared in 1507 on a map produced by a German cartographer, Martin Waldseemüller. The name applied to all of the lands known as the 'New World' or the 'Indies' and was coined to honour the Italian navigator Amerigo Vespucci, who had undertaken voyages to the Indies between 1499 and 1502. The map of the world produced by the Flemish cartographer Gerardus Mercator in 1538 helped further to establish the name, which was used to refer to both South and North America. While it is technically incorrect to use 'America' or 'American' when referring exclusively to the United States, custom and tradition have generally made the usage acceptable.

American Academy of Arts and Letters   Society that promotes American arts in a variety of ways, and which honours individual writers by election to membership. Originally founded in 1904, the academy was enlarged in 1976 after amalgamation with the American Institute of Arts and Letters. The American Academy of Arts and Sciences, founded in 1780, also seeks to promote American literature, and annually presents the Emerson-Thoreau Medal to a writer.

American Dream   Encompassing the Puritan belief in 'calling', Thomas Jefferson's ideal of an open society, the Protestant belief in work, Benjamin Franklin's financial opportunism, Emerson's self-reliance and Horatio Alger's fictional trajectory of rising in the world, the American Dream has been perhaps the primary ideological means by which Americans have defined themselves in contrast to other nations. In its purest form the American Dream is an ideal for society rather than for the individual, being a vision of a society that permits individuals to develop their potential without reference to their background or origins. Thus it is about a society that fosters opportunity and fulfilment, and not about individual success or accumulation of wealth. The term 'American Dream' was used in its modern sense in the 1930s, and the historian James T. Adams is credited with popularizing it. In *The Epic of America* (1931) he wrote:

> [the] American dream that has lured tens of millions of all nations to our shores in the past century has not been a dream of merely material plenty, though that has doubtless counted heavily. It has been much more than that. It has been a dream of being able to grow to fullest development as man and woman, unhampered by the barriers which had slowly been erected in older civilizations, unrepressed by social orders which had developed for the benefit of classes rather than for the simple human being of any and every class.

In *Facing Up to the American Dream* (1995), Jennifer L. Hochschild usefully identifies four tenets of the dream. They are: that everyone may participate equally in society; that everyone may have a reasonable anticipation of success; that success comes from one's own efforts, and that failure is a result of lack of talent or will.

The American Dream is the subject of innumerable American texts. The immense popularity of works such as those of Alger testifies to the power of belief in the dream. It has also been much criticized in literature, on various grounds, for example: that the material aspect of the dream is a corruption of its social vision; that it is an illusion through which inequalities are maintained and class realities are concealed; that it fosters individual achievement at the expense of social progress; that it supports ruthless plutocracy; that it equates personal fulfilment with material gain, and that it results in a narrowly selfish definition of success.

American epic   See Epic.

American Indian Movement (AIM)   Group founded in Minneapolis, Minnesota, in 1968 to defend the rights of Native Americans. At first AIM focused on the injustices experienced by urban-based American Indians, then it developed into an organization campaigning for the rights of all Native Americans. It has especially sought to draw attention to the United States government's breaking of treaties regarding American Indian autonomy and land rights, and to the exploitation of lands and resources by the mining and forestry industries. AIM has organized a series of high-profile protests, including occupations of Alcatraz Island (1969–71), Wounded Knee (1973) and areas of the Black Hills (1981). AIM's use of illegal methods has led to the imprisonment of many members. The most prominent and controversial of these is Leonard Peltier, who was sentenced to two life sentences after two FBI agents were killed during a shootout on Indian land in 1975.

AIM and its campaigns are often referred to in contemporary Native American writing. Louise Errich (b. 1954) fictionalizes Leonard Peltier as a TRICKSTER in *Love Medicine* (1984, 1993), and Peter Matthiessen (b. 1927) examines the Peltier case in *In the Spirit of Crazy Horse* (written 1983, published 1991). Russell Means's autobiography *Where White Men Fear to Tread* (1995) provides a valuable insight into the movement.

American Literature   Leading quarterly journal that publishes critical articles on American literature. It was founded in 1929 as the publication of the American literature division of the MODERN LANGUAGE ASSOCIATION and is published by Duke University.

American Renaissance   Term applied to the period *c.* 1830–65 during which American writing flourished. This period saw the development of a native writing that dealt with American themes in idioms that were specifically American rather than being imitative of British writing. These themes included the legacy of American history, a confrontation with the American landscape, the frontier, the nature of DEMOCRACY, and a fresh awareness of America's place in the world. A more confident use of American idiom and language was also characteristic of the period. Some of the most enduring and influential works of American literature were produced at this time. Key writers include COOPER, EMERSON, POE, HAWTHORNE, STOWE, MELVILLE, WHITMAN and DICKINSON, and TRANSCENDENTALISM was the most influential single literary movement. Although there had been previous references to a 'rebirth' of American writing, it was F. O. Matthiessen's influential study *American Renaissance* (1941) that coined the term for this period.

'The American Scholar'   Address by Ralph Waldo EMERSON, given to the Phi Beta Kappa society at Harvard University in 1837 and published later that year. The address is an important and influential statement of the role of the intellectual in American life and of the need for indigenous American thinking and writing.

There are three major strands of thought in 'The American Scholar'. Each is closely interwoven with the others and is also expressed in other essays, notably 'The

Divinity School Address' (1838), 'Self-Reliance' (1841) and 'The Poet' (1844). Each is also an aspect of Emerson's TRANSCENDENTALISM. The first strand is the ideal of 'Man Thinking', a realized individual who is independent from the thoughts of others and not awed by past achievements. Man Thinking is not a 'bookworm' but an imaginative reader; there is a need for 'creative reading as well as creative writing'. The second theme is the need for the creative imagination to embrace the local rather than the distant. This is expressed in two ways; firstly in a desire to write of the everyday: 'I embrace the common, I explore and sit at the feet of the familiar, the low.' Secondly, Emerson states the need for a writer who will express the here and now, who will find new forms appropriate to America: 'We have listened too long to the courtly muses of Europe.' Emerson's third theme is the need for American intellectual autonomy; this aspect led Oliver Wendell Holmes (1809–94) to call the address America's 'intellectual Declaration of Independence'. 'We will walk on our own feet; we will work with our own hands; we will speak our own minds,' is Emerson's rousing exhortation.

The ideas in 'The American Scholar' are echoed by many of Emerson's contemporaries and by later writers, including Henry David THOREAU (who was in the audience), Walt WHITMAN, Herman MELVILLE, Emily DICKINSON and Wallace STEVENS.

Anarchism   Although it may be narrowly defined as a political movement dedicated to the belief that society works best without authority or government, anarchism is better considered a moral or social position than a strictly political one. In the United States it has taken many forms, including the anti-institutional writings of Henry David THOREAU, some 19th century UTOPIAN works, the radical socialism of Emma Goldman (1869–1940), the beliefs of a series of groups dedicated to the violent overthrow of the state, and various 1960s movements opposed to the VIETNAM WAR. Politically, anarchism was most prominent in the period 1880–1914. This period saw several notorious acts of anarchist violence, notably the 1886 killing of seven police officers during the Haymarket riots in Chicago, and the assassination of President McKinley in 1901. Repressive measures followed McKinley's assassination, including a law barring foreign-born anarchists from the United States, and Emma Goldman was imprisoned and later deported. In the 1960s anarchism resurfaced in a less militant way as part of the decade's revaluation of authority, articulated in the writings of Paul Goodman (1911–72).

Antinomianism   Although the term refers to movements that existed in the early Christian church and during the Reformation, it is most often applied to a group of New England PURITANS led by Anne Hutchinson (1591–1643). The group believed in 'immediate revelation' – that is, that God spoke directly to individuals. It followed from this that individuals should obey personal intuition rather than church laws. The antinomians also believed in an extreme form of predestination: because God had predestined all of human history, it had also been decided irrevocably who was to be saved and who damned. Good works could not bring redemption; this contradicted the Puritan belief in a 'covenant of works' – that is, that moral conduct and charitable actions might be a 'preparation' for grace. Hutchinson and her followers were considered heretical and a threat to the existence of the church; consequently in 1637 she was tried, excommunicated and eventually banished. Hutchinson and her family moved to Rhode Island and later to Long Island, where she was killed in an Indian raid.

Anti-trust legislation   The 1880s saw the formation of trusts, which were effectively the consolidation of different, nominally independent companies. Public concern over the consequent threat of monopolies in particular industries led to state anti-trust legislation, but these laws proved ineffective, partly because corporations then created holding companies that functioned as the trusts had. In 1890 the United States Congress responded to concern by passing the Sherman Anti-Trust Act. For a decade the act was ineffective against corporations, but in the early years of the century a series of high-profile trusts were broken up. These included the Northern Securities Company (1902), the Du Pont Corporation (1907), the American Tobacco Company (1911) and Standard Oil (1911). The growth and power of trusts and monopolies were frequently scrutinized in contemporary literature, notably in the novels *The Octopus* (1901) by Frank Norris and *The Jungle* (1906) by Upton Sinclair (1878–1968), and in muckraking literature.

Apocalypse   In Jewish and in Christian tradition, apocalypse, meaning 'revelation', is the catastrophic intervention of God bringing the end of the world, the last judgment and the disclosure of divine mystery. Two biblical books, the Book of Daniel and the Book of Revelation, form the foundation for this tradition. Although apocalypse is the catastrophic end of the world, it is also about seeing a pattern to history and finding meaning for every event within that pattern. From colonial times to the present, apocalyptic writing has been a consistent and important strain in American literature and culture. Much of it has had a religious foundation, but a tradition of secular apocalyptism has also developed.

Within Puritanism, the apocalypse formed part of an overall belief in God's design for the universe and a belief in life as purpose and progress. One of the most widely read of all Puritan works, the poem *The Day of Doom* (1662) by Michael Wigglesworth (1631–1705), is apocalyptic, and so are many Puritan sermons and prose works. The writing of Jonathan Edwards (1703–58) in particular is suffused with a belief in the nearness of the apocalypse. Although over time such belief in the literal apocalypse waned, as did the influence of Puritanism, the apocalypse continued to hold a prominent place in many belief systems. During the 19th century it was explicitly developed in millennialism, but in the same period apocalypse was also increasingly secularized, as writers represented the world's end without God's intervention. Metaphorically represented, apocalypse was bound up with deep pessimism over America's future in works by Edgar Allan POE, Herman MELVILLE and Mark TWAIN. The non-religious apocalypse also became a feature of much SCIENCE FICTION, and remains so today. Another significant rhetorical troping of apocalypse originating in the 19th century has been in AFRICAN AMERICAN LITERATURE. Much African American oratory and writing about SLAVERY, for example, represented the apocalypse as God's promised retribution for the sin of slavery. This tradition continued after slavery, and apocalypticism figures strongly in the writing of Ralph ELLISON, James BALDWIN and Imamu Amiri BARAKA.

While apocalyptic writing was evident in the first half of the 20th century, notably in the novels of Nathanael West (1903–40), the very real possibility of the world's destruction by nuclear weaponry led to a renewed urgency in apocalyptic writing during the COLD WAR. While this is especially evident in science fiction, notably in the work of Kurt Vonnegut (b. 1922), it also motivated a wide range of writers, such as Robert LOWELL, Thomas PYNCHON and Bob Dylan (b. 1941). A further development of apocalyptic writing has been 'survivalist' literature, exploring the reshaping of human society after ecological or nuclear catastrophe. Notable examples in this large category include *The Long Tomorrow* (1955) by Leigh Brackett (b. 1915), *A Canticle for Lebowitz* (1960) by Walter M. Miller (1922–96) and *The Stand* (1978, 1989) by Stephen KING. For all its transformations, however, some modern apocalyptic writing has maintained a religious and spiritual dimension, for example in the novel *Love in the Ruins* (1971) by Walker Percy (1916–90) and the poem *The Changing Light at Sandover* (1983) by James Merrill (1926–95).

Further reading

After the End (1999) by James Berger; *Nuclear Annihilation and Contemporary American Poetry* (1996) by John Gery; *The Bang and the Whimper* (1984) by Zbigniew Lewecki; *Trials of the Word* (1965) by R. W. B. Lewis; *Imagining Apocalypse* (2000), edited by David Seed, and *Writing the Apocalypse* (1989) by Lois Parkinson Zamora.

Ariel   Posthumous collection of forty poems by Sylvia PLATH, first published in 1965. The American edition included an introduction by Robert LOWELL. *Ariel* explores a nightmarish world of menace, HORROR and repression in which an individual self, closely aligned with Plath herself, struggles to maintain integrity and resist the temptation to surrender to the forces that threaten to shape or destroy it. The book's tone varies between angry resentment, resignation, grim comedy, affection and hope for the future. The poems are highly sophisticated in formal terms and are imaginatively connected through recurrent imagery and through references to Shakespeare's Ariel from *The Tempest*. Although deeply personal at times, the collection has a significant public dimension, reflecting Plath's concern with public matters such as the aftermath of WORLD WAR II and the proliferation of nuclear weapons, although her use of imagery drawn from the HOLOCAUST has been heavily criticized. *Ariel*'s popularity did much to influence and define CONFESSIONAL poetry.

The book's publication has been somewhat controversial. Plath's widower Ted Hughes made the final selection of poems, and he included poems that Plath wrote after she considered *Ariel* complete, excluded others, and altered her proposed order for the poems. (Plath's list of *Ariel*'s contents is included in the notes to her *Collected Poems*.) Plath had planned *Ariel* as a sequence that started with the word 'Love' and ended with the word 'spring', in which a woman's terrible crisis and experience of mental illness would be dramatized, but also worked through towards resolution. One effect of Hughes's arrangement was to reduce the sense of dramatic sequence, thereby minimizing the context that certain poems required and also implying a movement in the book towards Plath's own death.

Further reading

Sylvia Plath: The Wound and the Cure of Words (1990) by Steven Gould Axelrod; Sylvia Plath and the Theatre of Mourning (1999) by Christina Britzolakis; Poetic License (1990) by Marjorie Perloff, and Inviolable Voice (1982) by Stan Smith. Hughes's poetry collection Birthday Letters (1998) provides an illuminating perspective on Ariel.

Armory Show   Name given to the International Exhibition of Modern Art, a major show of painting and sculpture held at the armoury of the 69th Regiment in New York City in 1913 and travelling later to Boston and Chicago. Although the display included American art, it was the European exhibits that caused a sensation, giving most Americans their first opportunity to see avant-garde works by the impressionists, postimpressionists and cubists. In addition to stimulating American art, the show was profoundly significant in the development of American literary MODERNISM.

Ashbery, John   Poet, born in Rochester, New York, in 1927. Ashbery attended university at Harvard and at Columbia, then worked in New York as an editor and copywriter before moving to Paris in 1955, where he worked as an art critic. Since returning to New York in 1965 he has taught at Brooklyn College and has received many distinguished awards and fellowships.

A member of the NEW YORK SCHOOL, Ashbery's first major publication was *Some Trees* (1956), followed by an experimental transitional work, *The Tennis Court Oath* (1962). Further collections, notably *Rivers and Mountains* (1966), *The Double Dream of Spring* (1970) and a long PROSE POEM, *Three Poems* (1972), consolidated his growing reputation before he published what are widely considered his two finest books, *Self-Portrait in a Convex Mirror* (1975) and *Houseboat Days* (1977). His other poetry collections include: *A Wave* (1984); *April Galleons* (1987); the long poem *Flow Chart* (1991); *Hotel Lautréamont* (1993); *And the Stars Were Shining* (1994); *Can You Hear, Bird* (1995); *Wakefulness* (1998); *Girls on the Run* (1999) and *Your Name Here* (2000). He has also published collections of essays on art and on poetry (notably *Other*

Traditions, 2000), several plays and a comic novel, *A Nest of Ninnies* (1969), co-written with James Schuyler (1923–91).

In a 1968 lecture Ashbery spoke of the importance of 'not planning the poem in advance, but letting it take its own way; of living in a state of alert and being ready to change your mind if the occasion seems to require it'. Typically his poems are suggestive discursive meditations which follow thought processes, accommodate apparent digressions and interruptions and do not present a subject in a conventional manner. A major POSTMODERN poet, his work encompasses a wide variety of styles with wit and insight; a poem may shift abruptly between heightened language and the demotic, between references to high art and popular culture and between the playful and the elegiac. He writes both in free-flowing unstructured verse and in highly challenging forms, as well as being a major exponent of the prose poem. Hostile to CONFESSIONAL poetry, Ashbery uses personal material reticently and obliquely, though there are occasional references to his homosexuality. Given their fluidity, their openness to interruptions, and their shifts in subject and tone, his poems may seem forbiddingly difficult to the reader looking for paraphrasable meanings – a fact that has generated some critical hostility.

Further reading

Modern Critical Views: John Ashbery (1985), edited by Harold Bloom; *John Ashbery and American Poetry* (2000) by David Herd; *Beyond Amazement: New Essays on John Ashbery* (1980) edited by David Lehman, and *On the Outside Looking Out* (1994) by John Shoptaw.

Asian American literature　Term coined in the late 1960s and now used to describe a wide variety of writing by Americans of Chinese, Filipino, Japanese, Korean, South Asian or Vietnamese background. Asian American literature is strongly and perhaps inevitably linked to the situation of Asians in American history and their often deeply racist representation in mainstream American culture; as Elaine Kim has stated, it is a literature that 'elucidates the social history of Asians in the United States'. It has been specifically concerned with IMMIGRATION, assimilation and intergenerational relationships. In generic terms, the novel and the SHORT STORY have been predominant, although the last two decades have seen the emergence of influential dramatists and poets. There has also been a strong emphasis on AUTOBIOGRAPHY, although some, notably Frank Chin (b. 1940), have argued that autobiography represents a Western and Christian tradition rather than an Asian one. Nevertheless, for a minority culture whose public history is unavailable or absent, autobiography performs a valuable service.

Broadly, Asian American literature has existed in two phases; the first characterized by claiming a visible identity in American culture, the second by asserting multiplicity and cultural fusion. As King-Kok Cheung has put it, there has been a broad shift from 'claiming America' to 'writing diaspora'. The first phase may be seen as a necessary response to the invisibility or the racist stereotyping of Asians in America. In the 19th century the Chinese were the first Asians to come to the United States in large numbers, although they were not permitted to become citizens, and the 1882 CHINESE EXCLUSION ACT outlawed immigration. The legal difficulties faced by the Chinese are often explored in Chinese American writing. Recurring motifs include the 'sojourner' (a labourer who does not intend to stay in the United States) and the 'paper son' (a fraudulent claim to naturalization rights made possible after the destruction of immigration records in the 1906 San Francisco earthquake and fire). One of the most remarkable collections of American poetry is that 'written on the walls', poems composed by Chinese immigrants temporarily detained for examination at Angel Island, San Francisco, between 1910 and the closing of the centre in 1940.

For the Chinese American writer the task of 'claiming America' has particularly involved emphasizing the part played by the Chinese in the settlement of the West, especially in the building of the transcontinental railway. Notable Chinese American works include: *Fifth Chinese Daughter* (1945) by Jade Snow Wong (b. 1922); *Eat a Bowl of Tea* (1961) by Louis Chu (1915–70) and *The Joy Luck Club* (1989) by Amy Tan (b. 1952). *THE WOMAN WARRIOR* (1976) by Maxine Hong KINGSTON has been considered a key text of Asian American literature. Not only was it acclaimed and accepted into mainstream American literature, but it also articulated the duality of identity confronted by Asian Americans while demonstrating the potential for intercultural fusion and enrichment. The last two decades have seen emerging voices in poetry and in drama; Cathy Song (b. 1955) and Li-Young Lee (b. 1957) are prominent poets, and Wakako Yamauchi (b. 1924) is a significant dramatist.

Where Chinese American literature has explored the twin themes of invisibility and immigration, Japanese American writing has often focused on intergenerational conflict, and on the treatment of Japanese Americans during WORLD WAR II. Japanese immigration mostly took place in the early years of the 20th century. First-generation immigrants are known as the *Issei* and the American-born second generation as the *Nisei*. After the outbreak of war between the United States and Japan, a loyalty oath was administered to Japanese Americans and many were interned in camps. This unjust and racist treatment has frequently been the subject of Japanese American writing, especially as it also involved conflict between the Issei and the Nisei. See especially the autobiography *Nisei Daughter* (1953) by Monica Sone (b. 1919) and the novel *No-No Boy* (1957) by John Okada (1924–71). The nature of the Japanese American community is explored in the short story collection *Yokohama, California* (1949) by Toshio Mori (1910–80), in stories by Hisaye Yamamoto (b. 1921) and the novel *All I Asking for is my Body* (1975) by Milton Murayama (b. 1923).

At first Chinese American and Japanese American writing tended to define Asian American literature; this was evident in the important anthology *Aiiieeeee!* (1974), edited by Frank Chin, Jeffery Paul Chan, Lawson Fusao Inada and Shawn Wong. *The Big Aiiieeeee!* (1991), and the anthology *Charlie Chan is Dead* (1993), edited by the

Filipino poet and dramatist Jessica Hagedorn (b. 1949), offered a broader representation of Asian Americans. This move directly reflected changing immigration patterns; there was much Filipino immigration from the 1920s onwards, and immigration from Asia rose after the 1965 Immigration and Nationality Act removed the quotas that had favoured Western European immigrants. *America Is in the Heart* (1946) by Carlos Bulosan (1913–56) is an influential Filipino text. The increasing diversity of Asian American writing that King-Kok Cheung has noted is reflected not only in the varied ethnic origins of the writers, but also in the multiple styles, voices and genres in which they work.

Further reading

An Interethnic Companion to Asian American Literature (1997), edited by King-Kok Cheung; *Asian American Literature: An Introduction to the Writings and their Social Context* (1982) by Elaine Kim; *Imagining the Nation: Asian American Literature and Cultural Consent* (1998) by David Leiwei Li; 'Emergent Literatures' by Cyrus R. K. Patell, in *The Cambridge History of American Literature*, Volume VII (1999), edited by Sacvan Bercovitch, and *Asian American Literature: A Brief Introduction and Anthology* (1996) edited by Shawn Wong.

Atlantic Monthly   Literary and current affairs journal founded in Boston in 1857 by Moses Dresser Phillips and Francis H. Underwood. The journal was especially associated with the BRAHMINS of New England. It was first edited by James Russell Lowell (1819–91), and later editors included William Dean Howells (1837–1920), who used it to champion REALISM. During the 1920s the magazine broadened its coverage of political issues, and since 1981 has been officially known as the *Atlantic*. Contributors have included Ralph Waldo EMERSON, Henry Wadsworth Longfellow (1807–82), Oliver Wendell Holmes (1809–94), Harriet Beecher STOWE, Thomas Wentworth Higginson (1823–1911), Mark TWAIN, Bret Harte (1836–1902), Henry Adams (1838–1918), Henry JAMES, Sarah Orne Jewett (1849–1909) and Kate CHOPIN. The classic novella *Life in the Iron Mills* by Rebecca Harding Davis (1831–1910) was first published in the journal in 1861.

Autobiography   Defined by Phillipe Lejeune in 'The Autobiographical Pact' (1971) as a 'retrospective prose narrative written by a real person concerning his own existence, where the focus is his individual life, in particular the story of his personality'. Appropriately for a culture that values self-becoming, individuality and self-expression, autobiography has had a significant place in American literature. This is evident not only in the number and quality of conventional autobiographies but also in the large number of autobiographical gestures in poetry and in fictional prose, and in the value attached to authenticated personal narrative such as the journal, the CAPTIVITY NARRATIVE and the SLAVE NARRATIVE.

In PURITANISM autobiography was an appropriate form of self-examination in order to ascertain God's purpose and design. Much Puritan writing has a strongly personal, self-scrutinizing dimension, and two of the most influential American autobiographies, *A Personal Narrative* (1740) by Jonathan Edwards (1703–58) and *Autobiography* (1818, 1867) by Benjamin Franklin, are both shaped by Puritan concerns with tracing the workings of God's design in the history of the self. With its analysis of self-realization and fulfilment, Franklin's work is one of the texts that define American autobiography. However, autobiographical writing has served a wide variety of purposes. This is especially evident in autobiographies by members of minority groups and immigrants. Often the minority autobiography affirms the self's presence and thereby validates the existence of the group. This was certainly among the functions of the slave narrative, but has also been performed by a wide variety of autobiographies. Such a list includes *The School Days of an Indian Girl* (1900) by Gertrude Bonnin (1876–1938), *Up From Slavery* (1903) by Booker T. Washington (1856–1915), *Bread Givers* (1925) by Anzia Yezierska (1885–1970), *Black Boy* (1945) by Richard Wright, *The Autobiography of Malcolm X* (1964) by Malcolm X (1925–65) and Alex Haley (1921–92), *I Know Why the Caged Bird Sings* (1970) by Maya Angelou (b. 1928) and *The Woman Warrior* (1976) by Maxine Hong Kingston. A significant development in minority autobiography has been a challenge to the ideal of cultural assimilation, and an assertion of difference and a corresponding need to acknowledge the various cultures that exist under the term 'American'.

Other ways in which conventional American autobiography has expanded include the development of the 'relational' autobiography, in which the author writes primarily of a relation with another or with a group. Although this has long been considered a feature of autobiographies by American women, it is also used by men, in writing either of one other, as in *Patrimony* (1991) by Philip Roth, or of a family, as in *A Heartbreaking Work of Staggering Genius* (2000) by Dave Eggers (b. 1971). There has also been the development of 'fictive autobiography' in which the boundaries between the novel and autobiography are unclear. Many literary autobiographies illustrate this category, including *A Small Boy and Others* (1913) by Henry James, *Dust Tracks on a Road* (1942) by Zora Neale Hurston, *The Autobiography of Alice B. Toklas* (1933) by Gertrude Stein, *Speak, Memory* (1966) by Vladimir Nabokov (1899–1977) and *World's Fair* (1985) by E. L. Doctorow (b. 1931). Confessional poetry may also be considered a form of autobiography.

Where definitions and categories of American autobiography once seemed relatively stable, the intense variety of modern autobiography has challenged such stability. By the same token, however, the wide range of autobiographies testifies to the vitality and centrality of the genre.

Further reading

Fictions in Autobiography (1985) and How Our Lives Become Stories (1999) by Paul John Eakin; Studies in Autobiography (1988) edited by James Olney; Autobiographical Inscriptions (1999) by Barbara Rodriguez; The Autobiographical I (1992) by Liz Stanley, and Studies in Modern American Autobiography (1983) by Gordon O. Taylor.

The Autobiography of Alice B. Toklas   The most widely read and accessible work of Gertrude STEIN, first published in 1933. Told as if written by Stein's lover Toklas, the book is an informative and sometimes playful account of the life that the two women shared in Paris, of their intimacy with the leading figures in artistic and literary circles, and of Stein's aesthetic beliefs and writing practices. Although the memoir may be read for its representation of artistic life, its adoption of Toklas's point of view, its narrative technique, the deliberate inclusion of some factual inaccuracies and the book's challenge to standard autobiographical development all mean that it raises some searching questions regarding the nature and practice of AUTOBIOGRAPHY.

Further reading

'Gertrude Stein and the Problems of Autobiography' by James E. Breslin, reprinted in *Critical Essays on Gertrude Stein* (1986), edited by Michael J. Hoffman; *Gertrude Stein and the Making of Literature* (1988), edited by Shirley Neuman and Ira Nadel, and *Gertrude Stein, Modernism and the Problem of Genius* (2000) by Barbara Will.

B

Baldwin, James   An influential novelist and essayist, Baldwin was born in Harlem in 1924, and during a troubled childhood he was for a brief period (at the age of 11) a storefront preacher. He began publishing stories and essays in the 1940s. Richard WRIGHT encouraged Baldwin, but Baldwin's 1949 essay 'Everybody's Protest Novel', which was critical of *NATIVE SON* and the protest tradition, ended their friendship. Between 1948 and 1957 Baldwin lived in France. Returning to the United States he became active in the CIVIL RIGHTS MOVEMENT. After 1969 he divided his time between Europe and the United States, where he held a series of academic appointments. He died in France in 1987.

Baldwin wrote frequently about interracial sexual experiences and often about homosexuality. He published six novels, and the first three are usually considered the best. *Go Tell it on the Mountain* (1953) is semi-autobiographical; *Giovanni's Room* (1956) involves a homosexual white American in Paris, and *Another Country* (1962), set in New York, concerns the suicide of a black jazz musician. Much of Baldwin's finest writing however is in his essays, collected in *The Price of the Ticket* (1985). He incisively and eloquently analysed the contemporary racial situation, often adopting the role of explainer of African American culture to whites. Baldwin attempted to demythologize race, writing in 1965 that 'One of the things the white world does not know, but I think I know, is that black people are just like everybody else' and observing that appalling social injustice has its roots in racist mythologizing. He was against SEGREGATION, but was also wary of the separatist aspirations of black national-ists. In his 1953 essay 'Stranger in the Village' he wrote, 'The time has come to realize that the interracial drama acted out on the American continent has not only created a new black man, it has created a new white man, too.' Gradually Baldwin became more APOCALYPTIC in his outlook, predicting violence and social upheaval if white America failed to acknowledge the anger and frustration of blacks. This vision is particularly evident in *The Fire Next Time* (1963).

Further reading

James Baldwin (1994) by David Adams Leeming and *James Baldwin* (1978) by Louis H. Pratt. *Talking at the Gates: A Life of James Baldwin* (1991) by James Campbell and *Stealing the Fire: The Art and Protest of James Baldwin* (1989) by Horace A. Porter are critical biographies.

Ballad   Usually a song telling a story that often involves tragic events, the ballad is an ancient form rooted in ORAL TRADITIONS. American ballads have often been adaptations of European ones, made to relate to American incidents and scenes, and typically focusing on the lives of common people; one of the most famous ballads to have orig-inated in the United States is 'Frankie and Johnny'. Particular groups, notably COWBOYS, have valued ballads very highly, and the form has been much used in African American song. Some poets have used the ballad form in seeking a popular idiom; these include John Greenleaf Whittier (1807–92), Henry Wadsworth Longfellow (1807–82), Carl Sandburg (1878–1967) and Stephen Vincent Benét (1898–1943). Several novelists have used aspects of the ballad, notably Eudora Welty (1909–2001) in *The Robber Bridegroom* (1942) and Carson McCullers (1917–67) in *Ballad of the Sad Café* (1951). The tradition of the 'broadside' ballad, dealing with outlaws, social injus-tice and protest has been very strong in the United States, evident in songs by Woody Guthrie (1912–67), Bob Dylan (b. 1941) and Bruce Springsteen (b. 1949). The ballad form is used especially powerfully in the two poems 'A Bronzeville Mother Loiters in Mississippi. Meanwhile a Mississippi Mother Burns Bacon' and 'The Last Quatrain of the Ballad of Emmett Till' (1960) by Gwendolyn BROOKS.

Baraka, Imamu Amiri   Influential African American playwright, novelist, poet and essayist, a leading figure in the BLACK ARTS MOVEMENT. Baraka, whose original name was Everett LeRoi Jones, was born in Newark, New Jersey, in 1934 and attended Howard University. He achieved recognition at first through his poetry, especially *Preface to a Twenty Volume Suicide Note* (1961) and *The Dead Lecturer* (1964). His one-act play *Dutchman* (1964) was a critical success and led to Baraka founding the Black Arts Repertory Theatre in 1965. His deepening interest in African American culture is reflected in his studies *Blues People: Negro Music in White America* (1963) and *Black Music* (1967). (In 1987 he published *The Music: Reflections on Jazz and*

Blues.) During the 1960s Baraka became a black nationalist and was increasingly interested in the African heritage of American blacks; this led to his change of name in 1965. He also became an important spokesman for black militancy, advocating violence through his writing and founding the Black Community Development and Defence Organization in 1968. In addition to his many plays, Baraka published a novel, *The System of Dante's Hell* (1965), and *The Autobiography of LeRoi Jones/Amiri Baraka* in 1984. During the 1970s he modified his black nationalist stance. He has taught at various universities.

Baraka's early writing, influenced by the BEATS, is expressly apolitical, but during the 1960s his work comes to express the anger and frustration of blacks in white America and also explores and exposes racial mythology. This is particularly evident in *Dutchman*, in which a white woman and a black man interact in the surreal setting of the subway. Although an often controversial figure, Baraka is essential to recent developments in African American writing.

Criticism on Baraka includes *Imamu Amiri Baraka* (1978) edited by Kimberly W. Benston; *Amiri Baraka* (2001) by Jerry Gafio Watts, and *Amiri Baraka/LeRoi Jones* (1978) by Werner Sollors.

Barnum's American Museum   In 1842 the showman Phineas T. Barnum (1810–91) took over John Scudder's American Museum in New York City and made it an extremely popular centre exhibiting the exotic and the unusual. The museum also staged plays, lectures and musical entertainments. Some of the most famous exhibits were hoaxes, such as the Fiji mermaid, though others were genuine, including the original conjoined ('Siamese') twins (Chang and Eng), 'General Tom Thumb' (Charles S. Stratton) and the Drummond light. The museum closed in 1868 after two serious fires. Barnum, the museum and its exhibits are often represented in literature. Herman MELVILLE referred frequently to Barnum and the museum, notably in *The Confidence-Man* (1857), Mark TWAIN was fascinated by Chang and Eng, and the young Henry JAMES was a frequent visitor to the museum. Barnum's *The Life of P.T. Barnum, Written by Himself*, first published in 1855 and much revised, is reckoned to have been one of the most popular books of the 19th century.

The Bay Psalm Book   The familiar name for *The Whole Booke of Psalmes Faithfully Translated into English Metre*, printed by Stephen Day in Cambridge, Massachusetts, in 1640. Produced by a committee of ministers, the book was a literal translation of the Old Testament psalms intended for use by PURITAN congregations. *The Bay Psalm Book* was the first book published in the English North American colonies. Over the next century there were around twenty-five further editions.

The translations of the psalms were literal, in accordance with the Puritan belief in 'plain style', in which metaphor and elaborate imagery were regarded as dangerous distractions. In the preface, probably written by Richard Mather, a defence of the use of music in Puritan worship was given, and a rationale for the style of the translations. The preface states that the main objective was 'fidelity rather than poetry' and that 'If therefore the verses are not always so smooth and elegant as some may desire or expect; let them consider that God's Altar needs not our polishings.' Sometimes the plain renderings were ungainly, as in the version of Psalm 23:

> The Lord to me a shepherd is
>> Want therefore shall not I.
> He in the folds of tender grass
>> Doth cause me down to lie:
> To waters calm me gently leads,
>> Restore my soul doth he,
> He doth in paths of righteousness
>> For his name's sake lead me.

In subsequent editions attempts were made to smooth out some of the roughness of the verses.

Beat movement   Literary group, also known as the Beats or the Beat generation, that flourished from the mid-1950s until the early 1960s. Its most prominent members were the novelists John Clellon Holmes (1926–88) and Jack Kerouac (1922–69), and the poets Allen GINSBERG, Lawrence Ferlinghetti (b. 1919), Philip Whalen (b. 1923), Gary Snyder (b. 1930) and Gregory Corso (1930–2001). William Burroughs (1914–97) was loosely associated with the group, which was mainly located in San Francisco and in Greenwich Village, New York City. Much Beat poetry was published by Ferlinghetti's 'City Lights' imprint, and his 'City Lights' bookstore in San Francisco was an important meeting-place for the group. Gregory Stephenson has suggested that the Beat movement had two distinct phases: the 'underground', from 1944 to 1956, and the public, 1956–62.

Holmes introduced the term 'Beat generation' in a 1952 essay on his novel *Go* (1952), and later Kerouac suggested that 'Beat' meant being socially marginalized and exhausted ('beaten down') and blessed ('beatific'.) There are also musical connotations to the name as many members were jazz enthusiasts. Socially the Beats, many of whom were homosexual or bisexual, extolled individual freedom and attacked what they saw as the materialism, militarism, consumerism and conformity of the 1950s; 'America, where everyone is always doing what they ought,' as Kerouac put it in one of Beat's defining works, the novel *On the Road* (1957). To this end they affected non-conformist styles of dress and speech and, avowedly anti-materialist, they cultivated mystical experiences by the use of drugs or by meditation – many members developed an interest in forms of mysticism and in Zen Buddhism. The Beats were politically radical, and to some degree their anti-authoritarian attitudes were taken up by activists in the 1960s. In their writing they encouraged direct and frank communication and, rejecting the formalist, impersonal writing encouraged by the NEW CRITICISM, they cultivated styles that gave the impression of spontaneity and improvization. Much Beat poetry was performance orientated (often read in public with jazz accompaniment). Although they have been much parodied and satirized, the Beats brought fresh energies to American writing and their influence has been significant.

Further reading

This is the Beat Generation (1999) by James Campbell; Beat Down to Your Soul (2001), edited by Ann Charters; The Beat Generation Writers (1996), edited by A. Robert Lee; A Different Beat: Writings by Women of the Beat Generation (1997), edited by Richard Peabody, and The Daybreak Boys (1990) by Gregory Stephenson.

Bellow, Saul   Novelist and short-story writer. Bellow was born near Montreal in 1915 into a Russian Jewish family, and brought up in Chicago. He attended Chicago and Northwestern universities before teaching at various colleges, and he has maintained strong links with the University of Chicago. Bellow's first two novels, *Dangling Man* (1944) and *The Victim* (1947), were written in an economic prose style and engaged with the theme of individual alienation and with the ambiguous relationship between a Jewish man and a Gentile. For his third, partly comic, picaresque novel, *The Adventures of Augie March* (1953), Bellow used a more exuberant style to explore the adolescence of the central character. Its opening phrase, 'I am an American, Chicago born', is one of the most famous in post-war fiction. *Seize the Day* (1956) returned to the style of the first novels, while *Henderson the Rain King* (1959), set in Africa, was less characteristic of Bellow's by now established style. In 1964 he published what is widely regarded as his finest work, *Herzog*. Focusing on a few days during the mental and emotional crisis of a middle-aged Jewish professor, Moses Herzog, the work encompasses an extraordinary range of sophisticated ideas and themes. Chief among them is one of Bellow's enduring concerns, the relation between the intellectual and contemporary society. Two subsequent novels, *Mr Sammler's Planet* (1969) and *Humboldt's Gift* (1975) – based to some extent on the character of the poet Delmore Schwartz (1913–66) – confirmed Bellow's status as the most important novelist of his generation, and in 1976 he was awarded the NOBEL PRIZE FOR LITERATURE.

Reception of Bellow's later work has been mixed. His engaging novel *The Dean's December* (1983) was adversely compared to *Herzog*, while the finely crafted and concentrated novellas *A Theft* (1989), *The Bellarosa Connection* (1989) and *The Actual* (1997) seemed to many to lack the richness of his earlier work. While *Ravelstein* (2000) continued Bellow's examination of the academy's place in society, it was considered too programmatic and too much a *roman-à-clef*. In addition to his novels Bellow has published several collections of essays and short fiction, and a play.

Although Bellow's critical stance towards radical and fashionable intellectualism has led to his being labelled a conservative, his work does not readily fit into narrow categories. Taken as a whole, it displays an incisive and passionate concern with the moral and intellectual climate of his time. Eschewing fashion in fiction, he has maintained a humanist belief in literature's power to educate and examine and in the duty of the novelist to deal with serious concerns. As he has said, 'I come of a generation, now largely vanished, that was passionate about literature, believing it to be an indispensable source of illumination of the present, of reflective power.'

Further reading

Bellow: A Biography (2000) by James Atlas; Saul Bellow: In Defense of Man (1979) by John Jacob Clayton; A Room of His Own (2001) by Gloria L. Cronin; Saul Bellow: Vision and Revision (1984) by Daniel Fuchs; Saul Bellow and the Decline of Humanism (1991) by Michael K. Glenday, and Saul Bellow and History (1984) by Judie Newman.

Beloved   Novel by Toni Morrison, published in 1987 and awarded the 1988 Pulitzer Prize. Set in Ohio during Reconstruction the novel concerns the rehabilitation of Sethe, who as a runaway slave attempts to murder her four children rather than allow them to go into slavery. She succeeds in killing her unnamed elder daughter, referred to as 'Beloved', whose ghost 18 years later arrives at Sethe's home, where she lives with her other daughter Denver. Having been ostracized by her community because of the killing, Sethe gradually dedicates herself to Beloved as reparation for the killing, and this further isolates her until Denver initiates contact with the community. In a symbolic repetition of the scene of the original killing, Beloved is expelled and the restoration of Sethe begins. The novel includes references back to slavery at Sweet Home in Kentucky and the experiences of other slaves on the farm, especially Sethe's lover Paul D. and her preacher mother-in-law Baby Suggs. Thematically, the novel's major concern is with finding a liveable negotiation between the need to forget or suppress a wounding past in order to function in the present, and the necessity of remembering a past without being paralysed by it. Although Morrison makes use of the slave narrative and also refers to an actual case of slave infanticide, *Beloved*'s narrative is fragmented and non-linear, reflecting the problems that the characters must confront in creating order and coherence in their lives. Stylistically the novel has affinities with magic realism as well as with the work of Poe and Faulkner.

For criticism, see *Toni Morrison* (1990), edited by Harold Bloom; *Toni Morrison's Fiction* (1997), edited by David L. Middleton, and *Toni Morrison, Beloved* (1998), edited by Carl Plasa.

Best-sellers   A best-seller is usually defined as a book that is selling more than any others within a give period, usually a week or a month. In the United States lists of best-sellers were introduced in 1895 by the magazine *Bookman*; currently the weekly list produced for the *New York Times* is considered the most authoritative. Best-selling books are divided into fictional and non-fictional, and the non-fictional categories, which include books on self-improvement, sports, celebrity autobiographies and cookbooks, are generally more popular than fiction, which in turn is considerably more popular than poetry. The Bible remains the largest-selling book ever, although it is excluded from best-seller lists. Generally, the biggest-selling fictional works have been those that fit into recognizable popular traditions (this tends to allow literary critics to regard best-sellers as formulaic writing). The major categories are CHILDREN'S LITERATURE, WESTERNS, ROMANCES, historical romances, religious romances, HORROR, war, adventure stories, SCIENCE FICTION, crime and DETECTIVE NOVELS. Although many best-sellers prove ephemeral, and consequently tend to be ignored by literary critics, it is worth remembering that works by some of the major authors of American literature have been best-sellers; these include works by Harriet Beecher STOWE, Herman MELVILLE, Mark TWAIN, Vladimir Nabokov (1899–1977), John Steinbeck (1902–68), Ernest HEMINGWAY, Willa CATHER, Richard WRIGHT, Ralph ELLISON, J. D. Salinger (b. 1919), Kurt Vonnegut (b. 1922), Norman Mailer (b. 1923), Joseph Heller (1923–99), Truman Capote (1924–84), E. L. Doctorow (b. 1931), Toni MORRISON and Alice WALKER. While sales of poetry do not compete with the sales of best-selling novels, the FIRESIDE POETS and Robert FROST have produced best-selling works.

Although the poem *The Day of Doom* (1662) by Michael Wigglesworth (1631–1705) and the *NEW ENGLAND PRIMER* were popular Puritan works, it is usually reckoned that modern American best-sellers begin with *Charlotte Temple* (1791) by Susanna Rowson (1762–1824), and with the works of James Fenimore COOPER and Washington IRVING, even though the situation regarding COPYRIGHT tended to hinder the sales of American books. In the mid 19th century there are a series of important best-sellers, the most prominent being *The Wide, Wide World* (1851) by Susan Warner (1819–85), Stowe's *Uncle Tom's Cabin* (1852) and *The Lamplighter* (1854) by Maria Susanna Cummins (1827–66). Subsequent major best-selling novels include *Ben-Hur* (1880) by Lew Wallace (1827–1905) *In His Steps* (1897) by Charles Sheldon (1857–1946); *Gone with the Wind* (1936) by Margaret Mitchell (1900–49); *The Robe* (1942) by Lloyd C. Douglas (1877–1951); *Valley of the Dolls* (1966) by Jacqueline Susann (1918–74), and *The Godfather* (1969) by Mario Puzo (1920–99). The major best-selling authors associated with particular categories of fiction are Horatio ALGER, Zane Grey (1872–1939), James Michener (1907–97), Louis L'Amour (1908–88), Irwin Shaw (1913–84), Herman Wouk (b. 1915), Harold Robbins (1916–97), Irving Wallace (1916–90), James Jones (1921–77), Anne Rice (b. 1941), Stephen KING, Danielle Steel (b. 1947) and John Grisham (b. 1955).

Bill of Rights   The first ten amendments to the CONSTITUTION, adopted together in 1791. The amendments guarantee a variety of individual rights, such as rights to petition and to bear arms, to trial by jury, to free speech, to freedom of religion and freedom of assembly. Although they have much in common with established British rights, the amendments are often quoted as distinctively American.

In full, the amendments are:

Amendment One

Congress shall make no law respecting an establishment of religion, or prohibiting the free exercise thereof; or abridging the freedom of speech, or of the press; or the right of the people peaceably to assemble, and to petition the government for a redress of grievances.

Amendment Two

A well regulated militia, being necessary to the security of a Free State, the right of the people to keep and bear arms, shall not be infringed.

Amendment Three

No soldier shall, in time of peace be quartered in any house, without the consent of the owner, nor in time of war, but in a manner to be prescribed by law.

Amendment Four

The right of the people to be secure in their persons, houses, papers, and effects, against unreasonable searches and seizures, shall not be violated, and no warrants shall issue, but upon probable cause, supported by Oath or affirmation, and particularly describing the place to be searched, and the persons or things to be seized.

Amendment Five

No person shall be held to answer for a capital, or otherwise infamous crime, unless on a presentment or indictment of a Grand Jury, except in cases arising in the land or naval forces, or in the militia, when in actual service in time of war or public danger; nor shall any person be subject for the same offence to be twice put in jeopardy of life or limb; nor shall be compelled in any criminal case to be a witness against himself, nor be deprived of life, liberty, or property, without due process of law; nor shall private property be taken for public use, without just compensation.

Amendment Six

In all criminal prosecutions, the accused shall enjoy the right to a speedy and public trial, by an impartial jury of the State and district wherein the crime shall have been committed, which district shall have been previously ascertained by law, and to be informed of the nature and cause of the accusation; to be confronted with the witnesses against him; to have compulsory process for obtaining witnesses in his favor, and to have the assistance of counsel for his defense.

Amendment Seven

In suits at common law, where the value in controversy shall exceed twenty dollars, the right of trial by jury shall be preserved, and no fact tried by a jury, shall be otherwise re-examined in any court of the United States, than according to the rules of the common law.

Amendment Eight
Excessive bail shall not be required, nor excessive fines imposed, nor cruel and unusual punishments inflicted.

Amendment Nine
The enumeration in the Constitution, of certain rights, shall not be construed to deny or disparage others retained by the people.

Amendment Ten
The powers not delegated to the United States by the Constitution, nor prohibited by it to the States, are reserved to the States respectively, or to the people.

Bishop, Elizabeth   Poet, born in Worcester, Massachusetts, in 1911. Bishop's father died when she was aged 8 months, and after her mother was committed to a mental hospital when Bishop was 5 years old, she was raised by her grandparents in Nova Scotia and her aunt in Boston. She attended Vassar College, graduating in 1934. Having befriended the poet Marianne Moore (1887–1972), an important mentor, she lived in various places, notably in Florida and in Mexico, and for an extended period near Rio de Janeiro with her lover, Lota de Macedo Soares. Leaving Brazil, Bishop taught creative writing at several universities, including Harvard (1970–77). She died in Boston in 1979. Never a prolific poet, Bishop's first book, *North & South*, was published in 1946 and reprinted with her second, *A Cold Spring*, in 1955; her other collections were *Questions of Travel* (1965) and *Geography III* (1976). Each book was highly acclaimed and contributed to the considerable reputation she now holds. *The Complete Poems 1927–79* was published in 1983, *The Collected Prose* in 1984, and a generous selection of letters, *One Art*, in 1994.

'Surely there is an element of mortal panic and fear underlying all works of art?' Bishop asked in her essay 'Efforts of Affection'. In a manner comparable to Robert Frost, Bishop used the formal properties of poetry to counteract the chaos and disruption that otherwise threatened to overwhelm. She has rightly been acclaimed for her luminous observation of the world's details and for her considered sense of locality, but this concentration serves a purpose for her, in temporarily counteracting feelings of estrangement, displacement and despair that are often immediately underneath the surface of her poetry. Bishop is a reticent poet, and was made uneasy by the personal revelation evident in the work of her friend Robert Lowell. Although she wrote only obliquely about her own experiences and was guarded about her lesbianism, her work generates a powerful sense of personal witness.

Elizabeth Bishop: Life and the Memory of It (1993) by Brett C. Millier is a critical biography. Critical studies include: *Elizabeth Bishop: Questions of Mastery* (1991) by Bonnie Costello; *Elizabeth Bishop: The Biography of a Poetry* (1992) by Lorrie Goldensohn; *Becoming a Poet* (1989) by David Kalstone, and *Elizabeth Bishop and her Art* (1983), edited by Lloyd Schwartz and Sybil P. Estess.

Black Arts Movement Sometimes called the 'second black renaissance' (the HARLEM RENAISSANCE being the first), the Black Arts Movement (BAM) began in the mid-1960s and flourished until the mid-1970s. As well as stimulating much powerful writing, it has had a lasting influence on subsequent African American art, criticism and politics.

The BAM emphasized the racial distinction of the black, and fostered writing that was specifically black, speech-based, radical, confrontational, anti-assimilationist and dedicated to revolutionary social change – as Imamu Amiri BARAKA wrote in his poem 'Black Art' (1969), 'We want "poems that kill"'. Similarly, in their Introduction to *Afro-American Writing: An Anthology of Prose and Poetry* (1972) Richard A. Long and Eugenia A. Collier wrote, 'There is no wall between the academy and the street. Our books are our weapons and the only ones which are likely to enable us to survive.' Broadly, the BAM shared the aims of the separatist militant black nationalists; in his seminal 1968 essay 'The Black Arts Movement' Larry Neal (1937–81) stated, 'Black Art is the aesthetic and spiritual sister of the Black Power concept.' This was seen particularly in the expression of pride in blackness and in locating an African rather than an American heritage and identity. This aim often led to the adoption of African or Muslim names rather than names deriving from American slavery (Baraka's name had previously been LeRoi Jones). It was also evident in preferences for African styles in clothing, hair and jewellery.

BAM stimulated creativity in many areas, but especially in poetry and writing for the theatre. Writers most associated with BAM include Baraka and Neal, who co-edited *Black Fire: An Anthology of African American Writing* (1968), Malcolm X (1925–65), Etheridge Knight (1931–85), Sonia Sanchez (b. 1934), June Jordan (1936–2002), Eldridge Cleaver (b. 1935), Lucille Clifton (b. 1936), Haki R. Madhubuti (b. 1942), Nikki Giovanni (b. 1943), Angela Davis (b. 1944) and Ntozake Shange (b. 1948).

Black Mountain Poets Small group of avant-garde experimental poets in the 1950s who were associated with Black Mountain College in North Carolina. Charles Olson (1910–70), who became the college's rector, was the group's most influential member, and his essay 'Projective Verse' (1950) may be regarded as the group's manifesto. Strongly influenced by the ideas of Ezra POUND and William Carlos WILLIAMS, Olson argued in 'Projective Verse' that poetry should be based on the 'breath' of the poet; that is, line lengths and phrasing should have an immediacy deriving from the poet's presence. The poem should be in 'open form', improvisatory and exploratory rather than closed or settled: 'form is never more than an expression of content' and 'one perception must immediately and directly lead to a further perception'. These statements had an important effect on the development of poetry after MODERNISM, and Olson's 1950 poem 'The Kingfishers' is sometimes called the first American POSTMODERNIST poem. Black Mountain poetry tended to be minimalist and truncated rather than expansive, and very much concerned with poetic technique. Other poets in the group included Robert Duncan (1919–88), Denise Levertov (1923–97) and Robert Creeley (b. 1926). The school was represented in two journals: *Origin* (1951–6) and *Black Mountain Review* (1954–7). Black Mountain College had been founded as a community college in 1933 and became an experimental liberal arts college. It closed in 1956.

Further reading

Black Mountain (1972) by Martin Duberman; *Understanding the Black Mountain Poets* (1995) by Edward Halsey Foster, and *Olson's Push* (1978) by Sherman Paul.

Blue laws   Phrase in use since the 18th century to refer to laws in the PURITAN colonies (especially Connecticut) that outlawed specific activities on Sundays. Most of the laws had to do with the restriction of sport, labour and trade, especially in alcohol and tobacco, although towards the end of the colonial period such restrictions were increasingly relaxed. The phrase 'blue law' is often used derisively to refer to any restrictive or supposedly Puritanical legislation.

Blues   The blues originated with African American performers in the Mississippi Delta of Louisiana in the late 19th or early 20th century, and became a written musical form in 1912. The blues are secular vocal folk music, although they partly derive from African American SPIRITUALS and partly from a tradition of work songs such as the 'field holler'. It has been suggested that the form has an African origin. W. C. Handy (1873–1958), who composed standards such as 'St Louis Blues' and 'Memphis Blues', was the first to publish blues music. The blues were immensely popular from the 1920s onwards, and there were many celebrated performers such as 'Ma Rainey' (Gertrude Melissa Nix Rainey, 1886–1939), Bessie Smith (1894–1937) and Louis Armstrong (1901–71). Individual performance and creative improvisation are essential to the blues. Although distinctly African American, the blues have been taken up by performers internationally, and have maintained their prominence in popular music, as well as being key influences in the development of both JAZZ and rock and roll music.

In musical terms the blues usually consist of three or four chords and a twelve-bar pattern. In the style of African American folk singers, the third or the seventh tone of the scale is slightly flattened, or 'blue' – hence the term 'Blues'. Blues songs are lyrical and reflective (rather than narrative) in form. Typically, the stanza pattern of a song is of three end-stopped lines in which the first line is repeated, sometimes with slight variation, and the third is an elaboration of the sentiment of the first. The first two lines usually have a strong caesura, evident in performance rather than on the printed page. Here, for example, are three lines from 'St Louis Blues': 'Feeling tomorrow, like I feel today / Feeling tomorrow, like I feel today / I'll pack my trunk, and make my get-away.'

However, it is the performative vocal element of blues that makes them distinctive. The blues commonly express feelings of alienation, frustration, loss, loneliness and marginalization; this has led the musicologist Paul Oliver to say that they are 'both a state of mind and a music which gives voice to it'. Although individualized by the single voice, like other forms of folk music the blues are expressive of collectively held sentiments.

From the HARLEM RENAISSANCE onwards African American writers have made much creative use of blues forms and idioms, although some writers involved in the BLACK ARTS MOVEMENT were critical of the blues for their passive acceptance of injustice. Langston Hughes (1902–67) and Zora Neale HURSTON were among the first writers to engage creatively with the blues, and many later writers such as Richard WRIGHT, Ralph ELLISON, James BALDWIN, Amiri BARAKA, Alice WALKER and Toni MORRISON have done so in various ways. Ellison in particular has written on the form, and his 1952 novel INVISIBLE MAN is often regarded as the finest example of a 'blues novel' in terms of its allusive, non-linear and associative narrative. In his 1945 essay 'Richard Wright's Blues' Ellison defined the blues as 'an autobiographical chronicle of personal catastrophe expressed lyrically'. Some critics, notably Albert Murray and Houston A. Baker, have argued that the blues are essential to African American literary traditions, particularly with regard to the non-sequential and improvisational aspects of prose narrative.

Further reading

Blues, Ideology and African American Literature (1984) by Houston A. Baker; Looking Up at Down (1989) by William Barlow; Blues People (1963, 1995) by LeRoi Jones (Baraka); Stomping the Blues (1976) by Albert Murray; Blues Fell This Morning (1960, 1990) by Paul Oliver, and The Blues Aesthetic (1989) by Richard J. Powell.

Bollingen Prize   Award given for distinguished poetic achievement. The prize was instituted in 1948 and funded by the philanthropist Paul Mellon through the Bollingen Foundation. (The name Bollingen refers to the Swiss village associated with the psychoanalyst Carl Jung, whom Mellon particularly admired.) Originally the award was administered by the Library of Congress and was presented annually, but since 1950 it has been administered by Yale University, and since 1964 it has been given biennially. At first worth $1,000, it is now worth $50,000 to the recipient.

In 1949 the first award aroused intense controversy as it was given to Ezra POUND for *The Pisan Cantos* (1948). Pound's extreme political views and his indictment for treason inflamed opposition to his receiving the award, and poets and critics were deeply divided over the issue. Because of the controversy, the United States Congress directed the Library of Congress to dissociate itself from the prize.

Borden, Lizzie Lizzie Andrew Borden (1860–1927) was accused of murdering her father and stepmother, who had been killed in the family home in Fall River, Massachusetts, in August 1892. She was tried in June 1893, and although she was acquitted, widespread belief in her guilt persisted. The case was sensational and remains mysterious. It has inspired many BALLADS, plays and novels, as well as non-fictional examinations. There is a well-known verse about the case: 'Lizzie Borden took an axe, / Gave her mother forty whacks. / When she saw what she had done, / Gave her father forty-one.'

Bradstreet, Anne Puritan poet, born Anne Dudley in England around 1612. In 1628 she married Simon Bradstreet and in 1630 they and her parents were part of the first major Puritan emigration to Massachusetts on board the *Arbella*. Simon Bradstreet held several important administrative positions in the MASSACHUSETTS BAY COLONY and the Bradstreets lived in various towns before eventually settling in Andover in 1645. Without her knowledge, Bradstreet's brother-in-law John Woodbridge took a manuscript of her poems with him to London, where they were published in 1650 under the title *The Tenth Muse Lately Sprung Up in America*. This was the first book of poetry to be published by a resident of the North American British colonies. (A revised and expanded edition with the title *Several Poems Compiled with Great Variety of Wit and Learning* was published posthumously in Boston in 1678.) Bradstreet raised eight children. She died in Andover in 1672.

Bradstreet's poetry is typically meditative, abstract and discursive, intended to illustrate PURITAN beliefs and doctrines, and written in the conventional forms and metres of the time. In his 1953 poem *Homage to Mistress Bradstreet* John Berryman (1914–72) described it as 'bald / abstract didactic rime'. But there are other poems, on personal subjects, which modern readers have found particularly interesting. In these poems, and in the series of short prose 'Meditations' that Bradstreet wrote for her family, there is often an evident tension between her identity as a woman, mother and grandmother and the Puritan doctrines that she accepted. Her poems remain prayer-like, in the approved Puritan convention, but they also reflect a searching, sometimes troubled mind. Sometimes her poems are defensive, anticipating criticism from those who saw writing poetry as an inappropriate activity for a woman and a kind of worldly vanity antithetical to the Puritan endeavour; perhaps fearing censure, she never published poetry willingly. However, it is worth remembering that Puritanism valued personal testimony, and that the leading Puritan Cotton Mather wrote in 1712, with Bradstreet in mind, that women 'have wrote such things as have been very valuable; especially relating to their own experiences'.

Further reading

Critical Essays on Anne Bradstreet (1983), edited by Pattie Cowell and Ann Stanford; *Anne Bradstreet Revisited* (1991) by Rosamond Rosenmeier, and *Anne Bradstreet: The Worldly Puritan* (1974) by Ann Stanford.

Brahmins   Term used to describe a group of well-born men of letters in 19ᵗʰ century New England. (The reference is to the Hindu caste system, in which the Brahmins are the highest or priestly caste.) The Brahmins included Henry Wadsworth Longfellow (1807–82), Oliver Wendell Holmes (1809–94) and James Russell Lowell (1819–91), who were based in Boston, associated with Harvard University and often assumed European models for their poetry and prose. The terms Brahmin and Brahminism are sometimes used, unfairly, to suggest fastidious, genteel writers producing light verse and fiction. The phrase 'the Brahmin caste of New England' appears in the novel *Elsie Venner* (1861) by Holmes.

Brook Farm   Formed in 1841 in West Roxbury, near Boston, Brook Farm was an experimental commune made up of around seventy members. It was founded by George Ripley (1802–80) and in some respects was a test of the optimistic social theories of TRANSCENDENTALISM. The community's main ideal was to live simply, find a balance between physical activity and intellectual reflection and debate, and establish a model for an egalitarian society. All of the members performed manual labour on the farm and there was a progressive school for the children. The financial arrangements were co-operative; effectively, each member was a stockholder, and received one share for each day's labour performed. It was intended that a measure of self-sufficiency would be achieved, and income was to be generated from the sale of farm produce and from the school. Although financially troubled, the farm was considered a success by most of its members. In 1844 the community adopted FOURIERISM and began to remodel itself according to that doctrine, terming itself a 'phalanx' and agreeing to the erection of a large communal building called a 'phalanstery'. Brook Farm broke up shortly after fire destroyed the newly erected phalanstery in 1847.

   Brook Farm was one commune among many such experiments at the time, but it was prominent because of the involvement of the transcendentalists. Both Ralph Waldo EMERSON and Margaret Fuller (1810–50) were interested in the project, and Nathaniel HAWTHORNE lived there for 6 months. He wrote a critical account of it in *The Blithedale Romance* (1852), in which the character of Zenobia is supposedly based on Fuller.

Brooks, Gwendolyn   Poet, born in Topeka, Kansas, in 1917. An African American, Brooks grew up in Chicago's south side, whose neighbourhoods are the localities for much of her writing. Brooks published her first collection, *A Street in Bronzeville*, in 1945, and her early poems both demonstrated her formal control and established her sympathies with the poor and the marginalized. Her second book *Annie Allen* (1949) confirmed her early promise; especially notable is the sonnet sequence 'The Children of the Poor'. In 1950 Brooks became the first African American to win the PULITZER PRIZE. In her later poetry Brooks became more experimental, using styles and rhythms derived from popular music and from black vernacular as well as maintaining her skill in traditional forms. She always sought a broad audience for her poetry, and in the 1960s she worked with a teenage street gang, the Chicago Blackstone Rangers. She also insisted on the poet's duty to comment on public events, and her poems on SEGREGA- TION and on the murder of Emmett TILL are especially powerful. In addition to her poetry she has published a novel, *Maud Martha* (1953), a book for children, *Bronzeville Boys and Girls* (1956), and two autobiographical sketches, *Report from Part One* (1972) and *Report from Part Two* (1996). In 1985 Brooks became the first African American woman to be Poetry Consultant to the Library of Congress. She died in Chicago in 2000.

Further reading

Urban Rage in Bronzeville (1999) by B. J. Bolden; *A Life of Gwendolyn Brooks* (1990) by George E. Kent; *A Life Distilled: Gwendolyn Brooks, Her Poetry and Fiction* (1987), edited by Maria K. Mootry and Gary Smith, and *Gwendolyn Brooks* (1980) by Harry B. Shaw.

Brown, Charles Brockden   Novelist, born in Philadelphia in 1771. Of QUAKER back- ground, Brown trained as a lawyer, but never practised, devoting himself to writing. His first novel, *Wieland*, was published in 1798 (a supplement, *Memoirs of Carwin, the Biloquist*, was published as a serial, 1803–05). His other major novels are *Ormond* (1799), *Edgar Huntly* (1799) and *Arthur Mervyn* (1800). In 1810 he died of tuberculo- sis in Philadelphia.

   Brown is sometimes called 'the father of American fiction'. Using American settings, he wrote in the developing tradition of GOTHIC and was a significant influence on the development of both Gothic and ROMANCE in American literature. Although his work is uneven in terms of plotting and style, he made significant use of indeterminacy and inconclusiveness and is an important precursor of Edgar Allan POE and Nathaniel HAWTHORNE. The fragility of identity and the precarious nature of rationality are recur- rent themes in his novels. In *Wieland*, for example, a trickster's deceptions lead the central character to self-doubt, despair and eventually murder. The power of the irra- tional and the nature of the nightmare are explored in *Edgar Huntly*. *Arthur Mervyn* is especially memorable for its depiction of Philadelphia during a plague of yellow fever.

Further reading

Charles Brockden Brown: An American Tale (1983) by Alan Axelrod; *Critical Essays on Charles Brockden Brown* (1981), edited by Bernard Rosenthal, and *The Romance of Real Life* (1994) by Steven Watts.

Brown v. Board of Education of Topeka   Landmark SUPREME COURT ruling of 1954 which declared that racial SEGREGATION in schools was unconstitutional. Segregation had been permitted after the 1896 Plessy v. Ferguson decision, so long as public facilities provided for blacks and whites were equal; the 1954 ruling declared that the 'separate facilities' for blacks were 'inherently inferior'. The Brown v. Board of Education decision required the racial integration of public schools, which was much resisted in the South, notably in Little Rock, Arkansas. While the decision was restricted to the public schools, it was understood to apply to all public services.

Bureau of Indian Affairs Known as the BIA, the bureau was founded in 1824 by the secretary of war, John C. Calhoun (1782–1850). Its main functions then were the management of treaties and the settling of disputes between Native Americans and settlers. Since 1849 the BIA has been part of the Department of the Interior, and it is now the largest bureau there. Its duties have gradually expanded and changed over time, and since the 1950s it has been run mostly by Native Americans. The BIA is currently responsible for the administration of social services, law enforcement, education, agricultural and land improvement programmes for Native American peoples. Its stated main objectives are the development and maintenance of autonomy for Native Americans, the mobilization of public and private aid, and the provision of life opportunities.

Burlesque Technically, a piece of writing in which another work or attitude is travestied for comic purposes, usually by treating an elevated subject in a low manner. Burlesque is distinguished from parody by being more broad in its humour, and is less likely to imitate skilfully the form of the targeted work. More generally, burlesque refers to a highly popular form of theatrical entertainment that was introduced in New York in the 1860s. Aimed particularly at masculine audiences, and having a reputation for being risqué, burlesque evolved from the format of the MINSTREL SHOWS, and consisted of comic sketches, songs, dances and acrobats. Some burlesques included boxing or wrestling matches, and, later, striptease acts. Burlesque continued in various forms, including VAUDEVILLE, until the 1950s.

Calvinism Body of ideas generated by the French theologian John Calvin (1509–64) which became central to PURITANISM and important to other Protestant reformed churches such as the Baptists and to PRESBYTERIANISM. Calvin's theology appears in his *Institutes of the Christian Religion* (1536), and was systematized in 1619. Calvinism stressed that all humans were in a fallen state because of the fall of Adam and Eve; that all were divided into either the redeemed (elect) or the damned; that God had predestined all human events, had chosen who was elect, and that it was impossible to be redeemed through one's own efforts. Calvinism also advocated the creation of a theocracy, that is, a 'city of God': a state or community in which civil would be the same as church law.

Calvinism was modified or adapted by other church groups. The Puritans remained closest to orthodox Calvinism, but tended to modify the doctrines of predestination and the inability to achieve salvation (by receiving grace) through individual effort. This modification was known as 'preparationism' and represented the belief that although one could not be saved through the earning of grace, one could prepare to receive grace by acting morally. Various religious groups in America, including the Puritans, have shared the Calvinist ideal of creating a theocracy but this has never been realized.

The Cantos Collection of densely allusive poems that forms the major work of Ezra POUND and is widely considered to be one of the major poetic achievements of the 20th century. Although it seems that Pound conceived of the poem as early as 1905, he began writing the cantos in 1915, published a section of them in 1919 and published the first sequence of them, *A Draft of XVI Cantos*, in 1925. Sections of cantos appeared over the next 35 years, and the whole sequence, consisting of 117 cantos, was published as one volume in 1970. The poems are not in set forms, and are almost entirely in FREE VERSE, and some involve significant use of earlier poetic styles.

Although Pound described *The Cantos* as 'a record of struggle', the collection can be described in various ways, and it evolved considerably over the long period of its composition. Broadly, the sequence is Pound's record of his absorption in history, in the world's past literature, in economic affairs and in contemporary politics. At times the poetry becomes opaque; some cantos are dense with allusions that are private or arcane, while some utilize many foreign languages and Chinese ideograms. Some are deeply personal while others deal with matters of public history. In spite of their general opacity, many individual cantos possess great lyric power and some are reasonably accessible. Some of the unified individual sequences are especially important, notably the Malatesta Cantos (8–11), the Chinese History Cantos (53–61), the Adams Cantos (62–71), the Pisan Cantos (74–84) and 'Thrones' (96–109). Given Pound's abhorrent political ideas, the award of the BOLLINGEN PRIZE to *The Pisan Cantos* in 1949 caused much anger.

Further reading

The Genesis of Pound's Cantos (1976) by Ronald Bush; *Ezra Pound's Cantos: The Story of the Text* (1979) by Barbara Eastman; *Ezra Pound and the Cantos* (1980) by Wendy Stallard Flory; *Pound's Cantos* (1985) by

Peter Makin, and *Ezra Pound and the Monument of Culture* (1991) by Lawrence S. Rainey. *Ezra Pound: The Cantos* (1989) by George Kearns is a useful brief introduction, while the two-volume *A Companion to the Cantos of Ezra Pound* (1980, 1984) by Carroll Terrell is invaluable for serious study of the collection.

Captivity narrative   Type of prose writing that originated as part of PURITAN LITERATURE, recounting the experience, usually that of women, of being held hostage by Native Americans. The form originated in 1682 with the account by Mary Rowlandson (?1635–1711) of her captivity in 1676 by Wampanoag Indians during KING PHILIP'S WAR. Rowlandson and her three children, along with twenty other people, were captured, and after 11 weeks she was ransomed to her husband for £20. One of her children, Sarah, died during the captivity; the others were released after Rowland. The full title of Rowland's narrative indicates the importance attached to interpreting the captivity as a religious experience: *The Sovereignty and Goodness of God, Together with the Faithfulness of His Promises Displayed; Being a Narrative of the Captivity and Restoration of Mrs Mary Rowlandson, Commended by her to all that Desire to Know the Lord's Doings to, and Dealings with Her. Especially to her Dear Children and Relations.* Rowlandson's narrative was extremely popular, as well as being the first major piece of prose written by a woman in the colonies. Her narrative became a model for many others, in which the American Indians were usually represented as devils, and in which the captivity could be interpreted simultaneously as a parallel to biblical captivities and as a personal ordeal leading to the experience of God's mercy. Other prominent captivity narratives include 'Narrative of a Notable Deliverance from Captivity' by Hannah Duston (1657–1736), published by Cotton Mather in *Humiliations Followed by Deliverances* (1697); *A Narrative of the Captivity of Mrs Johnson* (1796) by Susannah Johnson (1729–1810) and a QUAKER narrative, *God's Mercy Surmounting Man's Cruelty* (1728), by Elizabeth Hanson (1684–1737).

The captivity narrative was influential in the development of ROMANCE fiction. Its later manifestations include novels such as *The Last of the Mohicans* (1826) by James Fenimore COOPER, *Typee* (1846) by Herman MELVILLE, and the SLAVE NARRATIVE, particularly *Incidents in the Life of a Slave Girl* (1861) by Harriet JACOBS. The novel *Sanctuary* (1931) by William FAULKNER is often considered one of the foremost examples of a 20th century version of the captivity narrative.

Further reading

Flintlock and Tomahawk: New England in King Philip's War (1966) by Douglas E. Leach; So Dreadfull a Judgement (1978) by Richard Slotkin and James Folsom, and Puritans Among the Indians: Accounts of Captivity and Redemption 1676–1724 (1981), edited by Alden T. Vaughan and Edward W. Clark.

Carver, Raymond   Renowned for his mastery of the SHORT STORY, Carver was born in Clatskanie, Oregon, in 1938. He married when he was 19 and worked at various unskilled jobs. After attending a creative writing course at Chico State College he studied at Humboldt State College in Arcata, California, graduating in 1963. He began publishing short stories in the early 1960s and his collection *Will You Please Be Quiet, Please?* was acclaimed on its appearance in 1976. The collections *What We Talk About When We Talk About Love* (1981), *Cathedral* (1983) and *Where I'm Calling From* (1988) followed. Previously uncollected writing was published in *Call if you Need Me* (2000). He also published five books of poetry, collected in *All of Us* (1996). After the failure of his first marriage Carver married the poet Tess Gallagher (b. 1943). Until 1983 Carver taught creative writing at the University of California in Santa Cruz. He died of cancer in 1988, in Port Angeles, Washington.

Although Carver's work is clearly part of the existing American short-story tradition, notably that of HEMINGWAY, he developed it in intense ways. Though many stories may seem like fragments or sketches, they are actually highly organized and crafted, very much in the style of his acknowledged master, the Russian Anton Chekhov. Carver's language is concentrated, spare, understated and MINIMALIST; metaphor and ornate language are scarcely used. Typically, his unheroic characters are drawn from the poor working or lower middle classes, and they engage with searching questions to do with love, commitment, loss and community. Frequently his characters are baffled, aware of their marginal status yet unable to escape this and assert control over their lives. ALCOHOLISM, from which Carver suffered, often features.

Further reading

Conversations with Raymond Carver (1990), edited by Marshall Bruce Gentry and William L. Stull; *The Stories of Raymond Carver* (1995) by Kirk Nesset, and *Reading Raymond Carver* (1992) by Randolph Runyon.

Cather, Willa   Novelist and SHORT-STORY writer, born in Winchester, Virginia, in 1873 and brought up in Nebraska. Cather attended the University of Nebraska, graduating in 1896. She moved to Pittsburgh and later to New York, working as an editor and a teacher, eventually becoming managing editor of MCCLURE'S MAGAZINE (1908–12). She published a book of poetry in 1903 and in 1905 a collection of short stories, *The Troll Garden*. In 1912 she published her first novel, *Alexander's Bridge*, but it was with the second, *O Pioneers!* (1913), in which she focused on FRONTIER life on the Great Plains, that she established what would become her major theme. Cather portrayed the experiences of pioneer life, including the experiences of pioneer women, acknowledging the European ethnic backgrounds of the settlers. In her finest works, *My Ántonia* (1918), *One of Ours* (1922) and *A Lost Lady* (1923), this theme is presented with a powerful combination of REALISM and nostalgia. Elsewhere, notably in the novels *Song of the Lark* (1915) and *Lucy Gayheart* (1935), in the novellas in *Obscure Destinies* (1932) and in the collection of short stories *Youth and the Bright Medusa* (1920), she wrote in an obliquely autobiographical manner of restrictive small-town frontier life. Other notable novels are set outside of Nebraska: *The Professor's House* (1925) and *Death Comes for the Archbishop* (1927) in New Mexico, and *Sapphira and the Slave Girl*

(1940) in 19th century Virginia. Cather's essays, collected in *Not Under Forty* (1936), offer a valuable perspective on her art. She died in New York in 1947.

Cather cultivated a limpid, straightforwardly elegant prose style that lent immediacy to all her subjects. She was extremely reticent about her personal life, and her supposed lesbianism and its possible representation in her fiction have been the subject of much speculation and controversy.

Further reading

Willa Cather and the Politics of Criticism (2000) by Joan Acocella; *Willa Cather's Sexual Aesthetics* (1999) by John P. Anders; *Willa Cather: Queering America* (1999) by Marilee Lindemann; *Willa Cather in Context* (1996) by Guy Reynolds, and *Willa Cather's Imagination* (1975) by David Stouck. Biographies include *Willa Cather: A Life Saved Up* (1989) by Hermione Lee and *Willa Cather: The Emerging Voice* (1987) by Sharon O'Brien.

Chandler, Raymond   Novelist and SHORT-STORY writer celebrated for his seven novels set in Los Angeles and featuring the private detective Philip Marlowe. Chandler was born in Chicago in 1888 and lived in England from 1896 to 1912. During WORLD WAR I he served in the Canadian army and air force. Until the DEPRESSION he was a successful oil executive, and he began writing for a living in the 1930s. His first publications were in PULP MAGAZINES, and in 1939 he published the first Marlowe novel, *The Big Sleep*. *Farewell, My Lovely* (1940), *The High Window* (1942), *The Lady in the Lake* (1943), *The Little Sister* (1949), *The Long Goodbye* (1953) and *Playback* (1958) followed. *Poodle Springs*, which Chandler had left unfinished, was completed by Robert B. Parker and published in 1989. Chandler published several short-story collections and worked in Hollywood as a screenwriter; he worked on two classic films, *Double Indemnity* (1944) and *The Blue Dahlia* (1946). He also wrote an important essay, 'The Simple Art of Murder' (1944), on DETECTIVE FICTION and on the ideal private eye. Chandler died in California in 1959.

Philip Marlowe is the archetypal American detective, and Chandler's intricate plotting, vivid characterization and lively prose style have been much imitated. In spite of his flaws Marlowe is an honest and moral guide in an often brutal, violent landscape. Chandler's depiction of the modern city with is stark 'mean streets' (as he calls them in 'The Simple Art of Murder') has also been influential.

Further reading

The Life of Raymond Chandler (1976) by Frank MacShane; *Raymond Chandler* (1981) by Jerry Speir, and *Something More than Night* (1985) by Peter Wolfe.

Chautauqua movement   Programme that developed from the LYCEUM MOVEMENT and was similarly dedicated to fostering adult education and debate. The movement was adapted from annual Methodist meetings held at Lake Chautauqua, New York, for the purpose of training Sunday school teachers and other church workers. After 1874 these were gradually enlarged to include the study of various disciplines and many other 'Chautauqua' meetings were instituted. These were usually held annually in camps, and were specifically designed for intellectual and artistic outreach to rural communities. A Chautauqua meeting would typically include entertainment, theatrical and musical events as well as lectures and debate. The movement reached a peak of popularity in 1924 and declined thereafter.

Chicago School   Influential tradition of sociology which had notable affinities with the urban REALISM of novelists such as Theodore DREISER. The first department of sociology in the United States was instituted at the University of Chicago in 1892, and the Chicago School became renowned particularly for empirical, field-study research. Robert Park (1864–1944) was its leading figure.

Chicano/Chicana literature   The adjective 'Chicano' is most likely derived from the Spanish 'Mejicano' (Mexican), and is used to refer to Mexican Americans. Since 'Chicano' is a masculine adjective, the feminine 'Chicana' is often preferred when the reference is to Mexican American women. Not all Mexican American writers readily accept the term 'Chicano' and some prefer to use 'Hispano', 'Spanish American' or 'Mexicano'. Chicano and Chicana are also sometimes used loosely to include Latino and Latina writers.

Although there was earlier writing in Spanish, Chicano/Chicana literature is usually considered to begin after 1848, when the United States acquired vast Mexican territories in the West and Southwest that included around 80,000 Spanish-speaking Mexican inhabitants. Julio A. Martínez and Francisco A. Lomelí usefully divide Mexican American writing into four distinct periods after 1848: Transition, 1848–1910; Interaction, 1911–42; Adjustment, 1943–64, and Renaissance, post-1965. The periods clearly reflect the historical position and social conditions of Mexican Americans, and the 'Chicano Renaissance' is very much part of the movement towards full civil rights and higher social visibility for Mexican Americans since the 1960s. Poetry, drama and prose fiction have all been well represented in Chicano/Chicana literature, and it has flourished in particular areas, especially the Southwest and parts of California.

The Transition period of Chicano/Chicano literature reflects the transition that Mexican inhabitants of the United States were making. The dominant form in this period is the narrative BALLAD known as the 'corrido', part of an extensive ORAL TRADITION. The corrido typically represents the border conflicts between Mexicans and Anglos, especially in terms of COWBOY disputes. Collectively the corrido have been considered a form of EPIC. Many later writers have made use of the corrido tradition. The Interaction period of Chicano literature starts after 1910, when the Mexican Revolution led to the ending of the dictatorship and the founding of a constitutional republic. The revolution immediately stimulated immigration to the United States, and by the 1930s over a million Mexicans had migrated. While the corrido remains the dominant form, its subject now tends to focus on the problems of the immigrant who is defined by the Anglo as a second-class citizen. The corridos of this period form the basis of later works, and they begin to establish some of the recurrent themes in Chicano writing: the experience of immigration, the recognition of oppression, the pressure to assimilate to Anglo culture, bilingualism, the reformulation of the traditional family, and the relation between Roman Catholicism and contemporary social reality.

Although it may seem quiet in terms of the literature produced, the Adjustment period of Chicano writing is in some respects crucial to the subsequent surge of literature. This period is primarily one of consolidation of Chicano identities within the United States: significantly, one of the period's key texts was a critical analysis of the corrido tradition, *With His Pistol in His Hand* (1958) by Américo Paredes (b. 1915). The folk history *We Fed them Cactus* (1953) by Fabiola Cabeza de Baca Gilbert (1894–1991) and the novel *Pocho* (1959) by José Antonio Villareal (b. 1924) are other important works written in this period. Although later Chicano writers have reacted with ambivalence or hostility to it, *Pocho* was especially significant in helping to establish the presence of Chicano writing.

Undoubtedly, the most important period of Chicano/Chicana literature is the post-1965 'Renaissance'. The Renaissance developed as part of the Chicano civil rights movement known as La Causa, which from 1962 included strikes by and agitation on behalf of farm workers and fruit pickers, some of which were led by César Chávez. Drama played a significant role in this movement: in 1965 Luis Valdez (b. 1940) founded El Teatro Campesino ('The Farm-workers' Theatre'), a company that produced short one-act plays ('actos') dealing with the strikes and with labour conditions. The company also devised the dramatic form, the 'mito' or 'myth' play, which used parable and ritual. The groups El Teatro de la Esperanza ('Theatre of Hope') and Women in Teatro have also been important in the development of drama, which has proved crucial in the recognition given to Chicano/Chicana writing. Important dramatists include Denise Chavéz (b. 1948) and Cherríe Moraga (b. 1952). Valdez's *Zoot Suit* (1978) and Chavéz's *The Last of the Menu Girls* (1986) have been popular plays.

To a large extent the emergence of Chicano/Chicana literature was a consequence of a perceived need for such a body of literature and of a conscious attempt to bring it into existence. In 1969 the journal *El Grito* was founded at the University of California-Berkeley by a group of academics known as Quinto Sol. To help develop Chicano writing three annual Quinto Sol prizes were awarded from 1971. The three prize-winning authors are among the most important Chicano writers: Rolando Hinojosa (b. 1929), Rudolfo A. Anaya (b. 1937) and Tomás Rivera (1935–84). Their works have helped define much Chicano writing, especially Rivera's sketches ...*y no se lo tragó la tierra* [*And the Earth Did Not Part*] (1971), Hinojosa's *Estampas del valle*

[*Sketches of the Valley*] (1973) (both written in Spanish), and Anaya's novel *Bless Me, Ultima* (1972). Other key literature includes the novels *The Autobiography of a Brown Buffalo* (1972) and *Revolt of the Cockroach People* (1973) by Oscar Zeta Acosta (1935–74) and *The Rain God* (1984) and *Migrant Souls* (1990) by Arturo Islas (1938–91), the AUTOBIOGRAPHIES *Hunger of Memory* (1982) by Richard Rodriguez (b. 1944) and *The House on Mango Street* (1983) by Sandra Cisneros (b. 1954), and the poetry, fiction and essays in *Borderlands/La Frontera* (1987) by Gloria Anzaldúa (b. 1942). There have been several important anthologies of Chicano/Chicana literature, such as *This Bridge Called my Back* (1981), edited by Gloria Anzaldúa and Cherríe Moraga, and Anzaldúa's *Making Face/Making Soul* (1990). As well as those mentioned above, John Rechy (b. 1934), Estela Portillo-Trambley (b. 1936), Ricardo Sánchez (1941–95), Ana Castillo (b. 1953) and Helena Maria Viramontes (b. 1954) are prominent Chicano/Chicana writers.

Further reading

Chicano Authors (1980) by Juan Bruce-Novoa; Criticism in the Borderlands (1991), edited by Héctor Calderón and José David Saldívar; Chicano Literature: A Reference Guide (1989) edited by Julio A. Martínez and Francisco A. Lomelí; Chicano Theatre (1982) by Jorge Huerta, and Chicano Narrative (1990) by Ramon Saldivar.

Children's literature   Writing specifically intended for children has a long tradition in America. Broadly, it has developed in four major overlapping phases: the didactic, prominent from the PURITANS onwards; the representation of childhood as a special space in the 19th century; the development of fantasy towards the end of the 19th century, and from the mid 20th century, the development of literature dealing realistically with the difficulties of childhood and growing up. These kinds of children's literature overlap considerably, and there are many recurring and enduring elements in writing for children, such as the FANTASTIC, animal stories, DETECTIVE FICTION, SCIENCE FICTION, adventure fiction, and the retelling of existing stories and legends. The term 'children's literature' covers a wide range of writing that includes illustrated books for infants and works suitable for young adults. It is also important to bear in mind that the tastes of children often transgress international boundaries: British children's writing, for instance, has enjoyed considerable popularity in the United States. Furthermore, the boundaries between children's and adult literature are frequently blurred, since many works intended for an adult readership, such as Fenimore COOPER's LEATHER-STOCKING TALES and Harriet Beecher STOWE's *Uncle Tom's Cabin* (1852) have been enthusiastically taken up by children. Typically, however, children's literature represents the world from the child's point of view, and tends to represent children as essentially misunderstood by adults. Since children's literature plays a crucial role in the child's assimilation of social norms, there have been bitter disputes concerning its racial and gender stereotyping and the appropriateness of theme and content. Children's literature is the most censored of all literature.

The Puritans developed children's literature for the purpose of instruction, and this was broadly the function of the NEW ENGLAND PRIMER. But the pleasure to be gained from reading was also recognized, and there were many traditional stories available to children during the 18ᵗʰ century, one of the most renowned being *Songs from the Nursery* (1719). It was during the mid 19ᵗʰ century, though, that children's literature began to flourish, with many magazines aimed at a young audience, and a number of best-selling books. Major landmarks of 19ᵗʰ century children's literature include the series of novels published from 1827 by various writers using the pseudonym 'Peter Parley'; *The Wide, Wide World* (1850) by Susan Warner (1819–85); *Hans Brinker* (1865) by Mary Mapes Dodge (1831–1905); *Little Women* (1868) and its sequels by Louisa May Alcott (1832–88); *The Peterkin Papers* (1880) by Lucretia Hale (1820–1900); *The Story of a Bad Boy* (1870) by Thomas Bailey Aldrich (1836–1907); *What Katy Did* (1872) by Susan Coolidge (1845–1905) and the 'Uncle Remus' stories (1879 onwards) as told by Joel Chandler Harris (1848–1908). There has been much discussion over whether Mark TWAIN's *The Adventures of Tom Sawyer* (1876) and THE ADVENTURES OF HUCKLEBERRY FINN should be classed as children's literature. While they have been read and enjoyed by children, they do largely provide an adult perspective on childhood. However, it is significant that Twain represents childhood as separate from the adult world and also represents it as both subversive and threatened. This largely endorses the representation of childhood in many adult texts (such as *The Catcher in the Rye* (1951) by J. D. Salinger (b. 1919)), as well as in those intended for children.

Many enduringly popular novels for children were published towards the end of the 19ᵗʰ and early in the 20ᵗʰ century, notably *Little Lord Fauntleroy* (1886), *A Little Princess* (1905) and *The Secret Garden* (1911) by Frances Hodgson Burnett (1849–1924); the Oz stories of Frank L. Baum (1856–1919), beginning with *The Wonderful Wizard of Oz* (1900); *Rebecca of Sunnybrook Farm* (1903) by Kate Douglas Wiggin (1856–1923), and *Pollyana* (1913) by Eleanor Porter (1868–1920). This period also saw the establishment of syndicated popular series focused on characters such as Tom Swift, Nancy Drew, the Hardy Boys and the Bobbsey Twins. From the 1920s historically based realist fiction proved popular, most famously represented now by the 'Little House on the Prairie' novels (1932–43) of Laura Ingalls Wilder (1867–1957), but also evident in the work of Esther Forbes (1891–1967). Just as it did for adults, science fiction became increasingly popular in children's writing in the 1950s and 1960s, but this period also saw a new realism, with many authors focusing on the problems confronted by children. In particular, the novels of Joseph Krumgold (1908–80), and *From the Mixed-Up Files of Mrs. Basil E. Frankweiler* (1968) by E. L. Konigsburg (b. 1930) are considered especially influential, while the Earthsea Quartet (1968–90) of Ursula K. Le Guin (b. 1929) is a significant work of FANTASY. Prominent contemporary writers of children's literature include Natalie Babbitt (b. 1932), Virginia Hamilton (1936–2002) and Judy Blume (b. 1938), while the 'Babysitter's

Club' novels by Ann M. Martin (b. 1955) have been phenomenally popular. E. B. White (1899–1985), Theodor Geisel ('Dr. Seuss', 1904–91) and Maurice Sendak (b. 1928) also wrote enduringly popular works for children. Since 1922 the prestigious John Newbery Medal has been awarded annually for the best American book for children.

Further reading

What Katy Read (1995) by Shirley Foster and Judy Simons; *Criticism, Theory and Children's Literature* (1991) by Peter Hunt; *American Childhood* (1994) by Anne MacLeod, and *Trust Your Children* (1988) by Mark I. West.

Chinese Exclusion Act   Act passed by Congress in 1882, forbidding the IMMIGRATION of Chinese labourers for 10 years, and explicitly confirming that Chinese already in the United States were ineligible for American citizenship. The act was a response to anti-Chinese lobbying in California after the recession of the 1870s; an earlier act had been vetoed by President Hayes in 1879. A further series of anti-Chinese laws followed, and in 1892 the 1882 act was renewed for a further 10 years. After that, Chinese immigration was suspended indefinitely. The act not only signalled the beginning of restrictions on immigration into the United States, but was the only immigration act to define and discriminate against a particular ethnic group. It was repealed in 1943.

The series of anti-Chinese laws is important for much Chinese American writing. Maxine Hong KINGSTON presents the background to them in *China Men* (1981).

Chopin, Kate (Katherine O'Flaherty)   Novelist and short-story writer, born in 1851 in St Louis, Missouri. On marrying in 1870 she moved to Louisiana, which provides the setting for most of her fiction. After the death of her husband in 1882 she returned to St Louis and began writing for publication. She died in 1904.

Chopin's early work, the novel *At Fault* (1890) and the short-story collection *Bayou Folk* (1894), gave her a reputation as a LOCAL COLOUR writer. French writing, especially the work of Guy de Maupassant, influenced her, and her short stories commonly end with the type of plot twist characteristic of him. During her lifetime she published another collection of stories, *A Night in Acadie* (1897), and the novel *The Awakening* (1899) for which she is best known today. *The Awakening* was strongly influenced by the 1857 French novel *Madame Bovary* by Gustave Flaubert and was considered scandalous. A posthumous collection of stories, *A Vocation and a Voice*, was published in 1991. Chopin's work was little known until the 1960s, when it was seen to anticipate many of the concerns of modern FEMINIST writers.

Chopin worked mainly in the ROMANTIC tradition, although *The Awakening* interestingly explores tensions between romanticism and NATURALISM. Her prose style makes heavy use of symbolism and often has a lyrical, poetical quality. Thematically she frequently examines the married woman's lack of fulfilment and control in life; this is especially evident in *The Awakening*, in which Edna Pontellier's frustration leads her to adultery and suicide.

Further reading

Kate Chopin Reconsidered (1992), edited by Lynda S. Boren and Sara deSaussure Davis; *Kate Chopin: A Critical Biography* (1969) by Per Seyersted, and *Kate Chopin* (1990) by Emily Toth.

Citizenship   Under the Fourteenth Amendment to the CONSTITUTION (1868), all persons born or naturalized in the United States are citizens of the United States. To be naturalized as a citizen the applicant must be aged 18 years or over, have been resident in the United States continuously for 5 years (3 years if married to a United States citizen), be 'a person of good moral character', display an understanding of the English language, and be able to demonstrate 'knowledge and understanding of the fundamentals of the history, and the principles and form of government, of the United States'. The applicant must also swear a special oath of allegiance to the United States and the Constitution.

Civil rights movement   Mass campaign in the Southern states, generally led by African Americans, but with significant support from Northern whites. The movement's aims were to end SEGREGATION and to ensure full citizenship rights for African Americans, many of whom had been effectively disenfranchised in some Southern states. The campaign's success led to the passing of the Civil Rights Act (1964) and the Voting Rights Act (1965), and it became a model for many other movements. Prominent groups in the movement included the Southern Christian Leadership Conference (led by Martin Luther KING Jr), the Student Nonviolent Coordinating Committee, the NAACP and the Congress of Racial Equality.

The movement effectively began in Montgomery, Alabama, in 1955, with a boycott of the city's buses after a black woman, Rosa Parks (b. 1913), was arrested for refusing to surrender her seat to a white man on a racially segregated bus. Martin Luther King emerged as a leader during the boycott, and became the most prominent activist. The boycott led to many other actions, typically public demonstrations, marches and sit-ins that, under King's leadership, were non-violent. One of the campaign's highlights was a march on Washington in August 1963, during which King delivered his renowned 'I have a dream' speech. Throughout, the protesters' dignified passive restraint generated support and international admiration, especially when contrasted to the violence of some Southern whites. Public opinion was notably shaped by events such as white aggression over the attendance of nine black pupils at a high school in Little Rock, Arkansas, in 1957 and over the attempts of a black student, James H. Meredith, to register at the University of Mississippi in Oxford in 1962. White atrocities included the murder of a black leader, Medgar Evers, in 1963, the bombing of a church in Alabama that resulted in the deaths of four black girls in 1963, and the killing of three civil rights workers in Mississippi in 1964.

The movement generated drama, stories, poems and plays that fostered public awareness of injustice. This rich body of work includes poems by Gwendolyn BROOKS and Margaret Walker (1915–98), essays by James BALDWIN and songs by Bob Dylan (b. 1941). There are two classic autobiographies by civil rights activists: *Nigger* (1964) by Dick Gregory (b. 1932) and *Coming of Age in Mississippi* (1968) by Anne Moody (b. 1940). Alice WALKER's 1976 novel *Meridian* offers a valuable perspective on the movement.

Further reading

Parting the Waters (1988) by Taylor Branch and *Another Chance* (1981) by James B. Gilbert.

Civil War   The war started in 1861 after the SECESSION of the eleven CONFEDERATED STATES OF AMERICA, chiefly over fears that the recently elected President Lincoln would abolish SLAVERY. The shelling of Fort Sumter, South Carolina, by Confederate forces on 12 April actually began the war. Although its vastly superior communications, technology and industry gave the North a considerable advantage, the South, under the command of Robert E. Lee, was initially victorious in a series of battles, notably two at Bull Run. This almost persuaded the British, with their interests in the Southern cotton trade, to declare support for the Confederacy. However, the Union forces rallied after the second battle of Bull Run, and crucially survived a three-day battle at Gettysburg in July 1863, generally considered the war's turning point. Although many of the Civil War battles were intense and resulted in exceptionally heavy casualties, neither side held a clear advantage until, after the fall of Vicksburg in 1863, the North, now under the command of General Ulysses Grant, was able to begin marching on the South. Having captured Atlanta, General Sherman began his 'March to the Sea' in autumn 1864, which devastated a considerable area and led by January 1865 to the fall of Georgia and Tennessee. Federal forces then concentrated on routing the Confederates in North and South Carolina and in Virginia. On 9 April 1865 General Lee surrendered to General Grant at Appomattox Court House, and the war was over.

The war had an extraordinarily high casualty rate: about half of all the men who served in it were killed or wounded. This was partly because the firepower of the armies gave enormous advantage to defensive strategies and made any advance difficult without sustaining heavy losses. The total war dead is estimated at up to 650,000, with a total of about 500,000 wounded. Most of these were conscripts: although both sides began the war with volunteers, both had introduced conscription by early 1863 (this caused anti-draft riots in New York). The cost of the war has been estimated at over $15 billion. The war's official name is the War of the Rebellion, while in the South it is sometimes referred to as the War Between the States.

Prominent writers who served in the war include Thomas B. Thorpe (1815–78),

Fitz-James O'Brien (1828–1862), Thomas Wentworth Higginson (1823–1911), John William De Forest (1826–1906), Lew Wallace (1827–1905), Sidney Lanier (1842–81) and Ambrose Bierce (1842–?1914), while Walt WHITMAN, Louisa May Alcott (1832–88) and Constance Fenimore Woolson (1840–94) worked voluntarily as nurses during it. Mark TWAIN fought briefly for the South and recounts the experience in his sketch 'The Private History of a Campaign that Failed' (1885).

Whitman's view that 'The real war will never get in the books' seemed prophetic, since at first the war stimulated mainly poetry, with distinguished poems by John Greenleaf Whittier (1807–92), Henry Wadsworth Longfellow (1807–82), James Russell Lowell (1819–91) and William Gilmore Simms (1806–70), as well as two major masterpieces, Whitman's *Drum-Taps* (1865) and Herman MELVILLE's *Battle-Pieces* (1866). After 1865 sketches and memoirs were frequently published, and they include a series by Whitman (published in 1882 as *Specimen Days*) and Higginson's *Army Life in a Black Regiment* (1870). There was some reflective fiction set during the war, notably Lanier's *Tiger-Lilies* (1867) and De Forest's *Miss Ravenel's Conversion from Secession to Loyalty* (1867), and the war formed a significant background in a variety of novels, such as Louisa May Alcott's *Little Women* (1869). Henry Adams (1838–1918) would wryly present his first-hand experience of the tense diplomatic situation in London in *The Education of Henry Adams* (1906/1918).

Strikingly, however, it was a later generation with no first-hand Civil War experience that began to treat it as a major literary subject, perhaps partly encouraged by the development of NATURALISM and of REALISM. The most influential later-generation writer was Stephen CRANE, with his IMPRESSIONISTIC novel *The Red Badge of Courage* (1895) and several stories. The war gradually began to generate a large amount of popular writing, including the narrative poem *John Brown's Body* (1928) by Stephen Vincent Benét and the novel *Gone with the Wind* (1936) by Margaret Mitchell (1900–49). As part of his representation of troubled Southern history, the war and its aftermath feature significantly in several important works by William FAULKNER, notably *Absalom, Absalom!* (1936) and *The Unvanquished* (1938). Several of the writers associated with the AGRARIANS wrote on the war, notably Allen Tate (1899–1979) in his 1930 poem 'For the Confederate Dead', itself repeating a title that had been used by Henry Timrod (1828–67). The war remains an important subject for many writers, and continues to be explored in a considerably wide range of texts.

Further reading

The Unwritten War (1973) by Daniel Aaron and *Patriotic Gore* (1962) by Edmund Wilson. The war's origins are examined in *The Impending Crisis* (1976) by David M. Potter and Don E. Fehrenbacher. Histories of the war include *Battle Cry of Freedom* (1989) by James M. McPherson and *The American Civil War* (1975) by Peter J. Parish.

Cold War Term coined in 1947 by the presidential adviser Bernard Baruch (1870–1965) to describe the post-WORLD WAR II relationship between the United

States and the communist Soviet Union. The potentially devastating global effects of war between the two intensified after 1949, when the Soviets developed atomic weaponry and a massive build-up of nuclear arms began. To a large extent Cold War policies were devoted to maintaining a balance between the two powers, by containment of the other's sphere of influence and by offering (usually covert) support for resistance to the other's regime. During the Cold War a series of crises threatened to upset the balance of power and precipitate direct confrontation: this included the Soviet suppression of revolts in Hungary (1956) and Czechoslovakia (1968), the CUBAN MISSILE CRISIS (1962), the American military campaigns in Korea and VIETNAM, and the Soviet invasion of Afghanistan (1979). The Cold War ended abruptly in 1991 after a series of internal reforms led to the break-up of the Soviet Union.

In the United States the Cold War stimulated fear of communism, anxiety over nuclear devastation, and a growing alienation from and distrust of the government. Many American writers directly explored these aspects of the war, notably Saul BELLOW, E. L. Doctorow (b. 1931) and Robert Coover (b. 1932), while others, such as Thomas PYNCHON, focused on the absurdity that the war seemed to generate. Recently, writers such as Philip ROTH and Don DeLILLO have re-engaged with aspects of the Cold War from a fresh perspective.

Further reading

Restrained Response (1990) by Arne Axelsson; *Monsters, Mushroom Clouds and the Cold War* (2001) by M. Keith Booker; *Cold War Poetry* (2001) by Edward Brunner, and *American Fiction in the Cold War* (1991) by Thomas H. Schaub.

Compromise of 1850   Set of measures through which the sectional interests of slave and free states were balanced after new territories were acquired by the United States as a consequence of the MEXICAN WAR. The Compromise agreement, which included the passing of the 1850 FUGITIVE SLAVE ACT, enabled California to join the Union as a free state. Abolitionists deplored the Compromise, and in his 1850 poem 'Ichabod!' John Greenleaf Whittier (1807–92) attacked the appeasements made by Daniel Webster in its passing.

Confederated States of America   Formed in 1861, the Confederacy was the group of eleven Southern states that seceded from the Union and passed its own constitution. The Confederacy eventually comprised the states of North and South Carolina, Georgia, Alabama, Florida, Mississippi, Louisiana, Arkansas, Tennessee, Virginia and Texas. Jefferson Davis was the president, and the Confederate States had their own money and flag. Vice-President Alexander H. Stephens said that the 'cornerstone' of the Confederacy was 'the great truth that the negro is not equal to the white man'. In its Constitution, the right to possess slaves was guaranteed, although four border slaveholding states (Delaware, Missouri, Kentucky and Maryland) neither joined the

Confederacy nor seceded. After defeat in the Civil War the Confederacy ended and the Confederate States eventually rejoined the Union. The Confederacy has frequently been romanticized in literature of the South.

Confessional poetry   Term used in 1967 by M. L. Rosenthal to describe an influential trend apparent in poetry since the 1950s. In confessional writing the poet's personal experience is accorded particular prominence and the conventional gap between poet and poetic persona seems to have been extinguished. The poetry of Robert Lowell, John Berryman (1914–72), Anne Sexton (1928–74), Sylvia Plath, and to a lesser degree, of Theodore Roethke (1908–63), Randall Jarrell (1914–65) and Allen Ginsberg, has been called confessional, and the books *Heart's Needle* (1959) by W. D. Snodgrass (b. 1926) and Lowell's *Life Studies* (1959) are often taken as initiating the style.

Although confessional poetry varies considerably, there are shared aspects. The poets termed confessional were among the first to undergo psychoanalysis and to incorporate it into their poetry; for instance, by exploring childhood experience as the source of adult difficulties. Accordingly, 'confessional' is sometimes used to describe the representation of extreme, personal, possibly painful, experience, for therapeutic or cathartic effect. However, confessional poetry is not merely private, and the writers were often at pains to stress this: Berryman said he responded to the label 'with rage and contempt' and Plath emphasized that there was a crucial distance between herself and the personae of her poems. Much confessional poetry actually demonstrates an engagement with public, social and political concerns, and explores how these impinge on the individual. It is also important to emphasize that confessional poetry exists within a strong American tradition. Although the articulation of personal experience was revolutionary in directly countering the style of objective, impersonal poetry that had been encouraged by the New Criticism, confessionalism restored a tradition of personal witness and authenticity that had been initiated in Puritan literature and developed by many later writers, such as Walt Whitman.

Further reading

The Psycho-Political Muse (1987) by Paul Breslin; 'Confessionalism' by Lucy Collins in *A Companion to Twentieth Century Poetry* (2001) edited by Neil Roberts, and *The New Poets* (1967) by M. L. Rosenthal.

Confidence man   The confidence man has been a significant recurring figure in American literature, and has often been considered an admirable archetype in a culture that values self-representation, confidence, ingenuity and resourcefulness; as Gary Lindberg has suggested, he is 'a covert cultural hero'. Literary works about confidence men are often concerned with the relationship between appearance and reality, the nature of trust, the social implications of confidence and the power of self-fashioning.

The term 'confidence man' was first used in the late 1840s, although the figure had long been a familiar one, and the 19th century interest in confidence tricks is evident from the enduring popularity of the much-revised 1855 autobiography of Phineas T. Barnum (1810–91). Edgar Allan Poe considered the confidence man in the essay 'Diddling Considered as One of the Exact Sciences' (1843), and in his novel *The Confidence Man* (1857) Herman Melville combined the figure with the character of the TRICKSTER in an incisive analysis of contemporary society. Notable confidence men include Mark Twain's Colonel Sellers (in *The Gilded Age*, 1873, and *The American Claimant*, 1892) and William Faulkner's Flem Snopes (in *The Hamlet*, 1931, *The Town*, 1957 and *The Mansion*, 1959), while many novels and dramas depict various confidence tricks. The plays and screenplays of David Mamet frequently focus on confidence men, especially *The Shawl* (1985), *House of Games* (1987) and *The Spanish Prisoner* (1998).

Further reading

Confidence Men and Painted Women (1982) by Karen Halttunen; Fast Talk and Flush Times (1985) by William E. Lenz; The Confidence Man in American Literature (1981) by Gary Lindberg, and The Confidence Game in American Literature (1975) by Warwick Wadlington.

Congregationalism   Protestant religious movement that originated in England at the end of the 16th century and which was of special significance in the organization and the development of Puritanism in colonial New England. While acknowledging the necessity of a church structure, the Congregationalists advocated that each individual church community should have a high level of autonomy from a centralized church. The Puritans who founded the Massachusetts Bay Colony were Congregationalists who also wished to retain contact with the Anglican church, whereas those who founded the Plymouth Colony were separatists. In 1648 the two groups agreed on the 'Cambridge Platform', which endorsed the Congregationalist principle of autonomy. Congregationalism has been called the 'established religion of New England' and the movement was behind the founding of the universities of Harvard and Yale. As a consequence of disagreements after the Great Awakening Congregationalism became sharply divided in the early 19th century with the rise of Unitarianism.

Connecticut Wits   Also known as the Hartford Wits, the Connecticut Wits were a group of poets associated with Yale who flourished in the early years of the republic. The three most prominent members were John Trumbull (1750–1831), Timothy Dwight (1752–1817) and Joel Barlow (1754–1812). The group was nationalistic in outlook, and wrote public poetry on American themes, often collaborating in mock-heroic satirical verse on contemporary politics. The Wits imitated the styles of the British poets they most admired, particularly Alexander Pope and John Dryden. They also aspired to write the American EPIC, believing that the new nation's origins and ethos should be commemorated in the style of Virgil's *The Aeneid*. Barlow's *The*

Vision of Columbus (1787) represented such an attempt; the poem was enlarged and revised later as *The Columbiad* (1807) and is often considered an important precursor of later American epic writing. Noteworthy writing by the Wits includes Trumbull's *M'Fingal, A Modern Epic* (1776, revised 1782) and Dwight's *Conquest of Canaan* (1785).

Constitution debate   Series of pamphlets, letters and articles appearing in newspapers and journals in the period 1787–8, addressing the issue of whether the draft CONSTITUTION should be ratified by the thirteen states. However, the scope of the debate is much broader than the question of ratification alone and deals with fundamental issues regarding the nature of the republic and the future of the state. The debate was primarily between the Federalists, who urged ratification and were in favour of a strong centralized government, and the anti-Federalists who supported relative autonomy for individual states and were distrustful of centralized administration. James Madison (1751–1836) and Alexander Hamilton (1755–1804) were prominent Federalists, while Patrick Henry (1736–99) and Thomas Jefferson (1743–1826) were among the anti-Federalists, who eventually formed the first Republican Party. The articles published during the debate were usually published under *noms de plume* that echoed ancient Roman debates on the form of government; for instance, although written by three people, all of the *FEDERALIST PAPERS* appeared under the name 'Publius' while the anti-Federalists often used the name 'Brutus'.

The Library of America two-volume *Debate on the Constitution* (1993), edited by Bernard Bailyn, is a valuable collection of material.

Constitution of the United States of America   Designated as the 'supreme Law of the Land' the Constitution defines the United States' form of government, the role of its political institutions (including the presidency and the SUPREME COURT) and the rights of citizens. It was drafted at a special convention in Philadelphia in 1787, which met to revise the existing Articles of Confederation that had served as the Constitution since 1781. The draft owed much to the views of James Madison (1751–1836), known as the 'father of the Constitution'. It had to be ratified by two-thirds of the thirteen states, and the intense CONSTITUTION DEBATE ensued, especially focused on the nature of federalism. The *FEDERALIST PAPERS*, mostly written by Alexander Hamilton (1755–1804), were published to encourage adoption. By 1788 the necessary number of states had ratified the draft and the Constitution was adopted in 1789.

The Constitution allows for amendments if these are proposed by at least two-thirds of both Houses of Congress and subsequently ratified by at least two-thirds of the states within a time-limit set by Congress. There have been twenty-seven amendments, the first ten of which, known as the BILL OF RIGHTS, were adopted together in 1791. Notable amendments include the THIRTEENTH (1865), which abolished SLAVERY in the Confederated States; the Fourteenth (1868), which guaranteed the rights of the individual in all states; the Fifteenth (1870) which established the right to vote regardless of race; the Nineteenth (1920) establishing women's suffrage and the Twenty-sixth (1971), which established the right to vote for all over the age of 18. PROHIBITION was introduced with the Eighteenth Amendment (1919) and abolished with the Twenty-first (1933).

Contraband   Term used during the CIVIL WAR for a captured or fugitive slave, indicating that he or she was property without an owner.

Cooper, James Fenimore   The first major American novelist. Cooper was born in Burlington, New Jersey, in 1789. His father, William Cooper, founded a settlement in upstate New York (now called Cooperstown, after him), and Cooper was brought up there (he retained the name Fenimore in honour of his mother, Elizabeth Fenimore). Cooper was expelled from Yale College in 1805, then enlisted in the navy but resigned when he married in 1811. His first novel, *Precaution*, was published in 1820. With his second, *The Spy* (1821), he began to establish a national and international reputation and became a professional novelist. Cooper was involved in various New York literary circles, and lived in Europe for an extended period (1826–33). Returning to Cooperstown he became increasingly involved in conservative politics. His frequent lawsuits and his stance against modern American DEMOCRACY led to a diminishment of his earlier popularity in the United States, but he continued to write and publish prolifically. He died in Cooperstown in 1851, having published thirty-two novels, various collections of political commentary, essays and travel writing and a history of the American navy.

Cooper was the first American novelist able to support himself from the sales of his novels, which were enthusiastically received both in the United States and, significantly, in Europe. Furthermore, he was the first novelist to make successful use of the American landscape and of uniquely American situations. His reputation today rests mainly on the series of five LEATHER-STOCKING TALES (1823–41) and on his creation of the character of Natty Bumppo, but he also published an impressive series of sea novels, a number of significant works set during the revolutionary war, and one of the first American anti-Utopian novels, *The Crater* (1847). His novels set in Europe are little known today.

Cooper was called the 'American Scott' because of his Walter Scott-like ROMANCE narratives of historical events, and his commitment to the novel of adventure. Taken together, his romances of early American experience are often considered versions of American EPIC. His FRONTIER novels influenced the development of the WESTERN, although during his lifetime he was criticized for his romanticization of the frontier hero and for his depiction of the Native American as noble savage. While Cooper's prose style and plotting often seem awkward to modern readers (both were mercilessly attacked by Mark TWAIN in his celebrated essay 'Fenimore Cooper's Literary Offences' (1895)), Cooper remains important both in his own right and for the influence he exerted on later developments in American literature.

See the biography *James Fenimore Cooper* (1990) by Robert Emmet Long, and the critical works *James Fenimore Cooper: The American Scott* (1967) by George Dekker; *James Fenimore Cooper: A Collection of Critical Essays* (1979), edited by Wayne Fields; *Cooper's Americans* (1965) by Kay S. House, and *The American Abraham* (1987) by Warren Motley.

Copyright law   Under the Copyright Act of 1790, works of American-born authors were copyrighted to them in the United States for 28 years after first publication or performance. Since no international copyright agreement existed, works of foreign-born authors were not in copyright in the United States. Effectively, American publishers were able to print copies of non-American works without payment to their authors. As printing technology improved in the early 19th century, this situation came to be considered severely detrimental to the development of American literature, because many publishers preferred to print British works (especially those of Walter Scott and Charles Dickens) for which they knew there was a ready market, rather than risk money on American works. (Some publishers were able to bring out a pirated edition of a novel within twenty-four hours of receiving it.) The pirating issue worked both ways; American authors were not usually able to copyright their works abroad, unless there had been prior publication abroad or a period of residence there. This situation led to some American writers, like Washington IRVING, establishing residence in Europe, and to many novels (including *MOBY-DICK*) being published first in Britain rather than America. Any popular American novel could be pirated in Britain, as was the case with Harriet Beecher STOWE's *Uncle Tom's Cabin* (1852).

Until 1856 the copyright situation for drama was even more problematic. Foreign plays could be performed without payment of royalty, and for the American playwright copyright covered only a play's publication, not performance. Thus, once a dramatist had been paid a fee for the work, no royalty was due, no matter how many performances took place. The authors of some extremely popular American plays, Samuel Woodworth (1785–1842) and John Augustus Stone (1800–34), both died in poverty, having made very little money from their work. The 1856 Copyright Act rectified this by protecting performance as well as publication.

From the 1820s onwards there was much agitation by both British and American writers for an international copyright law, although some publishers strongly opposed reform. In the 1860s and 1870s a series of informal agreements helped curb the most extreme abuses, and the 1887 Berne Convention established international copyright for several European countries. The United States did not subscribe to the convention, but in 1891 passed a new Copyright Act that outlawed the pirating of foreign works.

Consequently, 1894 was the first year in which more American than foreign novels were published in the United States. After revisions to copyright law in 1978, a work is in copyright for 50 years after the death of the author, or at least 75 years after publication in the case of anonymous or pseudonymous works.

Cowboy   Historically the cowboy flourished in the period 1865–90, when cattle were herded on vast open ranges, especially in Texas, before the enclosure and settlement of the land. The cowboy developed special skills for the management of herds, and these are often celebrated in COWBOY POETRY. The first stories depicting cowboys appeared in the 1880s, and the cowboy became a staple of the WESTERN, typically a heroic figure although often seen in conflict with settlers and with Native Americans over the ownership and use of the land. An archetype of self-reliant manly heroism, the fictional cowboy's appeal lay primarily in his unequivocal masculinity, and popular cowboy stories often focus on aspects of male freedom that can find its fullest expression beyond the influence of women. As Zane Grey (1872–1939) put it in *The Light of the Western Stars* (1913), cowboys are 'great big simple boys'. As well as in Grey's work, significant representations of the cowboy can be found in *The Virginian* (1902) by Owen Wister (1860–1938), *The Log of a Cowboy* (1903) and *Cattle Brands* (1906) by Andy Adams (1859–1935), and in Westerns by Max Brand (1892–1944) and Louis L'Amour (1908–88). The 20th century transformation of the cowboy into dude rancher or professional rodeo rider has been examined in various texts, notably in the stories collected in *Close Range* (1999) by Annie Proulx (b. 1935).

Cowboy poetry   Style of poetry that developed in the 1870s and was particularly popular in the early 20th century. David Stanley describes it as 'a hybrid of folk and popular kinds of poetry [that] borrows deftly from popular and commercial images of the West, appropriating, parodying and critiquing'. Strongly related to work songs and the BALLAD, the poetry was usually written by cowboys, typically in set forms and dealing with the nature of the cowboy's life, focusing on work, sometimes celebrating the cowboy's skills and way of life, but also examining how far this lifestyle was being threatened. Although very much part of an ORAL TRADITION, cowboy poetry was widely published in newspapers, and there were several popular anthologies, notably *Songs of the Cowboys* (1908) edited by N. Howard Thorp, and *Cowboy Songs* (1910), edited by John Lomax. Significant cowboy poets include Lawrence Chittenden (1862–1934), James Barton Adams (1843–1918), Bruce Kiskaddon (1878–1949), Charles Badger Clark (1883–1957), Curly Fletcher (1892–1953) and Carlos Ashley (1903–93). There has been a recent revival of interest in cowboy poetry, with several critical studies and the anthologies *Cowboy Poetry: A Gathering* (1985) and *New Cowboy Poetry: A Contemporary Gathering* (1990), both edited by Hal Cannon, and *The Big Roundup* (2001), edited by Margo Metegrano.

Further reading

The Cowboy (1992) by Blake Allmendinger and *Cowboy Poets and Cowboy Poetry* (2000), edited by David Stanley and Elaine Thatcher.

Cracker   Offensive slang term for a white person, now used mainly by African Americans. It was formerly used more specifically to describe the poor white backwoodsman of Georgia or Florida. The name derives from cracked corn, the supposed subsistence diet of poor whites.

Cracker-barrel humour   Comic writing style that makes use of rustic directness and simplicity masquerading as profundity. It is primarily associated with mid 19th century New Englanders, but the term has been used to cover comic writing from all regions. Seba Smith (1792–1868), Josh Billings (pseudonym of Henry Wheeler Shaw, 1818–85) and Artemus Ward (pseudonym of Charles Farrar Browne, 1834–67) were celebrated humourists in this style, which is also used in the early writing of Mark Twain. The term derives from the practice of men exchanging gossip and opinion around the cracker barrel in the local general store.

Crane, Stephen   Novelist, short-story writer and poet, born in Newark, New Jersey, in 1871. Crane was the youngest of fourteen children, whose father, a Methodist minister, died when Crane was 9 years old. Crane attended Syracuse University for a year before going to live in New York City. There he worked for several newspapers and published his first novel, *Maggie, A Girl of the Streets*, pseudonymously in 1893 (revised edition, 1896). In 1895 he published his second novel *The Red Badge of Courage* and a book of poems, *The Black Riders*. *The Red Badge of Courage* was a popular success. Crane was hired as a roving reporter in the West and New Mexico, an experience that led to several Western stories and sketches. After a period back in New York he was hired in 1896 to cover the Cuban rebellion against Spain. However he was shipwrecked sailing to Cuba, an experience forming the basis of his short story 'The Open Boat' (1897). He then went to Greece to report on the war between Turkey and Greece, returning to the United States to cover the Spanish–American War. His writing on this war was collected in *Wounds in the Rain* (1900). In 1897 he and his lover Cora Howorth Steward (a former brothel-owner whom he had met in Florida) settled in England, where he became friendly with his neighbours Joseph Conrad and Henry James. He visited Ireland in 1897, subsequently writing a series of sketches and a novel (co-written with Robert Barr), titled *The O'Ruddy* (1903). His second book of poems, *War is Kind*, was published in 1899. Crane died of tuberculosis in Badenweiler, Germany, in 1900.

In his notebook Crane observed, 'The true artist is the man who leaves behind pictures of his time as they appear to him.' This statement is deceptively simple. Behind it are a series of beliefs: there is no universal truth; environment and circumstance determine the nature of reality; the artist has a responsibility to bear witness rather than merely entertain, and the artistic vision is inevitably subjective. Crane began as a writer firmly in the developing style of NATURALISM, and *Maggie* is a classic of that genre. However, as he became more interested in individual perception he moved away from naturalism. This is evident in *The Red Badge of Courage*, in which he impressionistically explores the growing awareness of Henry Fleming. Although Crane insisted on the need to live without illusions (one of the themes of 'The Open Boat'), some of his later work such as 'The Blue Hotel' (1898) explores the enduring need for belief. Crane is a complex writer, often exploring alienation, isolation and social injustice with a sharp sense of irony. His use of understatement, the often spare, laconic language of his poetry and prose, and his overall belief in the need to witness events first-hand were influential on many later writers, especially Ernest HEMINGWAY.

Further reading

Stephen Crane's Artistry (1975) by Frank Bergon; *The Pluralistic Philosophy of Stephen Crane* (1993) by Patrick K. Dooley; *The Color of the Sky: A Study of Stephen Crane* (1989) by David Halliburton, and *Stephen Crane: A Biography* (1968) by R. W. Stallman.

Creole literature   Derived from the Spanish 'criollo' and the French 'créole' (indigenous), the term Creole is used in Louisiana to refer to the group of Louisianan whites who claim descent from the original French or Spanish settlers of the region, in contrast to the Acadians ('Cajuns'), who arrived from French Nova Scotia. George Washington Cable (1844–1925), Kate CHOPIN, Grace Elizabeth King (1851–1932) and Alice Nelson Dunbar (1875–1935) are among those providing vivid accounts of Creole culture.

The Crisis   Monthly magazine published since 1910 by the NAACP. From its founding until 1934 it was edited by W. E. B. DU BOIS and during the HARLEM RENAISSANCE it published work by Jean Toomer (1894–1967), Arna Bontemps (1902–73), Langston Hughes (1902–67) and Countee Cullen (1903–46).

The Crucible   Play in four acts by Arthur MILLER, first performed in 1953. It was both critically acclaimed and popular from the first and it remains Miller's most frequently produced play. Its subject is the 1692 SALEM WITCH TRIALS, which Miller researched carefully, and from which he took the play's characters, although he stated he was more concerned with exploring the 'central nature' of the events than with accurate transcription of historical fact. The play's action centres on John Proctor, a farmer whose wife Elizabeth is among those accused of witchcraft by Abigail Williams, a teenaged girl once employed by him and with whom he had an adulterous relationship. In court Proctor confesses to the adultery as a means of exposing Abigail, but he is then himself accused of witchcraft. In the play's climax Proctor is at first willing to confess in order to escape hanging, but he refuses to testify against others. He eventually renounces his confession and is executed.

The play deals with what Miller called 'a paradox in whose grip we still live'. That is, the community's defence of itself against 'ideological enemies' turns to repression, which then threatens to destroy the community it was formed to save. Miller himself draws attention to the analogy between the witch-hunts and McCarthyism, but the play has a much wider thematic resonance, exploring issues of self-awareness and integrity, the nature of power and interpretation.

Further reading

Twentieth Century Interpretations of The Crucible (1972), edited by John H. Ferres, and *The Crucible in History and Other Essays* (2000) by Arthur Miller.

Cuban missile crisis Confrontation during the COLD WAR in 1962 between the United States and the Soviet Union, which seemed as though it would lead inevitably to nuclear devastation.

In 1959 the communist revolution in Cuba resulted in Fidel Castro gaining power, supported by the Soviet Union led by President Khrushchev. Perceiving a communist Cuba as a threat, President Kennedy supported an invasion of the island by exiles in April 1961. The offensive, known as the 'Bay of Pigs', failed ignominiously. In the meantime, the Soviet Union had begun to ship nuclear weapons to Cuba. President Kennedy ordered a blockade on Cuba in October 1962, stating that the US was prepared to seize any nuclear weaponry being supplied by Soviet ships. For ten days nuclear destruction seemed a real possibility, but the crisis was averted on 29 October when Khrushchev agreed to dismantle the existing Cuban missile sites. After a subsequent series of mutual concessions the crisis was resolved.

The crisis gave fresh urgency to fears of nuclear destruction and this was reflected in a number of APOCALYPTIC works, including the BALLAD 'A Hard Rain's A-Gonna Fall' by Bob Dylan (b. 1941). *Thirteen Days* (1969) by Robert F. Kennedy is a celebrated account of the crisis, which often appears in works set in the early 1960s: see, for instance, *Couples* (1968) by John Updike (b. 1932). The Bay of Pigs invasion plays a significant role in *American Tabloid* (1995) by James Ellroy (b. 1948).

D

Declaration of Independence   The key text of the American Revolution, which also articulates some of the ideals of the United States. Meeting in Philadelphia in June 1776, during the Revolutionary War, the Second Continental Congress of the Thirteen Colonies created a committee to draft a statement justifying the colony's independence from Britain, in case Congress should agree to this course of action. The committee was made up of Thomas Jefferson, John Adams, Benjamin Franklin, Roger Sherman and Robert R. Livingston. Jefferson wrote the first draft of the document that became the Declaration of Independence, although it was enlarged and revised by the committee and by Congress (which, among other changes, deleted a condemnation of the African slave trade). Congress voted for independence on 2 July and ratified the declaration on 4 July (thus, the 4 July holiday commemorates the adoption of the declaration rather than the vote for independence). Although the introduction to the declaration states that it is 'The Unanimous Declaration of the Thirteen United States of America', this was not the case, since the New York delegates had abstained, believing that they lacked their colony's authorization to vote for independence (they received this and ratified the document on 15 July).

The declaration is specifically a product of the Enlightenment, particularly in its assumption of a social contract from which the authority of the state arises, and its political philosophy is directly traceable to the ideas of the English thinker John Locke (1632–1704). The declaration is often seen to represent some of the ideals and aspirations of the United States, especially in its opening assertions 'that all men are created equal, that they are endowed by their Creator with certain unalienable Rights, that among these are Life, Liberty and the pursuit of Happiness'. The fact that the declaration was framed and ratified by the male representatives of a slave-owning country has been frequently noted as ironic. (See, for instance, the pastiche of the declaration in Chapter 157 of the 1849 novel *Mardi* by Herman Melville, and the 1852 speech 'What to the Slave is the Fourth of July?' by Frederick Douglass.) In 1848 the women's movement ratified its own version of the declaration at the Seneca Falls Convention.

Deference   In racial terms, deference was one of the informal means by which whites maintained authority over blacks in the South after emancipation. Deference involved a set of unwritten rules regarding the attitude blacks had to adopt in social interactions with whites; they included for instance respectful formal address, the removal of a hat, the avoidance of eye contact and the submissive acceptance of a patronizing form of address. An individual's failure to obey the unwritten rules of deference was extremely dangerous and likely to have serious consequences; lynching might well result from a perceived failure to defer. The system of deference gradually ended in the 1960s with the civil rights gained by blacks.

The most important study of racial deference is in *Caste and Class in a Southern Town* (1937) by the sociologist John Dollard. Dollard observed that while deference supports racial inequality and injustice it is also a means of preserving some kind of social equilibrium in a community and that any individual refusal to defer potentially destabilizes communal black–white relations. Deference is a theme in much writing about black–white relations, and is treated specifically by William FAULKNER in his 1948 novel *Intruder in the Dust*.

DeLillo, Don Novelist, born in New York City in 1936. DeLillo graduated from Fordham University in 1958 and worked for several years in advertising. He published his first novel, *Americana*, in 1971, followed by *End Zone* (1972) and *Great Jones Street* (1973). He began to receive critical attention with *Ratner's Star* (1976), and after several other novels (*Players*, 1977; *Running Dog*, 1978; *The Names*, 1982), the publication of *White Noise* in 1985 brought him widespread acclaim. Three ambitious and important novels followed: *Libra* (1988), *Mao II* (1991) and *Underworld* (1997). A novella, *The Body Artist*, was published in 2001.

A public and politically engaged writer, DeLillo's major work incisively analyses post-1945 American society and historical events such as the KENNEDY ASSASSINATION (*Libra*) and the beginning of the atomic age (*Underworld*). The rituals of American life fascinate him, and he has written powerfully of ecological threats and of the secrecy and subterfuge involved in political and social power. DeLillo can be a darkly comic writer, notably in his earlier work, but he also offers a thoughtful insight into menace and conspiracy, and in *Underworld* especially there is a breadth of vision and an ambition unusual in contemporary novels. Typically his novels are engaging and unsettling hybrids of different prose styles and kinds of writing, such as the detective story, the thriller and the farce. Wendy Steiner has referred to his work as 'generic cacophony', and Frank Lentricchia has observed that DeLillo's novels are 'montages of tones, styles, and voices that have the effect of yoking together terror and wild humor as the essential tone of contemporary America'.

Further reading

Introducing Don DeLillo (1991), edited by Frank Lentricchia; American Magic and Dread: Don DeLillo's Dialogue with Culture (2000) by Mark Osteen, and Critical Essays on Don DeLillo (2000), edited by Hugh Ruppersburg and Tim Engles.

Democracy Although a commitment to representative democracy now seems a defining principle of the United States, democracy itself has frequently been a controversial subject. In the 18th and early 19th centuries many commentators feared that the form of democratic republic established by the CONSTITUTION would mean rule by the mob, while others saw democracy as an interesting experiment, which provoked much analysis and speculation, most significantly by Alexis De Tocqueville (1805–59) in DEMOCRACY IN AMERICA. The United States' claim to be a democracy at all has been challenged, with critics pointing out that from the beginning the franchise was seriously restricted by property qualifications and by the exclusion of women and various minorities. The franchise was gradually widened, especially during the 1830s with the presidency of Andrew Jackson, and later after the abolition of SLAVERY and the granting of the vote to women in 1920.

As a literary subject, democracy has been treated in a variety of ways. Some writers, notably James Fenimore COOPER, expressed a patrician mistrust of the concept. Others, though, embraced it wholeheartedly; none more so than Walt WHITMAN, the self-styled 'Bard of Democracy'. As well as his expressions of trust in the democratic republic he also developed a style of poetry that he considered appropriate to democratic and libertarian principles, using FREE VERSE and having an inclusive rather than a selective range of subjects. (To a remarkable degree Whitman's work fulfilled De Tocqueville's speculation that a democracy would produce poetry that was energetic, rough, untutored and passionate.) There is also a considerable American tradition of writers – including Whitman himself at times – exposing the fallacy of democratic representation and the prevalence of corruption: *Democracy* (1880) by Henry Adams (1838–1918) and *Democracy* (1984) by Joan Didion (b. 1934) are major novels in this style.

Democracy in America   Influential and much-cited French commentary on the United States, written by Alexis De Tocqueville (1805–59). *De la démocratie* was published in four volumes (1835–40) following De Tocqueville's nine-month visit to the United States (1831–32), and was soon translated into English. Its scope is broad and the analysis often incisive: De Tocqueville wrote, 'I confess that in America I saw more than America; I sought the image of democracy itself, with its inclinations, its character, its prejudices, and its passions, in order to learn what we have to fear or hope from its progress.' The work attractively combines political science, social observation, travel writing and speculation on the nation's future. De Tocqueville considers a wide range of aspects of American life, including political participation, individualism, the professions, the penal system, the future of the arts, racial concerns and the role of women, and considers how these have been determined and will be affected by DEMOCRACY.

Depression (or Great Depression)   The most severe economic recession in history began in October 1929 with the WALL STREET crash. The 1920s had seen a boom and for some time before 1929 intense and uncontrolled speculation had driven up share prices to unprecedented and unrealistic levels. The 1929 crash resulted in a severe decline in industrial production and in mass unemployment. By 1933 almost half of the nation's banks had failed and up to 15 million people (about 30 per cent of the workforce) were unemployed. Farmers, already under pressure, were especially badly hit and many lost their farms. Without any system of social security the unemployed relied on charity and on soup kitchens to keep them from starvation. Many became homeless, or migrated to cities, often living on the outskirts in camps known as 'Hoovervilles' in mocking reference to the then president. The programmes initiated after 1933 under President Roosevelt's NEW DEAL mitigated the Depression's effects, but it was not until later in the 1930s with the European demand for armaments during WORLD WAR II that the Depression began to end, and it was completely over by 1941 when the United States entered the war. During the Depression many writers were assisted by New Deal programmes such as the FEDERAL THEATRE PROJECT and the FEDERAL WRITERS' PROJECT.

The Depression forms an important background to much writing set in the 1930s by writers such as William FAULKNER, John Dos Passos (1896–1970), Richard WRIGHT and Nathanael West (1903–40), and its effects were powerfully described in much contemporary writing, typically through the technique of social realism and often with a radical edge. Examples include the novels *Somebody in Boots* (1935) by Nelson Algren (1909–81), *The Grapes of Wrath* (1939) by John Steinbeck (1902–68), the Studs Lonigan trilogy of J. T. Farrell (1904–79), and the plays and stories of Clifford Odets (1906–63) and William Saroyan (1908–81). During this period in which the failure of capitalism was evident, many writers and intellectuals became aligned with Marxism, and the Depression saw a fresh interest in depicting the American proletariat. The Depression also profoundly affected many writers who grew up during it, featuring in important writings by Studs Terkel (b. 1912), Tillie Olsen (b. 1913), Arthur MILLER, William Kennedy (b. 1928) and E. L. Doctorow (b. 1931).

Further reading

The Great Depression and the Culture of Abundance (1995) by Rita Barnard; *The American Stage and the Great Depression* (1997) by Mark Fearnow, and *The Crucial Era* (1992) by Gerald D. Nash.

Detective story   Defining the detective story as one in which the investigator is the narrative's main figure distinguishes it from other stories involving crime or mystery. While the detective story is a variation of ancient tales that involve the solving of a mystery, the detective is a specifically modern figure, usually providing reassurance by discerning a rational pattern to what are apparently inchoate and possibly menacing events. Edgar Allan POE's detective, C. Auguste Dupin, functions in this way, and the first detective story is 'The Murders in the Rue Morgue' (1841). The detective featured in the DIME NOVEL, notably in the figure of Nick Carter created by John Russell Coryell (1848–1924), and there were also detective novels, such as *The Leavenworth Case* (1878) by Anna Katharine Green (1846–1935), but the detective story really developed after the 1880s with the immense popularity of Arthur Conan Doyle's character Sherlock Holmes, based partly on Dupin.

The detective story in American literature tends to be 'hard-boiled', involving violence and action rather than only intellectual crime-solving; this is partly because of its roots in the dime novel and PULP MAGAZINE. The work of James M. Cain (1892–1977), Dashiell Hammett (1894–1961), Raymond CHANDLER and Chester B. Himes (1909–84) developed from these traditions but took them in various directions, particularly in the representation of the city and the detective as a figure of moral authority. Along with Hammett's Sam Spade and Nick and Nora Charles, and Chandler's Philip Marlowe, other famous fictional detectives include Nero Wolf, introduced by Rex Stout (1886–1975); Philo Vance, by S. S. Van Dine (Willard Huntingdon Wright, 1888–1939); Perry Mason, by Erle Stanley Gardner (1889–1970); Ellery Queen, by co-authors Frederic Dannay (1905–82) and Manfred B. Lee (1905–71); Mike Hammer, by Mickey Spillane (b. 1918); Vic Warshawski, by Sara Paretsky (b. 1947), and Easy Rawlins by Walter Mosley (b. 1952). Writers not especially associated with the genre have also used the detective novel, including Mark TWAIN, with *Pudd'nhead Wilson* (1894) and *Tom Sawyer, Detective* (1896), and William FAULKNER, with *Intruder in the Dust* (1948).

The period since 1970 has seen a phenomenal rise in the numbers and popularity of detective novels. Prominent contemporary writers include Elmore Leonard (b. 1925), Ed McBain (Evan Hunter, b. 1926), Amanda Cross (Carolyn G. Heilbrun, b. 1926), Lawrence Block (b. 1938), Michael Connelly (b. 1946), James Ellroy (b. 1948) and Patricia Cornwell (b. 1956).

Further reading

Multicultural Detective Fiction (1999), edited by Adrienne Johnson Gosselin; The Woman Detective (1988) by Kathleen Gregory Klein; The Poetics of Murder (1983), edited by Glenn W. Most and William W. Stowe; The Naked City (1996) by Ralph Willett, and Detective Fiction: A Collection of Critical Essays (1988), edited by Robin W. Winks.

Determinism   Philosophical theory holding that human free will is an illusion, since actions are determined by forces beyond the individual's control. These forces may be social, economic, environmental or biological. Determinism originated in the 18th century, but its greatest period of influence was during the mid to late 19th century, as the social sciences were developing a systematic exploration of the forces that shape identity and behaviour. In American literature, the theory was fundamental to NATU-RALISM, but was also explored in a range of works, including *Puddn'head Wilson* (1894) by Mark TWAIN and *The Awakening* (1899) by Kate CHOPIN.

The Dial   The first *Dial* was the quarterly journal dedicated to TRANSCENDENTALISM. Published in Boston from 1840 until 1844, it was edited for a time by Margaret Fuller

(1810–50) and later by Ralph Waldo EMERSON. It published a range of poetry and essays, and its contributors included key transcendentalists such as Bronson Alcott (1799–1888) and Henry David THOREAU.

Another journal with the name *The Dial* began publication in Chicago in 1880 and moved to New York in 1920, becoming a key journal for the publication of MODERNIST writing. (Important contributions included the first American appearance of *THE WASTE LAND* by T. S. ELIOT.) It ceased publication in 1929, having been edited by Marianne Moore (1887–1972) since 1925.

Dickinson, Emily   Poet, born in Amherst, Massachusetts, in 1830. Dickinson was one of three children in a locally distinguished family. She attended Amherst Academy and Mount Holyoke Female Seminary. Dickinson did not marry; she lived in the family home all her life, scarcely ever left Amherst and after the 1860s became increasingly reclusive. As well as a poet Dickinson was an intensive reader and an assiduous letter-writer. Her earliest preserved poetry dates from the early 1850s, and she was most prolific during the period 1860–5. Only a handful of her poems were published during her lifetime, primarily it seems because she resented the editorial interventions that publication involved. Dickinson preserved much of her work in hand-sewn booklets called fascicles, and after her death in 1886 small selections of her work started to be published. In 1955 the first scholarly complete edition of her poems was published, edited by Thomas H. Johnson. This edition includes almost 1,800 poems.

Stylistically and thematically, Dickinson's poetry has an unsettling, challenging effect. It seems fragmented, with its use of dashes, its occasionally dislocated syntax, unusual rhymes and metres, and irregular capitalization of words. Furthermore, her language is concentrated and frequently approaches the epigrammatic, while her vocabulary tends towards the abstract; increasingly so over time. The style is appropriate for a poet who so incisively questions and refuses the comfort of fixed ideas and beliefs. As she wrote to a friend, Abiah Root in 1850, 'The shore is safer, Abiah, but I love to buffet the sea . . . I love the danger!' Her poetry can simultaneously manifest joy in the freedom of the imagination and terror at the unknown. Thematically there is often ambivalence and tension regarding questions of religious belief and death. Although her family, educational and communal background was strongly religious, in the PURITAN tradition, Dickinson refused to make the profession of faith that would permit her to join the church. Her poetry explores the attractions and possibilities of religious faith yet also manifests scepticism towards those who claim confident certainty of belief. Death, which she called 'a great adventure', is a significant and recurring subject for her. In representing the limit of human consciousness it may be at once attractive because of the demands that it makes on the imagination, while also terrifying in marking the absolute boundary of human understanding.

Dickinson's life has sometimes been represented as restricted, or as a series of refusals: refusal to accept orthodox Christianity, to marry, to conform to expectations, to publish her work. But such representations can lead to an under-valuing of the searching questions that she asks and of the way that her rich and intense inner life informs her work. They can also devalue the freedom that she finds in her imagination and in poetry's capacity to explore a multiplicity of identities and possibilities.

Further reading

The Undiscovered Continent (1983) by Suzanne Juhasz; *Feminist Critics Read Emily Dickinson* (1983), edited by Suzanne Juhasz; *Emily Dickinson: A Poet's Grammar* (1987) by Cristanne Miller; *Emily Dickinson: Monarch of Perception* (2000) by Domhnall Mitchell; *Dickinson: The Anxiety of Gender* (1984) by Vivian R. Pollack, and *Rowing in Eden* (1992) by Martha Nell Smith. *The Only Kangaroo Among the Beauty* (1979) by Karl Keller and *The Life of Emily Dickinson* (1974) by Richard B. Sewall are important critical biographies.

Dime novels   The mass-marketed dime novel was introduced in 1860 by Beadle and Company of New York, with a reprint of *Malaeska: The Indian Wife of the White Hunter* (1839) by Ann Stephens (1810–86). With various partners, Beadle's became the major publisher of dime novels, publishing over 7,000 in the period 1860–97. The novels were mostly in the WESTERN tradition, heavily influenced by the LEATHER-STOCKING series of James Fenimore COOPER, but there were also adventure, sports and DETECTIVE STORIES. The prolific author Edward Z. C. Judson (1823–86), whose pseudonym was Ned Buntline, is known as 'the father of the dime novel'. Judson collaborated with William F. Cody (1846–1917) in the invention of Buffalo Bill, one of the most popular dime-novel characters, based to some extent on Cody (fictitious adventures of historical figures such as Davy Crockett, Daniel Boone, Kit Carson and Jesse James were dime-novel staples). Many famous fictional characters were introduced by one author but taken up by others, including in-house writers. Three major characters, Deadwood Dick, Calamity Jane and Hurricane Nell, were invented by Edward L. Wheeler (?1854–?85). Some characters survived from dime novels into the PULP MAGA-ZINES that replaced them, notably the athletic Frank Merriwell, the invention of William G. ('Gilbert') Patten (1866–1945), and the detective Nick Carter, introduced by John Russell Coryell (1848–1924) and Ormond G. Smith (1860–1933). Other prominent writers included Edward S. Ellis (1840–1916) (inventor of the character Seth Jones), Prentiss Ingraham (1843–1904), Frances Auretta Fuller Victor (1826–1902) and her sister Metta Victoria Fuller Victor (1831–85), who wrote a celebrated anti-slavery dime novel, *Maum Guinea, and Her Plantation 'Children'* (1862). Louisa May Alcott (1832–88) wrote several dime novels under the pseudonym A. M. Barnard. The popularity of dime novels declined sharply after the 1890s because of competition from pulp magazines, and then from radio and film.

Although rarely taken seriously as literature, the dime novels indicate the tastes of a mass audience and were significant in shaping many of the myths of the West. Some characters have often provided a significant fund of reference for later writers.

Further reading

Reading the West (1997), edited by Bill Brown; *Mechanic Accents* (1998) by Michael Denning; *Virgin Land* (1950) by Henry Nash Smith; and *Pioneers, Passionate Ladies and Private Eyes* (1996), edited by Larry E. Sullivan and Lydia Cushman Sherman.

Dirty realism   Term coined by the literary editor Bill Buford in 1987 for an edition of *Granta* magazine, to describe fiction written in a MINIMALIST, generally non-metaphorical writing style. Especially associated with the SHORT STORY, dirty realism is usually laconic and understated, and frequently deals with the frustration and lack of fulfilment felt by marginalized characters. The short stories of Ernest HEMINGWAY are significant precursors of dirty realism, and writers associated with the style include Raymond CARVER, Richard Ford (b. 1944) and Tobias Wolff (b. 1945).

Donner Party   In the winter of 1846 a wagon train of eighty-seven people led by the brothers George and Jacob Donner was trapped by heavy snow in the Sierra Nevada mountains while travelling to California. The party was stranded there for the winter and thirty-nine of the group died. Some of those who were rescued in the spring had survived through cannibalism. The Donner Party is frequently referred to in literature of the Westward migration and it is the subject of the 1943 novel *The Mothers* by Vardis Fisher (1895–1968).

Double consciousness   The self-estrangement resulting from competing allegiances in racial or ethnic terms. The term is most associated with W. E. B. Du BOIS, who used it in the first chapter of *The Souls of Black Folk* (1903) to denote the typical condition of post-emancipation African Americans. Regarding the conflict experienced between being black and being American, Du Bois wrote:

> It is a peculiar sensation, this double-consciousness. . . . One ever feels his two-ness, – an American, a Negro; two souls, two thoughts, two unreconciled strivings; two warring ideals in one dark body, whose dogged strength alone keeps it from being torn asunder. The history of the American Negro is the history of this strife, – this longing to attain self-conscious manhood, to merge his double self into a better and truer self. In this merging he wishes neither of the older selves to be lost. . . . He simply wishes to make it possible for a man to be both a Negro and an American, without being cursed and spit upon by his fellows, without having the doors of Opportunity closed roughly in his face.

In the same book, Du Bois articulated the cost of assimilation to individual identity when he wrote 'the price of culture is a Lie'.

   Double consciousness has been a significant theme for many writers, especially for those exploring assimilation and its costs. In addition to being evident in the work of many African American writers, it is relevant to some NATIVE AMERICAN writing, and is especially prominent in the writing of second-generation immigrants, whose perceived cultural task may be to become American yet also to maintain an ethnic identity that may be devalued or not recognized in mainstream American culture.

Douglass, Frederick   Leading 19th century African American reformer and intellectual (1818–95) whose first autobiography, NARRATIVE OF THE LIFE OF FREDERICK DOUGLASS, AN AMERICAN SLAVE, WRITTEN BY HIMSELF (1845), was a best-seller and is one of the classic SLAVE NARRATIVES. Douglass was born a slave in Maryland; he never knew the date of his birth and was never certain about the identity of his father. His mother was a slave called Harriet Bailey; he assumed the surname Douglass after his escape from slavery. After his experiences as a slave and the escape to freedom described in the *Narrative*, Douglass went to Massachusetts in 1838. There he worked from 1841 for the anti-slavery cause as a lecturer and orator, travelling to England and Ireland before returning to Massachusetts in 1847, purchasing his freedom and founding the anti-slavery newspaper *North Star*. In 1853 he published a novella, 'The Heroic Slave'. During the CIVIL WAR he helped to organize two regiments of black troops, and after it he became an influential spokesman for African Americans. Douglass was a sophisticated and moving writer and was often considered the leading African American in the United States and an important example of the intellectual, spiritual and creative potential of blacks. As well as his work for racial equality, he campaigned for women's rights (being present at the 1848 SENECA FALLS CONVENTION). Douglass wrote two autobiographies after the *Narrative* – *My Bondage and My Freedom* (1855) and *Life and Times of Frederick Douglass* (1881) – and served in various public offices, including that of minister to Haiti (1889–91).

Further reading

Critical Essays on Frederick Douglass (1991), edited by William L. Andrews; *Frederick Douglass: A Critical Reader* (1999), edited by Bill E. Lawson and Frank M. Kirkland, and *Frederick Douglass* (1991) by William S. McFeely.

Dred Scott decision   With the assistance of abolitionists the slave Dred Scott (?1795–1858) sued for his freedom, on the grounds that he had been taken by his master to live in the free state of Illinois and then to the Minnesota territory which had been declared free soil by the MISSOURI COMPROMISE. The case Dred Scott v. Sandford was initiated in Missouri in 1846 and eventually reached the SUPREME COURT, which in 1857 (with two dissensions) ruled that Scott remained a slave. It declared that since he was legally defined as property and not as a citizen, Scott had no right to sue, and that since they were property, slaves could not be freed by the actions of Congress, because the Fifth Amendment to the CONSTITUTION guaranteed property rights. Chief Justice Roger B. Taney wrote that blacks were 'not intended to be included under the word "citizens" in the Constitution' and that they had 'no rights which any white man was bound to respect'. Effectively, the Dred Scott decision meant that slavery was legal in the territories and that the Missouri Compromise (which had been repealed in 1854) was unconstitutional. The case was violently controversial, inflaming the ABOLITION movement and increasing North–South antagonism prior to the CIVIL WAR.

Dreiser, Theodore   Novelist whose work was central to the development of NATURAL-ISM and of the urban REALIST novel. Dreiser was born in Terre Haute, Indiana, in 1871 into a large family. His father, a German immigrant, was an often-unemployed factory worker. Dreiser spent a year at the University of Indiana and then worked as a journalist in Chicago and Pittsburgh before moving to New York in 1894. He married in 1898, but the marriage ended in separation in 1912. Dreiser published his first novel, *Sister Carrie*, in 1900. This naturalistic classic is a frank, realistic and non-judgmental analysis of rural-born Carrie Meeber's move to Chicago and her use of her sexuality to fulfil her ambitions. Although its first edition sold poorly, the novel represented a new specifically anti-ROMANTIC urban realism, and exhibited Dreiser's absorption of SOCIAL DARWINISM. Dreiser's next novels, *Jennie Gerhardt* (1911), *The Financier* (1912) and *The Titan* (1914), were less original, although the later two were among the first American novels to focus on the figure of the businessman. Along with the weaker novel *The Stoic* (1947), they formed a trilogy centred on a speculator called Frank Cowperwood. After an autobiographical novel, *The 'Genius'* (1915), Dreiser published plays, travel books, two autobiographies, and collections of essays and short stories in the following decade. Returning to the novel, he published his masterpiece, *An American Tragedy*, in 1925. It was both critically acclaimed and a best-seller. Closely based on a notorious 1906 murder, trial and execution, it followed naturalist principles in analysing how a combination of social environment and biological forces shape human actions. Dreiser never repeated the artistic or popular success of *An American Tragedy*. He dedicated much energy to social reform, and apart from the short stories collected in *A Gallery of Women* (1929) and a frank autobiography, *Dawn* (1931), his later work shows a marked decline. He died in California in 1945.

Dreiser's attention to detail and the ability to create memorable scenes are rooted in his journalistic skills. His style has been criticized for its ponderous awkwardness and for its authorial interventions, but the power of the overall work compensates for these faults. Although best known for his commitment to naturalism, Dreiser was a pioneer of the fact-based fiction that later writers would develop as the NON-FICTION NOVEL.

Further reading

Theodore Dreiser Revisited (1992) by Philip Gerber; *Theodore Dreiser: Beyond Naturalism* (1995), edited by Miriam Gogol, and *The Novels of Theodore Dreiser* (1976) by Donald Pizer. Richard Lingeman's two-volume critical biography, *Theodore Dreiser: At the Gates of the City* (1986) and *Theodore Dreiser: An American Journey* (1990), is highly recommended.

Du Bois, W. E. B. (William Edward Burghardt)   Essayist, historian, sociologist and fiction writer, one of the most influential African American intellectuals of the 20th century.

Du Bois was born in Great Barrington, Massachusetts, in 1868. He attended Fisk University and then studied history at Harvard. In 1895 he became the first African American to graduate from Harvard with a PhD. In 1903 he published *The Souls of Black Folk*, a book of essays on post-emancipation African American culture. There he began the formulation of key concepts such as DOUBLE CONSCIOUSNESS and the TALENTED TENTH and started his disagreement with Booker T. Washington (1856–1915) over the optimum means of fully assimilating African Americans into American society. Over the next 40 years, based mostly at the University of Atlanta, Du Bois published widely in a variety of genres. His prolific writing includes collections of essays, poetry, novels, a biography of the ABOLITIONIST John Brown, socio-historical studies of African American culture, and two autobiographies. He was a key member of the NAACP and edited its magazine *THE CRISIS*. However, Du Bois grew critical of the ideal of assimilation and developed an interest in Marxism, resigning from the NAACP in 1934. His communist sympathies prompted an indictment against him in 1951. In 1961 Du Bois left the United States and later renounced his American citizenship. He died in Ghana in 1963.

While he was often a controversial figure, Du Bois's achievement and influence were considerable. His energetic campaigning on behalf of reform and civil rights and his restless, incisive and lyrical interrogation of African American cultures were crucial to African American history from the turn of the century to the HARLEM RENAISSANCE and the BLACK ARTS MOVEMENT.

Further reading

Seizing the Word (1994) by Keith E. Byerman; *W. E. B. Du Bois: Biography of a Race* (1993) by David Levering Lewis, and *The Art and Imagination of W. E. B. Du Bois* (1976, 1990) by Arnold Rampersad.

Eighteenth Amendment   The amendment to the CONSTITUTION which led to the passing of the Volstead Act and the introduction of PROHIBITION. The amendment was ratified in 1919 and prohibited the 'manufacture, sale, or transportation of intoxicating liquors within, the importation thereof into, or the exportation thereof from the United States and all territory subject to the jurisdiction thereof'. It was repealed when the Twenty-first Amendment was ratified in 1933.

Elegy   Since the 16ᵗʰ century, elegy has referred to a meditative lyric poem on the death of an individual. In Greek and Roman poetry, the term had denoted a reflective poem, devoted to any subject, written in elegiac couplets, that is, one line written in dactylic hexameter and the next in dactylic pentameter. PASTORAL elegy is a refinement of elegy, and in it the poet obeys certain conventions. The muse is invoked, nature is represented as mourning, the dead person is portrayed as a shepherd, a procession of mourners is included, as is a judgment on contemporary events, and the poem concludes with a consolatory statement regarding death. Generally, elegy serves to lament and praise the subject while consoling the bereaved.

The elegy has long been a significant form for American poets. It was especially appropriate in PURITAN LITERATURE, in providing a space where personal lament, public concern and pious expression could co-exist. Anne BRADSTREET, Urian Oakes (1631–81) and Benjamin Tompson (1642–1714) were prominent elegists. The elegy continued as a vehicle for popular sentiment, especially apparent in the proliferation of elegies after the death of George Washington in 1799. Modern American elegy begins with Walt WHITMAN's poem on Abraham Lincoln, 'When Lilacs last in the Dooryard Bloom'd' (1866). Whitman reworks pastoral elegy in a sophisticated way, and finally the elegized subject includes the unnamed Lincoln and all the CIVIL WAR dead. Though rooted in tradition, this powerful combination of the intimate with the public characterizes modern American elegy, evident in poems as varied as 'Ode to the Confederate Dead' (1928) by Allen Tate (1899–1979), 'The Quaker Graveyard in Nantucket' (1946) and 'For the Union Dead' (1964), both by Robert LOWELL, and *Kaddish* (1961) by Allen GINSBERG. Some key 20ᵗʰ century poetry collections have been strongly elegiac, notably Lowell's *LIFE STUDIES* (1959), *The Dream Songs* (1968) of John Berryman (1914–72) and *The Changing Light at Sandover* (1983) by James Merrill (1926–95). Still a vital and important form, significant commemorative elegies have been written by many American poets, notably William Carlos WILLIAMS, Elizabeth BISHOP, Amy Clampitt (1920–94), Anthony Hecht (b. 1923), Anne Sexton (1928–74), Sharon Olds (b. 1942) and Jorie Graham (b. 1951).

Further reading

Elegiac Romance (1983) by Kenneth A. Bruffee; *The American Puritan Elegy* (2000) by Jeffrey A. Hammond, and *Beyond Consolation* (1997) by Melissa F. Zeiger.

Eliot, Thomas Stearns   One of the major MODERNIST poets, a dramatist and an important critic. Eliot was born in St Louis in 1888 into a family that had significant New England roots. He graduated from Harvard in 1910 and after studying in Paris he returned to Harvard to study philosophy, writing a thesis on the philosophy of F. H. Bradley. Living in London, Eliot married Vivian Haigh-Wood in 1915, although the marriage proved difficult and the couple separated in 1932. Vivian, who underwent periods of mental illness, died in a sanatorium in 1947. During the early 1920s Eliot was briefly a schoolteacher and a bank officer as well as editing a journal, *The Criterion* (1922–39), and writing poetry, critical essays and reviews. He also began a lifelong association with the publishing company that later became Faber and Faber, first as editor and then as a director. In 1957 he married Valerie Fletcher.

With the guidance of Ezra Pound, Eliot published his first poems and his first collection, *Prufrock and Other Observations* (1917), which included 'The Love Song of J. Alfred Prufrock'. This dramatic monologue proved revolutionary in the development of 20th century poetry. In 1919 Eliot published *Poems*, and in 1920 *The Sacred Wood*, a collection of critical essays that included two major essays, 'Tradition and the Individual Talent' and 'Hamlet and His Problems', in which Eliot developed the idea of the 'objective correlative' as a means of expressing emotion in poetry. In 1922 he published *The Waste Land*, widely considered the most important single modernist poem. Its reception was sensational, and it immediately gave Eliot an international reputation. During the 1920s Eliot became increasingly drawn to Christianity, and in 1927 he was received into the Church of England and also became a British subject; in 1928 he described himself as 'classicist in literature, royalist in politics and Anglo-Catholic in religion'. Much of his poetry after 1927 has a strong religious element, and this reaches its greatest expression in *Four Quartets* (1943). The book's four sections are an intense and profound meditation on how God may be experienced in human time. For many readers, though, Eliot's poetry after 1927 seemed to lack the sense of radical urgent enquiry into the age that had characterized his earlier work and which had helped to shape modernism. Increasingly Eliot wrote verse drama that touched on religious themes. His plays, which were mostly popular successes, include *Murder in the Cathedral* (1935), *The Family Reunion* (1939) and *The Cocktail Party* (1949). In 1948 Eliot was awarded the Nobel Prize for Literature. He died in 1965.

Further reading

Mastery and Escape: T. S. Eliot and the Dialectic of Modernism (1994) by Jewel Spears Brooker; T. S. Eliot: A Study in Character and Style (1984) by Ronald Bush; The Invisible Poet (1959) by Hugh Kenner, and Thomas Stearns Eliot, Poet (1994) by A. David Moody. T. S. Eliot: A Life (1984) by Peter Ackroyd and Eliot's Early Years (1977), Eliot's New Life (1988) and T. S. Eliot: An Imperfect Life (1999) by Lyndall Gordon are recommended critical biographies.

Ellison, Ralph (Waldo)   Novelist, short-story writer and essayist who was one of the most widely read African American authors of the 20th century.

Ellison was born in Oklahoma City in 1914 and won a scholarship and went to Tuskegee Institute to study music, although he left without a degree in 1936 and worked in New York under the Federal Writers' Project. He served in the military in World War II. In 1952 his novel *Invisible Man* was published to great acclaim, winning the 1953 National Book Award and bringing Ellison to public prominence. Ellison lectured at various universities, and wrote essays and reviews that were collected in two books, *Shadow and Act* (1964) and *Going to the Territory* (1986). (*Collected Essays* appeared in 1995.) He also worked on a novel that was left uncompleted at his death, although a first chapter had appeared in 1965. A version of the novel, called *Juneteenth*, was edited by John F. Callahan and published in 1999. Ellison died in New York in 1994.

Ellison explored the shaping of individual identity through confrontation both with history and with contemporary social power structures. He considers questions that arise from the ideal of the African American's assimilation into mainstream American culture and questions how far assimilation may be achieved without loss of an identity deriving from an African American past. This theme is prominent in *Invisible Man* and in *Juneteenth*, which concerns the assassination of a racist senator, Adam Sunraider (Bliss) who is actually PASSING as white. Ellison updated long-standing debates about African American identity, such as the one between Booker T. Washington (1856–1915) and W. E. B. Du Bois. (Washington is a significant presence in *Invisible Man*.) He also researched and made both thematic and formal use of African American styles and folklore, writing incisively on JAZZ and BLUES as well as on the survival of African culture evident in figures such as the TRICKSTER and the use of masks. Some African American intellectuals were highly critical of Ellison, especially during the 1960s, for his anti-separatism, his perceived conservatism and his commitment to aesthetics.

Further reading

Speaking for You (1987) by Kimberly W. Benston; *Ralph Ellison* (1986), edited by Harold Bloom; *Invisible Criticism* (1988) by Alan Nadel, and *Heroism and The Black Intellectual* (1994) by Jerry Gafio Watts.

Emancipation Proclamation   Issued by Lincoln in September 1862, to take effect from 1 January 1863, the proclamation freed the slaves in the CONFEDERATE states, and made provision for legislation to free slaves in the four slave states that remained in the Union. While it was primarily symbolic, the proclamation was important in several respects. It effectively made the CIVIL WAR into a war about slavery rather than about saving the Union, since it was clear that if the North won slavery would be abolished (crucially, this prevented any possible intervention in the war by European powers on the side of the South). It also meant that when Union forces entered Confederate areas the slaves were freed, and that ex-slaves could join the Union army. Slavery was actually abolished by the THIRTEENTH AMENDMENT in December 1865. Lincoln said in February 1865 that the Emancipation Proclamation was 'the central act of my administration, and the greatest event of the nineteenth century'. Considering the centenary of the proclamation in 1963, James BALDWIN wrote in *The Fire Next Time* that 'the country is celebrating one hundred years of freedom one hundred years too soon'.

Emerson, Ralph Waldo   Poet and essayist, a major figure in the shaping of American thought and literature. Emerson was born in Boston in 1803, the son of a UNITARIAN minister who died when Emerson was aged 8. He attended Harvard, graduating in 1821, and taught for a period before being ordained a Unitarian minister in 1829. He married in 1829 but his wife, Ellen Louisa Tucker, died of tuberculosis in 1831. Her death came at a time when Emerson had started having doubts regarding Unitarianism, and in 1832 he resigned his ministry. He spent the subsequent year travelling in Europe, where he met Samuel Taylor Coleridge, William Wordsworth and Thomas Carlyle. Returning to the United States he settled in Concord, and started to develop a considerable reputation as a public speaker and lecturer. In 1835 he married Lydia Jackson. Emerson's first (and anonymous) publication, *Nature* (1835), was an important influence on the development of TRANSCENDENTALISM, and he met frequently with the TRANSCENDENTAL CLUB and edited *THE DIAL*. After publishing two volumes of *Essays* (1841, 1844) Emerson became one of the most influential and widely read figures of his day and spent much of his time touring and lecturing, including a visit to England in 1847–8. He lectured on a wide range of subjects and also came to support ABOLITION, being particularly critical of the FUGITIVE SLAVE ACTS. His other publications include *Poems* (1846), *Representative Men* (1849), *The Conduct of Life* (1860) and another poetry collection, *May-Day* (1867). He effectively withdrew from public life in 1877 and died in Concord in 1882.

'Trust thyself: every heart vibrates to that iron string,' wrote Emerson in 'Self-Reliance'. Emerson's philosophy is non-doctrinaire and can be contradictory at times, expressed as it is through his exploratory, heuristic essays. Nevertheless he continually stated his belief in the 'infinitude of the private man' and the need to identify and trust one's own feelings and instincts. This belief emerged as combination of ROMANTICISM and religious thought, since he came to believe that a part of God's nature, the 'over-soul', is present within all individuals and in nature. Accordingly, the search for God is also a quest for self-understanding and acceptance. His views have a notable social dimension, since he argued that learning to trust in one's own beliefs would lead to social reform. Although sometimes criticized for his assumption of innate goodness, this belief was an influential and positive alternative to PURITAN thought. Emerson's criticism of materialism and conformity and his eloquent articulation of individualism and SELF-RELIANCE have guaranteed his enduring influence. As well as having a crucial bearing on the direction of American literature, Emerson specifically influenced various writers, notably Henry David THOREAU and Walt WHITMAN.

Further reading

Ralph Waldo Emerson: A Collecton of Critical Essays (1993), edited by Laurence Buell; American Renaissance (1941) by F. O. Matthiessen; Emerson in his Journals (1982), edited by Joel Porte; Emerson and Literary Change (1978) by David Porter, and Emerson: The Mind on Fire (1995) by Robert D. Richardson.

Enlightenment International movement that began in 18th century Europe and exerted a profound influence on the formation of the United States.

The Enlightenment was a combination of diverse areas of thought: developments in physics and mathematics, typified by Sir Isaac Newton; fresh attempts to understand the workings of the mind, as in the work of John Locke; the political insights of Thomas Hobbes; the rationalism of René Descartes, and the vigorous scepticism of Voltaire. Enlightenment thought placed reason, experience and scientific enquiry at the centre of human understanding of the universe, displacing the authority of theology, received ideas and dogma. The age of Enlightenment encouraged the discovery and empirical demonstration of the natural laws governing the physical universe; it also envisioned social progress and the triumph of the rational.

In colonial America, the Enlightenment played a crucial role in the move away from strict PURITANISM during the early 18th century, in the growing challenge to colonial subordination to Britain, and eventually in the very definition of the republic. The ideas and attitudes of Benjamin FRANKLIN, Thomas Jefferson (1743–1826) and Thomas Paine (1737–1809) embodied the scientific, political and social dimensions of Enlightenment thought. In particular, Jefferson's DECLARATION OF INDEPENDENCE expresses Enlightenment attitudes towards human rights and the 'social contract'; it is this fact that led the historian Henry Steele Commager to comment, 'The Old World imagined, invented, and formulated the Enlightenment, the New World . . . realized it and fulfilled it.' More controversially, the Enlightenment has been considered an instrument of social injustice in the United States, because of the distinction that it made between human and non-human, 'civilised' and 'savage'. The Enlightenment belief that humans were characterized by their capacity for reason, language and abstract thought led to a designation of enslaved African Americans as non-human, while the definition of the civilized as cultivators of the land was used to justify the dispossession of the Native Americans.

Further reading

The Empire of Reason (1978) by Henry Steele Commager; The American Enlightenment 1750–1820 (1997) by Robert Ferguson (also in The Cambridge History of American Literature, Volume I (1994), edited by Sacvan Bercovitch); The Enlightenment in America (1976) by Henry May, and Iron Cages (1990) by Ronald Takaki.

Epic   In its narrowest definition, a long poem narrating heroic actions relating to an elevated subject, usually dealing with the myths or history of a people (in his *ABC of Reading* Ezra POUND calls the epic 'a poem including history'). More broadly, 'American epic' may refer to creative work in any genre that involves events on a large scale; this definition is wide enough to include prose works such as *MOBY-DICK*, *U. S. A.* (1937) by John Dos Passos (1886–1970) and *The Grapes of Wrath* (1939) by John Steinbeck (1902–68); the poems, Whitman's *LEAVES OF GRASS* and Pound's *THE CANTOS*, and films such as *Birth of a Nation* (1915) and *Gone with the Wind* (1939).

The epic has been of special significance in American writing, in which a modern form of epic has developed. After the founding of the United States the need for a poetic national epic was perceived, and there were various attempts to produce a poem that would narrate and celebrate the nation's founding. The most significant attempts at this kind of poetry epic were *The Conquest of Canaan* (1785) by Timothy Dwight (1752–1817) and *The Columbiad* (1807) by Joel Barlow (1754–1812) (a revision of his 1787 poem *The Vision of Columbus*). Henry Wadsworth Longfellow (1807–82) made use of epic elements in his lyrical narratives of American history, especially in *The Song of Hiawatha* (1855). But it was Walt WHITMAN who transformed and modernized the poetry epic, making it a form appropriate to forward-looking American DEMOCRACY. In 'Song of Myself' (1855, later revised) he uses epic elements, such as battles, public history, the myths of the nation, but he does so in a highly personal manner. He celebrates his own individuality and simultaneously seeks an inclusive approach to history, commemorating the defeated as well as the triumphant. Effectively, he himself becomes the epic hero, absorbing and articulating the myths and history of the nation and expressing these in a single poem. Whitman's version of epic was extremely influential and laid the foundations for the five major 20th century poetry epics of American poetry: *The Bridge* (1930) by Hart Crane (1899–1932); *Paterson* (1946–58) by William Carlos WILLIAMS; *The Maximus Poems* (1953–60) by Charles Olson (1910–70); *The Cantos*, and *The Dream Songs* (1968) by John Berryman (1914–72). *The New World: An Epic Poem* (1985) by Frederick Turner (b. 1943) is a recent attempt to revive the non-personal epic.

Before Whitman, the persistent difficulties of adapting the poetry epic to the American scene had led to the development of the epic in prose fiction. The LEATHER-STOCKING TALES (1823–41) of James Fenimore COOPER are the fullest embodiment of the American prose epic. Cooper makes use of epic elements: the hero (Natty Bumppo) who embodies the nation's beliefs and aspirations; historical incidents that were significant to the nation's origins, and the American landscape. In the 20th century the epic as a large-scale examination of American history was often mediated through film, notably in the works directed by D. W. Griffith (1875–1948) and by John Ford (1895–1973).

Further reading

The Inadvertent Epic (1980) by Leslie Fiedler; The American Epic (1989) by John P. McWilliams; The Continuity of American Poetry (1961) by Roy Harvey Pearce, and Bardic Ethos and the American Epic Poem (1989) by Jeffrey Walker.

Episcopalian church   Originally part of the Church of England, the Episcopalian church has had a presence in the colonies since the settling of JAMESTOWN, although on key doctrinal points, such as the recognition of the sacraments, it differed sharply from other Protestant churches, including PURITANISM. Also, in contrast to CONGREGATIONALISM and PRESBYTERIANISM, the Episcopalians maintained a strongly hierarchical church structure involving administration by the ordained, and government by bishops. The church's English associations led to many of its clergy taking the side of the LOYALISTS during the REVOLUTIONARY WAR.

Epistolary novel   A novel written in the form of letters, usually involving an exchange of letters by various correspondents. The epistolary novel is most associated with English writing in the 18ᵗʰ century, but some modern American writers have written in the form. *Wake Up, Stupid* (1959) by Mark Harris (b. 1922), *Letters* (1979) by John Barth (b. 1930), *The Color Purple* (1982) by Alice WALKER and *The Mixquiahuala Letters* by Ana Castillo (b. 1953) are distinguished examples.

Equal Rights Amendment   Unratified proposed amendment to the CONSTITUTION. First proposed in 1923 in a text written by the suffrage leader Alice Paul, the amendment was passed by the Senate in 1972. To become a constitutional amendment, it subsequently had to be ratified by thirty-eight states before 1982. It failed to do this, being ratified by thirty-five states. The proposal, which would have become the Twenty-seventh Amendment to the Constitution, stated, 'Equality of rights under the law shall not be denied or abridged by the United States or by any State on account of sex.'

Exceptionalism   The belief in the uniqueness of the United States in terms of its historical origins, political system and historical destiny. Exceptionalism may be seen to have originated with the PURITAN belief in God's intervention in history that gave a mission to the colonists. Although the religious sense of being a 'redeemer nation' gradually weakened, exceptionalism was intensified after the revolutionary period, in that the founding of the new nation and the experiment in democratic republicanism were considered fulfilments of historical destiny. Foreign visitors to the United States commonly made claims for American exceptionalism, and Alexis De Tocqueville famously did so in his *DEMOCRACY IN AMERICA* (1835–40). Exceptionalism was strongest during the 19ᵗʰ century, evident in both the concept of MANIFEST DESTINY and the FRONTIER THESIS, and receiving literary expression in the writings of Ralph Waldo EMERSON and Walt WHITMAN. Exceptionalism was also deeply criticized, however, especially by those who saw it as an ideological justification for territorial annexation. Although much modified, American exceptionalism persists as a strongly held belief.

Further reading

Reflections on American Exceptionalism (1994), edited by David K. Adams and Cornelis A. van Minnen; American Exceptionalism (1996) by Seymour Martin Lipset, and American Exceptionalism (1998) by Deborah L. Madsen.

Existentialism   Philosophy which emphasizes the individual's alienation from others, the absence of sustainable belief systems, and the responsibility of the individual to choose identity. Although existentialism exists in various forms, it was the work of Jean-Paul Sartre (1905–80) that was most familiar in the United States from the 1940s onwards. For Sartre, humans are born into 'nothingness' and must choose either to remain there passively or to create meaning and identity. Identity is therefore made, not given; in his celebrated formulation, 'existence precedes essence'.

Existentialism had a significant influence on writing in continental Europe, especially in the development of the ABSURD. Although less evident in the United States, it has been a presence, and was especially important in the work of some African American writers. The existential emphasis on nothingness and the consequent need to create identity was seen to be of special relevance to African Americans. As James BALDWIN put it in 'The Black Boy Looks at the White Boy' (1961), 'to become a Negro man . . . one had to make oneself up as one went along. . . . The world had prepared no place for you, and if the world had its way, no place would ever exist.' Ralph ELLISON explored the possibilities of existentialism in *INVISIBLE MAN*, but it was Richard WRIGHT who most enthusiastically took up existentialist thought. Wright became a friend of Sartre, and his novel *The Outsider* (1953) is a key statement of existential philosophy. Other works which explore existentialism include: *Dangling Man* (1944), *The Victim* (1947) and *Seize the Day* (1956) by Saul BELLOW; 'The White Negro' (1957) by Norman Mailer (b. 1923); *The Floating Opera* (1956) and *The End of the Road* (1958) by John Barth (b. 1930), and *The Moviegoer* (1961) by Walker Percy (1916–90).

Experimental theatre Term generally applied to drama that uses various non-naturalistic techniques and which often explores social and political concerns. Experimental theatre has tended to be associated with periods of cultural and social change or crisis; tellingly it was prominent during the late 1920s and 1930s and in the politically charged 1960s. Experimental drama has been considered an appropriate form for the marginalized in its implicit challenge to dominant modes and its publicizing of issues. In the 1930s, for instance, the Harlem Experimental Theatre produced drama dealing with racial concerns, such as *Climbing Jacob's Ladder* (1931) by Regina M. Anderson (b. 1901). In the 1960s groups such as the Living Theatre, Joseph Chaikin's Open Theatre and Richard Schechner's Performance Group produced experimental works by Edward Albee (b. 1928), Imamu Amiri BARAKA, Adrienne Kennedy (b. 1931), Lanford Wilson (b. 1937) and Ntozake Shange (b. 1948) in off-Broadway or off-off-Broadway productions. Generally non-commercial, experimental drama has often proved of great significance to the overall development of American theatre.

Further reading

The Eye of Prey (1987) by Herbert Blau; The Death of Character (1996) by Elinor Fuchs, and The Other American Drama (1994) by Marc Robinson.

Expressionism   Term that originated in art criticism of the early years of the 20th century, and is used broadly to refer to a style of writing in which representation of the writer's emotions and subjectivity is privileged over the representation of surface objective reality. Since a tenet of expressionism is that the work's form should be determined by the author's subjective vision rather than predetermined or shaped from without, expressionist works have usually been experimental and often anti-REALIST. In American writing, expressionism developed as part of the MODERNIST movement, and was especially important in the development of drama. Prominent examples of expressionistic drama include *The Adding Machine* (1923) by Elmer Rice (1892–1967), the early plays of Eugene O'NEILL, and works by Thornton Wilder (1897–1975), Tennessee WILLIAMS and Arthur MILLER. William FAULKNER uses expressionist techniques in his early novels, as does T. S. ELIOT in *THE WASTE LAND*.

F

Fantastic   Broadly defined by W. R. Irwin as 'the overt violation of what is generally accepted as possibility', the fantastic is a development of ROMANCE, and shares attributes with other styles of writing, such as GOTHIC, HORROR, SCIENCE FICTION, UTOPIAN literature and speculative fiction. The purposes and effects of the fantastic are extremely broad and varied; they include entertaining the reader, perhaps through escapism, exploring psychological states and impulses and providing a perspective on contemporary social reality.

Prominent American writers of fantastic literature include Edgar Allan POE, Frank L. Baum (1856–1919), Charlotte Perkins Gilman (1860–1935), Ray Bradbury (b. 1920), Kurt Vonnegut (b. 1922), James Merrill (1926–95), Ursula K. Le Guin (b. 1929), John Barth (b. 1930), Donald Barthelme (1931–89), Robert Coover (b. 1932), Thomas PYNCHON, Joanna Russ (b. 1937) and James Tate (b. 1943).

Further reading

Alien to Femininity (1987) by Marleen S. Barr; Bodies in Pieces (1996) by Deborah A. Harter; Fantasy and Mimesis (1984) by Kathryn Hume; The Game of the Impossible (1976) by W. R. Irwin, and Fantasy (1981) by Rosemary Jackson.

Faulkner, William   One of the most important American novelists and SHORT-STORY writers. Faulkner was born in New Albany, Mississippi, in 1897 and grew up in Oxford, Mississippi. Towards the end of WORLD WAR I he trained as a pilot in the Royal Air Force in Canada, although he did not go to Europe or see action. After the war he worked in Mississippi and briefly in New York, and published a collection of poems, *The Marble Faun*, in 1924. He spent much of 1925 in Europe, returning to Oxford to work again at a variety of jobs. He published his first novel, *Soldier's Pay*, in 1926, and his second, *Mosquitoes*, in 1927. Faulkner then completed a third novel, *Flags in the Dust*, which was unpublished in his lifetime, though it formed the basis for *Sartoris* (1929). In 1929 he married and bought a house, Rowan Oak, near Oxford. Between 1929 and 1936 he published four novels that are major works of American fiction: THE SOUND AND THE FURY (1929); *As I Lay Dying* (1930); *Light in August* (1932), and *Absalom, Absalom!* (1936). Technically innovative and challenging, these novels established Faulkner's major recurring themes, notably the ambiguous relation of the Southern past to its present and the tragic burdens imposed by a particular heritage. During this period he began to work as a scriptwriter in HOLLYWOOD and published two other novels, the consistently underrated *Sanctuary* (1931) and *Pylon* (1935), as well as short stories and another collection of poems.

In the 1930s Faulkner invented Yoknapatawpha County, Mississippi, as a setting for his work, calling it his 'postage stamp of native soil'. His preoccupation with the history and characters of this fictional county makes much of his work densely interconnected. His experimentations with form continued, notably with the short-story cycle *The Unvanquished* (1938) and the novel *The Wild Palms* (1939), with its two intertwined narratives, though he wrote more conventionally in *The Hamlet* (1940), the first of the 'Snopes trilogy' of Yoknapatawpha novels tracing the rise of Flem Snopes. The other Snopes novels are *The Town* (1957) and *The Mansion* (1959). In 1942 he published another short-story cycle, *Go Down, Moses*, which is his most accomplished work on the relation between the Southern past and present, while his searing personal ambivalence towards racial SEGREGATION is evident in the novel *Intruder in the Dust* (1948). Two significant later works show Faulkner's range as a novelist. In the partly dramatic *Requiem for a Nun* (1951) he explores the aftermath of some of the events depicted in *Sanctuary*, and further examines Yoknapatawpha's history. *A Fable* (1954), meanwhile, is unusual for Faulkner; set in France in World War I, it is largely an allegorical reconsideration of Christ's death.

American acclaim came relatively late to Faulkner, helped by his significant reputation in Europe and by the publishing of a selection of his work, *The Portable Faulkner* (1946), edited by Malcolm Cowley. In 1949 he received the NOBEL PRIZE FOR LITERATURE, and gave a celebrated acceptance speech in which he spoke of literature's capacity to help humanity to endure. After the Nobel Prize, Faulkner became a more public figure than before and was often quoted on issues of race and the South. Long an alcoholic, and leading a life of considerable turmoil, he died in July 1962.

The critic Hugh Kenner has wondered whether Faulkner is the 'Last Novelist'; that is, although Faulkner's technique makes special demands on his readers, he maintains the humanistic belief that the novel should deal with important public and social concerns, and, in the manner of Charles Dickens or Thomas Hardy, he creates an absorbing and intensely real fictional world. Although his style has sometimes been criticized for its supposed prolixity and unnecessary obscurity, and his fiction for rehearsing a series of racial stereotypes, Faulkner remains the most important 20th century American novelist.

Further reading

The Ink of Melancholy: Faulkner's Novels (1990) by André Bleikasten; *William Faulkner: Toward Yoknapatawpha and Beyond* (1978) by Cleanth Brooks; *The Achievement of William Faulkner* (1966) by Michael Millgate; *Faulkner and Modernism* (1990) by Richard Moreland; *Faulkner and Southern Womanhood* (1994) by Diane Roberts; *Faulkner: The House Divided* (1983) by Eric J. Sundquist, and *William Faulkner and Southern History* (1993) by Joel Williamson. *Faulkner* (1974) by Joseph L. Blotner and *The Life of William Faulkner* (1994) by Richard Gray are recommended critical biographies.

Federal Theatre Project   Formed during the DEPRESSION under the same programme as the FEDERAL WRITERS' PROJECT, the Federal Theatre Project operated from 1936 to 1939 and was responsible for the production of over 1,000 plays. Productions included classical plays, revivals, musicals, children's plays, radio plays and puppet shows as well as new drama. In addition to providing employment for the various professions involved in theatrical production, it is especially noteworthy for helping to develop the work of young dramatists. It also produced 'The Living Newspaper', experimental dramatizations commenting on current events. The politically radical aspect of some of the project's productions led to an investigation by Congress and this resulted in its termination.

Federal Writers' Project   Operating between 1935 and 1939 the project was initiated by Congress as part of the NEW DEAL, and was designed to provide assistance during the DEPRESSION for unemployed writers. The project was one of four administered by the Works Progress Administration, the others being the FEDERAL THEATRE PROJECT, the Federal Music Project and the Federal Arts Project. Various projects were sponsored, including guidebooks to regions and individual states and a collection of memories of SLAVERY. Writers employed under the project included Conrad Aiken (1889–1973), Nelson Algren (1909–81), Saul BELLOW, John Cheever (1912–82), Ralph ELLISON, Zora Neale HURSTON, Weldon Kees (1914–55), Claude McKay (1889–1948), Margaret Walker (b. 1915), Richard WRIGHT and Frank Yerby (1916–91).

Federalist Papers   A collection of eighty-five essays, published during 1787 and 1788 during the CONSTITUTION DEBATE. Most were written by Alexander Hamilton (1755–1804), and the rest by James Madison (1751–1836) and John Jay (1745–1829), although all appeared under the *nom de plume* 'Publius'. The essays were published in newspapers and collected in book form in 1788. They attempted to persuade New York state voters to ratify the proposed Constitution, and argued for centralizing the administration and strengthening federal government. Politically, the major premise of the papers is that only a strong centralized government with appropriate checks and balances can guarantee individual rights and liberties, by minimizing the effects of faction and self-interest that will inevitably develop under any social system.

Feminist movement   Modern feminism, sometimes referred to by the earlier term the 'women's liberation movement', began in the United States in the 1960s, perhaps most obviously with the founding of the National Organization for Women in 1966, and the beginning of university courses in women's studies in 1969. Whereas earlier women's movements tended to be devoted primarily to enfranchisement, feminism remains dedicated to a range of social and political objectives. These include: the raising of social awareness of the position of women; the ending of legal and social discrimination based on gender; validation of women's right to participate fully and compete equally in the workplace and in any profession; the recognition of women's authority over their own bodies and the legal right to ABORTION, and an end to media stereotyping of women as sexual objects or as having an existence wholly within a domestic sphere. The feminist movement has sometimes been criticized for its white, middle-class bias, and it has made various attempts to include women of colour and working-class women. Given the differences between European and American feminism, the movement's diversity, and a series of sometimes bitter conflicts within the feminist movement, many now prefer to use the term 'feminisms' rather than 'feminism', or consider 'gender studies' a more appropriate designation.

As a literary critical approach feminisms characteristically seek to validate women's literature, especially kinds of writing that have been marginalized or altogether excluded from the male-centred literary canon, to explore differences between masculine and feminine styles of writing, to encourage the realistic representation of women's experience, to reject essentialist views of gender, and to develop a literature that offers role models for women. Feminist literary criticism frequently draws on insights and methodology from a variety of disciplines, especially psychoanalysis and sociology.

Letters on the Equality of the Sexes (1838) by Sarah Moore Grimké (1792–1873), *Woman in the Nineteenth Century* (1845) by Margaret Fuller (1810–50) and *Women and Economics* (1898) by Charlotte Perkins Gilman (1860–1935) were important works defining feminism in the 19th century. Twentieth-century feminism was shaped by a series of influential texts such as Simone de Beauvoir's *The Second Sex* (1949), *The Feminine Mystique* (1963) by Betty Friedan (b. 1921), *Sexual Politics* (1970) by Kate Millett (b. 1934) and Germaine Greer's *The Female Eunuch* (1970). Many literary and critical works have been crucial to the definition, formation and dissemination of feminist thought. These include: the novels *Fear of Flying* (1973) by Erica Jong (b. 1942) and *The Women's Room* (1977) by Marilyn French (b. 1929); the studies *Feminist Theory* (1981) edited by Nannerl O. Keohane, Michelle Z. Rosaldo and Barbara C. Gelpi, and *Feminism Unmodified* (1987) by Catharine A. MacKinnon

(b. 1946); the critical works *A Literature of their Own* (1977) by Elaine Showalter, *The Madwoman in the Attic* (1979) by Sandra Gilbert and Susan Gubar, *Ain't I a Woman* (1981) and *Feminist Theory From Margin to Center* (1984) by bell hooks, *Sexual/Textual Politics* (1985) by Toril Moi, *Black Feminist Criticism* (1985) by Barbara Christian, and *Art and Anger* (1988) by Jane Marcus; poetry and essays by Adrienne RICH and Audre Lorde (1934–92), and the fiction and essays of Alice WALKER. Much contemporary feminist literary critical theory has been shaped by the European theorists Julia Kristeva, Luce Irigaray and Hélène Cixous.

Further reading

The Feminist Reader (1989), edited by Catherine Belsey and Jane Moore; *What is Feminism?* (1986), edited by Juliet Mitchell and Ann Oakley; *Literary Feminisms* (2000) by Ruth Robbins, and *Feminism on the Border* (2000) by Sonia Saldívar-Hull.

Fireside Poets   Label applied to an influential group of popular 19th century New England poets that included John Greenleaf Whittier (1807–92), Henry Wadsworth Longfellow (1807–82), Oliver Wendell Holmes (1809–94) and James Russell Lowell (1819–91). They were also known as the 'Schoolroom Poets'. 'Fireside' suggests poetry appropriate for reading in a family setting, and the group's poetry tends to be formally conservative, genteel and firmly in the lyrical-narrative mode. There is often also an instructive or didactic element to it, and Whittier especially developed this in his anti-SLAVERY poems. The term 'fireside' possibly derives from J. R. Lowell's 1864 collection of essays, *Fireside Travels*.

Fitzgerald, F. Scott (Francis Scott Key Fitzgerald)   Novelist and SHORT-STORY writer, born in St Paul, Minnesota, in 1896. From 1913 Fitzgerald attended Princeton University, where he enjoyed social success and popularity, although he left without graduating in 1917 and joined the army. While stationed near Montgomery, Alabama, Fitzgerald met and became engaged to Zelda Sayre (1900–48). Although she ended the engagement, the considerable success of Fitzgerald's first novel, *This Side of Paradise* (1920), led to reconciliation and the couple were married in 1920. Their only child, Frances (known as Scottie), was born in 1921. Fitzgerald's second novel, *The Beautiful and Damned*, was published in 1922. Taken together, the first two novels and Fitzgerald's short stories helped to define the JAZZ AGE and conveyed a vivid sense of a new generation. Although these early works lack Fitzgerald's later maturity and grasp of narrative technique, they have a stylish freshness and they spoke directly to their contemporary readers.

With Scott's writing generating a considerable income, the Fitzgeralds became celebrity figures in New York and seemed to personify the new age. In 1924 they moved to France, dividing their time between Paris and the Riviera. There Fitzgerald finished his most brilliant achievement, *THE GREAT GATSBY* (1925), which, though a commercial failure, showed a remarkable development from the earlier writing in terms of thematic focus and technical sophistication. This maturity was also largely evident in the 1926 collection of short stories, *All the Sad Young Men*. However, Fitzgerald began to struggle with ALCOHOLISM, while Zelda underwent a series of mental breakdowns that resulted in long periods in sanatoriums. Against this background the couple returned to the United States and Zelda published her only novel, *Save Me the Waltz* (1932), while Fitzgerald published *Tender is the Night* (1934). Set almost entirely in Europe, *Tender is the Night* is chiefly concerned with the marriage between a psychiatrist, Dick Diver, and the psychologically damaged Nicole Warren. It explores Diver's gradual decline, caused partly by loss of ambition as he enters Nicole's world of the wealthy leisured class, and partly by his infatuation with a young actress, Rosemary Hoyt. Although it is structurally problematic (Fitzgerald tried several times to revise it, and a different version was published in 1948), the novel contains some of his finest writing. With Zelda residing in various nursing homes, Fitzgerald worked as a screenwriter in HOLLYWOOD, living with a newspaper columnist, Sheilah Graham. Although he had mixed success as a screenwriter, his Hollywood experiences generated some significant fiction: a critically underrated series of stories about an alcoholic hack writer, Pat Hobby, and one of the most important Hollywood novels, *The Last Tycoon*. Although unfinished, this is a significant achievement. Focusing on a gifted film producer, Monroe Stahr, the novel rehearses familiar Fitzgerald themes: how an imaginative visionary is brought down by materialism, and how promise may be unfulfilled and unrepeatable. 'There are no second acts in American lives,' as Fitzgerald wrote in the novel's manuscript. A version of the novel, edited by Edmund Wilson, was published in 1941; it has also been edited by Matthew J. Bruccoli and published as *The Love of the Last Tycoon: A Western* (1993). Fitzgerald died of a heart attack in Hollywood in 1940. Zelda, whose contribution to Scott's writing is now generally acknowledged, died in 1948 during a fire at her nursing home in Asheville, North Carolina.

While understandable, the tendency to associate Fitzgerald primarily with the Jazz Age can obscure his more enduring achievements. Always a gifted writer of attractive lyrical prose, he developed remarkably while always maintaining a clear sense of the times in which he lived; and these included the DEPRESSION as well as the 1920s. In spite of the amount of flawed and unfinished work, he remains a major American novelist.

Further reading

Some Sort of Epic Grandeur (1981) by Matthew J. Bruccoli; The Illusions of a Nation (1972) by John F. Callahan; F. Scott Fitzgerald and the Craft of Fiction (1966) by Richard D. Lehan; F. Scott Fitzgerald: His Art and His Technique (1967) by James E. Miller, and F. Scott Fitzgerald and the Art of Social Fiction (1980) by Brian Way.

Folklore   Defined by Archer Taylor as 'the material that is handed on by tradition, either by word of mouth or by custom and practice', folklore is an ever-evolving body of stories, myths, legends, versions of historical events, and entertainments. American folklore has been studied seriously since the end of the 19th century, and the American Folklore Society was founded in 1888. Inevitably, much American folklore is adapted from European sources, although some has distinctively American origins. Folklore has been used in various ways by American writers, for instance in the LOCAL COLOUR and TALL TALE traditions, or as a serious analysis of myth. Folklore exists today in many forms, including rituals, jokes, apocryphal stories, stories of celebrities and urban myths.

Much European-American folklore has to do with the landscape of the FRONTIER and the development of the West, evident in mythic characters such as Johnny Appleseed, Paul Bunyan, Mike Fink and Casey Jones. The ORAL TRADITION through which folklore has generally been transmitted lies behind the BALLAD and the tall tale, which made folklore heroes of the frontiersmen Davy Crockett and Daniel Boone and OUTLAWS such as Billy the Kid. In this respect popular forms such as the DIME NOVEL and the pictorial comic book have been significant in the formation and transmission of American folklore. It is important to note that folklore may be especially significant for minority groups and for groups who are disadvantaged or oppressed. Folklore stories may exist as parables concerning power, perhaps deriving from particular social conditions and providing insight into them. The creation of outlaw heroes such as Billy the Kid and Bonnie and Clyde has often been explained in terms of social deprivation.

For Americans of colour, folklore may be especially significant in providing continuity to an otherwise occluded or severed past. Certainly there has been an adaptive tendency in much ASIAN AMERICAN and CHICANO writing, in which existing folklore is fused with contemporary situations and events in the United States. This tendency is even more marked in NATIVE AMERICAN and AFRICAN AMERICAN literature. For example, the writing of Paula Gunn Allen (b. 1939), N. Scott Momaday (b. 1934), Leslie Marmon SILKO, Louise Erdrich (b. 1954) and Sherman Alexie (b. 1966) is persistently concerned with the affirmative restoration of links between a folkloric Native American past and contemporary life. Since the HARLEM RENAISSANCE African American writers have shown an immense interest in the collection and use of folklore derived from Africa. Arna Bontemps (1902–73), Countee Cullen (1903–46) and Zora Neale HURSTON all worked on collecting folklore material, and Hurston's *Mules and Men* (1935) is a classic account of African folklore survivals. Furthermore, some of the most influential African American novelists have represented folklore as a means of affirming cultural identity. Works such as Hurston's *Their Eyes Were Watching God* (1937), Ralph ELLISON's *INVISIBLE MAN* and Toni MORRISON's *Song of Solomon* (1977) contain important elements of African-based folklore.

Further reading

Spider Woman's Granddaughters (1989), edited by Paula Gunn Allen; *Making Face, Making Soul=Haciendo Caras* (1990), edited by Gloria Anzaldúa; *Readings in American Folklore* (1979), edited by Jan Harold

Brunvand; 'Folklore' by Arthur Palmer Hudson, in *The Literary History of the United States* (1974), edited by Robert E. Spiller et al.; *Liberating Voices* (1991) by Gayl Jones, and *Myths, Legends, and Folktales of America* (1999), edited by David Leeming and Jake Page.

Fordism Closely associated with the 'scientific management' methods known as TAYLORIZATION, Fordism refers primarily to the labour system developed by the automobile manufacturer Henry Ford (1863–1947). Ford pioneered the assembly-line process, in which a product is put together by a series of semi-skilled workers who each repeatedly perform only one of the production tasks required. Critics of Fordism claimed that the price of efficient production was the fragmentation and dehumanization of the workforce. More broadly, the term Fordism has been used to describe post-1945 American society, characterized by large centralized organizational units, a strongly hierarchical structure, and the rationalized regulation of social, political and cultural life.

Four freedoms In his 1941 State of the Union Address President Franklin D. Roosevelt stated that there were four fundamental freedoms to which all people were entitled: freedom of speech and expression; freedom to worship God in their own way; freedom from want, and freedom from fear. Norman Rockwell (1894–1978) produced four famous paintings representing the freedoms, and during WORLD WAR II these were widely distributed by the Office of War Information.

Fourierism Social system devised by the French social reformer Charles Fourier (1772–1837). Fourier, who never visited the United States, proposed that society be organized in a system of communes, known as phalanxes, each with a population of 1,620. Ideally each phalanx would become self-sufficient through agriculture and handicrafts, and labour would be organized on an egalitarian model, with each person finding a balance between manual and non-manual work. Members of each phalanx would live in a large communal building, the phalanstery.

Many in the United States became interested in Fourierism after it was popularized by Albert Brisbane (1809–90) in the 1840s. Brisbane, who had studied with Fourier in France, published a book, *Social Destiny of Man* (1840), and many articles on Fourierism, which he termed 'Associationism'. There were approximately fifty attempts to establish Fourier-type communes in the United States in the 1840s, although they were on a much smaller scale than Fourier's plan. The most well known was BROOK FARM, which was already established as a commune before deciding to use the Fourier model. On average, communes lasted about 2 years before being broken up, although the North American Phalanx in Redbank, New Jersey, survived for 11 years (1843–54). Interest in Fourierism declined sharply in the 1850s, though the concept of a model small community has remained a powerful one in American life.

Fourteenth Amendment This amendment to the CONSTITUTION, ratified in 1868 during RECONSTRUCTION, had three important elements. It recognized former slaves as US citizens (since they were 'persons born or naturalized in the United States, and subject to the jurisdiction thereof'), forbade any state from denying the 'equal protection of the laws' to any citizen, and banned from public office anyone who had joined the CONFEDERACY having previously sworn allegiance to the Constitution. Taken together, the Fourteenth and the Fifteenth Amendments (1870), which enfranchised former slaves, were crucial in the attempt to grant full and equal citizenship to this group, but a series of subsequent voting laws in Southern states effectively nullified the amendments. The Fourteenth Amendment proved crucial to the CIVIL RIGHTS MOVEMENT in the 1950s and 1960s, however, as the phrase 'equal protection' was invoked in a series of important SUPREME COURT decisions, such as that of BROWN V. BOARD OF EDUCATION OF TOPEKA.

Franklin, Benjamin Diplomat, printer, inventor, scientist and public figure, one of the most famous of all Americans, often considered the epitome of American inventiveness, pragmatism and ingenuity.

Born in Boston in 1706, Franklin worked with his brother on a newspaper until they quarrelled. Franklin moved to Philadelphia in 1723; his arrival there as described in his *Autobiography* (1818; full edition 1867) is one of the iconic scenes in American literature. After various jobs, and a period spent in London, Franklin had by 1748 made a fortune as a printer in Philadelphia. He also wrote many pamphlets and satires, addressing topics such as the relation between Britain and her colonies, and many practical issues. In the spirit of the ENLIGHTENMENT he constantly attacked superstitions, notably those regarding witchcraft. He became particularly well known for publishing *Poor Richard's Almanac* (1733–58), memorable for its maxims and proverbs. Increasingly Franklin became a public figure, instrumental in organizing a lending library, a police force and a fire-fighting service for Philadelphia. His scientific experiments with electricity brought him international renown. From 1757 he represented the Pennsylvania Assembly in London, where he lived almost entirely until 1775, usually agitating for American interests. Back in Philadelphia in 1776 he was one of the committee that drafted the DECLARATION OF INDEPENDENCE, and he spent most of the REVOLUTIONARY WAR working for the Congress in Paris. He was popularly acclaimed in France as typifying American values of simplicity, rationality and straightforwardness, and internationally as a representative of the Enlightenment. Franklin remained in France until 1785, having been much involved in the negotiations that ended the Revolutionary War. Returning to his home in what was now the United States, he continued in public service, working on the committee that produced the CONSTITUTION and petitioning for the abolition of SLAVERY. He died in Philadelphia in 1790.

Franklin's engaging intellectual curiosity and wide-ranging interests are evident in his best-selling *Autobiography*, which, along with some of his satires, forms his considerable legacy to American literature. The *Autobiography*, which is unfinished, influenced the subsequent writing of American AUTOBIOGRAPHY. It is Franklin's reflective interpretation of his life, not merely a chronicle. Possessing a religious, didactic element, it demonstrates a trajectory of self-realization and offers an example of how to obtain success through a combination of astuteness, thrift, industry and the ability to recognize opportunity. The *Autobiography* is also significant in being an *American* narrative. When Franklin began it in 1771 it was primarily a private memoir, but when he resumed it in 1785 it became more self-consciously the presentation of a public and representative figure.

Further reading

Benjamin Franklin: An American Man of Letters (1964) by Bruce Ingham Granger; Benjamin Franklin in American Thought and Culture (1994) by Nian-Sheng Huang; Studies in Classic American Literature (1923) by D. H. Lawrence, and Benjamin Franklin (1938) by Carl Van Doren.

Free verse   Rendering of the French term 'vers libre' ('free line') used since the 1880s to describe unrhymed poetry written according to speech cadence rather than to a set metre; that is, in which there is no set pattern to the relation between stressed and unstressed syllables. The line length in free verse may vary considerably, and the stanzaic organization typical of more conventional poetry is abandoned, sometimes replaced by the 'verse paragraph'. In American poetry, free verse is especially associated with Walt WHITMAN, for whom it embodied a bardic style deriving from biblical idiom, a rejection of the formalism that he considered characteristic of European writing, and an expansiveness appropriate to his vision of the American landscape. One justification for the American poet's use of free verse appears in Ralph Waldo EMERSON's 1844 essay 'The Poet'. Emerson asserts 'it is not metres, but a metre-making argument, that makes a poem – a thought so passionate and alive, that, like the spirit of a plant or an animal, it has an architecture of its own, and adorns nature with a new thing.' Stephen CRANE wrote in free verse, but it was the poets Amy Lowell (1874–1925), Ezra POUND, H. D. (Hilda Doolittle) (1886–1961), T. S. ELIOT, William Carlos WILLIAMS, Carl Sandburg (1878–1967), Langston Hughes (1902–67) and later, Allen GINSBERG, who were its most important and influential practitioners in the 20th century. Free verse is closely linked with IMAGISM, as is evident from Pound's urging that the imagist poet should 'compose in sequence of the musical phrase, not in sequence of the metronome'. Commenting on Sandburg's poetry, Robert FROST famously remarked that writing free verse was 'like playing tennis with the net down'.

Free Soil Party   This small but influential political party was formed in 1848 in opposition to the expansion of slavery into the territories acquired by the United States after the MEXICAN WAR. Its slogan was 'free soil, free speech, free labor, and free men'. The poet John Greenleaf Whittier (1807–92) was a prominent member. Eventually in 1854 it was absorbed into the new Republican Party.

French and Indian Wars Term applied to a series of conflicts fought between Britain and France in the American colonies in the period 1690–1760, sometimes involving intricate shifting alliances with various Native American groups. The main territory in dispute was Canada and the Ohio Valley. There were four colonial wars in this period, each related to wars in Europe. They were: King William's War (1690–97); Queen Anne's War (1701–13); King George's War (1745–48), and the French and Indian War (1754–60). The French and Indian War was the most crucial in determining the ascendancy of the British. Under the terms of the Treaty of Paris (1763), the agreement that settled the war, the British were granted Canada and all of the French land east of the Mississippi, and Florida was ceded from Spain. (The French granted the Mississippi Valley and New Orleans to Spain to compensate for the loss of Florida.) Although so much was won by the British, the French and Indian War has often been considered crucial to the subsequent REVOLUTIONARY WAR, in giving the colonial forces confidence in their own abilities.

The classic history of the wars is the eleven-volume *France and England in North America* (1851–92) by Francis Parkman (1823–93). James Fenimore COOPER used the French and Indian War as historical background to several of his novels, notably *The Last of the Mohicans* (1826).

Frontier Consideration of the shifting boundary between white European settlement and wilderness has been a significant factor in much American writing, and the historical experience of the frontier has been considered a key element of the American character, as expressed in Frederick Jackson Turner's FRONTIER THESIS. While for early settlers the frontier was simply the land beyond the settlement, to later generations it became a challenge to be overcome so that the MANIFEST DESTINY of the United States could be fulfilled. By 1890 the report on the census stated that the spread of settlements meant that 'there can hardly be said to be a frontier line' any longer, and this has been taken to mean that frontier was closed. Nevertheless, the concept of the frontier has been repeatedly invoked and revised; for instance, in President Kennedy's invocation of a 'New Frontier' of internal reform and international responsibility, and in the concept of outer space as the 'final frontier', famously expressed in the television series *Star Trek*.

A great deal of WESTERN and DIME NOVEL writing is concerned with the frontier, which also shaped the TALL TALE, a great deal of FOLKLORE, and a particular kind of humour. James Fenimore COOPER's LEATHER-STOCKING TALES are the earliest sustained examination of the frontier as it moves westward from the eastern seaboard. The significance of the frontier is notably examined in works by Mark TWAIN (especially *Roughing It*, 1872), Hamlin Garland (1860–1940), Sinclair Lewis (1885–1951) and Willa CATHER.

Further reading

> Frontier: American Literature and the American West (1965) by Edwin S. Fussell; *The Lay of the Land* (1975) by Annette Kolodny; *The Frontier Experience and the American Dream* (1989), edited by David Mogen, Mark Busby and Paul Bryant; *Virgin Land* (1950) by Henry Nash Smith, and *Regeneration through Violence* (1973) and *Gunfighter Nation* (1992) by Richard Slotkin.

Frontier thesis   Argument put forward by the historian Frederick Jackson Turner (1861–1932), in which the struggle with the FRONTIER is seen as the most important single factor in creating a distinctive American character, in terms of fashioning individualism, DEMOCRACY, optimism and SELF-RELIANCE. Turner presented the thesis in a paper entitled 'The Significance of the Frontier in American History', which he gave in Chicago in 1893. He stated that:

> to the frontier the American intellect owes its striking characteristics. That coarseness and strength combined with acuteness and inquisitiveness, that practical, inventive turn of mind, quick to find expedients, that masterful grasp of material things, lacking in the artistic but powerful to effect great ends, that restless, nervous energy, that dominant individualism, working for good and for evil, and withal that buoyancy and exuberance which comes with freedom – these are traits of the frontier, or traits called out elsewhere because of the existence of the frontier.

Although the thesis has often been challenged and discredited as history it has functioned significantly as myth.

Frost, Robert   Poet, born in San Francisco in 1874 and raised in New England. Frost briefly attended Dartmouth College and later Harvard, but did not graduate. He married in 1895. From 1900 Frost combined teaching jobs with poultry farming in Derry, New Hampshire. In 1911, determined on a literary career, he sold his farm and moved with his family to England. While there he published his first two books, *A Boy's Will* (1913) and *North of Boston* (1914). Frost's considerable reputation rests largely on the poems in these two works. He and his family returned to the United States in 1915. He resumed farming and taught at the University of Michigan and at Amherst College. In 1916 he published *Mountain Interval*, and in 1923 *New Hampshire*. Increasingly Frost's work was popularly acclaimed and he was awarded numerous honorary degrees and literary prizes. As a public figure he represented the United States on several trips abroad, and, famously, read 'The Gift Outright' at President Kennedy's inauguration in 1961. Frost also played a significant role in the release of Ezra POUND from confinement in a mental hospital. He died in Boston in 1963.

Pound's description of Frost as 'VURRY Amur'k'n' goes some way towards identifying his achievement and his enduring appeal. As well as rooting his poems in the New England rural landscape, Frost used American speech patterns as the basis of his blank verse. His apparently casual, colloquial poems may combine the simple with the profound but they always provide a point of entry for the reader – a 'door' as Frost called it – in contrast to the sometimes forbidding poems of his MODERNIST contemporaries. Frost's work is anti-ROMANTIC, typically representing human efforts to make a home in hostile, indifferent nature. Frost considers such struggles as a defining characteristic of the human, and as simultaneously heroic and tinged with futility. He wrote that a poem was 'a momentary stay against confusion', the phrase indicating both the joy of making the poem and the knowledge that it can only provide temporary comforting order in an otherwise confusing and unknowable world. Critics have often focused on this bleak, pessimistic aspect of Frost and have considered it as sharply at odds with the developed persona that is at the basis of his popular appeal.

Further reading

Robert Frost (1986), edited by Harold Bloom; *Toward Robert Frost* (1992) by Judith Oster; *Robert Frost, The Work of Knowing* (1977, 1990) by Richard Poirier; *Frost: A Literary Life Reconsidered* (1984) by William H. Pritchard, and *The Ordeal of Robert Frost* (1997) by Mark Richardson.

The Fugitives   Literary group that began meeting in Nashville, Tennessee, in 1921, largely under the influence of the poet-critics John Crowe Ransom (1888–1974) and Allen Tate (1899–1979). In spite of the later concerns of its members, the Fugitives were not overtly political, and existed mainly to try and help develop Southern writing. The group produced a journal, *The Fugitive*, between 1922 and 1925 and published poetry by a range of contributors, including Robert Graves and Laura Riding (1901–91). Members of the Fugitives included Donald Davidson (1893–1968) and Robert Penn Warren (1905–89). Several of the group were later key members of the AGRARIANS, a group that was much more politically defined than the Fugitives.

Further reading

The Fugitive Legacy (2001) by Charlotte H. Beck and *The Fugitive Group* (1959) by Louise Cowan.

Fugitive Slave Acts   The two acts, of 1793 and 1850, were intended to ensure the return of runaway slaves who had escaped to a non-slave state or territory. As anti-slavery feeling grew, so did defiance of the 1793 act, both individually and more systematically through the UNDERGROUND RAILROAD. As part of the COMPROMISE OF 1850, a more severe Fugitive Slave Law was introduced, as a consequence of which slaves could be arrested without warrant and were denied trial by jury, while those helping runaway slaves became liable to heavy penalties. Even freed blacks were threatened by the act, fearing that they might be kidnapped back into slavery. Liberal Northerners were outraged by the 1850 act, and in a celebrated 1851 address Ralph Waldo EMERSON said that the act 'enacts the crime of kidnapping' and that 'it must be made inoperative … must be abrogated and wiped out of the statute-book; but whilst it stands there, it must be disobeyed'. Henry David THOREAU's 1854 address 'Slavery in

Massachusetts' is also critical of the act. The act, which was repealed in 1864, sharply increased sectional divisions before the CIVIL WAR.

The Fugitive Slave Laws form an important background to much writing about slavery. The figure of the slave-catcher, for instance, is a familiar one in anti-slavery works such as Harriet Beecher STOWE's *Uncle Tom's Cabin* (1852), and the 1850 act occasioned the deferring of liberty in Harriet JACOBS' *Incidents in the Life of a Slave Girl* (1861).

Fundamentalism   Movement within Protestantism, founded on literal interpretation of the Bible and specifically opposed to Charles Darwin's theory of evolution. As a conservative force Fundamentalism has been a notable presence in American public life since the 1920s. There are various churches within the Fundamentalist movement, and since 1930 they have been affiliated to the Independent Fundamental Churches of America. The movement's name derives from a series of twelve pamphlets titled *The Fundamentals*, published between 1910 and 1915.

G

Gilded Age   Term used to describe the period 1865–1880, derived from the novel *The Gilded Age* (1873) by Mark TWAIN, written in collaboration with Charles Dudley Warner (1829–1900). The period is characterized by an increasing materialism and also by speculation and political corruption. It is also often represented as a time of transition in which the innocent original idealism of the United States is lost. Many writers, notably WHITMAN and MELVILLE, felt alienated from this new America, and some channelled their anger into novels of social criticism, which are a striking feature of the period. Key works set during the Gilded Age include *Democracy* (1880) by Henry Adams (1838–1918) and *The Rise of Silas Lapham* (1885) by William Dean Howells (1837–1920).

Ginsberg, Allen   Poet, born into a Jewish family in Newark, New Jersey, in 1926. Ginsberg attended the University of Columbia, where he met William Burroughs (1914–97) and Jack Kerouac (1922–69). Although his academic progress was interrupted he graduated in 1948 and worked at a variety of jobs before moving to San Francisco, where he became a leading member of the BEATS. In 1956 he published his first book, *Howl and Other Poems*. Although its critical reception was mixed, the book, and especially the poem 'HOWL', proved influential in the development of American poetry. No subsequent book by Ginsberg had the same impact. The title poem of *Kaddish and other Poems* (1961) is a moving elegy for his mother, who had experienced periods of madness. Other books include *Reality Sandwiches* (1963), *Planet News* (1968), *The Fall of America: Poems of These States* (1972), *Mind Breaths* (1978), *White Shroud* (1986) and *Cosmopolitan Greetings* (1994). *Collected Poems* appeared in 1984. From the 1960s onwards Ginsberg became a celebrity who travelled widely and spoke eloquently for many social causes. He died in 1997.

Ginsberg absorbed a wide range of influences, notably William Blake, Walt WHITMAN and William Carlos WILLIAMS, and his poetry reflects his often troubled engagement with the contemporary political and social situation. Using often-robust vocabulary, his poems can shift impressively between outrage, comic self-regard, APOCALYPTIC prophecy, satire and tenderness. Ginsberg tended to use speech-based FREE VERSE in long lines, but as he became increasingly interested in creative fusions of poetry and music, he considered the poem as a public utterance requiring performance. His writing is highly innovative and yet also self-consciously traditional, restoring a bardic, prophetic voice to poetry. Overall, his work is driven by his personal and social concerns, such as his intense sympathy for the marginalized, his disgust with materialism and with the spiritual vacancy that he considered characteristic of post-war consumerist America, his homoeroticism and his varied interests, such as Buddhism. Consistent with the bardic tradition, his ambition was for poetry that would raise political consciousness and effect social change.

Further reading

On the Poetry of Allen Ginsberg (1980), edited by Lewis Hyde; *Allen Ginsberg in America* (1969) by Jane Kramer, and *Ginsberg: A Biography* (1989) by Barry Miles.

Godey's Lady's Book   Illustrated monthly magazine founded in Philadelphia in 1830 and published until 1898. It flourished under the editorship of Sarah Josepha Hale (1788–1879), who edited it for 40 years (1837–77). *Godey's* was among the most successful of all monthly magazines, and at its peak in the 1850s it had up to 150,000 subscribers. It was aimed at women readers and as well as poetry, short fiction and book reviews it included domestic advice, recipes and articles on fashion and manners. Hale expressly tried to encourage women writers, and although much of the verse included may seem sentimental she did publish significant work by Catharine Sedgwick (1789–1867) and Harriet Beecher STOWE, as well as by male contributors, including EMERSON, William Gilmore Simms (1806–70), Henry Wadsworth Longfellow (1807–82) and Edgar Allan POE.

Gold rush   Term applied to any of a series of discoveries of gold which led to a sudden and dramatic influx of prospectors. Typically, a discovery of gold would be followed by the speedy arrival of individual prospectors; a mining camp would develop, housing prospectors, families and those providing services; a rough town might then be built, until overcrowding and diminishing returns of gold would mean a crisis. Towns that had other natural resources might survive while others would become ghost towns after the gold rush.

The first major rush was in 1849, after gold was discovered in Sutter's Mill, California, in January 1848. It is estimated that over 80,000 prospectors came to the area in 1849 (the so-called 'forty-niners'), and that more than 250,000 had arrived by 1853. Although the gold rush was over by 1854, the influx of migrants into California precipitated the territory's transformation into a state. The next rushes were in Colorado in 1858, which attracted over 50,000 prospectors, and in Nevada in 1859. This rush followed the discovery of several precious metals, including gold and silver, and resulted in the sudden growth of Virginia City. This was the most enduring rush, because the richness of the 'Comstock Lode' made long-term working profitable. Discovery of a small amount of gold, and rumours of much more, in the Black Hills of the Dakotas in 1874 was more significant in opening up lands to settlers than in the amount of gold mined. The discovery, made by army prospectors, was on land that was sacred to the Lakota and which had been promised to them in perpetuity. The arrival of prospectors led to the breaking of this promise, to a series of battles with the Lakota and eventually to Congress taking the Black Hills and 40 million acres from the Lakota. The last major gold rush was in the Klondike in 1896. This led to an influx of prospectors to the Yukon and the creation of the town of Dawson, but the rush was over within 3 years. In addition to major gold rushes there were innumerable minor ones, including many in Idaho, Arizona and Montana.

The gold rush and the life of the prospector have formed subjects for many writers and have been considered integral to the development of FRONTIER writing. The gold mine and the promise of gold have been staples of much popular WESTERN literature, while several writers have used the life cycle of the mining camp or town to explore particular themes. These include works as various as the California stories of Bret Harte (1836–1902) and the Western *Welcome to Hard Times* (1960) by E. L. Doctorow (b. 1931). Mark TWAIN wrote memorably of Virginia City in *Roughing It* (1872). Jack London (1876–1916) went to the Yukon in the 1896 gold rush and wrote short stories based on his life there, and set several novels, notably *Call of the Wild* (1903) and *White Fang* (1906), in Alaska.

Gothic   Variation of ROMANCE in which there is much emphasis on lurid, supernatural, fantastic, mysterious and horrific events. Gothic writing developed in England in the mid 18th century. (It was called Gothic because of its cultivation of elements connected with the medieval period in Europe, a time associated with the Goths, a Germanic tribe.) The style proved very popular, and as it developed, certain typical features emerged. These include: secluded settings; wild landscapes; ruined buildings (especially castles); haunted houses; a desolate, gloomy atmosphere and monsters or monstrous events.

Gothic has a long and significant history in American literature. *The Asylum* (1811) by Isaac Mitchell (1759–1812) is usually considered the first American Gothic romance, but it was the novels of Charles Brockden BROWN that made Gothic both popular and influential. Gothic occupied a central place in the work of Edgar Allan POE, and was a prominent feature in the work of a wide diversity of writers, including Nathaniel HAWTHORNE, Emily DICKINSON, Ambrose Bierce (1842–1914), Henry JAMES and Edith Wharton (1862–1937). (The SLAVE NARRATIVE has also been called a variation of Gothic fiction.) Women writers have often used Gothic in significant ways, and 'The Yellow Wallpaper' (1892) by Charlotte Perkins Gilman (1860–1935) and *The Haunting of Hill House* (1959) by Shirley Jackson (1919–65) are classics of the genre. In the 20th century writers took Gothic in different directions. H. P. Lovecraft (1890–1937) was influential in combining it with SCIENCE FICTION, while others, such as Stephen KING, developed it into a genre dealing primarily with HORROR and the super-natural. However, traditional Gothic remained prominent, especially in the work of William FAULKNER and writers associated with SOUTHERN GOTHIC. Gothic remains a popular and influential style of writing, and fiction by James Purdy (b. 1923), Joyce Carol Oates (b. 1938) and others has been labelled 'New American Gothic'.

In concentrating on insecurity, terror, the irrational and the continuing burden of the past, Gothic offers a defiant alternative to optimistic, ROMANTIC, progressive American narratives. It is an anti-ENLIGHTENMENT style of writing. It has been argued that Gothic is a devious means of subverting dominant modes at specific historical moments; as Teresa A. Goddu has written, 'Instead of fleeing reality, the Gothic registers its culture's contradictions, presenting a distorted, not a disengaged, version of reality.'

Further reading

Through the Pale Door: A Guide to and Through the American Gothic (1990) by Frederick S. Frank; *Gothic America* (1997) by Teresa A. Goddu; *Redefining the American Gothic* (1989) by Louis Gross; *The Gothic Tradition in Fiction* (1979) by Elizabeth MacAndrew; *New American Gothic* (1962) by Irving Malin; *American Gothic* (1998), edited by Robert K. Martin and Eric Savoy, and *American Gothic* (1982) by Donald Ringe.

Graveyard school Term applied to a style of writing, especially poetry, prevalent in the early nineteenth century. The graveyard school originated in 18th century Britain, with the work of Edward Young, Robert Blair and Thomas Gray, and was taken up in the United States by Philip Freneau (1752–1832), Washington IRVING and William Cullen Bryant (1794–1878) among others. Graveyard writing is reflective and melancholy, perhaps morbid to modern sensibilities in its focus on death. The poems 'The Indian Burying Ground' (1787) by Freneau and 'Thanatopsis' (1817) by Bryant are outstanding examples of the style. The earliest work of Emily DICKINSON is in the graveyard tradition, and its influence may also be seen in many commemorative poems by the bereaved; certainly, the tradition lasted until the 1880s, when Mark TWAIN parodied it through the figure of Emmeline Grangerford in *The Adventures of Huckleberry Finn*.

Great Awakening Series of religious revivals that took place mainly in New England during the 1730s and in other parts of the colonies shortly afterwards. A major figure in the revivals was Jonathan Edwards (1703–58), whose sermon 'Sinners in the Hands of an Angry God' (1741) became famous. Edwards wrote on the Great Awakening in his essays 'A Faithful Narrative of the Surprising Work of God' (1737) and 'Some Thoughts Concerning the Present Revival of Religion in New England' (1742). The awakening provoked controversy partly because during a period of ENLIGHTENMENT it was seen to foster emotionalism rather than rational enquiry, and because much emphasis was placed on damnation. There was also division among those involved with the revivals, notably between the 'Old Lights' such as Edwards, who returned to an older form of evangelical Protestantism, and the 'New Lights' represented by Charles Chauncey, who embraced a more liberal approach. The New Lights eventually moved towards UNITARIANISM. Some historians have argued that the Great Awakening contributed to the American Revolution by breaking down respect for institutions. There was a much smaller 'Second Great Awakening' in the first decades of the 19th century.

The Great Gatsby Novel by F. Scott FITZGERALD, published in 1925. Set in New York and narrated by Nick Carraway, the novel explores the self-transformation of Jimmy Gatz from modest Mid-Western origins to the wealthy and mysterious Jay Gatsby of Long Island whose ambition is to regain his former lover Daisy, now the wife of Tom Buchanan, and Carraway's cousin. The novel ends with Gatsby, having been exposed as a bootlegger, killed by a garage owner, George Wilson, who mistakenly believes that Gatsby has had an affair with his now-dead wife, Myrtle. The story is not told in a straightforwardly chronological manner, but unfolds as Carraway learns more about Gatsby.

The novel's primary concern is with the duplicitous nature of the AMERICAN DREAM, as Fitzgerald explores Gatsby's inability to enter the world of the Buchanans, which depends on inherited rather than on earned wealth. In this respect the novel explores the failure of the American Dream, and this is powerfully reinforced by images Fitzgerald draws from T. S. ELIOT's *The Waste Land* and by the ELEGIAC ending in which the American continent is envisioned at the moment when its aspirational promise is about to be corrupted by material desire. However, Gatsby becomes heroic precisely because of his belief in dreams: in this respect, it is important to acknowledge that Carraway creatively shapes his representation of Gatsby to make him into a necessarily heroic figure embodying a deeply held American ROMANTIC belief in the ability to transform dreams into realities. Thus the novel is finely balanced between the will to believe in the promises of America and recognition that they are corruptible and worthless illusions. Fitzgerald's narrative device (and his seductively lyrical prose) ensures that this balance is maintained. In a fundamental way Fitzgerald examines the need for belief in order to animate life and give it direction and meaning, even if the object of that belief turns out to be unattainable or illusory. As he wrote, the novel's theme is 'the loss of those illusions that give such color to the world so that you don't care whether things are true or false as long as they partake of the magical glory'.

Further reading

New Essays on The Great Gatsby (1985), edited by Matthew Bruccoli; *Twentieth Century Interpretations of The Great Gatsby* (1968), edited by Ernest Lockridge, and *The Great Gatsby* (Critics Debate Series) (1990) by Stephen Matterson.

Great Migration   The move made within the United States by African Americans from the rural South to the urban North, especially in the years 1917–30. In 1910 almost 90 per cent of African Americans lived in the South, but by 1930 up to 2 million blacks had moved to cities of the North, Northwest and Mid-West (especially to New York, Chicago, Detroit and Philadelphia). This internal migration has been compared to the western migration of the 19th century in its transformation of the social landscape of the United States. The migration took place mainly because of the better economic opportunities provided by the North and because of racial injustice in the South. As well as profoundly affecting the Northern cities the migration transformed the African American population from a predominantly rural one to an urban one.

Migration from the South is a recurring trope in African American literature. Since the time of SLAVERY the move north had been represented as a move to freedom, while after slavery it most often represents opportunity for self-fulfilment and the realization of a true identity. ('New York! That's not a place, it's a dream,' Ralph ELLISON writes in *INVISIBLE MAN*.) Richard WRIGHT's story 'The Man Who Was Almost A Man' (1939) is a parable of the Great Migration, and Wright collaborated on *Twelve Million Black Voices* (1941), a picture essay on the migration and its place in African American culture.

Guggenheim Fellowships   Annual awards made by the Guggenheim Foundation, usually with a view to permitting artists and scholars to spend a period of between 6 and 12 months outside the United States. The awards were established in 1925 by Simon Guggenheim (1867–1941), one of a family of philanthropists whose wealth originated in the mining industry. Notable recipients have included Nella Larsen (1891–1964), Hart Crane (1899–1932), Countee Cullen (1903–46) and James Dickey (1923–97). Fellowships now provide funds of around $30,000 to the recipient and no special conditions are attached.

Harlem Renaissance   The first major movement of African American literature, beginning around 1923 and flourishing until the Depression, but providing a stimulus that lasted through the 1940s.

The renaissance mainly involved a group of writers and intellectuals associated (often loosely) with Harlem, the district of Manhattan that, during the Great Migration of African Americans from the rural South, became the major centre for urbanized blacks. Harlem was described by Alain Locke (1886–1954) as 'not merely the largest Negro community in the world, but the first concentration in history of so many diverse elements of Negro life'. The renaissance was associated with the New Negro Movement, so called because of the anthology *The New Negro* (1925) edited by Locke, whose introductory essay 'The New Negro' is the closest to a manifesto or statement of ideals that the Harlem Renaissance has. In it he writes of the Negro who is no longer apologetic for blackness but who takes a new pride in a racial identity and heritage, of the 'renewed self-respect and self-dependence' felt in the contemporary black community, which is 'about to enter a new phase'. Elsewhere Locke urged writers to examine the meaning of an African past and to utilize this in their art. This urging coincided with a growing interest among whites at the time in primitivism, evident for example in Eugene O'Neill's plays *The Emperor Jones* (1920) and *All God's Chillun Got Wings* (1924). The Harlem Renaissance was partly fostered by the existence of this interest, and by the concurrent development of American modernism and the readiness to accept experimentation and to expand the breadth of artistic expression. The renaissance was greatly assisted by several whites, especially Carl Van Vechten (1880–1964), whose enthusiasm for African American culture was reflected in his popular 1926 novel *Nigger Heaven*. Locke had explicitly called for social and artistic interracial co-operation in 'The New Negro', commenting that, 'The fiction is that the life of the races is separate, and increasingly so. The fact is that they have touched too closely at the unfavorable and too lightly at the favorable levels.'

One characteristic of the Harlem Renaissance was a move towards so-called 'high art' in black writing, rather than the use of folk idioms, comic writing and vernacular that had often been considered the special realm of African American writing up to that time. In some respects this shift mirrors the change from rural to urban life for many blacks in this period. However, several of the Harlem writers made powerful use of folk idioms such as the blues, particularly Langston Hughes (1902–67). The Harlem writers also engaged in an intense debate regarding the place of the African American in American life, and on the role and identity of the African American artist. In this sense the Harlem Renaissance is by no means a monolithic movement with a single purpose. For example, the artistic differences between Hughes and the poet Countee Cullen (1903–46) are instructive. Cullen believed that an African American poet should be free to write in mainstream established traditions, and need not racialize poetry. 'I want to be a poet, not a Negro poet,' he said, and wrote in forms such as the sonnet and became a translator of Euripides. Hughes, on the other hand, saw this attitude as a betrayal of racial identity, an aping of white European-ness, and sought in his work to accept and explore his blackness using forms and idioms that he associated with it. Both are major poets but their differences point to the relative breadth of the movement and to the development of quite different kinds of African American writing in the Harlem Renaissance.

Prominent Harlem Renaissance writers include James Weldon Johnson (1871–1938), Jessie Redmon Fauset (1882–1961), the Jamaican-born Claude McKay (1889–1948), Zora Neale Hurston, Nella Larsen (1893–1964), Jean Toomer (1894–1967), Arna Bontemps (1902–73), Gwendolyn Bennett (1902–81) and Helene Johnson (1907–95). In addition to the *New Negro* anthology, key works produced during the period of the renaissance or during its influence include Toomer's multi-generic *Cane* (1923), Hughes's *Weary's Blues* (1926), Larsen's *Quicksand* (1928) and *Passing* (1929) and Hurston's *Their Eyes Were Watching God* (1937).

Further reading

Color, Sex and Poetry: Three Women Writers of the Harlem Renaissance (1987) by Gloria Hull; *The Harlem Renaissance in Black and White* (1995) by George Hutchinson; *When Harlem was in Vogue* (1989) by David Levering Lewis, and *Women of the Harlem Renaissance* (1995) by Cheryl A. Wall. *Harlem Renaissance: A Historical Dictionary for the Era* (1984), edited by Bruce Kellner, is a valuable resource.

Harper's Monthly Magazine Founded in 1850 in New York and originally called *Harper's New Monthly Magazine*, this illustrated magazine was an important vehicle of publication for many important authors and was significant in the development of American literature. At first it published mainly reprints of British works but gradually it came to concentrate on American writing, particularly short fiction and serialized novels. Before the Civil War it was the most successful periodical in the country. Authors published in the magazine included Herman Melville, Henry James and Mark Twain. William Dean Howells (1837–1920) wrote an influential column for it (1901–20).

Hawthorne, Nathaniel Novelist and short-story writer, born in 1804 in Salem, Massachusetts. Hawthorne's ancestors had been prominent Puritans; more immediately, his father was a sea captain who died when Hawthorne was aged 4. Hawthorne attended Bowdoin College in Maine and in 1828 he published his first novel, *Fanshawe*. He later withdrew it from circulation and concentrated on writing short fiction. Hawthorne worked at various jobs, including a spell in the Boston custom house, and he lived in the Brook Farm community for 6 months in 1841. He married

Sophia Peabody in 1842 and moved to Concord, where he came into close contact with Ralph Waldo EMERSON and other prominent thinkers. Returning to Salem he worked at the custom house until a change in the political administration resulted in his dismissal. In 1850 he published *The Scarlet Letter*, which brought him acclaim; *The House of the Seven Gables* (1851) and *The Blithedale Romance* (1852) followed. When living in rural Massachusetts Hawthorne befriended Herman MELVILLE, for whom he embodied the idea that a writer could make a living from writing fiction while maintaining artistic integrity. (*MOBY-DICK* is dedicated to Hawthorne.) When Hawthorne's college friend Franklin Pierce ran for US president Hawthorne wrote a campaign biography of him, and on Pierce's election Hawthorne was appointed US consul in Liverpool (1853–7). He lived in Europe for several years and published his final novel, *The Marble Faun*, in 1860. He left several novels unfinished when he died in Plymouth, New Hampshire, in 1864.

Imagining his Puritan ancestors in 'The Custom-House', the introduction to *The Scarlet Letter*, Hawthorne declares, 'strong traits of their nature have intertwined themselves with mine'. In his tales and romances, he repeatedly plays out his ambivalence towards Puritanism, and although his work typically has a historical setting, he examines Puritanism as a contemporary force rather than a historical fact. In particular, he often explores the conflict between the attractions of ROMANTICISM or TRANSCENDENTALISM and the burden of a Puritan belief in humanity's fallen nature. In 'Hawthorne and His Mosses' (1850) Melville wrote that in Hawthorne's work there was a 'great power of blackness'; 'there really lurks in him [a] touch of Puritanic gloom'. Hawthorne's ambivalence is evident in his writing style. Rather than a novelist he called himself a writer of ROMANCE, and his use of symbolism and allegory frequently creates powerful ambiguities. The unstable and even duplicitous nature of his writing has often been noted.

Further reading

New Essays on Hawthorne's Major Tales (1993) by Millicent Bell; *The Province of Piety* (1984) by Michael J. Colacurcio; *American Renaissance* (1941) by F. O. Matthiessen; *Salem is my Dwelling-Place* (1991) by Edwin Haviland Miller; *Nathaniel Hawthorne* (1991) by Charles Swann; *Nathaniel Hawthorne: A Biography* (1980) by Arlin Turner, and *Hawthorne* (1955) by Hyatt Waggoner.

Hemingway, Ernest Novelist and SHORT-STORY writer, awarded the NOBEL PRIZE FOR LITERATURE in 1954. The son of a doctor, Hemingway was born in Oak Park, Illinois, in 1899, and after leaving school he trained as a newspaper reporter with the *Kansas City Star*. During WORLD WAR I he served as an ambulance driver in Italy and was seriously wounded, his experiences forming the basis of the novel *A Farewell to Arms* (1929). After a period at home Hemingway moved to Paris in 1921 as a correspondent for the *Toronto Star*, joining a group of American expatriates that included Gertrude STEIN, Ezra POUND and F. Scott FITZGERALD. Guided particularly by Stein and Pound he published his first works, notably the stories *In Our Time* (1925) and the novel *The Sun*

Also Rises (1926). Dealing with the lives of LOST GENERATION expatriates in Paris and Spain, the novel was a critical and popular success which brought Hemingway fame. A man of enormous energy and appetite for experience, Hemingway combined a remarkable range of physical activities while also producing carefully crafted fiction and poetry. Increasingly a celebrity, he won renown as a fisherman, big-game hunter and adventurer as well as a war-reporter, and he wrote an outstanding book on bull fighting, *Death in the Afternoon* (1932). He lived in various places, including Florida, Cuba and Idaho, and was married four times. He committed suicide in 1961 while ill and severely depressed.

Hemingway shared with Stephen CRANE a concern with the formation of identity in extreme circumstances, and a preoccupation with the nature of masculinity. Much of his work examines types of heroism that have to do with the formulation of a personal, non-institutional and secular moral code and a confrontation of experience without the comfort that illusion and self-deception may provide. At its best, Hemingway's prose style is simple and straightforward, tersely economical, concrete and understated rather than abstract, florid or extravagant. His short stories 'A Clean Well-Lighted Place', 'The Snows of Kilimanjaro' and 'Big Two-Hearted River', are some of the finest of the 20th century.

Hemingway's other major works are the novels *For Whom the Bell Tolls* (1940) and *The Old Man and the Sea* (1952), and the sketches in *Green Hills of Africa* (1935). A series of posthumous works has appeared, including the memoir *A Moveable Feast* (1964), the stories of *Islands in the Stream* (1970) and the unfinished novel *The Garden of Eden* (1986). *By-Line* (1967) is a collection of his journalism.

Further reading

Ernest Hemingway (1992) by Peter B. Messent; Ernest Hemingway (1963, 1986) by Earl Rovit; Ernest Hemingway: Six Decades of Criticism (1987), edited by Linda Wagner-Martin, and The Tragic Art of Ernest Hemingway (1982) by Wirt Williams. Ernest Hemingway: A Life Story (1969) by Carlos Baker, and Hemingway (1987) by Kenneth S. Lynn, are important biographies.

Hollywood   The motion-picture industry's headquarters in this area of Los Angeles, California, has been the setting for a particular body of American literature. Many prominent writers worked in Hollywood for varying periods of time and degrees of success, notably Theodore DREISER, F. Scott FITZGERALD, William FAULKNER, Dorothy Parker (1893–1967), Raymond CHANDLER, Joan Didion (b. 1934) and David MAMET. Fictional works set in or around the film industry belong to what is broadly known as the 'Hollywood novel' tradition. Typically the Hollywood novel examines American values, often in an absurd manner, while there is also a tradition of thriller and detective fiction set in and around Hollywood. Prominent Hollywood novels include *The Day of the Locust* (1939) by Nathanael West (1903–40); Fitzgerald's unfinished work *The Last Tycoon* (1941) (revised in 1993 by Matthew Bruccoli as *The Love of the Last Tycoon*); *What Makes Sammy Run?* (1941) and *The Disenchanted* (1950) by Budd

Schulberg (b. 1914); Chandler's *The Little Sister* (1949); *The Deer Park* (1955) by Norman Mailer (b. 1923); *Myra Breckinridge* (1968) by Gore Vidal (b. 1925); Didion's *Play it as it Lays* (1970); *Hollywood* (1989) by Charles Bukowski (1920–94), and *Get Shorty* (1990) by Elmore Leonard (b. 1925). The novels of James Ellroy (b. 1948) are often set in Hollywood, notably *The Black Dahlia* (1987), *The Big Nowhere* (1988), *Hollywood Nocturnes* (1994), and *L. A. Confidential* (1990). Other significant works that engage with aspects of Hollywood include Fitzgerald's *Pat Hobby Stories* (1962), the poetry collection *The Lost World* (1965) by Randall Jarrell (1914–65), and the plays *Angel City* (1976) by Sam Shepard (b. 1943) and *The Road to Nirvana* (1991) by Arthur Kopit (b. 1937).

Further reading

America's Dream-Dump (1999) by Bruce L. Chipman; The American Poet at the Movies (1994) by Laurence Goldstein; Writers in Hollywood (1990) by Ian Hamilton; The Hollywood Novel (1995) by Anthony Slide, and Hollywood in Fiction (1969) by Thomas Spatz.

Holocaust (Also termed the *Shoah*, from the Hebrew.)   The attempted genocide of European Jews under the Nazi regime, beginning with attacks on Jews in 1930s Germany and culminating in systematic extermination in concentration camps by 1945. It is believed that about 6 million people were killed in the Holocaust, including up to half a million gypsies as well as homosexuals and others who were considered deviants by Nazi ideology.

There are broadly two phases of American literature about the Holocaust. The first mainly involves historical and personal testimony and indirect reference. The second, beginning in the early 1960s, includes fiction, poetry and drama concerned with examining the Holocaust's psychological and historical consequences. In some respects, the first phase bears out the judgment of Lionel Trilling, who wrote in 1953 that the Holocaust could inspire only silence: 'The activity of mind fails before the incommunicability of man's suffering.' Before 1960 there are indirect references to the Holocaust in some works by Bernard MALAMUD, Saul BELLOW, Arthur MILLER and Philip ROTH, and in works by non-Jewish writers such as John Berryman (1914–72) and (controversially) Sylvia PLATH. After 1960 there is more direct representation of the Holocaust and more consideration of its effect on American Jews and second-genera-tion survivors. There are several reasons for this development, including the immense popularity of *The Diary of Anne Frank* (1952), and the televised trial of the Nazi Adolf Eichmann in 1961, both of which helped to end silence about the Holocaust. Also as they reached maturity the second generation of survivors began to consider what the Holocaust meant to them as Americans; as Hilene Flanzbaum has written, in the 1960s American Jews began 'to claim the holocaust'.

What is now a large body of fiction, testimony and drama includes: *Mila 18* (1961) by Leon Uris (b. 1924); *Touching Evil* (1969) by Norma Rosen (b. 1925); *Holocaust*

(1975) by Charles Reznikoff (1894–1976); *Sophie's Choice* (1979) by William Styron (b. 1925); *Gone to Soldiers* (1987) by Marge Piercy (b. 1936); *Broken Glass* (1994) by Arthur Miller, and *Elijah Visible* (1996) and *Second Hand Smoke* (1999) by Thane Rosenbaum. The work of Cynthia Ozick (b. 1928) is especially important, particularly the fictional works *Levitation: Five Fictions* (1982), *The Cannibal Galaxy* (1983), *The Shawl* (1989) and her play *Blue Light* (1994). The writings of Primo Levi (1919–87) and Elie Wiesel (b. 1928) have been influential on the overall development of American Holocaust literature.

Further reading

Crisis and Covenant (1985) by Alan Berger; *Children of Job* (1997) by Alan L. Berger; *The Americanization of the Holocaust* (1999), edited by Hilene Flanzbaum; *Witness through the Imagination* (1989) by S. Lillian Kremer, and *The Holocaust in American Life* (1999) by Peter Novick.

Homestead Act   Passed in 1862, the act opened up lands in the Mid-West and West to settlers. Any citizen (or intending citizen) who was either over the age of 21 or the head of a family was entitled to ownership of 160 acres of land for no charge, provided a $10 filing fee was paid and the land occupied for at least 5 years and a crop raised on it. The act was the culmination of a long campaign that was organized by the homestead movement and opposed by employers and landowners in the East. Between 1862 and 1900 over 8 million acres was granted to 600,000 claimants.

The Homestead Act is frequently referred to in WESTERN and pioneer writing, since it was the cause of considerable migration from the East, and subsequently of conflict between 'homesteaders', ranchers and Native Americans. It is of special significance in pioneer stories because of the challenge in occupying and cultivating the land as a condition of ownership. In the 'Little House on the Prairie' novels (1932–43) by Laura Ingalls Wilder (1867–1957), Pa refers to the act's conditions as his 'bet with Uncle Sam'.

Horror   Although horror is often taken to be synonymous with GOTHIC (and many Gothic writers are also horror writers), horror is a specific development of Gothic, tending to place more emphasis on the lurid and the FANTASTIC, and being more singular in its purpose of frightening its readers, often by objectifying and exploiting their latent fears. Typically, horror deals explicitly with external manifestations of the monstrous and the supernatural, whereas these are mainly implied or suggested in Gothic. A cast of familiar horror monsters includes ghosts, witches, vampires, werewolves, scientifically created beings, possessed creatures and various manifestations of the devil. There is also some crossover between horror and SCIENCE FICTION.

It was during the 19th century, and especially with the development of the SHORT STORY, that horror started to develop as a distinct style of writing. However, the origins of American horror writing may be seen in PURITAN LITERATURE, with its sometimes sensationalist depictions of hell, as in *The Day of Doom* (1662) by Michael Wigglesworth (1631–1705), and in the Puritan belief in the intervention of the supernatural in everyday life. Many later horror stories exploit the Puritan legacy in different ways, and a large amount of American horror fiction has a New England setting. Major writers of horror include Isaac Mitchell (1759–1812), Charles Brockden Brown, Edgar Allan Poe, H. P. Lovecraft (1890–1937), Robert Bloch (1917–94), Shirley Jackson (1919–65), Anne Rice (b. 1941) and Stephen King. Horror stories have been produced by a large number of American writers, notably Nathaniel Hawthorne, Henry James, Ambrose Bierce (1842–1914), F. Marion Crawford (1854–1909), Edith Wharton (1862–1937), William Faulkner and Joyce Carol Oates (b. 1938), writing as 'Rosamond Smith'.

Further reading

American Horror Fiction (1990), edited by Brian Docherty; *Horror* (1992) by Mark Jancovitch; *Danse Macabre* (1981) by Stephen King, and *The Literature of Terror* 2 vols, (1996) by David Punter.

'Howl'   Title poem of a collection by Allen Ginsberg, first published by the City Lights Press of San Francisco in 1956. A key work of the Beat movement, and one of the most widely read poems of the 20th century, its frank language caused its publisher, the poet Lawrence Ferlinghetti (b. 1919), to be tried for obscenity. He was acquitted in 1957.

In its final text (1986) 'Howl' comprises three sections and an epigraphic 'Footnote'. Dedicated to a mentally troubled friend, Carl Solomon, the poem asserts that his condition is a result of the intolerant repressive age. The poem ranges widely in tone and subject, angrily condemning the materialism and aggression of Cold War America, expressing an apocalyptic view of the future, both lamenting and affirming homosexual alienation, and declaring profound affection for Solomon and others. Much of the poem's success derives from Ginsberg's choice of an incantatory form that flexibly accommodates shifting moods and subjects. While giving the effect of revolutionary originality, the poem's form is a long-considered synthesis of established styles, sometimes discussed with William Carlos Williams (who wrote the collection's introduction). The form echoes some Old Testament writings, the poetry of Walt Whitman, the prophetic books of William Blake, and what Ginsberg called the 'elasticity of the long verse line' of the 18th century English poet Christopher Smart. As with much Beat writing, the poem is meant to seem spontaneous and improvisational, although the annotated 1986 facsimile edition indicates careful revision. In explicitly rejecting the then dominant academic, impersonal mode of American poetry, the poem helped establish a new readership for poetry and restored to it otherwise latent energies. In 1986 Ginsberg stated that he had wanted 'to leave behind after my generation an emotional time bomb that would continue exploding in U. S. consciousness in case our military-industrial-nationalist complex solidified into a repressive police bureaucracy'.

Further reading

On the Poetry of Allen Ginsberg (1980), edited by Lewis Hyde; *Allen Ginsberg, Howl: Original Draft Facsimile* (1986), edited by Barry Miles, and *Allen Ginsberg in the Sixties* (1972) by Eric Mottram.

Hudson Review   Quarterly journal published in New York, founded in 1948 by Frederick Morgan (b. 1922). The journal publishes poetry and fiction, and is especially distinguished for its critical articles.

Hudson River School   Influential grouping of landscape painters that flourished between 1825 and 1870, originally associated with the Hudson River Valley. The school depicted the American landscape as ROMANTIC or sublime, and was significant in asserting artistic independence from Europe. These characteristics linked the school with the aspirations of contemporary American writers, notably James Fenimore COOPER and William Cullen Bryant (1794–1878). The school's founding members were Thomas Doughty (1793–1856), Asher Durand (1796–1886) and Thomas Cole (1802–48), and others associated with it include George Inness (1825–94), Frederick Edwin Church (1826–1900), Albert Bierstadt (1830–1902) and Thomas Moran (1837–1926). Bierstadt and Moran were particularly important for their representations of Western landscapes.

Humour   Humorous and comic writing has formed a significant tradition in American literature, and several critics have argued for the centrality of humour to the development of a distinctly American literature and the formation of American identities. Although it may depend on antagonism and even hostility, humour can also perform a cohesive function; as Gregg Camfield points out, it 'very often cuts across the grain of obvious antagonisms [and finds] common grounds for agreement as well as disagreement'.

In the colonial period much humorous literature was witty or satirical, as is evident in the work of Benjamin FRANKLIN, though there was also more robust vernacular comedy, seen in some of the writings of William Byrd (1674–1744) and in the satirical poem 'The Sot-Weed Factor' (1708) by Ebenezer Cook (?1672–1732). The distinction between 'high' and 'low' comedy intensifies during the 19th century, as the subtly humorous writings of Royall Tyler (1757–1826), Washington IRVING and James Russell Lowell (1819–91), and the complex comedy evident in the writings of Nathaniel HAWTHORNE, Herman MELVILLE and Emily DICKINSON, diverges from the developing tradition of broad vernacular humour. YANKEE humour is an example of the vernacular, as seen in the character of Sam Slick, created by T. C. Haliburton (1796–1865); though the major development is FRONTIER or Southwestern humour.

Strongly rooted in ORAL TRADITIONS such as the TALL TALE, Southwestern humour originates as a written form in the 1830s, mainly associated with Augustus Baldwin Longstreet (1790–1870), Thomas Bangs Thorpe (1815–75) and George Washington

Harris (1815–69). The comic sketches of writers such as Bret Harte (1836–1902), Josh Billings (pseudonym of Henry Wheeler Shaw, 1818–85) and Artemus Ward (pseudonym of Charles Farrar Browne, 1834–67), and Mark TWAIN derive from oral comic performance, and use a mixture of exaggeration and puncturing of pretensions. This style is especially evident in Twain's early work, notably in *The Innocents Abroad* (1869), while the satirically deflating aspect of frontier comedy is also used in *THE ADVENTURES OF HUCKLEBERRY FINN*. Twain's increasingly mordant humour finds echoes in the work of writers such as Ambrose Bierce (1842–1914) and H. L. Mencken (1880–1956) and developed into a tradition of American dark humour that includes aspects of the ABSURD; this tradition is notably used by Nathanael West (1903–40).

Along with specific developments of Southwestern humour, the 20th century saw the growth of a particular style of refined urban-based American humour. This is exemplified by figures associated with *THE NEW YORKER*, such as Robert Benchley (1889–1945), Dorothy Parker (1893–1967), James Thurber (1894–1961) and E. B. White (1899–1985), but is also apparent in the witty songs of lyricists such as Irving Berlin (1888–1989), Cole Porter (1891–1964) and Ira Gershwin (1896–1983), the entertainments of S. J. Perelman (1904–79), the political satire of Finley Peter Dunne (1867–1936) and the comic verse of writers such as Don Marquis (1878–1937) and Ogden Nash (1902–71). Damon Runyon (1884–1946) and Ring Lardner (1885–1933) relocated the oral frontier sketch into urban settings, while the writers associated with SOUTHERN GOTHIC also made significant use of the frontier tradition. The 20th century saw a number of serious writers using humour in especially sophisticated ways. Examples include Vladimir Nabokov (1899–1977), Saul BELLOW, John Berryman (1914–72), Joseph Heller (1923–99) and Thomas PYNCHON, whereas other writers, notably John Cheever (1912–82), Kurt Vonnegut (b. 1922), J. P. Donleavy (b. 1926), John Barth (b. 1930), John Updike (b. 1932) and Philip ROTH, have reputations as comic novelists, even though their humour frequently serves serious ends. Tom Robbins (b. 1936), John Irving (b. 1942), Garrison Keillor (b. 1942), P. J. O'Rourke (b. 1947) and T. Coraghessan Boyle (b. 1948) are significant contemporary comic writers.

Although often critically undervalued or overlooked there has also been a considerable tradition of humorous writing by American women. As Nancy Walker has observed, women's humour exists as 'a direct response to women's cultural subordination' and has often focused on the frustrations of domesticity. Much comic writing and light fiction by Fanny Fern (pseudonym of Sara P. Willis, 1811–72), Frances Whitcher (1814–52), Marietta Holley (1836–1926), Anita Loos (1893–1981), Dawn Powell (1896–1965), Betty MacDonald (1908–58), Shirley Jackson (1919–65) and Erma Bombeck (1927–96) is in this tradition.

The American humour tradition includes well-established kinds of ethnic or minority humour, and the African American and the Jewish American traditions have been especially important. Along with many others, Charles W. Chesnutt (1858–1932), Zora Neale HURSTON, Langston HUGHES (1902–67), Dick Gregory

(b. 1932), Ishmael Reed (b. 1938) and Alice WALKER have helped develop a folk-based African American humour that often has a quality of exaggeration but with a wry effect that gives it a significant satirical aspect. There is a considerable tradition of Jewish American comic writing, often deriving from the rich fund of Yiddish humour: Leo Rosten (1908–97), Bernard MALAMUD and Woody Allen (b. 1935) are major Jewish American comic writers. Some Native American writers, notably Sherman Alexie (b. 1966), have also developed an existing comic tradition.

Further reading

Necessary Madness (1997) by Gregg Camfield; Comic Relief (1978), edited by Sarah Blacher Cohen; American Humor (1987), edited by Arthur Power Dudden and Peter M. Briggs; The Comic Imagination in American Literature (1974) edited by Louis D. Rubin, and A Very Serious Thing (1988) by Nancy A. Walker.

Hurston, Zora Neale   Novelist and anthropologist who has had a significant influence on the development of African American women's writing. Hurston was born in Alabama in 1891 (though she claimed to have been born in 1901), and grew up in the all-black community of Eatonville, Florida. She moved to New York in 1925 and became part of the HARLEM RENAISSANCE, working particularly with Langston Hughes (1902–67), with whom she collaborated on several plays. After graduating from Barnard College in 1928 she studied anthropology at Columbia University. Hurston travelled as a folklorist in the South collecting tales and songs; this resulted in the collections *Mules and Men* (1935) and *Tell My Horse* (1938). In 1934 she published her first novel, *Jonah's Gourd Vine*, and in 1937 her second, *Their Eyes Were Watching God*. She published her AUTOBIOGRAPHY, *Dust Tracks on a Road*, in 1942. Hurston's writing was popular but in 1948 she withdrew from public life after a scandal in which a false accusation was made against her. She worked at various jobs and in 1960 she died unrecognized and in financial hardship in Fort Pierce, Florida.

Hurston's studies of anthropology and FOLKLORE function along with her fiction as affirmations of black identity. The note for her attitude was struck early on; in her 1928 essay 'How it Feels to be Colored Me' she wrote: 'I do not belong to the sobbing school of Negrohood who hold that nature somehow has given them a lowdown dirty deal and whose feelings are all hurt about it.' This attitude is further evident in *Their Eyes Were Watching God*, an important FEMINIST novel involving the gradual self-acceptance and autonomy of its central character Janie Crawford.

The 1970s saw a significant revival of interest in Hurston, and her work has influenced many later writers. Alice WALKER was crucial to the rediscovery of Hurston, and Walker's *I Love Myself When I am Laughing* (1979) is an excellent selection of Hurston's writing.

Critical studies include *Zora Neale Hurston* (1986), edited by Harold Bloom; *The Character of the Word* (1987) by Karla F. C. Holloway; *Zora Neale Hurston* (1980) by Lillie P. Howard, and *Every Tub Must Sit on Its Own Bottom* (1995) by Deborah G. Plant. Robert E. Hemenway's *Zora Neale Hurston* (1977) is an important biography.

Imagism Poetic technique in which an image or series of images alone is intended to convey meaning. The imagists rejected narrative and what they regarded as redundant exposition, in favour of clear, concentrated, direct treatment of the subject, somewhat in the manner of the Japanese form haiku, although in freer verse. Imagism flourished from 1909 until about 1919 and was an international movement. The English aesthetician T. E. Hulme provided much of the intellectual theory supporting the imagists, while Ezra POUND and Amy Lowell (1874–1925) were two leading American members of the group. In 1913 Pound wrote that the principles of imagism were: 'Direct treatment of the "thing," whether subjective or objective'; 'To use absolutely no word that does not contribute to the presentation' and 'to compose in sequence of the musical phrase, not in sequence of the metronome'. In 1915 he further stated, 'the Image is more than an idea. It is a vortex or cluster of fused ideas and is endowed with energy.' Pound's two-line poem 'In A Station of the Metro' (1913) is often cited as the archetypal imagist poem. Pound edited the anthology *Des Imagistes* (1914), though he developed away from imagism soon afterwards. Lowell's interest was more consistent, and between 1915 and 1917 she edited three anthologies, each with the title *Some Imagist Poets*. (Pound then disparagingly referred to the movement as 'Amygism'.) Although at times imagism risked eroding the necessary common ground between poet and reader, and hence becoming recondite or obscure, it played a crucial role in the development of MODERNISM. American poets who made use of Imagism at some point in their work include Wallace STEVENS, William Carlos WILLIAMS and H. D. (Hilda Doolittle) (1886–1961).

Immigration There have been four major phases of immigration to the lands that now comprise the United States. The first was during the colonial period (1607–1776), which saw over a million Europeans come to the THIRTEEN COLONIES, the majority being British subjects. Up to half a million African slaves were forcibly brought to what became the United States (that is, approximately 5 per cent of all the Africans who were brought to the American continent) before the ending of the slave trade in 1808. Europeans also dominated the second major immigration period (1815–70), with over 6 million migrating during this time, of whom many were from Germany and Ireland. The third phase (1870–1914) was one of mass immigration. The overwhelming majority of immigrants were still Europeans, now from Southern and Eastern Europe, although there were also significant numbers of Asian migrants. During this period over 25 million immigrants arrived. In 1924 new laws effectively ended mass immigration by introducing an annual 'national origins' quota system. The total annual number of immigrants was fixed at 150,000, and allocations for each nation were linked to the proportion of American citizens originally from that nation. This meant that over 70 per cent of the annual quota was given to Britain, Germany and Ireland. Restrictions on immigration from Asia were also introduced (these had already featured in the CHINESE EXCLUSION ACT). In 1965 this form of allocation ended, and quotas were no longer linked to the national origins of American citizens. The annual quota was increased to 290,000, with 170,000 places available to applicants from outside the Western Hemisphere and 120,000 for applicants from the Western Hemisphere. Illegal immigration has been a major concern, and in 1986 laws were passed which permitted existing illegal aliens to apply for citizenship, while introducing more severe punishments for illegal immigrants.

The experiences of immigration and assimilation have been explored in numerous works of American literature, and have been notably examined in AUTOBIOGRAPHICAL writings, in which the tension between allegiance to a non-American heritage and the demands of assimilation has been a recurrent feature. The immigrant novel has been especially important to the development of JEWISH AMERICAN LITERATURE and ASIAN AMERICAN LITERATURE. Important works dealing with immigration include *The Rise of David Levinsky* (1917) by Abraham Cahan (1860–1951), *Bread Givers* (1925) by Anzia Yezierska (1885–1970), *Fifth Chinese Daughter* (1945) by Jade Snow Wong (b. 1922), *Nisei Daughter* (1953) by Monica Sone (b. 1919), *No-No Boy* (1957) by John Okada (1924–1971) and *THE WOMAN WARRIOR* (1976) by Maxine Hong KINGSTON.

Further reading

Ethnic Passages (1993) by Thomas J. Ferraro; Making Americans (2000) by Desmond King; Immigrant Subjectivities (1998) by Sheng-Mei Ma, and New Strangers in Paradise (1999) by Gilbert H. Muller.

Impressionism   Term derived from the 19th century movement in French painting. In a literary context, 'impressionistic' has a relatively loose meaning. It may be used broadly to describe any writing in which the existence of objective reality is challenged, as in many of the short stories of Edgar Allan POE and Nathaniel HAWTHORNE, or in which a restricted consciousness forms the dominant point of view, as for example in Herman MELVILLE's stories 'Bartleby the Scrivener' (1853) and *Benito Cereno* (1855). However the term is usually applied more narrowly to a development in prose writing of the late 19th and early 20th centuries, in which representation of impressions made on a receptive mind are privileged over the objective recording of events. The technique was used influentially by Stephen CRANE, notably in *The Red Badge of Courage* (1895), and by Henry JAMES. To a large extent, impressionism was a significant predecessor of the STREAM OF CONSCIOUSNESS technique. It also features in early MODERNIST poetry, in works by Ezra POUND, Amy Lowell (1874–1925) and T. S. ELIOT.

Individualism   Term first used by Alexis De Tocqueville (1805–59), referring to a humanistic philosophy that is considered central to American thought and attitudes.

Individualism is a belief in the rights of the individual and in the desirability of encouraging self-interest as a means of organizing society. It asserts that the state should not interfere in the individual's autonomous conduct in economic, religious and moral terms, and that the state's main function is to support the emergence and development of the individual. Individualism emerged in England during the 18th century, but it has found its fullest expression in the United States, where, as a broadly Protestant concept, it is often seen as part of Puritanism's legacy. Individualist philosophy is evident in the personal protections guaranteed by the Constitution and the Bill of Rights, in the characteristic American distrust of institutions and in the general American belief in individual responsibility and self-reliance.

Industrial Workers of the World (IWW)   Also known as the 'Wobblies', the IWW was a labour organization founded in Chicago in 1905. Under the leadership of William D. Haywood it developed into a revolutionary anti-capitalist movement and became notorious for its leadership in strikes, particularly in the 1912 strike of textile workers in Lawrence, Massachusetts. The ballad-writer Joe Hill, who was executed on a charge of murder in 1915, was an important member. Membership of the IWW has been variously estimated as up to 100,000 at its peak in 1917. However, its declared opposition to US involvement in World War I damaged the organization. After the war thirty-two states made membership of the IWW a criminal offence, and by 1925 it had become insignificant.

The IWW produced a large amount of verse and song, notably Joe Hill's 1911 song 'The Preacher and the Slave' with its famous lines 'Work and pray, live on hay, / You'll get pie in the sky when you die.' (See the 1997 study *Partisans and Poets* by Mark W. Van Wienen for an overview of IWW poetry.) The Wobblies appear often in literature set in the period 1905–17, notably in *The 42nd Parallel* (1930) by John Dos Passos (1896–1970).

Invisible Man   Novel by Ralph Ellison, published in 1952. It explores the experiences of an unnamed Southern black narrator, including his being awarded a scholarship to university, his leaving the university in disgrace and his move to New York. After an accident when working in a paint factory, he becomes involved in the Communist Party (called 'The Brotherhood') but leaves it after a series of confrontations. The killing of Tod Clifton, a former friend of his, sparks a riot in Harlem, exploited by the black nationalist Ras the Destroyer, and the novel ends (and begins) with Invisible Man hiding in a cellar.

The novel's main thematic concern is with Invisible Man's gradual realization about how power functions in a society, and how this works to keep blacks at a certain level. For instance, the award of his scholarship takes place during a ritual of humiliation designed to reinforce deference. Similarly, the college that he attends (based on Tuskegee Institute) appears to assist blacks to rise in society but actually functions to maintain a low social status for them. The Brotherhood seems to provide an outlet for anger but in fact is sponsored by those who wish to keep dissent in check. Eventually Invisible Man seeks reconciliation between his nostalgic desire for an identity formed from within, and the modern realization that this is an illusion and that a series of identities are already given to him, by his past, by his different communities, by racial mythology and by broader American society.

Much of the novel's significance derives from Ellison's creative handling of the difficulties blacks have historically confronted in attempting to survive and progress in American society. He utilizes many narrative conventions, including the flight narrative, the SUCCESS NARRATIVE, the story of Booker T. Washington (1856–1915), contemporary debates about assimilation, separatism and activism, and brings these together in an often surrealistic manner. There is considerable use of black idioms such as SIGNIFYING, JAZZ and BLUES, and reference to a broad range of American styles and literatures.

The novel was an immediate success, winning the 1953 NATIONAL BOOK AWARD, and it has remained an important and much-studied work. It has been criticized, though, particularly by writers involved in the BLACK ARTS MOVEMENT, for representing radical African American political movements as irrelevant.

Further reading

Speaking for You: The Vision of Ralph Ellison (1987), edited by Kimberley W. Benston; Invisible Man: Race and Identity (1988) by Kerry McSweeney, and New Essays on Invisible Man (1988), edited by Robert G. O'Meally.

Irving, Washington   Irving was born in 1783 in New York City, the youngest of eleven children. Having spent a period in Europe (1804–6), he began writing essays and sketches while training as a lawyer in New York. His first book, the burlesque *A History of New York by Diedrich Knickerbocker* (1809), enjoyed considerable success, but it did not lead directly to a literary career. Irving worked in Washington DC and in England on behalf of his brothers' hardware business. Returning to the United States, Irving served in the New York State Militia in the WAR OF 1812. In 1815 he went back to Europe, where he was to live until 1832. In 1820 he published *The Sketch Book of Geoffrey Crayon, Gent*. This enormously successful collection of satires, tales and sketches includes 'The Legend of Sleepy Hollow' and 'Rip Van Winkle'. Both were adaptations of German stories, given settings in rural New York. Now a celebrity, Irving published a sequel, *Bracebridge Hall* (1822). In Spain (1826–9), he was a diplomatic attaché and became particularly interested in Spanish and Moorish history. This led to a series of histories and sketches: *Columbus* (1828); *The Companions of Columbus* (1831); *A Chronicle of the Conquest of Granada* (1829), and *The Alhambra* (1832). After his return to the United States he published several more works, including *A Tour on the Prairies* (1835). He spent another period in Spain as a diplomat (1842–6), before returning to New York, where he died in 1859. His final work was the five-volume *Life of George Washington* (1859).

Irving cultivated an easy, attractive, graceful writing style. During his lifetime this won him many admirers, although some contemporaries, and later generations, criticized him for too closely imitating English models. Irving's importance lies in the enduring quality of his writing and in the role he played in both the development of the American short story and the professionalization of the American writer.

Further reading

Critical Essays on Washington Irving (1990), edited by Ralph M. Aderman; *Comedy and America* (1976) by Martin Roth, and *Adrift in the Old World: The Psychological Pilgrimage of Washington Irving* (1988), by Jeffrey Rubin-Dorsky.

Isolationism   Principle of non-intervention by the United States in world affairs, especially regarding military intervention. Isolationism was supported by a majority of Americans after WORLD WAR I, in the belief that involvement in the war had been a mistake. The principle guided American foreign policy during the interwar years, and was behind the passing of a series of Neutrality Acts (1935–7). It is especially associated with Senator William E. Borah (1865–1940), who successfully led resistance to the United States's joining the League of Nations.

J

Jacobs, Harriet Ann   African American author renowned for her SLAVE NARRATIVE *Incidents in the Life of a Slave Girl, Written by Herself* (1861). Jacobs was born into SLAVERY in Edenton, North Carolina, probably in 1813. In *Incidents* Jacobs uses the pseudonym Linda Brent and tells of her experiences in slavery, including her resistance to sexual coercion, her accepting the protection of a white man who fathers her two children, and her hiding in a tiny space (9 feet by 7 feet by 3 feet) in an attic for 7 years in the home of her free grandmother. Brent eventually escapes to the North (Jacobs went there in 1842), where her freed children join her, but her own freedom is deferred because of the FUGITIVE SLAVE LAW. *Incidents* is especially powerful in the appeal it makes to the white woman reader to assist the slave woman; Jacobs urges the transcendence of racial difference and emphasizes the potential unity of all women. The narrative is also important in representing the conditions of the slave woman; Jacobs argues that 'slavery is terrible for men; but it is far more terrible for women' because of sexual exploitation and because the children of a slave woman were also enslaved. She also considers that the virtues aspired to in the cult of true womanhood need to be reconsidered for the slave woman. *Incidents*, which was lightly edited by

Lydia Maria Child (1802–80), was neglected until the 1980s; the scholarship of Jean Fagan Yellin was invaluable in its rediscovery.

After her flight to the North, Jacobs worked for the anti-slavery cause and for the relief effort during the Civil War. After the war she moved to Washington DC, where she assisted in the formation of the National Association of Colored Women. She died in Washington in 1897.

Further reading

Incidents in the Life of a Slave Girl (1987), edited by Jean Fagan Yellin, is a valuable source of information. Criticism includes Mastering Slavery (1996) by Jennifer Fleischner; Harriet Jacobs and Incidents in the Life of a Slave Girl (1996), edited by Deborah M. Garfield and Rafia Zafar, and Doers of the Word (1995) by Carla L. Peterson.

James, Henry　One of the most important novelists as well as a figure of immense significance in the overall development of the novel as a genre, James was born in New York City in 1843. His father was Henry James, who wrote and lectured on philosophical and religious matters, and he was brother to the philosopher William James (1842–1910) and to the diarist Alice James (1848–92). The family was considerably wealthy, and James was privately schooled and spent much of his childhood and early years in Europe before studying law for a year at Harvard. Keenly interested in French realist fiction, James began publishing stories, essays and reviews in the 1860s. Due to an accident that resulted in what he called an 'obscure hurt', he did not serve in the Civil War. James published his first significant novels, *Roderick Hudson* (1876) and *The American* (1877), after living in Paris, where he came to know Ivan Turgenev, Gustave Flaubert, Émile Zola and Guy de Maupassant. From 1876 until his death in 1916 James lived in England, making frequent trips to continental Europe and several journeys to the United States. He became a British subject in 1915. James was highly sociable, acquainted with all of the leading literary figures in England, notably Joseph Conrad, Stephen Crane and H. G. Wells; Edith Wharton (1862–1937) was an especially close friend. James never married, and there has been much speculation about his sexual identity.

James was a prolific writer; as well as more than twenty novels he published numerous short stories and several novellas, as well as drama, literary criticism, travel writing and three autobiographical books. James's fiction is usually divided into three main stylistic periods: 1876–90, 1890–1901 and 1901–11. However, the subjects and themes that most attracted James remained fairly constant throughout his work. The majority of James's novels are set in Europe, though several important works, notably *Washington Square* (1881) and *The Bostonians* (1886), have American settings. Typically his fiction concentrates on a few characters in a domestic context and often involves interaction between Europeans and Americans, usually with Americans abroad in Europe, as in *Daisy Miller* (1879), or, as in *The Europeans* (1878), with Europeans in the United States. Interactions usually involve differences in modes of

111

thought and manners and frequently raise questions of commitment and identity. James particularly explores the interaction between innocent Puritanical and usually wealthy leisured Americans and sophisticated, aristocratic (and sometimes relatively impoverished) Europeans. In James's early fiction such interaction might be treated lightly in the 'comedy of manners' tradition, but in two of his greatest novels, *The Portrait of a Lady* (1881) and *The Golden Bowl* (1904), the theme assumes tragic intensity as James explores fractured and frustrated lives. Other major works of James do not touch so much on the 'international' theme, although he does frequently examine the nature of innocence. One of James's recurring subjects, evident in *Washington Square*, is the social and emotional constraints that women face, while in *What Maisie Knew* (1897) and *The Awkward Age* (1898) he concentrates on the moral and psychological transitions that girls make to womanhood. In some novels, such as *The Princess Casamassima* (1886) and *The Bostonians*, he explores contemporary social trends, while in several pieces of shorter fiction, notably 'The Turn of the Screw' (1898) and *The Sacred Fount* (1901), he made use of the ghost story and the uncanny. Another early theme that is found throughout his fiction is the position of the artist, and he also constantly explores the nature of reading and interpretation. For most critics James's major achievement is in the three late novels, *The Wings of the Dove* (1902), *The Ambassadors* (1903) and *The Golden Bowl*, which are widely considered to be among the greatest novels ever written. Although their plots are relatively straightforward, these novels of psychological realism are considerably complex in theme and dense in their style, which is characterized by labyrinthine sentences and paragraphs. After his last completed novel, *The Outcry* (1911), James left two unfinished works, *The Ivory Tower* and *The Sense of the Past*.

James's significant non-fiction includes his critical studies *Hawthorne* (1879) and 'The Art of Fiction' (1884), *The American Scene* (1907), an account of his return to the United States, and the autobiographical volumes *A Small Boy and Others* (1913), *Notes of a Son and Brother* (1914) and *The Middle Years* (1917). James put considerable energy into works for the stage but his only produced original play, *Guy Domville* (1895), was a failure. The eighteen prefaces that he wrote for the New York edition of his novels (1907–9) are important for an understanding of his work.

Further reading

A Woman's Place in the Novels of Henry James (1984) by Elizabeth Allen; Henry James and Masculinity (1994) by Kelly Cameron; Henry James and the Woman Business (1989) by Alfred Habegger; Henry James and the Imagination of Pleasure (2002) by Tessa Hadley; Henry James: History, Narrative, Fiction (1993) by Roslyn Jolly; Desire and Repression (1985) by Donna Przybylowicz, and Henry James and the Philosophical Novel (1993) by Merle A. Williams. Although it has come under severe critical scrutiny, Leon Edel's Henry James remains the most important biography. It was published in five volumes (1953–72), made available in two volumes (1977) and then revised and condensed into one volume, Henry James: A Life (1985).

Jamestown   The first capital of Virginia and site of the first successful British colony in what is now the United States. Named to honour James I, the colony was founded in 1607 by a group of around 100, including the adventurer John Smith (1580–1631). After initial severe hardships it survived because of the cultivation of tobacco. Jamestown was the site of the first colonial government, founded in 1619, and in the same year the first enslaved Africans in the colonies were brought there. The colony's population gradually decreased and it was abandoned in 1699. Smith, who left the colony in 1609, wrote various accounts of the settlement, which were collected in *The General History of Virginia, New England and the Summer Isles* (1624), in which he tells the story of Pocahontas interceding to save his life.

Jazz   While its origins are traced by some researchers back to Western Africa, jazz properly begins in New Orleans in the early years of the 20ᵗʰ century and its immediate roots are in African American musical traditions, both religious such as the SPIRITUAL, and secular, such as the work song. Although it is in this way associated with the BLUES, RAGTIME and boogie-woogie, jazz encompasses many varieties, including traditional, mainstream, modern, swing and big band. It may be entirely instrumental and may be played by an orchestra or by a quartet. While it is played all over the world it remains a distinctively African American idiom, and one that has stimulated many American writers.

At first, jazz was associated with 'low life' (the origin of the 'jazz' is perhaps from 'jass', supposedly New Orleans slang for sexual intercourse) and it has been a strongly urban form. It first became widely popular during the 1920s partly because this was music that embraced and celebrated modernity and its artefacts; a fact suggested by the term JAZZ AGE to describe the early 1920s. In this respect it differs sharply from the blues, and the jazz musician is recognizable as the 'new Negro' acclaimed during the HARLEM RENAISSANCE – assertive, positive and upbeat.

Formally, jazz is collaborative, with each band member playing off the others, while space is also allotted to each instrument for a 'break' or solo. The skill of the soloist lies in imaginative improvisation and embellishment of the established phrases of the musical piece. It is this technique that has led many to see an analogy between jazz and SIGNIFYING. For some writers, notably Ralph ELLISON, the jazz band has been used as an image of an ideal community, in which individual expression is encouraged but which also exists within a group framework. In his essay 'The Charlie Christian Story' (1958) Ellison wrote, 'true jazz is an art of individual assertion within and against the group. Each true jazz moment . . . springs from a contest in which each artist challenges all the rest; each solo flight, or improvisation, represents . . . a definition of his identity: as individual, as member of the collectivity and as a link in the chain of tradition.'

Many American writers have been fascinated with jazz, finding in it thematically a powerful assertion of the modern, and technically an alternative to European American poetics or narrative forms. MODERNIST poets imitated its syncopated rhythms in their writing, the BEATS sought a consonance between the poem and music, while the BLACK MOUNTAIN POETS saw that 1940s jazz provided an alternative to formal poetic traditions. African American writers in particular, including Ellison, Albert Murray (b. 1916), James BALDWIN, Imamu Amiri BARAKA and Toni MORRISON, have grounded their work in various jazz idioms.

Further reading

Blues, Ideology and African American Literature (1984) by Houston A. Baker; Shadow and Act (1964) by Ralph Ellison; The Signifying Monkey (1988) by Henry Louis Gates, Jr; The Jazz Revolution: Twenties America and the Meaning of Jazz (1989) by Kathy J. Ogren, and The Color of Jazz (1997) by Jon Panish.

Jazz Age   Term referring to a period of prosperity and of increased leisure time between 1919 and the WALL STREET crash of 1929. The decade is often represented as a period in which people (in spite of PROHIBITION) experienced a new sense of personal liberation, expressed hedonistically. This new sense was seen especially in the changing behaviour of women, who had achieved a new measure of independence. Women had the vote, after the ratification of the Nineteenth Amendment (1920), and the 'new woman' was in the labour force in unprecedented numbers. More daring fashions (including short skirts) and new hairstyles (notably the 'bob') contributed to a new sense of freedom for women, and the term 'flapper' was coined to describe the emancipated fun-loving woman. F. Scott FITZGERALD used the term 'Jazz Age' in 1922 for the title of a collection of short stories, and his fiction set in New York chronicles what he called 'the greatest, gaudiest spree in history'.

Jewish American literature   Although there has been a constant Jewish presence in America since 1654 with the arrival of groups from Spain and Portugal, the major Jewish IMMIGRATION began in the 19th century. An estimated 2.5 million Jews emigrated from Eastern Europe in the period 1882–1914, mostly leaving severe economic conditions, varying degrees of persecution, or legal discrimination. In the United States legal proscription against Jews has been rare, but for long periods there was institutional anti-Jewishness, and until the 1940s Jews were often excluded from membership of social clubs and academic and political organizations, while entry into certain professions was restricted.

While a tradition of Jewish writing in Yiddish has survived from the 19th century to the present, and was given high prominence by the fiction of Isaac Bashevis Singer (1904–91), the first phase of American Jewish writing in English began with several influential figures in the period 1880–1930: Emma Lazarus (1849–87), Abraham Cahan (1860–1951) and Anzia Yezierska (1885–1970). All were concerned, as might be expected, with themes of immigration, the shaping of identity and cultural assimilation. Lazarus's collection *Songs of a Semite* (1882) has been called the first important book of Jewish poetry in America, and her sonnet 'The New Colossus' is inscribed on the Statue of Liberty. Cahan wrote short fiction, as in *The Imported Bridegroom and Other Stories of the New York Ghetto* (1898), and novels, notably *The Rise of David Levinsky* (1917). His work realistically conveyed the everyday experiences of urban immigrant life in ways that prefigure much Jewish American writing. Yezierska wrote an important collection of short stories, *Hungry Hearts* (1920), and an outstanding AUTOBIOGRAPHICAL novel, *Bread Givers* (1925), in which she explores cultural assimilation from the viewpoint of a second-generation daughter. This period's concern with the relation between past, present and future is also evident in the writing of Mary Antin (1881–1949), especially *The Promised Land* (1912).

MODERNISM's relation to the American Jewish writer has been vexed, given the anti-Jewishness of some of modernism's major figures, but the work of Henry Roth (1906–95) and Isaac Rosenfeld (1918–56) has been called modernist. Roth's STREAM OF CONSCIOUSNESS novel, *Call it Sleep* (1934), influenced a later generation of writers. Nevertheless Jewish writing, especially during the DEPRESSION, maintained a concentration on urban life in the social realist style, evident in the widely read series of sketches *Jews Without Money* (1930) by Michael Gold (1893–1967). The 1930s also confirmed the strong links between the Jewish writer and radical or progressive politics. This had been evident from the earliest phase of Jewish writing and remains a powerful characteristic. It has been suggested that this connection was an amalgamation of the traditional Jewish concern for social justice with the poverty and unjust conditions experienced by urban-based Jews.

The period from 1945 to the present has seen an astonishing flourishing of Jewish American writing accompanied by a considerable broadening of its readership. Many suggestions have been made to explain these developments. They include the view that Jewish writers are dealing with urgent contemporary concerns such as alienation, identity, social justice and the meaning of history, and that they have maintained a belief, elsewhere challenged, in literature's ability to deal with profound moral issues. Another relevant point is that the Jewish American writers coming to maturity from the 1940s onwards represented the first generation to have had greater opportunities for university education and entry into a wide range of professions. The main emphasis in the post-1945 period has been on the novel, although poets and dramatists with a Jewish background have also been prominent. Poets include Charles Reznikoff (1894–1976), Louis Zukofsky (1904–78), Delmore Schwartz (1913–66), Muriel Rukeyser (1913–80), Karl Shapiro (1913–2000) and Allen GINSBERG. Lillian Hellman (1905–84), Arthur MILLER and David MAMET have been outstanding dramatists. Tillie Olsen (b. 1913), Bernard MALAMUD, Saul BELLOW, Grace Paley (b. 1922), Norman Mailer (b. 1923), Joseph Heller (1923–99), Cynthia Ozick (b. 1928), E. L. Doctorow (b. 1931), Philip ROTH, Erica Jong (b. 1942) and Paul Auster (b. 1947) are prominent among many other fiction writers. American Jewish writing on the HOLOCAUST has become evident since the 1960s.

However convenient the term 'American Jewish writer', it is in fact difficult to generalize convincingly about what is by now a widely diverse body of work, or even, perhaps, to say what is distinctively Jewish about certain works when the majority of Jewish writers are secular Jews. It is also worth noting that there are some writers with a Jewish background, notably Gertrude STEIN, J. D. Salinger (b. 1919) and Adrienne RICH, in whose work Jewishness plays little part. Broadly, however, it has been proposed that Jewish writers affirm a humanist tradition and demonstrate an ongoing belief in social progress and in the value of learning and scholarship. There is also a use of self-deprecating humour, and an eye for comic incongruity and absurdity, as is evident in the work of Nathanael West (1903–40), the novels of Heller, Philip Roth's early fiction and the comic monologues of Woody Allen (b. 1935).

Further reading

Defenses of the Imagination: Jewish Writers and Modern Historical Crisis (1977) by Robert Alter; *Not One of Them in Place* (2001) by Norman Finkelstein; *The Schlemiel Comes to America* (1983) by Ezra Greenspan; *The Jewish Writer in America* (1971) by Allen Guttmann; *The Conversion of the Jews and Other Essays* (1990) by Mark Shechner, and *Jewish American Literature since 1945* (1999) by Stephen Wade.

Jim Crow laws   Set of laws, at first informal but then formalized by individual states, operating from the 1870s until the 1960s to enforce the SEGREGATION of blacks from whites in public places, as well as in institutions such as the armed forces. The name derives from a minstrel routine, 'Jump Jim Crow', performed in the 1830s by the white minstrel player Thomas Dartmouth Rice (known as 'Daddy' Rice). 'Jim Crow' came to be a derogatory term for blacks, suggesting the racist stereotype of the 'comic darky', and later became a nickname for segregationist practices. The SUPREME COURT upheld the segregation laws in the PLESSY V. FERGUSON decision (1896) but segregation was declared unconstitutional in the BROWN V. BOARD OF EDUCATION OF TOPEKA judgment in 1954. Richard WRIGHT examines what he calls his 'Jim Crow education' in his memoir-essay 'The Ethics of Living Jim Crow, an Autobiographical Sketch' (1937).

John Brown's Raid   In October 1859 the militant ABOLITIONIST John Brown (1800–59) led a group of twenty-one men in a raid on the federal armoury at Harpers Ferry, Virginia (now West Virginia). Brown's intention was to establish a stronghold and initiate the freeing of slaves through armed intervention, but under attack from the United States Marines ten of Brown's men, including two of his sons, were killed and Brown was injured and captured. He was convicted on charges of murder, treason and slave insurrection, and was hanged, with six of his followers.

Prior to the Harpers Ferry Raid, Brown was a nationally known figure with a reputation for violence in the abolitionist cause. He had helped in running the UNDERGROUND RAILROAD and increasingly saw himself as divinely appointed to lead a holy war against SLAVERY. He moved to Kansas in 1855 with his five sons to oppose the extension of slavery, and in 1856 he led a group that murdered five pro-slavery settlers. This act, known as the 'Pottawatomie Massacre', gave Brown a national reputation. His trial and hanging made him one of abolitionism's martyrs.

Brown's raid, his trial and his execution were much written about. Lydia Maria Child (1802–80) tried to go to Virginia to nurse him in prison. Ralph Waldo EMERSON wrote in support of him before the execution and afterwards delivered a lecture, 'John Brown'. Henry David THOREAU wrote repeatedly of him and represented him as a martyr in his essay 'The Last Days of John Brown', while Herman MELVILLE depicted him as a prophet or 'weird' in his poem 'The Portent'. John Greenleaf Whittier (1807–92) commemorated him in the poem 'John Brown of Osawatomie' and the first draft of Harriet JACOBS's *Incidents in the Life of a Slave Girl* concluded with a tribute to him. The raid on Harpers Ferry is the subject of the famous CIVIL WAR song 'John Brown's Body', with words probably written by Thomas B. Bishop. Later representations of Brown include a commemorative speech on the raid given by Frederick DOUGLASS in 1881 (Douglass was a friend of Brown), a biography (1909) by W. E. B. DU BOIS, and a section of the long narrative poem *John Brown's Body* by Stephen Vincent Benét (1889–1943). *Cloudsplitter* (1998) by Russell Banks (b. 1940) is a recent fictional treatment of Brown.

Kansas–Nebraska Act   Passed in 1854, the act permitted the voters of the Kansas and Nebraska territories to decide whether or not they would allow SLAVERY. Under the terms of the 1820 MISSOURI COMPROMISE, lands acquired by the LOUISIANA PURCHASE that lay outside of Missouri north of the 36° 30′ parallel were closed to slavery, but the concept of popular sovereignty, championed by the Democratic senator Stephen A. Douglas, was held to supersede congressional decisions. The passing of the Kansas–Nebraska Act effectively repealed the Missouri Compromise, and led to violent conflict in Kansas because of the IMMIGRATION of pro- and anti-slavery factions. (The series of skirmishes is known as 'Bleeding Kansas', and over 200 poeple were killed prior to 1856.) Although intended to reduce the growing tension between North and South over slavery, the Kansas–Nebraska Act sharply increased it, and led directly to the establishment and growth of the Republican Party on an anti-slavery platform.

Kennedy assassination   On Friday 22 November 1963 President John F. Kennedy was fatally shot while visiting Dallas. Lee Harvey Oswald was arrested for the killing and was himself murdered by a nightclub owner, Jack Ruby, two days after the assassination. Kennedy, the fourth US president to be assassinated, was succeeded by Lyndon B. Johnson. In 1964 a commission of enquiry led by Earl Warren concluded that Oswald, located in the Texas School Book Depository, had killed Kennedy with two shots and that he had acted alone. However, there has been a persistent belief that there was more than one assassin, and that the assassination was a conspiracy involving either organized crime or the Central Intelligence Agency. Such beliefs were intensified in 1979 after a committee of the US House of Representatives reported that there was possibly a second gunman.

The Kennedy assassination and theories about it have provoked a vast literature, beginning with elegies for the president, such as *Formal Elegy* (1964) by John Berryman (1914–72). There have been a large number of fictionalizations of the killing and related events, notably *Libra* (1988) by Don DELILLO, *Oswald's Tale* (1995) by Norman Mailer (b. 1923) and *American Tabloid* (1995) by James Ellroy (b. 1948). Its effects on other people are examined in many novels set in the period, such as *Couples* (1968) by John Updike (b. 1932) and Alice WALKER's *Meridian* (1976). The assassination is often regarded as a pivotal event in American life, transforming Americans' perceptions of themselves, the media and governmental institutions. As DeLillo wrote in a 1983 essay, 'What has become unraveled since that afternoon in Dallas is ... the sense of a coherent reality most of us shared. We seem from that moment to have entered a world of randomness and ambiguity.'

Further reading

Not in Your Lifetime (1980, 1998) by Anthony Summers and *Covering the Body* (1992) by Barbie Zelizer.

Kenyon Review   Founded in 1939 by John Crowe Ransom (1888–1974), the review was a quarterly journal of criticism and creative writing, published at Kenyon College, Ohio. It was especially significant in the development and dissemination of NEW CRITICISM, and in the fostering of younger poets and novelists. Until 1959 Ransom edited the journal, which ceased publication in 1970 but was revived in 1979.

King, Martin Luther, Jr   Baptist minister and civil rights leader who won the Nobel Prize for Peace in 1964 and was assassinated in 1968. His achievements and his murder have often been the subject for various writers.

King was born in Atlanta, Georgia, in 1929. As a pastor in Montgomery, Alabama, he led opposition to SEGREGATION on buses in 1956, a key event in the development of the CIVIL RIGHTS MOVEMENT. A skilful orator, he gained international recognition as a leader, forming the Southern Christian Leadership Conference and advocating non-violent protest, a philosophy evident in his influential 'Letter from Birmingham Jail' (1963). In 1963 he delivered his famous 'I have a dream' speech during a massive march on Washington. King's leadership was influential in the passing of the Civil Rights Act in 1964, although there were African American intellectuals such as Malcolm X who were critical of his reliance on non-violent protest. A white man, James Earl Ray, assassinated King in Memphis, Tennessee.

King Philip's War   The most significant conflict in colonial New England between Native Americans and the colonists. Hostilities began in summer 1675 after the colonists in Plymouth executed three Wampanoag Indians, supposedly for murdering an informer. The Wampanoag leader Metacomet, known to the colonists as King Philip, had organized an alliance of the Narragansett, Abnaki, Nipmuck and Mohawk tribes, and after various provocations this grouping now undertook raids on colonial frontier settlements. The tribes became depleted, however, and the war ended in summer 1676 after Metacomet was killed in a skirmish. It has been estimated that the war resulted in the deaths of 3,000 Native Americans and 600 settlers, as well as much devastation of property. The war was decisive in establishing the ascendancy of the colonists in New England as defeat precipitated the decline of the Native American population.

Mary Rowlandson (?1635–1711) was abducted during the war, and her 1682 memoir of the incident is a well-known CAPTIVITY NARRATIVE. James Fenimore COOPER's 1829 novel *The Wept of Wish-ton-Wish* is set during the war, and *Eulogy on King Philip* (1837) by William Apess (1798–1839) is a polemic on it.

King, Stephen   Best-selling and prolific novelist. King was born in 1947 in Portland, Maine, and attended the University of Maine, where he later taught for a brief period. His first novel, *Carrie* (1973), quickly established his reputation as a HORROR writer and his work is almost exclusively in this tradition. His most prominent novels are *'Salem's Lot* (1975), *The Shining* (1977), *The Stand* (1978), *The Dead Zone* (1979), *Firestarter* (1980), *Christine* (1983), *It* (1986), *Misery* (1987), *The Dark Half* (1989), *Needful Things* (1991), *Dolores Claiborne* (1992), *Insomnia* (1994), *Desperation* (1996) and *Dreamcatcher* (2001). He has also published several SHORT-STORY collections, notably *Night Shift* (1978), and a study of horror, *Danse Macabre* (1981). There have been many film adaptations of his works and well over 100 million copies of his novels have been sold.

Although King's fiction is widely criticized for being undisciplined and stylistically inelegant, he is a significant writer with a keen awareness of the horror tradition in which he works and a rarely matched ability to entertain and involve the reader. 'The purpose of horror fiction', he stated in *Danse Macabre*, 'is not only to explore taboo lands but to confirm our own good feelings about the status quo by showing us extravagant visions of what the alternative might be.' Typically he sets his stories in apparently UTOPIAN suburbs or small communities in New England and at his best he explores the darker implications of everyday reality and the destructive aspects of supposedly normal desires; as he has said, 'the monster shouldn't be in a graveyard in decadent old Europe, but in the house down the street'.

Further reading

Reign of Fear (1991) by Don Herron; *The Dark Descent* (1992), edited by Tony Magistrale, and *Fear Itself* (1982), *Kingdom of Fear* (1986) and *Bare Bones* (1988), edited by Tim Underwood and Chuck Miller.

Kingston, Maxine Hong   Novelist, SHORT-STORY writer and poet whose work involves a profound examination of the history, experiences and identity of Chinese Americans. Maxine Hong was born to Chinese immigrant parents in 1940 in Stockton, California. She graduated from the University of California-Berkeley in 1962, married an actor, Earll Kingston, and went on to teach in California and Hawaii. Returning to California, she is now a professor at Berkeley.

Kingston's first book, THE WOMAN WARRIOR: MEMOIRS OF A GIRLHOOD AMONG GHOSTS (1976), received widespread acclaim, and won the National Book Critics' Circle Award for non-fiction. Strongly AUTOBIOGRAPHICAL, the work movingly explores the difficulties of first-generation Chinese immigrants, torn between two cultures and histories, yet it also examines the potential for personal strength deriving from a fusion between the two cultures. Its concentration on the experiences of Chinese and Chinese American women was balanced by her second book, *China Men* (1980), winner of the American Book Award for non-fiction. Kingston documented the exploited, impoverished lives of immigrant Chinese male labourers in the 19th century West, and recorded their considerable though unrecognized contributions to the making of the modern West, particularly through the building of the transcontinental railway. In a laconic, understated style she also publicized the deeply racist laws that affected the Chinese in America, including the fact that Chinese were not allowed to become American citizens, and that Chinese IMMIGRATION became illegal with the CHINESE EXCLUSION ACT. Kingston's third book, a novel, *Tripmaster Monkey: His Fake Book* (1989), received less acclaim. It involves the travels and development of Wittman Ah Sing and his attempts, sometimes successful, to improvise an amalgamation of Chinese and American literary traditions.

Despite their being labelled non-fiction, Kingston's first two books are similar to her third in fusing documentary realism, autobiography, history, fiction and myth in a brilliantly controlled prose style. While she frequently focuses on the pain and appalling injustices that have been a part of Chinese American identity, a concurrent theme in her writing is the adaptability of myth and its capacity to be imaginatively renewed and therefore to offer guidance, hope and strength. When criticized for her adaptations of Chinese myths, she has responded by arguing, 'myths have to change, be useful or be forgotten'.

Further reading

Articulate Silences (1993) by King-Kok Cheung; Maxine Hong Kingston (1999) by Diane Simmons; Critical Essays on Maxine Hong Kingston (1998), edited by Laura E. Skandera-Trombley, and Conversations with Maxine Hong Kingston (1998), edited by Paul Skenazy and Tera Martin.

Knickerbocker Magazine   Leading monthly magazine published in New York from 1833 until 1865, edited mainly by Lewis G. Clark (1808–73), with his twin brother Willis G. Clark (1808–41). The magazine grew out of a group of writers known as the

Knickerbocker Group, whose name was chosen in honour of Washington IRVING's comic character Diedrich Knickerbocker. It published work by James Kirke Paulding (1778–1860), Irving, James Fenimore COOPER, William Cullen Bryant (1794–1878), Nathaniel HAWTHORNE, Henry Wadsworth Longfellow (1807–82), Francis Parkman (1823–93) and John Greenleaf Whittier (1807–92). The *Knickerbocker Magazine* was considered Anglophile in its tastes and during the 1840s was attacked by the nationalistic YOUNG AMERICA movement. Some of those associated with the magazine and with the Knickerbocker group were assessed by Edgar Allan POE in his 1846 critical essay 'The Literati of New York City'.

Know-Nothing Party   Political grouping that originated in the late 1840s and which attracted large support until the mid-1850s. The party began in secret as an anti-IMMIGRATION and anti-Catholic organization. Although its official name was the American Party, its popular name derived from the fact that members had been instructed to reply that they 'knew nothing' when asked about their political affiliation. Support for the party grew during the 1850s when it seemed a viable alternative to the existing parties, which were sharply divided over SLAVERY. However, the party itself split as the slavery debate intensified and it never recovered popular support after 1855.

Ku Klux Klan   The first Ku Klux Klan was formed by CIVIL WAR Confederate veterans in Tennessee during 1866. (The name supposedly derives from the Greek *kuklos*, meaning circle.) It became the most powerful of several such organizations working against the federal occupation of the South and directing violence, particularly through LYNCH LAW, against blacks. It was characterized by its Masonic-like structure and costumes of white robes. The Klan was outlawed by Congress in 1871, declared unconstitutional by the SUPREME COURT in 1882, and virtually disappeared as white power was restored in the South; in his 1901 AUTOBIOGRAPHY *Up From Slavery* Booker T. Washington (1856–1915) commented that 'To-day there are no such organizations in the South, and the fact that such ever existed is almost forgotten by both races.'

The Ku Klux Klan was revived in 1915 in Georgia, at a time when white supremacy was perceived to be under threat. The new Klan was strongly influenced by the racist anti-miscegenation novels of Thomas Dixon (1864–1946), especially *The Leopard's Spots* (1902) and *The Clansman* (1905 – the basis of D. W. Griffith's 1915 film *The Birth of a Nation*), in which white Southern womanhood is under attack from black men. In addition to its terrorization of blacks the Klan, considering itself the defender of Protestantism and Anglo-Saxon racial 'purity', has victimized Roman Catholics, immigrants, Jews and organized labour. The Klan was estimated to have over 2 million members in the 1920s; though it sharply declined after 1945, it revived during the CIVIL RIGHTS MOVEMENT and, while increasingly marginalized, has retained a presence in American life.

Following her mentor Dixon, Margaret Mitchell (1900–49) romanticized the first Klan as defenders of the Old South in *Gone with the Wind* (1936). FAULKNER's murderous Percy Grimm in *Light in August* (1932) is a Klan member.

L

Language poetry   Critical and poetic movement originating in the mid-1970s (sometimes represented typographically as L=A=N=G=U=A=G=E poetry). Language poets emphasize both the non-transparent nature of language and the role language plays in perpetuating social and political structures. They challenge the ROMANTIC, subjective and lyrical-expressive traditions of poetry and often use techniques such as collage, fractured syntax and broken sentences to heighten the reader's awareness of inhabiting a linguistic realm. Since the connection between the commodification of language and the hegemonic processes of capitalism is emphasized, language poetry has a strong political dimension. Thus, one of the objectives of defamiliarization through the splintering of language is to make the poem an anti-commodity. As Bruce Andrews (b. 1948) and Charles Bernstein (b. 1950) have written, 'It is our sense that the project of poetry does not involve turning language into a commodity for consumption; instead, it involves repossessing the sign through close attention to, and active participation in, its production.' Much language poetry is published by small presses and journals, and has an experimental and sometimes forbidding quality. *L=A=N=G=U=A=G=E*, published between 1978 and 1982, was an influential magazine of poetry and essays. As well as Bernstein and Andrews, significant language poets include Susan Howe (b.1937), Lyn Hejinian (b. 1941), Ron Silliman (b. 1946) and Bob Perelman (b. 1947).

Further reading

Textual Politics and the Language Poets (1989) by George Hartley; *The Dance of the Intellect* (1985) by Marjorie Perloff, and *The New Sentence* (1987) by Ron Silliman. *The L=A=N=G=U=A=G=E Book* (1984), edited by Bruce Andrews and Charles Bernstein, is an important collection of essays and statements.

Leather-Stocking Tales   Series of five novels by James Fenimore COOPER following the adventures of the backwoodsman Natty Bumppo, who is known by various names, and is called Leather-Stocking in the first of the novels to be published. Taken together the novels are often considered the earliest version of American EPIC and were influential in the development of the WESTERN.

In order of publication, the novels are: *The Pioneers* (1823), *The Last of the Mohicans* (1826), *The Prairie* (1827), *The Pathfinder* (1840) and *The Deerslayer* (1841). However, the order of publication does not follow chronologically the lives of Natty and his American Indian 'sworn brother' Chingachgook. For instance in *The Pioneers* they are old men living in a settlement and Chingachgook, known as John Mohegan (he is 'the last of the Mohicans'), dies, whereas in *The Deerslayer* they are seen at their youngest. The fictive chronological sequence of the novels is: *The Deerslayer*, *The Last of the Mohicans*, *The Pathfinder*, *The Pioneers* and *The Prairie*, in which Natty dies. In chronological order he is referred to as Deerslayer, Hawkeye, Pathfinder, Leather-Stocking and 'the trapper'.

The Leather-Stocking novels trace the gradual westward movement of the FRONTIER, and insist on the historical inevitability of this movement. But simultaneously they lament the loss of wilderness and register the displacement of the Native American; this sense of loss is exemplified by the fact that *The Deerslayer* is the last in order of composition, yet is the earliest in terms of setting. In order of composition the novels gradually change from being historically based adventure narratives to ROMANTIC and ELEGIAC representations of a mythic past.

Much of the importance and enduring popularity of the Leather-Stocking tales derives from the character of Natty, who is partly based on the legends surrounding Daniel Boone (?1734–1820). Natty is the archetypal illiterate frontiersman who, although not being of mixed race (he is 'a man without a cross' as he insists in *The Last of the Mohicans*), combines the best traditions of both Europeans and Native Americans in his respect for the wilderness and his mastery of the skills required to live in the woods. (The French novelist Balzac called Natty 'a magnificent moral hermaphrodite between the savage and civilized states'.) Natty resents the wastefulness and careless attitude to nature demonstrated by the settlers – this is most evident in *The Pioneers* and *The Prairie* – and is aware that this attitude represents the civilizing future which will displace him.

Further reading

James Fenimore Cooper: New Critical Essays (1985), edited by Robert Clark; *Plotting America's Past* (1983) by William P. Kelly; *Fenimore Cooper: A Study of his Life and Imagination* (1978) by Stephen Railton, and *Cooper's Leather-Stocking Novels* (1991) by Geoffrey Rans.

Leaves of Grass   Collection of poems by Walt WHITMAN, first published anonymously in 1855 and undergoing considerable expansion and revision until the final authorized edition was published posthumously in 1892.

The first *Leaves of Grass* signalled a revolution in American poetry. Breaking audaciously with the formal, genteel poems of his contemporaries, the book consisted of twelve poems in unrhymed, flowing FREE VERSE. The language was a sometimes bizarre combination of slang, occasional coarse references, foreign phrases and lyrical, tender passages. The subject matter too was revolutionary, encompassing references to intense mystical experience, to New York City and its working-class people, to the poet's body, sexual longings and appetite for life. While there was a clear resonance between the poems and TRANSCENDENTALIST thought, there was also an expression of love for concrete reality and the small details of nature. Furthermore the twelve poems were introduced by a prose preface that boldly outlined a programme for American poetry and announced, 'The United States themselves are essentially the greatest poem.' *Leaves of Grass* embodied a philosophy of inclusive DEMOCRACY and attempted to realize this philosophy in aesthetic terms. The first edition was ridiculed and reviled as obscene, but Ralph Waldo EMERSON hailed it as a fresh beginning in American poetry. For subsequent editions Whitman tended to modify the bolder stylistic elements (for example by numbering the sections of the longer poems), and the language became smoother. Each edition was more than merely an expansion of the previous one; new poems were added but existing poems might be revised or placed in a different sequence. This alteration of context often provided new possibilities of meaning for particular poems. Overall, the changing editions suggest the idea of organic growth and the correspondence of the book with Whitman's life.

Further reading

The New Walt Whitman Handbook (1975) by Gay Wilson Allen; Leaves of Grass: One Hundred Years After (1955), edited by Milton Hindus, and A Critical Guide to Leaves of Grass (1957) by James E. Miller.

Leisure class   Term coined by the economist Thorstein Veblen (1857–1929) in his polemical and influential study *The Theory of the Leisure Class* (1899). Analysing the United States in the second half of the 19th century, Veblen explored the formation of a class that measured its value by its distance from labour and by what he called its 'conspicuous consumption'. Veblen satirized this class, and particularly its belief that ostentatious display denoted status, seeing it as a serious threat to American society's traditional values of work and thrift.

Lewis and Clark Expedition   Overland journey of a group led by Meriwether Lewis (1774–1809) and William Clark (1770–1838) to the Pacific Northwest and back (1804–6). President Thomas Jefferson commissioned the expedition in 1803, prior to the LOUISIANA PURCHASE. The expedition consisted of a group of about fifty people, mostly connected with the military, and it endured much hardship and privation during the trip of over 4,000 miles. Sacajawea (1786–?1812), the Shoshone Indian wife of a French interpreter, joined the expedition in 1805 and played an important role as interpreter, negotiator and guide. The expedition collected geological and other specimens, produced maps and recorded details of fauna and flora and of meetings with Native Americans. An abridged, edited version of the diaries of Lewis and Clark was published in 1814, but a standard edition was not available until 1905, when *The*

Original Journals of the Lewis and Clark Expedition was published, edited by Reuben Gold Thwaites.

The Liberator   Published from 1831 until 1865, *The Liberator* was the weekly newspaper founded and edited by William Lloyd Garrison (1805–79) and dedicated to ABOLITIONISM. Published in Boston, the paper had at most a circulation of about 3,000, though its readership was much higher. Writers associated with it include Frederick DOUGLASS, Henry David THOREAU and John Greenleaf Whittier (1807–92). The paper ceased publication when the THIRTEENTH AMENDMENT was ratified.

Library of Congress Poetry Consultancy   A one-year appointment given to poets by the Library of Congress. On appointment the poet, in return for a stipend, is expected to arrange poetry readings, deliver a lecture and to act as consultant to the library. The post was established in 1936 and notable holders have included Conrad Aiken (1889–1973), Karl Shapiro (1913–2000), Randall Jarrell (1914–65), Robert FROST, Gwendolyn BROOKS, Robert LOWELL, Elizabeth BISHOP and Anthony Hecht (b. 1923). The 1952 appointment of William Carlos WILLIAMS was blocked because of his supposed communist sympathies. Since 1985 the appointee has been officially termed the 'Poet Laureate Consultant in Poetry' and unofficially called the POET LAUREATE OF THE UNITED STATES.

Life Studies   Highly influential poetry collection by Robert LOWELL, first published in 1959. The book comprises four interrelated parts. The first is mainly devoted to historical figures; the second '91 Revere Street', is a prose memoir of Lowell's childhood; the third section comprises four poems on writers, and the final part, 'Life Studies', contains a sequence of poems on Lowell's own life. The book is broadly sequential, with recurring images, and there is a notable shift from dramatic monologue by assumed personae towards the poet speaking in his own voice and exploring personal, familial and public crisis. It was this aspect of *Life Studies* that accounted for its impact and led to its being considered a key work of CONFESSIONAL POETRY. Lowell explores various aspects of loss and breakdown in cultural, historical and individual terms, and examines how far these may result in the generation of significant energies. The book is also ELEGIAC to a large extent, and includes powerful poems on the deaths of Lowell's parents. Stylistically, Lowell moved away from the allusive, dense texture of his earlier poetry to a more informal, apparently freer style; he called *Life Studies* 'a book without symbols' and said that he wanted readers to feel they were 'getting the real Robert Lowell'.

Further reading

The Collected Prose (1987) by Robert Lowell; 'Robert Lowell: *Life Studies*' by Stephen Matterson, in *A Companion to 20ᵗʰ Century Poetry* (2001), edited by Neil Roberts, and *Critics on Robert Lowell* (1972), edited by Jonathan Price.

Little Review   Published in Chicago, the monthly *Little Review* was founded in 1914 and edited by Margaret Anderson (1886–1973). Dedicated to all the arts, it came to be especially associated with MODERNISM, and, for a spell with ANARCHISM, publishing work by Emma Goldman (1869–1940). Writers published in the magazine include Amy Lowell (1874–1925), Ezra POUND (who acted as foreign editor, 1917–19), Sherwood Anderson (1876–1941), Carl Sandburg (1878–1967), William Carlos WILLIAMS, Gertrude STEIN, Wallace STEVENS, T. S. ELIOT and Hart Crane (1899–1932). In 1918 James Joyce's *Ulysses* was serialized in the magazine and Margaret Anderson and her co-editor Jane Heap were consequently fined $50 each for publishing obscenity. The magazine ceased publication in 1929.

Local colour   Literary style associated with REGIONALISM that developed in the 1860s and flourished until the 1890s. While using fictive plots, local colourists wrote realistically of the landscape, customs, language and habits of particular areas. Local colour is especially associated with the novel and SHORT STORY, although poets also used it. The term 'local colourist' is sometimes unfairly used as a synonym for a minor writer. Significant local colourists include Bret Harte (1836–1902) and Mark TWAIN in the West, Harriet Beecher STOWE, Sarah Orne Jewett (1849–1909) and Mary Wilkins Freeman (1852–1930) in New England, Hamlin Garland (1860–1940) in the Mid-West and George Washington Cable (1844–1925) and Kate CHOPIN in the South. Local colour has undergone a recent revival, evident in the work of Annie Proulx (b. 1935), Richard Ford (b. 1944) and David Guterson (b. 1956).

Further reading

Regional Fictions (2001) by Stephanie Foote; Regions of Identity (1999) by Kate McCullough, and Regionalism and the Female Imagination (1985) by Emily Toth.

Long Day's Journey into Night   Play in four acts by Eugene O'NEILL, written 1940–1 and published in 1956. The play is strongly AUTOBIOGRAPHICAL, as O'Neill indicated in the dedication to his wife, where he described it as a work 'of old sorrow, written in tears and blood'.

The play has only five characters, four of whom belong to the Irish-American Tyrone family: James, an alcoholic actor, his wife Mary, who is addicted to morphine, and their sons the alcoholic Jamie and the tubercular Edmund. The fifth character is Cathleen, their servant. Each act is set in the family living room, and all of the action takes place on one day in August 1912. O'Neill frames the drama between combinations of the characters, brilliantly displaying the nature of the interactions between them. The major theme is one that O'Neill often explored: the ways that people react when forced to confront the nature of the illusions that sustain their lives. Each member of the Tyrone family is unfulfilled and broken in some way and is unable to acknowledge this truth. Each is in some measure willing to collude in the maintenance of the illusions of the other three family members and equally liable to accuse, shame and punish them for their self-deceptive acts. O'Neill particularly examines the nostalgic illusion of a stable defining past – the illusion that, in the words of Mary, 'Only the past when you were happy is real.' The play's closed, hermetic world gives the drama a remarkable claustrophobic intensity.

Further reading

Final Acts: The Creation of Three Late O'Neill Plays (1985) by Judith E. Barlow; Eugene O'Neill's New Language of Kinship (1982) by Michael Manheim, and Staging Depth: Eugene O'Neill and the Politics of Psychological Discourse (1995) by Joel Pfister.

Long poem Broadly, there have been two types of American long poem. The first involves a formal organization, a plot and an overall discernible pattern. It may be narrative or meditative. This tradition includes some of the earliest American poems, such as works by Anne BRADSTREET and, notably, *The Day of Doom* (1662) by Michael Wigglesworth (1631–1705). The narrative, meditative long poem flourished in the 19th century in the work of Joel Barlow (1754–1812), Henry Wadsworth Longfellow (1807–82), John Greenleaf Whittier (1807–92) and James Russell Lowell (1819–91). One of the most ambitious of American long poems, Herman MELVILLE's *Clarel* (1876), is also in this tradition, which was continued in the poetry of Robert FROST and exists today in the work of poets such as James Merrill (1926–95) and Robert Pinsky (b. 1940).

The second type of long poem is usually considered more distinctively American, and is generally seen to begin with the 1855 version of Walt WHITMAN's 'Song of Myself'. In this tradition the form may be improvisatory and the poem relatively plotless, heuristic and open-ended; in some cases it may be an accumulation of shorter lyrics. This kind of long poem is comparable to a living organism, always open to change and addition, although the poet may have a clear overall design in mind; certainly the enduring model for this organic long poem is Whitman's *LEAVES OF GRASS* (1855–92). There is usually an interweaving of personal and public concerns, and perhaps a consideration of American history and culture. Poems in this tradition include Ezra POUND's *THE CANTOS* (1919–72), *The Bridge* (1930) by Hart Crane (1899–1932), *The Maximus Poems* (1953–70) by Charles Olson (1910–70), 'A' (1928–78) by Louis Zukofsky (1904–78), *Paterson* (1946–63) by William Carlos WILLIAMS, *The Dream Songs* (1968) of John Berryman (1914–72) and Robert LOWELL's *History* (1973).

Further reading

Obdurate Brilliance (1991) by Peter Baker; On the Modernist Long Poem (1986) by Margaret Dickie; Discovering Ourselves in Whitman (1989) by Thomas Gardner, and The American Quest for a Supreme Fiction (1979) by James E. Miller, Jr.

Lost generation Term used to describe the generation of writers active immediately after World War I. Gertrude STEIN used the phrase in conversation with Ernest

HEMINGWAY, supposedly quoting a garage mechanic saying to her 'You are all a lost generation.' The phrase signifies a disillusioned post-war generation characterized by lost values, lost belief in the idea of human progress, and a mood of futility and despair leading to hedonism. The mood is described by F. Scott FITZGERALD in *This Side of Paradise* (1920) when he writes of a generation that found 'all Gods dead, all wars fought, all faiths in man shaken'. 'Lost generation' usually refers specifically to the American expatriate writers associated with 1920s Paris, especially Hemingway and Fitzgerald, and to a lesser extent T. S. ELIOT and Ezra POUND. Hemingway used the phrase 'You are all a lost generation' as the epigraph to his first novel *The Sun Also Rises* (1926), and the influential critic Malcolm Cowley (1898–1989) used 'lost generation' in various studies of expatriate writers.

Louisiana Purchase   Land transaction between the United States and France, by which the size of the United States more than doubled. In 1803 the United States agreed to purchase a vast area of over 828,000 square miles, comprising what are now the entire states of Arkansas, Iowa, Louisiana, Missouri, Nebraska, North Dakota, Oklahoma and South Dakota and most of the land in what are now the states of Colorado, Kansas, Minnesota, Montana and Wyoming. For this the United States agreed to pay a total of $15 million – a price of less than 3 cents an acre (although interest payments to Dutch and English banks meant that the final cost was over $27 million). The area had been officially under Spanish administration and had just been returned to France under Napoleon, who was willing to sell the land in order to concentrate on European interests. President Jefferson was concerned over whether the CONSTITUTION allowed for such an acquisition, but this issue was elided after the Senate approved the purchase.

Lowell, Robert   Among the most acclaimed and influential 20th century poets, Lowell was born in Boston in 1917. Both of his parents belonged to distinguished New England families, including, on his father's side, the poets James Russell Lowell (1819–91) and Amy Lowell (1874–1925). Lowell attended Harvard University but after a family quarrel he transferred in 1937 to Kenyon College, Ohio. In 1940 he became a Roman Catholic, and married the novelist Jean Stafford (1915–79). In 1943 he spent 5 months in prison for refusing to be drafted into military service. Lowell's first two books, *Land of Unlikeness* (1944) and *Lord Weary's Castle* (1946), earned him a considerable reputation. The poems exhibit tremendous technical mastery, indicating the influence of NEW CRITICISM. Thematically they express Lowell's religious, and at times APOCALYPTIC, world-view. During the 1950s Lowell underwent a series of life changes, which included his move away from Roman Catholicism, divorce and marriage to the critic Elizabeth Hardwick. There was also an increase in the frequency of the mental breakdowns and manic episodes which he had suffered since the early 1950s. In 1959 he published *LIFE STUDIES*, which signalled a significant change from his established style, both formally and in his use of AUTOBIOGRAPHICAL material. His subsequent collections are: *For the Union Dead* (1964); *Near the Ocean* (1967); *Notebook 1967–68* (1969), followed by an enlarged version, *Notebook* (1970), which Lowell later revised and republished as *History* (1973) and *For Lizzie and Harriet* (1973); *The Dolphin* (1973), and *Day by Day* (1977). His work maintained an autobiographical emphasis while being very much concerned with the politics and public issues of the times. At certain periods Lowell compulsively used certain forms, especially sonnet variations in the period 1969–73. His other work includes a collection of translations, *Imitations* (1961), and an acclaimed dramatic trilogy, *The Old Glory* (1968). His *Collected Prose* was published in 1987. Living chiefly in Boston and New York, Lowell taught at various universities, including Harvard and, from 1973, also at Essex University in England. He and Hardwick divorced in 1972 and he married Caroline Blackwood. He died of heart failure in New York in 1977.

Lowell's friend John Berryman (1914–72) memorably called him 'the Bostonian / rugged & grand & sorrowful'. Lowell was highly self-conscious about his New England literary and religious heritage, and his intense poems record both a private life and a historical period of doubt, turmoil and uncertainty. Although he wrote 'I want words meat-hooked from the living steer' his poetry was actually highly crafted and carefully revised while maintaining a vital and voracious attitude to experience.

Further reading

The Critical Response to Robert Lowell (1999), edited by Steven Gould Axelrod; *Robert Lowell: Life and Art* (1978) by Steven Gould Axelrod; *Robert Lowell: Nihilist as Hero* (1983) by Vereen Bell; *Robert Lowell: A Biography* (1982) by Ian Hamilton, and *Circle to Circle* (1975) by Stephen Yenser.

Loyalists   Those colonials who were loyal to the British before and during the American Revolution. It has been estimated that up to one third of the population of the colonies was loyal, and that the loyalists formed a majority in the states of New York and New Jersey. Up to 30,000 loyalists fought for the British during the REVOLUTIONARY WAR, and during and after the war up to 100,000 left the United States (usually for Britain or other British colonies in the Americas). Although they appear infrequently in American literature, the loyalists are represented in James Fenimore COOPER's novels that are set during the Revolutionary War, notably *The Spy* (1821), *Lionel Lincoln* (1825) and *Wyandotté* (1843).

Lyceum movement   Voluntary society that was dedicated to the provision of educational and informational programmes for adults. The first American lyceum was founded in 1826 in Millbury, Massachusetts, by the educational reformer Josiah Holbrook (1788–1854), who came to lead the movement. (The name 'lyceum' refers to the Athenian school founded by Aristotle in ancient Greece.) By 1834 over 3,000 lyceums had been established throughout the country, and these served as venues for debate, adult education and lecture series as well as occasional lectures. They were especially significant in stimulating discussion on current topics such as SLAVERY, REFORM and TEMPERANCE. Towards the end of the 19th century the CHAUTAUQUA MOVEMENT gradually took over the functions served by the lyceums. Many significant American writers were popular lyceum lecturers, notably Ralph Waldo EMERSON, Frederick DOUGLASS, Nathaniel HAWTHORNE, Henry David THOREAU and Mark TWAIN. Some of the key essays by Emerson and by Thoreau were originally given as lyceum lectures.

Lynch law   The word 'lynching' derives from the name of Captain William Lynch (1742–1820), who organized vigilante anti-LOYALIST groups in 18th century Virginia. Lynch law was commonly practised on the frontier as a rudimentary form of justice, and before the CIVIL WAR its victims were mostly white. During RECONSTRUCTION, however, lynching was racialized and ritualized as a method of victimization and intimidation. Lynching frequently involved torture and mutilation and was often a public spectacle. It is estimated that between 1876 and 1914 there were over 3,500 lynchings. Lynching took place mainly in the Southern states and the majority of the victims were black, both men and women. Contradicting the idea that lynching was a defence of the white woman, most lynchings of black men did not arise from allegations of sexual assault; approximately a quarter did, but lynching was the punishment for offences against common law, and for acts perceived as threatening to white supremacy. As Trudier Harris has observed, 'Lynchings were carefully designed to convey to black persons that they had no power and nothing else whites were obligated to respect.'

The NAACP campaigned vigorously against lynch law, and many writers, both black and white, condemned the practice. Ida B. Wells (1862–1931) wrote the classic anti-lynching polemic *A Red Record* (1895), and Mark TWAIN wrote bitterly of 'The United States of Lyncherdom' (1901). Lynching and the threat of it is a recurring theme in the work of many African American writers. *The Ox-Bow Incident* by Walter Van Tilburg Clark (1909–71) is a celebrated WESTERN about frontier lynching.

Further reading

Vengeance and Justice: Crime and Punishment in the 19th Century South (1984) by Edward L. Ayers; *Going to the Territory* (1986) by Ralph Ellison, and *Exorcising Blackness* (1984) by Trudier Harris-Lopez.

Magic realism   Term used since the 1940s to describe a form of prose writing in which the FANTASTIC is juxtaposed with the everyday. Some critics suggest that magic realism reflects the social and political situation of a colonized or powerless people, in demonstrating the manipulation and alteration of truth and the juxtaposition of harsh social reality and the absurd. The style has been mostly employed by Latin-American authors and to a lesser extent by some British and Anglo-Indian writers. In the United States magic realism was first used to refer to a style of painting, and it has been relatively unused in American literature, although it is a feature in works by various writers, including William Wharton (b. 1925) and Toni Morrison. A kind of magic realism may be considered an established feature of much Native American story-telling, and it is used to some extent by writers such as Louise Erdrich (b. 1954) and Sherman Alexie (b. 1966).

Malamud, Bernard   Novelist and SHORT-STORY writer, born in Brooklyn, New York, in 1914, to Russian Jewish immigrants. Malamud attended the City College of New York and Columbia University. After graduating he taught in high schools, then at universities in Oregon and Vermont. He died in New York in 1986. Malamud's first novel, *The Natural* (1952), deals with the career of a baseball player. Although it is in many respects untypical of his work, it does begin the combination of fantasy and REALISM that he would later develop in more sophisticated ways. He wrote seven novels in all, notably *The Assistant* (1957), *The Fixer* (1966) and *Dubin's Lives* (1979). *The Assistant* explores the relation between an elderly Jewish shopkeeper and his non-Jewish helper. Though *The Fixer* is based on a 1913 Russian crime and its aftermath, it refers obliquely to the HOLOCAUST through its exploration of Jewish scapegoating. *Dubin's Lives* concerns a middle-aged biographer who becomes infatuated with a young woman. Malamud is especially acclaimed for his short stories, collected in *The Magic Barrel* (1958), *Idiots First* (1963), *Pictures of Fidelman* (1969), *Rembrandt's Hat* (1973) and *The Stories of Bernard Malamud* (1983). His finest stories are realistic and unsentimental depictions of the bleakness and hardships of working-class immigrant urban life, which yet provide a sense of possible spiritual and emotional resonance, potentially giving luminous coherence to otherwise mundane and difficult existence.

Further reading

The Good Man's Dilemma (1981) by Iska Alter; Experimental Essays on the Novels of Bernard Malamud (1995) by Philip Davis; Jewish American Fiction (1992) by Stanford Pinsker, and Critical Essays on Bernard Malamud (1987), edited by Joel Salzberg.

Mamet, David   Dramatist, screenplay writer and film director. Mamet was born in Chicago in 1947 and attended Goddard College in Vermont. Returning to Chicago he worked at various jobs, some of which provided subjects for his early work. His first success, *Duck Variations* (1972), was followed by *Sexual Perversity in Chicago* (1974), *American Buffalo* (1975), *A Life in the Theatre* (1977) and *The Woods* (1977). Since 1981 Mamet has been prolific in a range of media. As well as the critically acclaimed plays *Glengarry Glen Ross* (1982), *Speed-the-Plow* (1987), *Oleanna* (1993) and *The Cryptogram* (1995), he directed films of his own screenplays *House of Games* (1987),

Things Change (1988), *Homicide* (1991) and *The Spanish Prisoner* (1998). He also wrote screenplay adaptations for a series of high-profile films, including *The Postman Always Rings Twice* (1981), *The Verdict* (1982) and *Wag the Dog* (1997). He has published a satirical novel, *The Village* (1994), two volumes of memoirs, and various collections of essays. In 1998 he co-founded a film production company, *Films of Atlantic.*

Mamet's plays are driven mainly by dialogue rather than action. While he uses natural speech rhythms, his language is highly stylized, with a distinctive use of echo and repetition. Thematically he is fascinated by interaction between individuals, by the human need for stories, by CONFIDENCE games, and by how groups define themselves in particular ways, such as language or manners or ethical codes. His work is often particularly concerned with male group identity and behaviour.

Further reading

David Mamet (1985) by C. W. E. Bigsby; *David Mamet: Language as Dramatic Action* (1990) by Anne Dean; *Weasels and Wisemen* (1999) by Leslie Kane, and *David Mamet in Conversation* (2001), edited by Leslie Kane.

Manifest destiny   Term coined by New York editor John L. O'Sullivan in 1845 to describe the ideal of the territorial expansion of the United States over the American continent, especially to the Pacific ocean. O'Sullivan wrote of 'our manifest destiny to overspread the continent allotted by Providence'. 'Manifest destiny' was significant in suggesting a view of United States history as destiny, thereby reinforcing a version of history that had existed in PURITANISM, and in being supported by contemporary racial theories that specifically made it the destiny of Anglo-Saxons. The concept was used to justify the annexation of Texas, Oregon, New Mexico and California in the name of historical inevitability.

Mason–Dixon Line   Symbolically the supposed boundary between the North and South. The line was actually the boundary mapped by two English surveyors, Charles Mason (1730–87) and Jeremiah Dixon (d. 1777), to resolve an 80-year-old boundary dispute between the Penns, owners of Pennsylvania, and the Baltimores, owners of Maryland. Mason and Dixon surveyed the boundary between 1763 and 1767 (though the work was completed by others), and the boundary between Pennsylvania and Maryland was ratified in 1769. The line later became significant as the division between FREE-SOIL states and SLAVE states. The reference to the South as 'Dixie' is often considered a reference to the Mason–Dixon line, though it derives more directly from the so-called Confederate anthem 'Dixie' composed by Dan Emmett in 1859, which became a marching song during the CIVIL WAR.

Massachusetts Bay Colony   Settlement founded by the PURITANS in 1630 under the leadership of John Winthrop. The Puritans had been granted a royal charter in 1629 that enabled the settlement to be created and almost a thousand people crossed the Atlantic in a small fleet headed by the *Arbella*. They first settled at Salem and later at Boston. The colony was much larger than PLYMOUTH COLONY, which had been founded by the *Mayflower* separatists in 1620. The colony was strongly though not exclusively Puritan, and Winthrop was its first governor. It grew quickly; 20,000 more immigrants arrived during the next decade in the so-called Puritan 'great migration'. As the colony prospered it began to assert greater independence from the crown, which resulted in the withdrawal of the royal charter in 1684. A new charter was granted in 1691, under the terms of which Plymouth Colony was absorbed into the Massachusetts Bay Colony.

Mayflower Compact   Agreement signed by forty-one of the male emigrants travelling from England to PLYMOUTH COLONY on the *Mayflower* in 1620. Those emigrants who devised the compact were separatists, a branch of extreme PURITANS believing in the need for absolute separation from the Church of England. The compact was designed to prevent the possible fragmentation of the group and to ensure the legitimacy of the settlement as 'a civil body politic'. It empowered the emigrants to pass 'such just and equal laws . . . as shall be thought most meet and convenient for the general good of the colony' and bound each settler to abide by the laws. Somewhat misleadingly, the compact is often referred to as the crucial social contract in the founding of America. For instance, in his 1980 acceptance speech to the Republican convention, Ronald Reagan called the act a 'voluntary binding together of free people to live under the law' that 'set the pattern for what was to come'.

McCarthyism   Term applied to the repressive political atmosphere of the years 1950–4 and more generally to any intolerant repression of dissent or unconventionality. After Senator Joseph R. McCarthy (1908–57) claimed to have a list containing 205 names of communists holding government posts, an investigation began. This intensified the so-called 'Red scare' that had begun in the previous decade and which eventually led to thousands of federal employees, especially teachers, losing their posts after being accused of affiliation with the Communist Party. The scare had also resulted in the jailing and blacklisting of 'The Hollywood Ten' – ten prominent motion-picture figures who had refused to testify before the House Un-American Activities Committee (HUAC) in 1947. McCarthy's inflammatory accusations generated an atmosphere of paranoia and suspicion, particularly because those called before his investigating committee were not only aggressively questioned about their own supposed affiliations but were challenged to 'name names' of others they suspected. McCarthy was most powerful between 1952 and 1954. His accusations became increasingly irresponsible and hysterical, culminating in a televised series of hearings when the army was accused of harbouring communists. He lost much support and in December 1954 the Senate censured him for unbecoming behaviour.

McCarthyism is addressed in numerous works by American writers. Notable examples include Arthur MILLER's play *THE CRUCIBLE* (1953) and Philip ROTH's novel *I Married A Communist* (1998).

Further reading

McCarthyism (1978), edited by Thomas Reeves and *Many are the Crimes* (1998) by Ellen Schrecker.

McClure's Magazine   Popular monthly magazine published in New York between 1893 and 1929. Founded by Samuel Sidney McClure (1857–1949), it was the first MUCKRAKING magazine, and published fiction by many contemporary writers. McClure helped to revolutionize the magazine industry by keeping cover prices low and appealing to the average rather than the specialist reader. Frank NORRIS reported for *McClure's* on the SPANISH–AMERICAN WAR, and Willa CATHER was its managing editor from 1908 until 1912.

Melting pot   Term describing the process by which various immigrant ethnic identities would be fused into a distinctly American race. The metaphor is drawn from the practice of mixing different metals at great heat to produce new compounds, and it appears in the 1908 play *The Melting Pot* by the English writer Israel Zangwill; 'America is God's Crucible, the great Melting Pot where all the races of Europe are melting and re-forming.' Although he did not use the phrase, J. Hector St John De Crèvecoeur (1735–1813) articulated the positive concept of the melting pot in *Letters from an American Farmer* (1782) when he wrote that in America 'individuals of all nations are melted into a new race of men'.

Melville, Herman . Novelist, SHORT-STORY writer and poet, born in New York City in 1819. Despite a distinguished background the Melville family was left in difficult financial circumstances following the bankruptcy and death of Melville's father in 1832. After a period spent in odd jobs, Melville sailed in 1841 on a whaling voyage. He jumped ship in the Marquesas Islands, however, where he lived for several weeks; this experience formed the basis of his first novel, *Typee* (1846). He then went to Hawaii where he lived for several months before enlisting in the United States Navy for a voyage back to the United States. He returned to his family in Massachusetts in 1844. There, Melville began to write fictionalized accounts of his experiences. *Typee* sold well and brought him some acclaim, which was consolidated by his second novel, *Omoo* (1847), also based on his South Sea adventures. In 1847 Melville married Elizabeth Shaw, daughter of the chief justice of Massachusetts. The couple had four children (their son Malcolm died in 1867 after shooting himself in ambiguous circumstances).

Melville's third novel, *Mardi* (1849), represented a considerable departure from his earlier work. Wholly fictive, it mixed satire, allegory, political commentary and philosophical speculation in a way that readers and critics found unacceptable. Although a critical and commercial failure, *Mardi* was an interesting experiment that opened up imaginative possibilities for Melville. He returned to experience-based fiction, and his next two novels, *Redburn* (1849) and *White-Jacket* (1850), helped repair his reputation. Melville was becoming increasingly frustrated by the discrepancy between what he wanted to write and what would sell. This dissatisfaction is evident in the letters he wrote to his neighbour in rural Massachusetts, Nathaniel HAWTHORNE, during the time that he was writing *MOBY-DICK*. To Melville, Hawthorne represented a writer who could remain true to an artistic vision while managing to please popular taste. Finding a similar balance proved increasingly impossible for Melville. *Moby-Dick* received mixed reviews and sold poorly; his next novel, *Pierre* (1852), puzzled and infuriated reviewers. However, the chance to write short fiction for *PUTNAM'S MONTHLY MAGAZINE*, with a guaranteed payment and a particular audience, led to some of Melville's finest work, including 'Bartleby the Scrivener' (1853) and *Benito Cereno* (1855). In 1857 Melville published *The Confidence-Man*. An incisive analysis of the social, economic and religious meanings of trust, this consistently underrated novel is in many respects his most considerable achievement.

Melville travelled to the Holy Land in 1857. Returning home he attempted to make a living from lecturing, but when this failed he became a customs inspector in New York. He worked at this job for 19 years and published no more prose fiction in his lifetime. He devoted his creativity now to poetry, and privately published several works, notably *Battle-Pieces and Aspects of the War* (1866), and the two-volume narrative poem *Clarel: A Poem and Pilgrimage in the Holy Land* (1876). In spite of Melville's considerable reputation, *Clarel* remains a little-known masterpiece (Melville called it 'eminently adapted for unpopularity'). He retired in 1885 and worked on *Billy Budd*. Left unrevised at his death in 1891, this was published in 1924. There were signs of a small revival of interest in Melville's work towards the end of his life, but he died a largely forgotten writer. Critical recognition of him began in the 1920s.

'I love all men who *dive*,' wrote Melville. He had the greatest admiration for those whose thought challenged received ideas, who refused the comforts of accepted beliefs, who took risks and had little regard for public opinion. His own remarkable development as a writer and his related tendency to show disdain for his early work indicate his intellectual restlessness, although they may also mask what is consistent in his writing. Melville was a social critic whose concern for social justice is evident throughout his work. He was a pessimist who mistrusted the promises of TRANSCENDENTALISM but simultaneously found APOCALYPTIC cynicism insufficient for his needs. He was suspicious of any kind of absolutism but at the same time was fascinated by scientific, metaphysical, religious and mythological attempts to understand and explain the world. Melville both represents such quests as ennobling and satirizes them as futile. Throughout, Melville's writing is carefully managed, sometimes moving smoothly between radically different styles. For instance, he can encompass the tragic and the comic in a single work, while also demonstrating his mastery of explicative, rhapsodic, meditative and scientific prose styles. At his best, Melville achieved exactly what he revered in other writers such as Hawthorne and Shakespeare – what he called (with a keen awareness of the phrase's paradox) 'the great Art of Telling the Truth'.

Further reading

The Melville Log (1969) by Jay Leyda; *Herman Melville: A Biography, 1919–1851* (1996) by Hershel Parker, and *Subversive Genealogy* (1983) by Michael Paul Rogin. Criticism includes *A Companion to Melville Studies* (1986), edited by John Bryant; *Melville's Later Novels* (1986) by William B. Dillingham; *Melville's Thematics of Form* (1968) by Edgar A. Dryden; *Symbolism and American Literature* (1953) by Charles Feidelson, Jr, and *Shadow over the Promised Land* (1980) by Carolyn L. Karcher.

Mesmerism   Technique of inducing a trance-like state, named after the Austrian physician Franz Anton Mesmer (1734–1815). Mesmer believed in the existence of 'animal magnetism', a force that originates in the stars, permeates the universe and influences individual actions. He believed that he possessed the gift of manipulating this force, and that it could be controlled for therapeutic purposes. Although mesmerism was scientifically suspect and often denounced as fraudulent, it was an important forerunner of hypnotism in permitting access to the unconscious.

Mesmerism was popular in the United States in the 19th century, both as a subject for exhibitions and as a therapeutic practice. Edgar Allan POE was especially interested in it, and it appears prominently in some of his work, notably in the stories 'Mesmeric Revelation' (1844) and 'The Facts in the Case of M. Valdemar' (1845).

Metafiction   Fiction that is concerned with fiction, that is, in which the nature of fiction itself is explored as a subject of the text. Rather than concealing literary artifice, the metafictional author exposes it. This strategy may have various effects. While often being used for comic or playful purposes, it may also work in making the reader self-conscious about fiction as a medium, emphasizing that no medium is natural or transparent, and, in some cases, that reality itself is determined by language and convention, and readers should be aware of their own positioning in language.

In its broadest terms, metafiction has a long international history that includes the work of the 18th century Irish-born writer Laurence Sterne, and in American literature, some of the narratives of Edgar Allan POE, Nathaniel HAWTHORNE and Herman MELVILLE. However, metafiction is usually regarded as an anti-REALIST POSTMODERNIST technique originating in the 1960s. Vladimir Nabokov (1899–1977) and the Argentinian writer Jorge Luis Borges (1899–1986) were important influences on those writers who have been most associated with metafiction in American literature: John Barth (b. 1930), Donald Barthelme (1931–89), Thomas PYNCHON and, to a lesser extent, Kurt Vonnegut (b. 1922) and Robert Coover (b. 1932). Pynchon's *The Crying of Lot 49* (1966) and Barth's *Lost in the Funhouse* (1968) and *Chimera* (1972) are among the key works of metafiction, along with Barthelme's short stories.

Further reading

Metafiction (1995) edited by Mark Currie; *Black Metafiction* (1997) by Madelyn Jablon; *The Metafictional Muse* (1982) by Larry McCaffery, and *Metafiction* (1984) by Patricia Waugh.

Metaphysical poetry   Style of poetry characterized by ingenuity, wit and bold, extravagant development of metaphor. The term 'metaphysical' was first used in a pejorative manner to describe the style of certain 17th century English poets, especially John Donne, George Herbert and Richard Crashaw. The metaphysical style was less evident in American poetry, partly owing to the PURITAN preference for plain style, but Edward Taylor (1645–1729) used it. T. S. ELIOT's praise for the metaphysical poets in the 1920s led to a new interest in their work, and their influence is evident in the bold images of his early poetry. The work of various poets, such as Joyce Kilmer (1886–1918) and Louise Bogan (1897–1970), has been considered metaphysical.

Mexican War   War between Mexico and the United States which had far-reaching consequences for the growth of the Union. Hostilities began with Mexican anger over the annexation of Texas in December 1845. After a series of incidents that the United States interpreted as aggressive, President Polk declared war in May 1846. The war ended after the United States forces captured Mexico City in September 1847 and the peace treaty of Guadalupe Hidalgo was signed in February 1848. Under its terms the United States received a vast territory of over 500,000 square miles, consisting of modern-day New Mexico, Utah, Nevada, Arizona, California, Texas and western Colorado. In return the United States paid Mexico $15 million and agreed to cancel further claims against it. The war made General Zachary Taylor a national hero and helped him to win the presidential election of 1848.

In spite of the resulting territorial gains, the war was costly for the United States, with over 13,000 casualties and a monetary cost of $100 million. It was also a divisive war in terms of public opinion. Though it was supported by expansionists who believed in MANIFEST DESTINY, Polk's political opponents, who called it 'Polk's War', condemned it. Anti-SLAVERY groups also opposed the war, fearing the expansion of slavery into any acquired territory (this issue led to the COMPROMISE OF 1850).

The war features in much writing of the time, notably in works by Ralph Waldo EMERSON and Herman MELVILLE. It is the subject of some of the poems in *The Biglow Papers* (1848) by James Russell Lowell (1819–91), and it is the starting point for the celebrated 1849 lecture 'Resistance to Civil Government' (commonly called 'Civil Disobedience') by Henry David THOREAU. (Opposition to the war was among Thoreau's reasons for refusing to pay his poll tax and consequently spending a night in prison.)

Millennialism   Term referring to the belief, held by a wide diversity of religious groups and movements, that God will return to earth in a 'second coming'. Evil will be defeated, and Satan imprisoned for a thousand years, during which time God will reign on earth over a society of justice and peace in a 'New Jerusalem' (or 'New Zion'). The belief derives from the Book of Revelation in the New Testament. While millennialism is an internationally held belief, it has had a strong presence in colonial America and in the United States. PURITANS, MORMONS, Jehovah's Witnesses, Shakers and Adventists are only some of the most prominent American millennialists, who see their task in America as one of preparation for the New Jerusalem. Since millennialism encompasses both a vision of APOCALYPSE and a vision of social justice it has been used to describe groups predicting the end of the world, as well as social reformers who may not be particularly religious in outlook. The Millerites, or Second Adventists, are an example of apocalyptic millennialists; led by William Miller, they convinced thousands of people that the world would end in October 1843. Conversely, millennialism is also a term used to describe a progressive, optimistic view of history and the future.

Miller, Arthur   Dramatist, born into a German Jewish family in New York City in 1915. His father's manufacturing business failed during the DEPRESSION. Miller attended the University of Michigan and wrote several short plays while there. He published a novel, *Focus* (1945), concerned with anti-Semitism, and won recognition for his drama *All My Sons* (1947). In its examination of a corrupt arms manufacturer, the play interweaves individual and familial concerns with public and political matters, in ways that would characterize Miller's drama. Two major works of American theatre followed: *Death of a Salesman* (1949) and *THE CRUCIBLE* (1953), his most-produced play. Both are ambitious examinations of the individual's relation to American cultural values. *Death of a Salesman* is highly innovative in terms of stagecraft, and realizes new possibilities for tragedy.

Under the atmosphere produced by MCCARTHYISM, Miller's long-standing sympathy with radical politics led to his being investigated by the House Un-American Activities Committee in 1956. His refusal to cooperate with the committee led to his being convicted of contempt, though he successfully appealed against this judgment. After the plays *A View from the Bridge* (1954) and *A Memory of Two Mondays* (1955) Miller wrote no drama until 1964. He married the film actress Marilyn Monroe in 1956, and worked on a screenplay, *The Misfits* (1961), in which she was to appear. They divorced in 1960, and although their relationship is obliquely represented in *After the Fall* (1964), it is only a small part of a play that raises significant moral issues, and Miller has long been reserved about the marriage.

Since the 1960s Miller's work has become increasingly wide-ranging in terms of subject and period, and explores Jewish identity much more directly than his earlier work. *Incident at Vichy* (1965) is set in Nazi-occupied France, *The Price* (1968) in contemporary New York, *The Archbishop's Ceiling* (1977) explores the situation of the dissident writer in Soviet Russia, *The American Clock* (1980) is set during the Depression and based on testimonies collected by Studs Terkel (b. 1912), *The Last Yankee* (1993) is set in a mental hospital, and *Broken Glass* (1994) is set in Germany in 1938 and is concerned with the beginnings of the HOLOCAUST. Despite the wide range of Miller's subjects, these plays share his abiding concern with questions about personal integrity under strain, with the role and limitation of individual responsibility, the human costs of compromise and the relation between private and public morality. His other writings include a short-story collection, *I Don't Need You Any More* (1967), *Theater Essays* (1977) and the AUTOBIOGRAPHY *Timebends* (1987).

Further reading

Arthur Miller: Social Drama as Tragedy (1985) by Santosh K. Bhatia; The Cambridge Companion to Arthur Miller (1997), edited by Christopher Bigsby; Arthur Miller (1982) by Neil Carson; and Miller, The Playwright (1983) by Dennis Welland.

Minimalism   Style of writing, especially in prose, in which expansive, elaborate and metaphorical expression is eschewed in favour of literal, direct, spare, even flat treatment of a subject. In American prose, minimalism emerged particularly in the 1970s, although its roots may be seen in the work of Stephen CRANE and Ernest HEMINGWAY. Prose minimalism is especially associated with Raymond CARVER, William Gass (b. 1924), Richard Ford (b. 1944), Tim O'Brien (b. 1946) and Paul Auster (b. 1947). In poetry, minimalism is linked with both IMAGISM and OBJECTIVISM, but is also characteristic of some of the work of William Carlos WILLIAMS, John Cage (1912–92) and Robert Creeley (b. 1926).

Minstrel shows   The shows originated in the 1840s and were popular in the United States and in Europe until the 1870s. The performers were white men in blackface, whose actions supposedly mimicked those of plantation slaves. Thomas Dartmouth Rice ('Daddy' Rice) was one of their originators, and other performers included Daniel Decatur Emmett and the Christy Minstrels. The format of the shows became stylized, with a first act featuring a comic routine, the second featuring songs and the finale being a dance or 'hoedown'. The comics in the first act would sit in a semicircle with two 'end men'. Tambo (with a tambourine) and Bones (with castanets), trading remarks with each other and with a central figure, the interlocutor. The songs were often sentimental, and some of the best-known, such as 'Oh! Susanna!', 'Old Folks at Home' and 'Camptown Races', were written by Stephen Foster for the Christy Minstrels. In spite of their offensive caricaturing, the shows were taken over by blacks after the 1870s and they provided a significant outlet for black performers.

The minstrel routine is frequently referred to in American writing, and the Tambo–Bones–Interlocutor relation is important in the poetic sequence *The Dream Songs* (1968) by John Berryman (1914–72). George C. Wolfe (b. 1954) utilizes the minstrel tradition in his 1986 drama *The Colored Museum* and it is the subject of the

1994 novel *Darktown Strutters* by Wesley Brown (b. 1945). In his 1958 essay 'Change the Joke and Slip the Yoke' Ralph ELLISON examines the tradition of black masking.

Further reading

Inside the Minstrel Mask (1996) by Anne Marie Bean, James V. Hatch and Brooks McNamara; *Raising Cane* (1998) by W. T. Lhamon, and *Tambo and Bones* (1930) by Carl Wittke.

Miscegenation   Coined in 1864 as a term of abuse denoting sexual relations, cohabitation and marriage between whites and blacks. Laws intended to restrict or forbid sexual relations between whites and non-whites existed in America from colonial times, and continued in sixteen states until the SUPREME COURT declared them unconstitutional in 1967. In spite of attempts to restrict 'intermingling', miscegenation was common, although it remained a largely taboo subject, and one that, for many, revealed the hypocrisy of whites in their claims to racial superiority and nullified the belief that there were essential differences between races.

Though commonly practised, miscegenation was considered dangerous because of the view that it 'stained' whiteness, as Thomas Jefferson put it, thereby weakening the white race. In spite of Jefferson's own extended relationship with his slave Sally Hemings, his *Notes on the State of Virginia* (1782) and his letters repeatedly emphasize fear of such 'contamination'. Mostly, laws against 'intermingling' were directed against relations between whites and African Americans rather than Native Americans, and this distinction sharpened with the racially driven defences of SLAVERY from the late 18th century onwards. Prejudice against miscegenation also intensified in the early 19th century with a growing belief in a hierarchy of races and in the species inferiority of the black. Some of the pro-slavery arguments exploited the fear of miscegenation by claiming that if the slaves were freed racial confusion would result; in this way pro-slavery groups characterized the ABOLITIONIST movement as supportive of miscegenation. During one of the debates with Stephen Douglas, Abraham Lincoln was careful to make a distinction between desiring emancipation and supporting miscegenation, conceding: 'There is a natural disgust in the minds of nearly all white people at the idea of an indiscriminate amalgamation of the white and black races.' Fear of miscegenation also created prejudice against the offspring of interracial relationships, with the mulatto or hybrid or 'half-breed' considered a monstrosity or a freak of nature.

The end of slavery by no means lessened white fears of miscegenation. In some respects hostility intensified, and LYNCH LAW arose partly from this hostility, supposedly justified by the need to protect white women from black men. During the 20th century anti-miscegenation feeling remained as a result of racial prejudice, though, again, the ironies involved in supposedly preserving racial distinctions in the face of the treatment of women slaves were apparent. (In a debate on the subject with a white Southern man, James BALDWIN said, 'You're not worried about me marrying *your* daughter, you're worried about me marrying your *wife's* daughter. I've been marrying your daughter ever since the days of slavery.')

Although miscegenation as a theme in literary works is now explored far less frequently than before, many writers have examined it, either directly or by considering the fate of the offspring of interracial relations. For those writing about slavery or during it, the focus is frequently on the appalling irony of there being laws against miscegenation while the rape or sexual coercion of female slaves by their masters was widely practised – and was made more reprehensible because children of such liaisons were also slaves. The absurdity of defending slavery on a racial basis when so many slaves were of mixed parentage was also pointed out: as Harriet JACOBS asked, 'Who *are* Africans? Who can measure the amount of Anglo-Saxon blood coursing in the veins of American slaves?' Writers have focused particularly on the children of interracial relationships, examining how their existence destabilizes the supposed binary opposition between white and non-white. The 'tragic mulatto' was once a common figure in American literature, and themes such as PASSING also often involve scrutiny of miscegenation. The relationships between black men and white women has been particularly examined by writers, for example by Richard WRIGHT in *NATIVE SON* (1940), Chester Himes (1909–84) in *If He Hollers Let Him Go* (1945), Ralph ELLISON in *INVISIBLE MAN* (1952) and Alice WALKER in *Meridian* (1976). Miscegenation is viewed positively in the novel *The Oxherding Tale* (1982) by Charles R. Johnson (b. 1948). One of the key earlier texts on the possible 'intermingling' of the races is *The Last of the Mohicans* (1826) by James Fenimore COOPER (1789–1851). Leslie Fiedler has claimed that miscegenation is the 'secret theme' of the novel, in which Cooper raises the possibility of a union between the pureblooded Mohican Uncas and Cora Munro, daughter of a European white father and a West Indian Creole mother who was 'descended, remotely' from an African slave. True to his time, however, Cooper disallows the relationship by having both characters killed, and extols the virtues of racial purity exemplified by Natty Bumppo, the man 'without a cross'.

Further reading

Dislocating the Color Line (1997) by Samira Kawash; Neither Black Nor White Yet Both (1997) by Werner Sollors, and New People (1980) by Joel Williamson.

Missouri Compromise   Passed by Congress in 1820, the compromise was the agreement by which the Missouri territory was allowed to apply for statehood. The compromise allowed the numbers of slave and free states in the Union to be balanced. SLAVERY would be permitted in the state of Missouri, but Maine would simultaneously enter the Union as a free state. Furthermore, slavery was prohibited in the LOUISIANA PURCHASE lands outside of Missouri north of the 36° 30′ parallel. The compromise was critical in the sectionalization of the United States over the issue of slavery and alerted many to the potentially disastrous implications that slavery had for the future existence of the Union; famously, Jefferson wrote in an 1820 letter that the Missouri situation 'like a fire bell in the night, awakened and filled me with terror. I considered it at once the knell of the Union.' The compromise was repealed in 1854 with the passing of the Kansas–Nebraska Act, and was declared unconstitutional by the Supreme Court in the Dred Scott decision (1857).

Moby-Dick Melville's novel was published in 1851, its English title being *The Whale* and its full American title *Moby-Dick; or, The Whale*. Although it was received without enthusiasm on its first publication, it is widely regarded as one of the greatest of all novels. Told by a narrator who asks us to call him Ishmael, the novel records his adventures as he goes to New Bedford and Nantucket to go on a whaling voyage, meets the harpooner Queequeg and signs up on the *Pequod* under the command of Captain Ahab. After the voyage starts Ahab reveals that he is seeking a white whale known as Moby Dick, which he intends to kill as revenge for a previous encounter in which Ahab lost a leg. To try and ensure success in the hunt Ahab has secretly brought on board a mysterious group led by Fedallah, a Parsee mystic. During the voyage Ahab becomes detached from humanity in his murderous and increasingly diabolical quest, which ends, after a three-day chase, with Moby Dick sinking the *Pequod*, and with the deaths of all of the crew except Ishmael.

Although based to some extent on an actual incident, an attack in 1820 by a whale that resulted in the sinking of the whale-ship *Essex*, and on legends surrounding a ferocious white whale known as Mocha Dick, the novel ranges widely, richly combining different writing styles and exploring various subjects to do with whales and the whaling industry and making many references to ancient myths, various philosophies and religions, and contemporary politics. Described as 'madness', Ahab's quest is the extreme of the human desire for absolute mastery of reality and the natural world. In this respect he has been seen as a romantic Promethean or Faustian hero challenging the boundaries of human knowledge and human limitations; Melville's references to Shakespeare's tragic heroes are important for this reading. Ahab has also been seen as the extreme of human rapaciousness and destructive attitudes towards nature. While Ahab and Ishmael are sharply contrasting characters, with Ahab's isolating monomania contrasting sharply with Ishmael's humour, sociability and relativism, Ishmael too has a quest, of trying to understand the whale encyclopaedically, through history, myth and science.

The novel, which is dedicated to Nathaniel Hawthorne, includes the characters of the three mates Starbuck (the chief mate, who tries to resist Ahab), Stubb and Flask, the three harpooners, Queequeg, Tashtego and Daggoo, the cook Fleece and the boy Pip. Others include the ship's Quaker owners, Peleg and Bildad, Bildad's sister, Aunt Charity, and the priest Father Mapple, who preaches a memorable sermon.

Further reading

Ishmael's White World (1965) by Paul Brodtkorb; *The Wake of the Gods* (1963) by H. Bruce Franklin; *Twentieth Century Interpretations of Moby-Dick* (1977), edited by Michael T. Gilmore; *Critical Essays on Moby-Dick* (1992), edited by Brian Higgins and Hershel Parker; *The Trying-Out of Moby-Dick* (1948) by Howard P. Vincent, and *The Salt-Sea Mastodon* (1973) by Robert Zoellner.

Modern Language Association   Founded in 1883, the MLA is open to all engaged in the study and teaching of modern literatures. In 1921 it instituted an American literature division and it also fosters various associations dedicated to American authors. Its activities include the sponsoring of scholarly editions of significant texts and the publication of its two-monthly journal, *Publications of the Modern Language Association* (*PMLA*), and of occasional collections of essays on American authors and texts. Each December the MLA organizes a large annual convention with many workshops and lectures, as well as interviews for academic positions.

Modernism   Although generally called a movement, it is more valid to see modernism as an international body of literature characterized by a new self-consciousness about modernity and by radical formal experimentation. Several literary movements and styles, notably IMAGISM and VORTICISM, were fostered within modernism, which flourished from around 1890 until 1940. There was also a period of so-called 'high modernism', 1920–5.

Generally, modernists were driven by the belief that the assurances once provided by religion, politics or society no longer sufficed. This belief intensified after WORLD WAR I, when it seemed to many that history itself was coming to an end and that modern life was horrific, chaotic and ultimately futile. Some modernists, notably T. S. ELIOT, expressed a deep sense of loss and despair. However, others responded with a fresh sense of both the freedom and the responsibilities of the artist in a new age. Ezra POUND in particular envisaged the possibility of a new society to which artists would contribute meaningfully. Many modernists shared an ambitious, aspirational belief in the role and place of the artist in contemporary life, believing that art had replaced religion in providing coherence, guidance and insight into the human condition. For some writers this meant a fresh sense of the possibilities of ancient myths, and a revaluation of the contemporary meanings of myth was typical of high modernism. Others, especially Gertrude STEIN, Robert FROST, William Carlos WILLIAMS, Wallace STEVENS and Ernest HEMINGWAY, were less convinced by the relevance of myth, believing that the creation of meaning and coherence was the task of the writer, performed in opposition to false and damaging external impositions of order. This overall sense of the serious responsibility of the artist helps to account for the large projects in which many modernists engaged, for instance the LONG POEM or the EPIC.

The modernist period also saw a radical experimentation in literary form and expression. In part this developed in response to new insights provided by recently established disciplines such as psychology. This was certainly true of the STREAM OF

143

CONSCIOUSNESS technique, and in many respects modernist prose narrative begins with the complex later novels of Henry JAMES. Experimentation was also partly a response to the new forms of expression that were developing in painting, sculpture and music; another of modernism's characterizing features was the intense interaction between literature and the other arts. A further reason for modernist experimentation lay in technological innovations, such as the telephone and the cinema, which were changing the forms and the very meaning of communication. New forms were needed, as was the reinvigoration of established forms. Pound's famous exhortation 'Make it new' is rightly considered one of modernism's mottoes, but as well as demanding novelty he was urging writers to apply new energy to established forms. A considerable amount of Pound's earlier poetry was written in antiquated forms as part of his attempt to revitalize and update tradition. At the same time, most modernists believed that literature should challenge and unsettle readers, and much modernist work may be demanding and difficult, alluding to a wide range of learning.

American modernism was broadly of two kinds. One was cosmopolitan, and created by expatriate writers, especially Pound, H. D. (Hilda Doolittle) (1886–1961), Stein and Eliot. Based in urban centres such as London and Paris, these writers sought to internationalize literature, often making powerful connections between their work and a broad range of past literature. Generally, they had little belief in the usefulness (or existence) of an American literary tradition. There was also a group of non-expatriate American modernists, even though several of them did spend time abroad. Stevens, Frost, Williams, Marianne Moore (1887–1972), F. Scott FITZGERALD, William FAULKNER and Hemingway developed a modernist literature that was connected to American traditions, and the heavy concentration on region and place in the work of Stevens, Frost, Faulkner and Williams marked them as radically different from Pound, Stein and Eliot. What all the modernists shared was a belief in literature's importance in the modern world, and the need for it to be continually vital.

Further reading

Modernism and the Harlem Renaissance (1987) by Houston A. Baker, Jr; *The Concept of Modernism* (1990) by Ástráður Eysteinsson; *The Pound Era* (1971) by Hugh Kenner; *Foreigners: The Making of American Literature 1900–1940* (1981) by Marcus Klein, and *Modernisms: A Literary Guide* (1995) by Peter Nicholls.

Molly Maguires   Secret organization led by Irish Americans, formed in the 1860s to fight the brutal exploitation of mineworkers in Pennsylvania and West Virginia. (The original Molly Maguires were a group of rural activists in Ireland and the name's origins are uncertain.) During a series of bitter strikes in the 1870s the 'Mollies' were suspected of a series of illegal acts, including the murder of sixteen people connected with the mines. Under cover, an agent of the Pinkerton private detective agency called James McParlan infiltrated the association and for 3 years gathered evidence that resulted in a series of trials in 1877. As a result, many members were imprisoned and twenty men were executed. The Molly Maguires have been frequently fictionalized, and they appear as 'the Scowrers' in Arthur Conan Doyle's Sherlock Holmes novel *The Valley of Fear* (1915).

Monroe Doctrine   Formulated in 1823 by President James Monroe, the doctrine was a statement of intent which helped to guide American foreign policy until the 20th century. The doctrine consisted of two principles: that the Americas are 'not to be considered as subjects for future colonization by any European powers'; and that the United States would not intervene in the internal affairs of European countries and their colonies. Although never ratified as official policy, the doctrine was important in effectively designating spheres of relevant influence for the United States and Europe.

Mormonism   The religion of the Church of Jesus Christ of Latter-day Saints, also known as the Mormons. The church was founded in 1830 after Joseph Smith (1805–44) claimed to have had a series of visitations from an angel called Moroni, over several years in upstate New York. Moroni eventually showed him where two inscribed golden plates were buried. Smith translated the writing on the plates and this became *The Book of Mormon* which, supplemented by Moroni's teachings and a series of revelations, forms the basis of Mormon beliefs. The book stated that one of the tribes of Israel came to America 600 years before the birth of Christ. The tribe divided, however, into two groups, the Nephites and the Lamanites, from whom Native Americans were descended. Mormon was a Nephite prophet who wrote down this history on the gold plates and prophesied a New Jerusalem built in America.

Mormonism grew rapidly and, in accordance with their belief in MILLENNIALISM and a desire for freedom in order to enact their own laws, the Mormons moved westwards. They first went to Ohio, then to Missouri and Illinois, where they founded a city called Nauvoo. Conflicts between the Mormons and others, though, resulted in Smith being murdered. The Mormons left for the territory of Utah under the leadership of Brigham Young (1801–77) and founded a settlement at Salt Lake City in 1847, where the church is now based.

The Mormons appear frequently in popular literature, such as Arthur Conan Doyle's Sherlock Holmes novel *A Study in Scarlet* (1888), and were often figures of mistrust because of their practice of polygamy (officially renounced in 1890), their attitude to 'gentiles' (i.e. all non-Mormons) and their secrecy. They appear significantly in *Roughing It* by Mark TWAIN (1872) and in *Riders of the Purple Sage* (1912) by Zane Grey (1872–1939). The WESTERN novels of Virginia Eggertsen Sorensen (1912–91) deal extensively with the Mormons.

Morrison, Toni (Chloe Anthony Wofford)   Born in 1931 in Lorain, Ohio, Morrison is a critically acclaimed author and a distinguished academic with a significant former career in publishing. She is the recipient of numerous awards and in 1993 she was awarded the NOBEL PRIZE FOR LITERATURE.

Morrison has written seven novels. Although each is distinctive in terms of theme, setting, historical situation and prose style, taken together they form an incisive inter-rogation of American history and of the relation of African Americans to historical circumstance. Often her focus is particularly on female experience, and she frequently explores the tensions involved in the conflict between 'African' and 'American'. Thus in her first novel, *The Bluest Eye* (1970), the child Pecola Breedlove desperately needs self-validation through alignment with valued elements of Euro-American culture which she has internalized. The tension between assimilative success and ethnic awareness is further evident in *Tar Baby* (1981), while the need to connect an African heritage and an American present is the perceived task in *Song of Solomon* (1977). Morrison has also focused on inescapable tensions within primarily black communi-ties, as in *Jazz* (1992) and *Paradise* (1998). There is a large historical sweep in Morrison's work, evident in *Sula* (1973), which is structured by given years between 1920 and 1965. She is also a creative and sophisticated user of existing narratives, as in her masterpiece BELOVED (1987), which utilizes the SLAVE NARRATIVE. While Morrison most often explores the experience of working-class or dispossessed characters, she does include middle-class experience, notably in *Song of Solomon*. Throughout her work there is a strong sense of neighbourhood as a site through which history is most meaningfully expressed.

Morrison's prose style is complex, intricate and sometimes dense, having affinities with that of FAULKNER, though she also makes occasional use of MAGIC REALISM. In 1991 she published *Playing in the Dark: Whiteness and the Literary Imagination*, an impor-tant work of criticism in which she eloquently argues for the presence of a potentially destabilizing blackness in white American literature.

Further reading

The Aesthetics of Toni Morrison (2000) edited by Marc C. Conner; Toni Morrison's Fiction (1996), by Jan Furman; Toni Morrison (1993), edited by Henry Louis Gates, Jr and K. A. Appiah; Toni Morrison's Fiction (2000), edited by David L. Middleton; Toni Morrison (2000) by Linden Peach, and Conversations with Toni Morrison (1994) by Danille Taylor-Guthrie.

Muckraking   Type of investigative journalism that flourished in the period 1902–12 and which had a counterpart in the novel of social protest. Muckraking journalism, which developed from YELLOW JOURNALISM, was typically concerned with the exposure of abuses, corruption or injustice in industry and politics. The muckraking novel shared this aim, and was usually written in a REALIST style, with the aim of informing the reader of abuses with a view to reform. *The Jungle* (1906) by Upton Sinclair (1878–1968) is the exemplary muckraking novel. Set in Chicago, it exposes the exploitative, corrupt and unhygienic practices in the stockyards. A best-seller, the novel contributed to the reform of laws governing the meat industry. David Graham Phillips (1867–1911), Robert Herrick (1868–1938) and Brand Whitlock (1869–1934) were leading muckraking novelists. Influential muckraking journalists included Ida

Minerva Tarbell (1857–1944), Lincoln Steffens (1866–1936), Ray Stannard Baker (1870–1946) and Samuel Hopkins Adams (1871–1958). The term 'muckraker' derives from a disapproving 1906 speech by Theodore Roosevelt in which he borrowed a term used in John Bunyan's *The Pilgrim's Progress* (1684).

NAACP (National Association for the Advancement of Colored People)
The NAACP is the oldest still extant organization dedicated to the advancement of African Americans in the United States. It was founded in 1909 after a series of violent race riots (including one in Lincoln's birthplace, Springfield, Illinois) and was pledged to work for the social equality of blacks. It campaigned particularly against LYNCH LAW and SEGREGATION, and for equal voting rights and better educational opportunities for blacks. At first it was mainly a white organization but this changed quickly and many important African American intellectuals, such as W. E. B. Du Bois, were key members. The NAACP has been particularly involved in the legal defence of black rights, and it was instrumental in the crucial 1954 Supreme Court BROWN v. BOARD OF EDUCATION OF TOPEKA decision, by which racial segregation in public schools was declared unconstitutional.

Narrative of the Life of Frederick Douglass, An American Slave, Written by Himself One of the classic SLAVE NARRATIVES, first published in 1845. The *Narrative* was written for the ABOLITIONIST cause and was a best-selling work. In it DOUGLASS relates his experiences of SLAVERY, into which he was born in Maryland in 1818, and his escape to freedom in 1838. The work was critically neglected until the 1960s.

While scholars have authenticated the incidents described in the *Narrative*, Douglass carefully shapes these and imaginatively uses recurrent imagery to foreground particular themes. Among these is the demonstration of 'how a man was made a slave'. Contrary to contemporary pro-slavery arguments, Douglass demonstrates, there is no racial characteristic in Africans making them suitable for slavery; he relates the loss of family and sense of self that lead to the brutalization of the human into the condition of the slave. Douglass also attacks the biblical justifications for slavery, claiming that 'religious slaveholders are the worst' and arguing that slavery morally contaminates the whites engaged in it. Much of the writing is vivid and powerful, particularly the description of the whipping of Aunt Hester and the fight that Douglass has with Covey, a 'slave-breaker' to whom he is hired out.

In emphasizing the achievement of self-reliance and manhood, the *Narrative* is comparable to a success narrative. Notably, though, in relating his struggles to become literate (at a time when it was forbidden to teach a slave to read and write), Douglass emphasizes that literacy did not bring him a sense of freedom. This, he says, emerged after the fight with Covey, which provided him with a true sense of manhood.

Further reading

To Tell a Free Story (1986) by William L. Andrews; *The Journey Back* (1980) by Houston A. Baker, Jr; *Frederick Douglass' Narrative* (1988), edited by Harold Bloom; *Prison Literature in America* (1989) by H. Bruce Franklin, and *Frederick Douglass: New Literary and Historical Essays* (1990), edited by Eric Sundquist.

Nashoba Community Located in Tennessee close to present-day Memphis, the community was founded in 1825 by the controversial reformer Frances Wright (1795–1852) in order to demonstrate the practicality of emancipating slaves. With some abolitionist support, thirty slaves were purchased then conditionally emancipated to work the land. Although Wright hoped to show that freed slaves would be industrious and socially responsible, the climate and the conditions led to failure. The community was dissolved in 1830 and the slaves were fully emancipated and resettled in Haiti. Nashoba is described in Frances Trollope's *Domestic Manners of the Americans* (1832).

Nat Turner's Revolt The slave and religious leader Nat Turner (1800–1831) led a group of about seventy slaves in a revolt in August 1831 in Southampton County, Virginia. Although the state militia swiftly quelled the revolt in a few days, an estimated fifty-nine whites were killed during it. Turner evaded arrest for about 2 months but was captured, tried and hanged in November 1831. Turner's insurrection, the most successful slave revolt, shocked and alarmed slave-owners, challenging the view that their slaves were complacent. Consequent hysteria led to the killing of innocent slaves and to repressive measures, including an increase of night patrols and proscriptions on slave education and assembly. (The closing of slave churches is referred to in Harriet Jacobs's *Incidents in the Life of a Slave Girl* (1861).) The charismatic figure of Turner was an inspiration for many contemporaries and for later generations of blacks, offering a militant version of Christian faith to counteract its supposed fostering of meek submissiveness.

Writers have often represented or considered Turner's revolt, beginning as early as 1831 with *The Confessions of Nat Turner to the Public* by Thomas R. Gray (a white lawyer who visited Turner in prison before his execution) and including the essay 'Nat Turner's Insurrection' (1861) by Thomas Wentworth Higginson (1823–1911). Fiction about the revolt includes *Dred: A Tale of the Great Dismal Swamp*, by Harriet Beecher Stowe (1856) and *The Confessions of Nat Turner* (1967) by William Styron (b. 1925). Styron's novel was controversial because of the use of a first-person narration by a white author. *Nat Turner Before the Bar of Judgement* (1999) by Mary Kemp Davis is a valuable survey of accounts of the Turner revolt.

National Book Awards Prestigious awards presented to authors of what are judged to be the best books of the year in the categories of fiction, poetry, young people's literature and non-fiction. The awards were established in 1950 by a consortium of publishing industry associations: the American Book Publishers Council, the American Booksellers Association, and the Book Manufacturers Institute. Only books written by Americans and published by American publishers are eligible for the awards, which carry a monetary value of $10,000. Between 1980 and 1987 the awards were known as the American Book Awards of the Association of American Booksellers, and the number of categories for awards has varied considerably. The award for young people's literature was introduced in 1996.

Native American literature While Native American cultures have a considerable ORAL TRADITION, Native American writing in English begins in the 17th century. It is therefore, to use Gerald Vizenor's term, a 'postindinan' literature, emerging only after the entry of Europeans into the American continent and their naming of the indigenous peoples as Indians. As such, Native American literature is necessarily hybrid. It has characteristically confronted and explored the tension between what seems to be the necessity of assimilation into the dominant culture and the maintenance of ethnic identities. Although the first Native American writers were Christians, this tension was to some degree evident in their work, and came to be more obvious in many subsequent works. From the 19th century onwards, Native American writers tended to be highly self-conscious about writing within a culture in which Native Americans were seen as inconvenient, non-amenable to enlightened civilization, and members of a dying race. (Since the 19th century the white cultural trope of the 'last' or 'vanishing' Indian has been extremely powerful, and Native American writers have resisted it in particular ways.) As well as developing a literature that counteracts negative images and claims a presence in America, many Native American writers have considered it equally important to counteract the romanticized version of the Native American – the so-called 'invented Indian' as noble savage that originates in the 18th century and which has been revived both in the counterculture of the 1960s and the New Age movement of the 1980s. It is also important to bear in mind that despite the common use of the adjectival phrase 'Native American' there is no monolithic American Indian culture. In spite of some broadly shared elements, the beliefs, history and communal identities of various Indian tribes or nations differ considerably.

Much 19th century writing by Native Americans was in the form of essays and oratory. The first notable Indian writer is Samson Occom (Mohegan) (1723–92), a Christian preacher whose most important work is the *Sermon at the Execution of Moses Paul* (1772). Another prominent figure is William Apess (Pequot) (1798–1839), who wrote several polemics, notably the *Eulogy on King Philip* (1837), and an AUTO-BIOGRAPHY, *A Son of the Forest* (1831). One significant feature of early Native American writing was the collaboration of the white, as editor, mediator or, in some cases, the transcriber of an oral account into written form. This collaboration begins in the 17th century, when speeches of Indians were put into written English, but it continues well into the 19th and even into the 20th century. The authenticity and the trustworthiness of texts resulting from such transcription have often been questioned. This has certainly been the case with *The Life of Black Hawk* (1833), *Geronimo: His Own Story* (1906), and, notoriously, *Black Elk Speaks* (1932), which, edited by John Neihardt, has been especially problematic given the popularity the work achieved in the 1960s. However, it can be pointed out that since autobiography does not exist in oral cultures, then the writing of one is for a Native American always an expression of acculturation. This is certainly true of some of the earliest significant autobiographies by Native Americans: the autobiographical sketches (1900–2) by Zitkala-Ša/Gertrude Bonnin (Yankton Nakota) (1876–1938), collected in *American Indian Legends* (1921), and *Indian Boyhood* (1902) and *From the Deep Woods to Civilization* (1916) by Charles Alexander Eastman (Wahpeton Dakota) (1858–1939). However, these autobiographies were important not only as forms of history that allowed questions of assimilation and identity to be considered, but also in providing insight and understanding into Native American lives.

The 19th century also saw the publication of fiction by Native Americans, notably with the work of Yellow Bird/John Rollin Ridge (Cherokee) (1827–67), especially the novel *The Life and Adventures of Joaquin Murieta* (1854). But it is with the novel *Cogewea, The Half-Blood* (1927) by Christine Quintasket/Mourning Dove/Humishuma (Okanagon) (1888–1936), and its focus on the strengths rather than the difficulties of hybridity, that some of the concerns of modern Native American writing begin to emerge. The novel *The Surrounded* (1936) by D'Arcy McNickle (Salish) (1904–77) is also seen as a precursor of modern Native American writing.

In spite of the significance of past writing, it is undoubtedly the contemporary period, the so-called Native American Renaissance, which has produced the most exciting and engaging writing by Native Americans. While it is misleading to generalize, there are many shared thematic and stylistic characteristics of Native American writing since 1968. These include: an adaptation of oral traditions to MODERNIST and POSTMODERNIST literary styles; an exploration of the enduring relevance of legends and older stories; an examination of the contrast between European and Native American perceptions of time and history; a strong sense of place; a critique of INDIVIDUALISM; an examination of the situation of the Native American in contemporary America, including an emphasis on endurance through adaptation rather than assimilation; an emphasis on the variety of Native American identities, and an exploration of the legacy of oppression and injustice. To a large degree, the Native American literary text itself embodies the endurance of Native American cultures through adapting whatever is to hand. Significantly, some of the techniques associated with oral traditions are also characteristic of those recognized as postmodernist or MAGIC REALIST.

Broadly, the Native American Renaissance begins during the 1960s when a new interest in Native Americans led to the publication of anthologies of FOLKLORE, fiction and poetry. This sense of a renaissance was most evident with the publication of three influential novels: *House Made of Dawn* (1968) by N. Scott Momaday (Kiowa) (b. 1934) (the novel won the PULITZER PRIZE); *Winter in the Blood* (1974) by James Welch (Blackfeet) (b. 1940), and *Ceremony* (1977) by Leslie Marmon SILKO (Laguna). Since then a large number of important Native American writers have emerged. These include Gerald Vizenor (Anishinabe) (b. 1934), Paula Gunn Allen (Laguna/Sioux) (b. 1939), Simon Ortiz (Acoma) (b. 1941), Louise Erdrich (Turtle Mountain Anishinabe) (b. 1954) and Sherman Alexie (Spokane-Coeur D'Alene) (b. 1966). Some of the most important texts published since 1968 are: Momaday's THE WAY TO RAINY MOUNTAIN (1969); Vizenor's *Darkness in Saint Louis Bearheart* (1978); Welch's *The Death of Jim Loney* (1979); Allen's *The Woman Who Owned the Shadows* (1983); Ortiz's *From Sand Creek* (1981); Silko's *Storyteller* (1981) and *Almanac of the Dead* (1991); Erdrich's tetralogy of novels, *Love Medicine* (1984, revised 1993), *The Beet Queen* (1987), *Tracks* (1988) and *The Bingo Palace* (1994), and Alexie's *Reservation Blues* (1995) and *Indian Killer* (1996).

Some indication of the considerable heritage of Native American poetry has been made available through various anthologies. Many of the writers mentioned above have also published poetry, and in some supposedly prose works, especially by Momaday, Ortiz and Silko, there is a considerable poetic element, either through the use of prose poems or by the inclusion of lyric poems. Other poets are Carol Lee Sanchez (Laguna Pueblo/Sioux) (b. 1934), Lance Henson (Cheyenne) (b. 1944), Linda Hogan (Chickasaw) (b. 1947) and Joy Harjo (Creek) (b. 1951).

Further reading

The Sacred Hoop (1986) by Paula Gunn Allen; Early Native American Writing (1996) edited by Helen Jaskoski; The Voice in the Margin (1989) by Arnold Krupat; Native American Renaissance (1983) by Kenneth Lincoln; Forked Tongues (1991) by David Murray; Manifest Manners (1994) by Gerald Vizenor, and Native American Literature (1985) by Andrew Wiget.

Native Son   Influential novel by Richard WRIGHT, published in 1940. Set in Chicago, the novel's protagonist is Bigger Thomas, a young black man from the ghetto who is hired as a chauffeur by the wealthy white Dalton family. Patronized by the Daltons' progressive daughter Mary, Bigger spends an evening out with her and her friend Jan, a member of the Communist Party. Returning to the Dalton house he accidentally kills the drunken Mary. Terrified, Bigger decapitates Mary and puts the corpse into a furnace before fleeing. He confides in his girlfriend Bessie Mears but when she panics he kills her. Bigger is eventually apprehended, put on trial for the killing of Mary and sentenced to death. He is represented by Max, who tries to persuade him that poverty and the social injustice of his environment have resulted in murder. Bigger refuses to accept this, saying before his execution, 'what I killed for, I *am!*' The novel is REALIST and in the NATURALIST tradition, notably comparable to *An American Tragedy* (1925) by Theodore DREISER.

Native Son was a popular success, selling 200,000 copies in under a month. Wright later co-wrote a successful stage adaptation, and played the role of Bigger in a screen version in 1951. It was a novel that transformed the nature of African American writing, bringing in a new voice of social protest that was a precursor of the BLACK ARTS MOVEMENT. Critics have however been deeply divided over the novel's artistic merits, some denigrating its crudity, others seeing this as an essential aspect of the aesthetic that Wright was developing.

Further reading

Critical works include *Richard Wright* (1987), edited by Harold Bloom, and *Critical Essays on Richard Wright's Native Son* (1997), edited by Keneth Kinnamon. James Baldwin wrote two important essays on the novel, 'Everybody's Protest Novel' (1949) and 'Many Thousands Gone' (1951).

Naturalism Although its origins were European, naturalism was an important movement in American literature from the 1890s until the 1920s. While it is strongly associated with REALISM, in the shared emphasis on depicting surface reality, naturalism is more than a literary technique, involving as it does the philosophy of DETERMINISM. Naturalism is anti-ROMANTIC in emphasizing the limited ability of humans to impose will upon their own destiny, and also in devaluing the imagination's embellishment of reality. For the naturalist, it is the duty of the writer to present to the reader reality without illusion, to offer a scientific, detached view of it rather than to adorn or mislead or simply please the reader. The writer is also seen to have a diagnostic function, scrutinizing the ills of society, and the scientific element of naturalism has its origins in the theories of Darwin and, after Marx, in the development of the social sciences during the nineteenth century. American naturalism developed broadly in two directions, one examining the social and political dynamics of American urban life and the other examining the biological aspects of deterministic thought. The influence of Marx is frequently evident in the former branch and that of Darwin in the second.

This diagnostic element of naturalism derives directly from the French novelist Émile Zola, the most important figure in the development of literary naturalism. American writers, notably Stephen CRANE, endorsed this view of the writer's responsibility to analyse, and Crane's novel *Maggie, A Girl of the Streets* (1893) is a classic of American naturalism. In it he shows that 'environment is a tremendous thing in the world, and frequently shapes lives regardless'. The novel presents the process of the disruption of Maggie's family, her descent into prostitution and her eventual suicide, and considers this process as an inevitable consequence of the limited choices offered by the poverty of her New York environment. *Maggie* exemplifies much American naturalistic writing in its use of an urban setting, its refusal to condemn or sentimentalize Maggie's prostitution, its depiction of slum life and its objective focus on scandalous or immoral subjects. The supposedly immoral nature of naturalistic writing should not be underestimated; as in France, much naturalistic writing in the US was considered scandalous and liable to censorship or prohibition. Although Crane later moved away from classic naturalism his work maintained its diagnostic anti-illusionist element.

The naturalistic emphasis on how economic and social forces determine human behaviour was developed by novelists such as W. D. Howells (1837–1920), Frank Norris and Theodore Dreiser, while elements of naturalism are present in the works of Upton Sinclair (1878–1968) and John Steinbeck (1902–68), who both brought a progressive socialist political commitment to the movement. The novels of Dreiser, notably *An American Tragedy* (1925), and of Norris (*McTeague*, 1899, *The Octopus*, 1901, *Vandover and the Brute*, 1895/1914), were particularly significant in exploring the fate of the individual during the rapid industrialization and urbanization of the United States; naturalist writing is closely linked to American social change during a period of dramatic capitalist growth and the rise of big business. Social Darwinism forms an important part of naturalism at the end of the 19th century.

The deterministic concern with biological forces is generally less evident in American writing than it is elsewhere, although it emerges in the 1890s novels of Mark Twain (especially *Pudd'nhead Wilson*, 1894) and in some women's writing. For example, in spite of the romantic tradition in which she wrote, Kate Chopin explored naturalistic ideas. This is especially so in *The Awakening* (1899), in which she expresses through the character Dr Mandelet the naturalist view that romantic love is an illusion damaging to women's social status since it determines for them the biological role of motherhood. The illusion of love, he says, is 'a provision of Nature; a decoy to secure mothers for the race'. In spite of this, Chopin's heroine Edna Pontellier maintains a romantic view of experience and her suicide, in sharp contrast to that of Crane's Maggie, is a triumphant expression of individual will over circumstance. Other writers associated with naturalism include Jack London (1876–1916), who often explored the Darwinian contiguity between humans and animals and how the otherwise buried animalistic survival instinct surfaces in extreme circumstances. This is exemplified in *The Sea-Wolf* (1904), but is frequently a theme in London's Klondike stories, and distinctions between human and animal behaviour were often blurred in his writing, as in *The Call of the Wild* (1903) and *White Fang* (1906).

Although naturalism was most influential in the period 1890–1925, aspects of it survived into MODERNISM; Hemingway's early work, for instance, often uses the naturalistic concept of the individual who is being tested by extreme circumstance and learning to live without self-delusion, and realist writers such as Sherwood Anderson (1876–1941) and Sinclair Lewis (1885–1951), made use of naturalistic idioms in their analyses of human motivation and circumstance.

Further reading

The Beginnings of Naturalism in American Fiction (1961) by Lars Ahnebrink; *American Literary Naturalism and its 20ᵗʰ Century Transformations* (1994) by Paul Civello; *Determined Fictions* (1989) by Lee Clark Mitchell; *The Theory and Practice of American Literary Naturalism* (1993) by Donald Pizer, and *Documents of American Realism and Naturalism* (1998), edited by Donald Pizer.

New Criticism   Literary critical practice that developed in the 1930s and was highly influential until the 1950s. Opposing biographical and historical approaches to the literary text, the New Critics encouraged close reading that paid particular attention to the text's special language. Seeing the text as an autonomous artefact, their readings often concentrated on its formal elements and on its irony and ambiguity. The approach especially influenced the way literature was taught, but also encouraged a style of poetry that was detached, impersonal and highly formal. New Criticism was never a movement with an agreed set of shared principles or a recognizable membership, although several of its leading figures, such as John Crowe Ransom (1888–1974), Allen Tate (1899–1979), Robert Penn Warren (1905–89) and Cleanth Brooks (1906–94), had been involved with the AGRARIANS. Journals connected to New Criticism included KENYON REVIEW and the SOUTHERN REVIEW. The term 'The New Criticism' attained wide circulation after Ransom used it for a book title in 1941.

Further reading

Literary Theory: An Introduction (1993) by Terry Eagleton; *The Cultural Politics of the New Criticism* (1993) by Mark Jancovich, and *A History of Modern Criticism*, Volume VI (1986), by René Wellek.

New Deal   Programme of state intervention in economic and social affairs, initiated in two phases by President Franklin D. Roosevelt between 1933 and 1938. The primary aim of the New Deal was to counteract the effects of the DEPRESSION. In its first phase it was directed towards providing relief for the unemployed and stimulating the revival of agriculture and industry. In its second phase, after 1935, it was more concerned with broader measures for social and economic reform. These included some state regulation of banks and stock exchanges, the provision of welfare through social security, the improvement of working conditions, and the alleviation of the effects of unemployment through work-relief projects. Under the authority of the Works Progress Administration, support was given to unemployed artists and writers through the FEDERAL THEATRE PROJECT and the FEDERAL WRITERS' PROJECT. The term 'New Deal' originated in Roosevelt's 1932 speech accepting the Democratic nomination to run for the presidency, in which he promised a 'new deal for the American people'.

New Directions   Publishing company founded in 1936 by James Laughlin (1914–97) which was significant in publishing new work by Ezra POUND, William Carlos WILLIAMS and Tennessee WILLIAMS, and for reissuing work by Henry JAMES and F. Scott FITZGERALD in the 1940s.

New England Confederation   The first attempt by the PURITAN English settlers in the colonies to form a federation. The confederation was formed in 1643 and consisted of Massachusetts, New Haven, Connecticut and Plymouth. It was formed primarily for the purposes of maintaining boundaries and for defence from the Native Americans, Dutch and French, but it formed a significant model of co-operation among the Puritans. The confederation was dissolved in 1684.

New England Primer   An illustrated collection of religious verses, moral precepts and prayers for children compiled by Benjamin Harris and published in the early 1680s. The primer was PURITAN in ethos and had the dual aim of helping children learn to read and inculcating religious doctrine: through study of the primer the child would be 'both instructed in his Duty, and encouraged in his Learning'. It was an extremely popular book, with many revised editions published before 1830. Overall it is reckoned to have sold over 5 million copies and is often considered significant in the development of CHILDREN'S LITERATURE.

New Formalists   Group of poets formed in the early 1980s. Reacting against FREE VERSE, experimental and CONFESSIONAL poetry, they write in traditional poetic forms and metres, often in a non-personal manner. Some members are associated with the conservative journal *New Criterion* ('staunch defender of the values of high culture'), under the poetry editorship of Robert Richman. The group includes Timothy Steele (b. 1948), Dana Gioia (b. 1950), Elizabeth Spires (b. 1952) and Brad Leithauser (b. 1953).

Further reading

See the collection of essays *Expansive Poetry* (1989), edited by Frederick Feirstein, and the poetry anthology *Rebel Angels: 25 Poets of the New Formalism* (1996) edited by Mark Jarman and David Mason.

New Harmony   Community in Indiana founded on rational principles by the Welsh socialist Robert Owen in 1825. A German sect, the Rappists, had earlier occupied the site. Over 1,000 settlers gathered in New Harmony, but they could not agree on a form of administration and the community was dissolved in 1828. The community's publication *The New Harmony Gazette* was absorbed by the progressive journal *The Free Enquirer*.

New historicism   Term first used in 1982 by the Shakespeare scholar Stephen Greenblatt, describing a critical practice which emphasizes a literary work's embeddedness in other forms of discourse contemporary with it. There is no single definition of new historicism, which exists primarily as a practice rather than a theory; as Gallagher and Greenblatt have written, 'new historicism is not a repeatable methodology or a literary critical program'. Nevertheless, H. Aram Veeser has identified a series of assumptions held by its practitioners; these include the beliefs that 'every expressive act is embedded in a network of material practices' and that 'literary and non-literary "texts" circulate inseparably'. New historicist studies often focus on how a society's economic, political and religious ideologies function within texts produced in that society.

Further reading

The New American Studies (1991), edited by Philip Fisher; Practicing New Historicism (2000) by Catherine Gallagher and Stephen Greenblatt, and The New Historicism (1989) and The New Historicism Reader (1994), both edited by H. Aram Veeser.

New Humanism A critical movement that flourished between 1910 and 1930, shaped primarily by Irving Babbit (1865–1933) and Paul Elmer More (1864–1937). New Humanists stressed the primacy of free will, rationality, classical restraint and decorum, and argued that literature assisted in the formation of the individual's moral sense. They were especially critical of the DETERMINISTIC ideology of NATURALISM and of what they considered the excessive subjectivism of ROMANTICISM. The New Humanists influenced some writers, notably T. S. ELIOT, and also played a significant role in the development of literary studies in universities.

New York School Term referring primarily to a loose grouping of ABSTRACT EXPRESSIONIST painters based in New York City, and also to a group of poets in the 1950s who were stimulated by the concepts they explored. The poets of the New York School are James Schuyler (1923–91), Kenneth Koch (1925–2002), Frank O'Hara (1926–66) and John ASHBERY. Their poetry is characterized by sophistication, wit, experimentation, pastiche and a tendency to shift between formal and informal styles. Several members of the group were art critics, and O'Hara was curator of the Museum of Modern Art, where Schuyler also worked.

The New Yorker Stylish and influential weekly magazine first published in 1925. Harold W. Ross (1892–1951) was the founder and he edited the magazine until his death. Although it changed ownership in 1985 and a new editorial style was developed after 1992, it has maintained its high reputation. From the first, *The New Yorker* cultivated a sophisticated, informed readership with its articles on current affairs, reviews and regular columns. It became especially renowned for its humorous drawings, notably those by James Thurber (1894–1961) and Charles Addams (1912–88), and for publishing distinguished fiction, poetry and essays. Some important works first appeared in full in the magazine. Prominent among these are: *Hiroshima* (1946) by John Hersey (1914–93); 'The Lottery' (1948) by Shirley Jackson (1919–65); *Pnin* (1957) by Vladimir Nabokov (1899–1977); *Franny and Zooey* (1961) by J. D. Salinger (b. 1919); 'The Fire Next Time' (1962) by James BALDWIN and *Snow White* (1967) by Donald Barthelme (1931–89). Frequent contributors have included Thurber, Dorothy

Parker (1893–1967), John O'Hara (1905–70), Eudora Welty (1909–2001), John Cheever (1912–82), Elizabeth Bishop, Amy Clampitt (1920–94), John Ashbery, John Updike (b. 1932), Bobbie Ann Mason (b. 1940) and Jorie Graham (b. 1951).

Nobel Prize for Literature   Nobel prizes were instituted in 1901 under the terms of the will of Alfred Bernhard Nobel, a Swedish industrialist. The prize for literature, the most prestigious literary prize in the world, is determined by the Swedish Academy and awarded annually, with the announcement of the winner usually being made in autumn. Winners receive a gold medal and a sum of money (usually over $1 million). They are expected to receive the award in person in Stockholm and to deliver an address.

Nine American writers have been awarded the prize for literature: Sinclair Lewis (1885–1951) in 1930; Eugene O'Neill in 1936; Pearl Buck (1892–1973) in 1938; T. S. Eliot in 1948; William Faulkner in 1949; Ernest Hemingway in 1954; John Steinbeck (1902–68) in 1962; Saul Bellow in 1976, and Toni Morrison in 1993. Two naturalized Americans have won the prize; the Polish-born fiction writer Isaac Bashevis Singer (1904–91), who wrote in Yiddish (1978), and the Lithuanian-born Czeslaw Milosz (b. 1911) for his poetry in Polish (1980). Faulkner's prize acceptance speech is much celebrated. The Nobel Prize features occasionally as a topic in American fiction, notably in *Bech at Bay* (1998) by John Updike (b. 1932).

Non-fiction novel   Term used by Truman Capote (1924–84) to describe a work in which the author has utilized the resources and techniques of fiction while exploring actual events and actual people. Capote saw the non-fiction novel as a synthesis of journalistic story-telling and fictional exploration of character and motive; 'Journalism always moves along a horizontal plane, telling a story, while fiction – good fiction – moves vertically, taking you deeper and deeper into characters and events,' he said in 1966. *An American Tragedy* (1925) by Theodore Dreiser and *Hiroshima* (1946) by John Hersey (1914–93) are notable precedents of the non-fiction novel, but Capote's *In Cold Blood* (1965), a meticulously researched account of a brutal crime and the consequent execution of the killers, is its greatest example. Other significant non-fiction novels include: *The Executioner's Song* (1979) and *Oswald's Tale* (1995) by Norman Mailer (b. 1923); *The Black Dahlia* (1987) and *American Tabloid* (1995) by James Ellroy (b. 1948) and *Blonde* (2000) by Joyce Carol Oates (b. 1938). Although the distinction is frequently blurred, the non-fiction novel's sustained focus on actual events and its supposed fidelity to fact distinguishes it from works such as *Ragtime* (1975) by E. L. Doctorow (b. 1931), in which actual characters and events are interwoven with fictional ones and are not the central focus, and in which facts are altered. The possible conflict between imaginative freedom and responsibility to historical fact has made the non-fiction novel controversial, especially when a claim is made for accuracy. Such controversy was especially evident in 1999 after the publication of a fictive biography, *Dutch: A Memoir of Ronald Reagan*, by Edmund Morris (b. 1940).

Norris, Frank Novelist in the NATURALIST tradition. Benjamin Franklin Norris was born in Chicago in 1870 and at the age of 14 moved with his family to California. He was an art student in Paris before studying at the University of California and at Harvard. As a journalist he reported on the Boer War from South Africa (where he was captured by the Boers) and from Cuba on the SPANISH–AMERICAN WAR. He worked as a publishing editor in New York and travelled frequently to the West to research his fiction. He died in San Francisco in 1902.

Although Norris wrote a series of ROMANTIC novels and stories, his most considerable work was in the emergent REALIST style. His mastery of realism and his absorption of naturalism were evident in an early novel, *Vandover and the Brute* (written in 1895 but not published until 1914), and later in *McTeague* (1899). Concerned with a dentist's murder of his wife, *McTeague* is conventionally naturalistic in examining the biological and environmental determination of behaviour. Increasingly Norris came to believe that the novel should be an instrument for social improvement and reform. In his 1902 essay 'The Novel with a "Purpose"' he asserted, 'The muse is a teacher not a trickster.' His planned trilogy 'Epic of the Wheat' was to embody this belief in a detailed examination of Western agriculture and its wider effects. Only the first two novels, *The Octopus* (1901) and *The Pit* (1903), were completed before Norris died. Both reflect contemporary unease over the growth of big business and the monopolizing tendencies of the trusts. *The Octopus* involves a struggle between Californian wheat farmers and the monopolizing Pacific and Southwestern Railroad. The company is the 'octopus' referred to in the title, spreading its tentacles over the state. Set in Chicago, *The Pit* involves a group of speculators, one of whom is ruined after the failure of his attempt to monopolize the wheat market. Together the two novels represent Norris's most substantial achievement.

Further reading

Frank Norris (1969) by William B. Dillingham; *Critical Essays on Frank Norris* (1980), edited by Don Graham, and *The Art of Frank Norris, Storyteller* (1988) by Barbara Hochman.

North American Review Literary, political and historical journal, founded as a quarterly in 1815 and published from Boston. Early on, it published significant work by William Cullen Bryant (1794–1878), but it flourished particularly in the period 1863–89, during the editorships of James Russell Lowell (1819–91), Henry Adams (1838–1918) and Allen Thorndike Rice (1851–1889). Writers published in the review included Ralph Waldo EMERSON, Henry Wadsworth Longfellow (1807–82), Walt WHITMAN, Francis Parkman (1823–93), Henry JAMES and Mark TWAIN. After 1878 it was published from New York City, and following a decline in circulation it ceased publication in 1940.

Nullification   The doctrine holding that each state of the Union possessed the right to declare null and void within the state any act of the federal government. This doctrine was strongly promoted by both Thomas Jefferson and James Madison as part of a vision of the United States as a voluntary social contract entered into by each state. Nullification was considered by South Carolina in the nullification crisis of 1832–3, over its disagreement with the protectionist federal tariff policy that had been instituted in 1828. However, President Jackson refused to permit nullification, declaring it treasonable and thereby making an intervention that anticipated the pro-Unionist anti-secessionist campaign prior to the CIVIL WAR. Daniel Webster's 1830 congressional anti-nullification speech concluded with the phrase 'Liberty *and* Union, now and forever, one and inseparable,' which was revived in support of the Union during the Civil War.

Objectivism   Style of poetry that began in the late 1920s. Rather than seeking to transform objects into metaphors or symbols the objectivists sought to present the object as an autonomous entity without subjective interpretation from the poet, and they also emphasized that the poem itself was like an object. As Carl Rakosi put it in 1969, the aspirations of objectivism were 'to present objects in their most essential reality [and] to make of each poem an object'. Louis Zukofsky (1904–78) coined the term 'objectivist' for a special issue of *Poetry* in 1931. Objectivism was not so much a movement as a loose grouping of individuals; leading figures were Zukofsky; Charles Reznikoff (1894–1976); Lorine Niedecker (1903–70); Rakosi (b. 1903), and George Oppen (1908–84). Oppen and his wife Mary ran the Objectivist Press (1933–6). William Carlos WILLIAMS had much in common with the objectivists. Philosophically, objectivism is associated with PHENOMENOLOGY in its insistence on the recalcitrant integrity of the object. In literary terms it was anti-ROMANTIC and was both a development of IMAGISM and anti-imagistic, being distrustful of imagism's metaphoric basis. It also tended to have a radical political dimension. Some aspects of objectivist thought were influential in the development of LANGUAGE POETRY.

Further reading

The Objectivist Nexus (1999) edited by Rachel Blau DuPlessis and Peter Quartermain.

O'Connor, (Mary) Flannery   Novelist and SHORT-STORY writer, born in Savannah, Georgia, in 1925. A Roman Catholic, O'Connor attended Georgia State College for Women and Iowa University before returning to her family home in Milledgeville, Georgia, where she lived for most of her life. From about 1952 she suffered from the debilitating effects of lupus, from which she died in 1964. O'Connor's first novel, *Wise Blood* (1952), is often considered her best. It explores the nature of religious belief through the central character, Hazel Motes, who attempts to make his life a living testimony to his denial of faith, founding the 'Church Without Christ'. The story's grotesque elements are matched by a writing style that brilliantly encompasses the comic and the serious. Similar themes are developed in O'Connor's second novel, *The Violent Bear It Away* (1960), in which Francis Marion Tarwater, like Motes, tries violently to deny his religious vocation but eventually fulfils his destiny as a prophet. Two critically acclaimed short-story collections, *A Good Man is Hard to Find* (1955) and *Everything that Rises Must Converge* (1965), firmly fixed O'Connor's reputation as a major exponent of SOUTHERN GOTHIC, characteristically using the rural South as a setting. Although typically represented as a religious writer whose primary subject is the role of faith in contemporary life, O'Connor was also deeply concerned with racial injustice and intolerance.

Further reading

The Art and Vision of Flannery O'Connor (1989) by Robert Brinkmeyer; Flannery O'Connor and the Mystery of Love (1989) by Richard Giannone, and Flannery O'Connor and the Language of Apocalypse (1986) by Edward Kessler. The Habit of Being (1979), edited by Sally Fitzgerald, is a valuable collection of O'Connor's letters.

One-drop rule   The ruling that 'one drop' of black blood disallows a person from being legally defined as white. The rule is inherently racist, because it derives from a belief in a hierarchy of races with the 'white' at the top, and therefore liable to 'contamination' or 'weakening' through MISCEGENATION, and because in a racially unequal society it seeks to preserve a set of privileges and benefits that are perquisites of whiteness. The rule also depends on the essentialist idea that race is an innate biological fact rather than a social construction.

Some way of defining the 'color-line' (the symbolic division between racial groups) was essential from colonial times onwards, because racist laws restricted citizenship, voting and property rights, determined who could be enslaved, and forbade interracial marriage. Attempts were repeatedly made to codify the proportion of 'black blood' that legally determined blackness, but in a great many cases where ancestry might be unknown, simple appearance of whiteness might be sufficient to ensure white legal status.

Such racial classification based on 'blood' has been and continues to be controversial and also potentially absurd. In 1983 Susie Guillory Phipps failed in her attempt to be classified as white, rather than black, because under Louisiana state law anyone with one thirty-second of 'Negro blood' is legally black. In literature, the one-drop rule has frequently been exposed as a dangerous fiction or satirized. *Pudd'nhead Wilson* (1894) by Mark TWAIN mordantly satirizes its absurdity, focusing on the character Roxy who is enslaved in spite of being one-sixteenth black, and her son (known as Tom) who, since the condition of being a slave was determined by the mother's status, is enslaved despite being one thirty-second black.

O'Neill, Eugene   Dramatist, born in New York in 1888 to Irish-American parents. His father was a renowned stage actor, and O'Neill spent much of his childhood travelling as his father toured. He briefly attended Princeton University but left and spent five years travelling and working as an ordinary seaman and at other jobs. During this period he drank heavily, and attempted suicide. In 1912 he contracted tuberculosis and was confined to a sanatorium for 6 months. It was immediately after this that he began writing drama, taking a course in playwriting at Harvard University. After several plays produced by the Provincetown Players, his first real success came with *Beyond the Horizon* in 1920, and he was soon an established dramatist with a considerable international reputation. The THEATRE GUILD, of which he was a founder member, produced many of his works. O'Neill wrote over thirty plays, among them the most important works of American theatre. These include: *The Emperor Jones* (1920); *Anna Christie* (1921); *The Hairy Ape* (1922); *All God's Chillun Got Wings* (1924); *Desire Under the Elms* (1924); *Strange Interlude* (1928); the three plays in *Mourning Becomes Electra* (1931), and *The Iceman Cometh* (written 1939, performed 1946). The relations between O'Neill and his father, mother and brother are explored in his corrosively AUTOBIOGRAPHICAL masterpiece LONG DAY'S JOURNEY INTO NIGHT (written 1940, published 1956). One of his planned projects was a cycle of eleven plays tracing the history of an American family from colonial times to the 20th century, although he completed only two of the plays. O'Neill was awarded the NOBEL PRIZE FOR LITERATURE in 1936, the only American dramatist to win the award. He led a turbulent and sometimes tragic personal life; he married three times, was estranged from his daughter, one of his two sons committed suicide and the other became mentally unstable. Towards the end of his life O'Neill suffered from a form of paralysis that made writing physically difficult. He became increasingly reclusive and died in Boston in 1953.

O'Neill was the first major American dramatist. He modernized American theatre, gave it an international reputation and exerted a profound influence on subsequent drama. Although his work was often experimental and EXPRESSIONISTIC, his most intense work was in the naturalistic tradition. He frequently created characters who require particular beliefs or illusions to sustain them, and explored the consequences when such beliefs are threatened or removed. His work is predominantly tragic, and one of his achievements was in maintaining the dramatic purity and intensity of Greek tragedy in a modern American idiom and setting.

Further reading

Eugene O'Neill: Beyond Mourning and Tragedy (1999) by Stephen Black; *Contour in Time: The Plays of Eugene O'Neill* (1987) by Travis Bogard; *The Plays of Eugene O'Neill* (1985) by Virginia Floyd, and *Eugene O'Neill's Century* (1991), edited by Richard F. Moorton, Jr. *O'Neill* (revised edition, 2000) by Arthur and Barbara Gelb is a comprehensive biography.

Oral traditions Although the oral transmission of culture is chiefly associated with societies without a written literature, various oral traditions have been important in American literature and continue to play significant roles. Oral traditions are particularly significant for HUMOROUS literature, the TALL TALE, and any kind of writing that interacts with FOLKLORE. But it is the traditions of AFRICAN AMERICAN, NATIVE AMERICAN, ASIAN AMERICAN and CHICANO writing that have been most prominent in maintaining and developing oral traditions in written form. For example, in the oral tradition of story-telling, the story (or poem) exists as an affirmation of community, does not distinguish between myth, history and memory, does not belong to one creator, is never in a final form (since each story-teller may adapt the story to ensure its contemporary relevance), may be improvisational, associative, and non-linear in its development, and has cumulative and adaptable rather than fixed meanings. These elements of story-telling have been of immense significance in the work of writers such as Zora Neale HURSTON, Toni MORRISON, Maxine Hong KINGSTON, N. Scott Momaday (b. 1934) and Leslie Marmon SILKO, who have each sought to represent characteristics of orality in written forms and frequently place special emphasis on the figure of the story-teller. Some contemporary poets, especially those who see their work as performance, also affirm the living importance of oral traditions.

Further reading

Oral Poetry (1992) by Ruth Finnegan; *Oral Tradition in Literature* (1986) edited by John M. Foley; *Retelling/Rereading* (1992) by Karl Kroeber, and *Orality and Literacy* (1982) by Walter Ong.

Outlaw The outlaw has been much celebrated in American culture, especially in FOLKLORE, the ORAL TRADITIONS, the DIME NOVEL, the BALLAD and the popular song. Although the outlaw tradition has much in common with stories of the English outlaw Robin Hood (always popular in the United States), admiration for the outlaw's daring and ingenuity develops specifically in WESTERN and FRONTIER writing and has been considered a specifically Western trait; as the English historian James Bryce observed in 1912, Westerners 'are tolerant of lawlessness which does not directly attack their own interests'. While many celebrated outlaws were actual historical figures, they quickly turned into legends. The James brothers, Frank (1843–1915) and Jesse (1847–82), Belle Starr (1848–89), John Wesley Hardin (1853–95), Henry McCarty/William H. Bonney, 'Billy the Kid' (1860–81) and the Dalton Brothers, Grat (1861–92), Bill (1863–94), Bob (1870–92) and Emmett (1871–1937), were among the most renowned frontier outlaws. In the 20th century admiration for outlaws was intensified during the DEPRESSION, perhaps in the belief that that outlaws were responding heroically to an inherently unjust society, or were driven to crime by poverty. Charles Arthur 'Pretty Boy' Floyd (1901–34), Clyde Barrow (1909–34) and Bonnie Parker (1911–34) are among the most renowned Depression outlaws, and the gangster figure is also largely within the outlaw tradition. During the 1950s the BEAT movement again made the outlaw into a heroic figure, notably so in the novel *On the Road* (1957) by Jack Kerouac (1922–69).

In addition to the considerable amount of imaginative literature devoted to actual outlaws, there is a strong tradition of fictional outlaws, among the earliest and most influential being James Fenimore COOPER's Natty Bumppo, introduced in *The Pioneers* (1823). As well as being staples of frontier and *noir* writing, outlaws recur in the fiction of William FAULKNER, John Steinbeck (1902–68) and Edward Anderson (1905–69). Bob Dylan (b. 1941) and Bruce Springsteen (b. 1949) often celebrate the outlaw in their songs.

P

Paris Review   Quarterly journal founded in 1953 by Harold L. Humes (1926–92) and Peter Matthiessen (b. 1927), and published in Paris and New York City. George Plimpton (b. 1928) has always been the editor, and others, including William Styron (b. 1925), have been advisory editors. As well as publishing significant poetry and short fiction, the review is especially renowned for its interviews with writers and it has published interviews with most major contemporary authors. Several collections of these have been published under the title Writers at Work.

Partisan Review   Founded in 1934 by William Philips and Philip Rahv (1908–73), who edited it until 1969, the review was at first explicitly associated with the Communist Party, and maintained a leftist position after it formally broke with the party in 1938. As well as poetry, prose and literary criticism it publishes articles on political and social matters. Delmore Schwartz (1913–66) was a co-editor from 1943 to 1955; the journal was mainly published bi-monthly but is now a quarterly published at Boston University. Wallace STEVENS, Vladimir Nabokov (1899–1977), Lionel Trilling (1905–75), Dwight Macdonald (1906–82), Saul BELLOW, Randall Jarrell (1914–65), Robert LOWELL, Norman Mailer (b. 1923), Philip ROTH, Susan Sontag (b. 1933) and Joyce Carol Oates (b. 1938) have been among its many distinguished contributors.

Passing The act by which members of a minority may surreptitiously enter and be accepted into a dominant majority group. Although it has been used to refer to various racial and sexual minorities, passing most frequently refers to the actions of African Americans whose skin is sufficiently light to enable them to be considered white. In a racist society the advantages of passing may be considerable, since belonging to the dominant racial majority provides better access to education and career opportunities and offers considerable material advantages. Although acts of passing may be seen as subversive on an individual level, they do in fact represent an acceptance of existing racial inequalities.

Passing has been an important theme in literature dealing with race. Some acts of passing during slavery are represented as essential acts of survival, as in *Uncle Tom's Cabin* (1852) by Harriet Beecher Stowe and in *Clotel* (1853) by William Wells Brown (?1814–84). Later African American writers often represented passing as a pragmatic action, perhaps as an extreme form of the ideal of assimilation but, tellingly, also one in which the status gains of entering white society might be offset by the loss of a sense of community, or in which the guilt of betraying one's racial origins is paramount. In this way, assimilative passing may be treated as a tragic necessity, or as an act that leads ultimately to lost identity and lack of individual fulfilment. Passing is the main theme of many works by African American writers, including *Iola Leroy* (1892) by Frances E. W. Harper (1825–1911) (where Iola, who could pass, refuses to); *The House Behind the Cedars* (1900) by Charles W. Chesnutt (1858–1932); *The Autobiography of an Ex-Colored Man* (1912, 1927) by James Weldon Johnson (1871–1938); *Passing* (1929) by Nella Larsen (1891–1964); the short story 'Passing' (1933) by Langston Hughes (1902–67); *Oxherding Tale* (1982) by Charles R. Johnson (b. 1948), and *Juneteenth* (1999) by Ralph Ellison (ed. John F. Callahan). Passing is also a key theme in Philip Roth's *The Human Stain* (2000). In addition to works dealing directly with passing, many novelists refer to it, for example, Kate Chopin, Zora Neale Hurston, Alice Walker and Toni Morrison.

Since the act of passing exposes racial identity as a social construct, some writers have taken it as a theme to explore the binary polarization of black and white and expose the potentially ludicrous aspect of racial labelling. This is evident in, for example, *Pudd'nhead Wilson* (1894) by Mark Twain, and both *Light in August* (1932) and *Intruder in the Dust* (1948) by William Faulkner.

Further reading

Slippery Characters (2000) by Laura Browder; *Passing and the Fictions of Identity* (1996), edited by Elaine K. Ginsberg, and *Crossing the Line* (2000) by Gayle Wald.

Pastoral Ancient mode in which rural life is represented as idyllic. The conventions of pastoral include praise of the simple life (usually in contrast to the complexities of urban existence) and the idealized depiction of shepherds. The mode is chiefly

European and pre-modern, and to some extent it was absorbed by ROMANTICISM, and varieties of it exist today. Pastoral has been less evident in American writing; PURITAN attitudes towards nature and the struggle with the land tended to discourage pastoral representation. There is a pastoral strain to some influential 18ᵗʰ century accounts of American life, such as *Letters from an American Farmer* (1782) by Hector St John De Crèvecoeur (1735–1813), *Notes on the State of Virginia* (1784/1787) by Thomas Jefferson (1743–1826) and *Travels* (1791) by William Bartram (1739–1823), and variations of pastoral are central to TRANSCENDENTALISM, the PLANTATION NOVEL and the WESTERN. However, pastoral has often been presented ironically, for instance in Herman MELVILLE's short stories concerning the hardships of rural existence, and in his novel *Pierre* (1852). Modern pastoral has been chiefly a nostalgic mode, expressing regret for lost simplicity or idealism, evident in the work of writers such as Willa CATHER and Garrison Keillor (b. 1942), and to some degree in the work of William FAULKNER and Ernest HEMINGWAY. F. Scott FITZGERALD makes powerful use of pastoral's elegiac mode at the close of *THE GREAT GATSBY*, where he invokes the simple innocent wonder of the continent's first settler as a contrast to the sordid, sophisticated present, and it is used similarly in Philip ROTH's novel *American Pastoral* (1997). Many modern idealized accounts of Native American life may also be considered variations of pastoral.

Further reading

The Environmental Imagination (1995) by Lawrence Buell; *Pastoral* (1999) by Terry Gifford; *The Machine in the Garden* (1964) by Leo Marx; *Nature Writing* (1996) by Don Scheese, and *The Green Breast of the New World* (1996) by Louise H. Westling.

Phenomenology   Philosophical movement that developed in the early 20ᵗʰ century, which aspires to experience and to mediate phenomena as they are, without the distortions caused by ideology, theory or preconception. Some aspects of phenomenology have implications for the study of ethics and alterity. Although they differ considerably, phenomenology is associated with the philosophers Edmund Husserl (1859–1938), Emmanuel Lévinas (1905–95), Maurice Merleau-Ponty (1908–61) and Paul Ricoeur (b. 1913), and with some of the early work of Jean-Paul Sartre (1905–80). In American literature, phenomenology has significant affinities with a non-symbolic, realist and empirical mode of writing, notably with the poetry of Wallace STEVENS, William Carlos WILLIAMS and the OBJECTIVIST movement.

Phrenology   So-called science in which specific emotions and attributes are linked to areas of the brain, and in which the character of an individual may be determined from a 'reading' of the skull. Although it is now scientifically discredited, phrenology was extremely popular in the early to mid 19ᵗʰ century in the United States; Edgar Allan POE and Walt WHITMAN were particularly interested in it and used it in their writings. Poe's interest is evident in his emphasis on the mind's division into different sections, and also in some of the descriptions of characters in his fiction, notably that of the head of Roderick Usher in 'The Fall of the House of Usher' (1839), and phrenology is central to his story 'The Imp of the Perverse' (1845). Whitman was friendly with two well-known phrenologists, the brothers Orson and Lorenzo Fowler. He found in phrenology reassurance of the naturalness of sexuality and of the connection between sexual expression and health, both significant themes in his poetry. Whitman also took over the vocabulary of phrenology in distinguishing between 'amativeness', that is, heterosexual love or passion, and 'adhesiveness', that is, homosexual or 'comradely' love.

Pike figure Popular stock character of FRONTIER literature from the mid-1860s until the 1890s. The figure supposedly comes to the frontier or to California from Pike County, Missouri, but is also associated with Illinois, north Texas and Arkansas. Although typically used for comic purposes, he does to some extent represent the WESTERN's emphasis on the common man. The Pike is usually somewhat cunning, acquisitive and keen to speculate, and is often the gullible and slow-witted target of confidence tricks and jokes; his speech is rendered in dialect for comic effect. The figure was popularized by the early poems and stories of Bret Harte (1836–1902) and by six dialect poems in *Pike County Ballads* (1871) by John Hay (1838–1905). Bayard Taylor (1825–78) describes the type in *At Home and Abroad* (1860). Mark TWAIN's allusion to the 'Pike County dialect' in the preface to THE ADVENTURES OF HUCKLEBERRY FINN indicates his indebtedness to the tradition.

Plantation novel Associated particularly with SOUTHERN LITERATURE, the plantation novel most often concerns the tranquil nature of leisured aristocratic life on the antebellum plantation. Although plantation writing appears in the 1820s and 1830s, notably with *Northwood* (1827) by Sarah J. Hale (1788–1879) and *Swallow Barn* (1832) by John Pendleton Kennedy (1795–1870), it was in reaction to *Uncle Tom's Cabin* (1852) by Harriet Beecher STOWE that the plantation novel emerged in the 1850s as a pro-slavery defence of the Southern way of life. *Woodcraft* (1854) by William Gilmore Simms (1806–70) was an influential example. Post-war plantation writers such as George Washington Cable (1844–1925) and Joel Chandler Harris (1848–1908) relied on and helped create nostalgia for the 'Old South'. *Gone with the Wind* (1936) by Margaret Mitchell (1900–49) is an extreme representation of the nostalgic plantation ROMANCE. The paternalistic view of slavery in the plantation novel has been much criticized. Plantation life is represented in a range of journals, notably that of Fanny Kemble (1809–93).

Plath, Sylvia Poet, born in Boston in 1932. Her father, who features significantly in some of Plath's key poems, was a professor of biology who died when Plath was aged 8. An outstanding student, Plath attended Smith College and then won a Fulbright

Fellowship to the University of Cambridge, England, where she met the poet Ted Hughes, whom she married in 1956. The couple lived in the United States until 1959, with Plath teaching at Smith. She published short stories in magazines, but her first significant publication was the poetry collection *The Colossus*, in 1960. Plath's highly formal, carefully organized poems indicated a significant talent, but it was when she began to develop AUTOBIOGRAPHICAL personae in her work that her qualities as a major poet became most apparent. In 1963 she published a novel, *The Bell Jar*, using the pseudonym Victoria Lucas. Strongly autobiographical, the novel depicts the mental illness, attempted suicide and recovery of Esther Greenwood as she is driven to confront the social limitations imposed upon her. The novel is usually considered to be of special significance in the development of women's writing in the 20th century. During 1962, living in England with two young children, Plath's marriage came under increasing strain, and after separating from Hughes she committed suicide in London in February 1963. Shortly before her death she had been writing the intense, often highly introspective poems that would be published posthumously in *ARIEL* (1965). Again using autobiography and psychoanalysis, Plath's late poetry has a directness and power matched by few of her contemporaries, and although the poems have a raw, wounded quality, their success depends on Plath's sure control of emotion and form. Other posthumous publications are the poetry collections *Crossing the Water* (1971), *Winter Trees* (1971) and *Collected Poems* (1981); a collection of sketches and stories, *Johnny Panic and the Bible of Dreams* (1977); *Letters Home* (1975), edited by Aurelia Schober Plath, and *The Journals of Sylvia Plath* (2000), edited by Karen V. Kukil (an enlarged version of the earlier edition).

Somewhat paradoxically Plath's poetic achievement has sometimes been obscured by the following her work has generated as well as by criticisms of her use of personal and public material. Significant aspects of her poetry have sometimes been overlooked by approaches that treat the poems as if they were merely transparent and unambiguous expressions of personal anguish leading up to her suicide. She is a lyric poet of great linguistic and formal control who uses female archetype and myth to explore public concerns, and uses a complex range of personae to examine aspects of the self.

Further reading

Plath's Incarnations (1983) by Lynda K. Bundtzen; The Art of Sylvia Plath (1970), edited by Charles Newman; Critical Essays on Sylvia Plath (1984), edited by Linda Wagner, and The Haunting of Sylvia Plath (1991) by Jacqueline Rose; Bitter Fame (1989) by Anne Stevenson and Sylvia Plath: A Biography (1987) by Linda Wagner-Martin are important critical biographies.

Pledge of Allegiance   Recited by American schoolchildren as an expression of patriotism. The pledge was devised in 1892 and was officially recognized by the United States government in 1942. The pledge reads: 'I pledge allegiance to the flag of the United States of America and to the Republic for which it stands, one nation under

God, indivisible, with liberty and justice for all.' The phrase 'under God' was added in 1954. The words of the original pledge are attributed to Francis Bellamy, an assistant editor of *The Youth's Companion*, in which it first appeared.

Plessy v. Ferguson   The SUPREME COURT decision of 1896 by which SEGREGATION was declared constitutional. The case itself involved a challenge to a railway company in Louisiana that maintained separate facilities for blacks and whites. In its judgment the court declared that the FOURTEENTH AMENDMENT to the CONSTITUTION was intended 'to enforce the absolute equality of the two races before the law' but that it could not have intended 'to abolish distinctions based on color, or to enforce social, as distinguished from political equality, or a commingling of the two races upon terms unsatisfactory to either'. The ruling that 'separate but equal' facilities were acceptable legitimized informal customs and practices known as the JIM CROW LAWS through which whites and blacks were kept apart in public transport, places of entertainment and other public facilities. The most significant area of segregation was in education, with the provision of entirely separate schools for blacks and whites. The Plessy v. Ferguson ruling was overturned in 1954 by BROWN V. BOARD OF EDUCATION OF TOPEKA.

Plymouth Colony   The first permanent settlement by the Europeans in North America, founded in 1620 by the separatist PURITANS, later known as the Pilgrims, who had emigrated from England on board the *Mayflower*. After initial hardships (it is estimated that about half of the settlers died during the first winter) the settlement was gradually established. It was absorbed into the MASSACHUSETTS BAY COLONY in 1691.

William Bradford (1590–1657), who was governor of the colony for most of the period 1622–56, wrote the *History of Plymouth Plantation* (published in full in 1856). The colony's early years have frequently supplied subjects for writers, such as Henry Wadsworth Longfellow (1807–82) in his 1858 poem *The Courtship of Miles Standish*.

Pocahontas   Generally used name of Matoaka, daughter of Wahunsonacock (known to the English as Powhatan), born perhaps in 1595 near what is now JAMESTOWN, Virginia. Chief of the Pamunkey tribe, Wahunsonacock headed a powerful confederacy of Indian tribes when Jamestown was settled. According to *The General History of Virginia, New England and the Summer Isles* (1624) by Captain John Smith (1580–1631), Pocahontas interceded to save his life during an incident in 1607. The story also appears in *The Historie of Travaile into Virginia Britannia* (written 1612, published 1849) by William Strachey (d. 1618). Although Pocahontas became friendly with the settlers, she was taken hostage by them in 1612. She was baptized as a Christian, taking the name Lady Rebecca, and married the planter John Rolfe (1585–?1622) in 1614. They had a son, Thomas, in 1615. The marriage resulted in a temporary peace between the settlers and the natives. In 1616 Pocahontas came to England with Rolfe and Thomas, where the 'Indian Princess' was a popular spectacle.

She died of smallpox in 1617, and was buried in Gravesend, Kent.

The actual circumstances of Pocahontas's rescue of Smith are extremely uncertain; some historians suggest that it was staged by Wahunsonacock, or it was part of a ritual that Smith misunderstood. Nevertheless the event and Pocahontas's conversion were enthusiastically transformed into a still powerful myth. Partly the myth is a ROMANTIC one, partly it involves the concept of the Indian who renounces her culture and chooses Christianity, and partly it indicates the potential for harmony between settler and native. Both directly and indirectly, the Pocahontas story has been the subject of much European American fiction, drama and poetry, especially in the 19th century. It was a popular subject for plays, such as *The Indian Princess* (1808) by James Nelson Barker (1784–1859) and *Pocahontas: A Historical Drama* (1837) by Robert Dale Owen (1801–77). The first novels in which Pocahontas features are both by John Davis (1775–1854): *The First Settlers of Virginia* (1805) and *Captain Smith and Princess Pocahontas* (1805). Other novels about her include *My Lady Pocahontas* (1885) by John Esten Cooke (1830–86). *Argall* (2001) by William T. Vollmann (b. 1959) is a significant contemporary version of the narrative. Pocahontas appears in many poems, for example: 'Pocahontas' (1833) by Lydia H. Sigourney (1791–1865); *Pocahontas: Princess of Virginia* (1841) by William Watson Waldron; 'Our Mother Pocahontas' (1917) by Vachel Lindsay (1879–1937); 'Cool Tombs' (1918) by Carl Sandburg (1878–1967), and *The Bridge* (1930) by Hart Crane (1899–1932). Pocahontas is also much represented in paintings.

Further reading

The Pilgrims and Pocahontas (1999) by Ann Abrams; The Return of the Vanishing American (1969) by Leslie Fiedler, and Pocahontas: The Evolution of an American Narrative (1994) by Robert S. Tilton.

Poe, Edgar Allan   One of the most influential of all American writers, Poe was born in Boston in 1809 to parents who were actors. After his father deserted the family in 1810, and the death of his mother in 1811, Poe was brought up by the wealthy Allan family in Richmond, Virginia, with a period (1815–20) spent in Britain. Poe had an uneasy relationship with the Allans, and his waywardness was evident in his leaving the University of Virginia in debt after less than a year and in his expulsion from the military academy West Point in 1831 after a short time spent as an enlisted soldier. For the rest of his life Poe's income depended on his writing, mainly as an editor and reviewer as well as a writer of short stories. He lived variously in New York, Richmond, Philadelphia and Baltimore, where he died in 1849. Although he had a reputation, heightened after his death, as a heavy drinker, a drug user and a philanderer, this legend has been much disputed. Poe and his 13-year-old cousin, Virginia Clemm, were married in 1836. Virginia died in 1847, and the couple were childless.

Poe's stories and poems were mainly published in magazines and collected in various editions. He was well known in his lifetime as a SHORT-STORY writer, literary critic and also as a poet, especially after the publication of his popular poem 'The Raven' (1844). While he published a novel, *The Journal of Arthur Gordon Pym* (1838), and an essay, *Eureka* (1848), which is simultaneously a PROSE POEM and imaginative scientific speculation, his influence and subsequent reputation stem primarily from his tales. These are traditionally divided into two types: tales of 'mystery and imagination' and tales of 'ratiocination'. In the former kind Poe builds on GOTHIC conventions and often suggests multiple, even indeterminate, meanings by looking beneath surface REALISM. He exploited both his fears and the fears of his readers in ways that have been imitated by innumerable HORROR writers. Stories such as 'Ligeia' (1838), 'The Fall of the House of Usher' (1839), 'William Wilson' (1839) and 'The Black Cat' (1843) belong in this category. Conversely, the tales of 'ratiocination' demonstrate the mind's capacity for rational ordering of the chaotic. Some of the stories in this category, especially 'The Murders in the Rue Morgue' (1841), 'The Mystery of Marie Rogêt' (1843) and 'The Purloined Letter' (1845), have led to Poe being designated the originator of DETECTIVE FICTION. Poe also had a strong interest in scientific discoveries, evident in many essays and, perhaps confusingly, also in a number of hoaxes that he wrote. The sharp division in his work between nightmarish horror and a belief in rational thought has often led critics to see Poe himself as a deeply divided figure exploring his own contradictions.

Poe's poetry has seldom received critical acclaim. Although he cultivated a lyrical-narrative style in the ROMANTIC tradition, his poetic effects have generally been considered clumsy and even trite. However, he had a remarkable influence on French writers, notably on the symbolist movement and on the poets Charles Baudelaire and Stéphane Mallarmé. His critical ideas about poetry appear in the lecture 'The Poetic Principle' (published 1850) and the essay 'The Philosophy of Composition' (1846), where he states, 'The death of a beautiful woman is, unquestionably, the most poetical topic in the world.'

The Poe Log (1987), by Dwight Thomas and David K. Jackson, and *Edgar A. Poe* (1991) by Kenneth Silverman are recommended biographical studies. Criticism includes: *Fables of Mind* (1987) by Joan Dayan; *Poe Poe Poe Poe Poe Poe Poe* (1972) by Daniel Hoffman; *Romancing the Shadow* (2001), edited by J. Gerald Kennedy and Liliane Weissberg, and *The American Face of Poe* (1995), edited by Shawn Rosenheim and Stephen Rachman.

Poet Laureate of the United States   Officially, the 'Poet Laureate Consultant in Poetry'. Position created by the United States Congress in 1985, replacing the post of LIBRARY OF CONGRESS POETRY CONSULTANT. The appointee receives a salary and is expected to attend certain public functions and to present a poetic work during the year. Robert Penn Warren (1905–89) was the first to hold the office, in 1986. Subsequent holders have included Richard Wilbur (b. 1921), Howard Nemerov (b. 1920), Mark Strand (b. 1934), Rita Dove (b. 1952) and Stanley Kunitz (b. 1905).

Poetry: A Magazine of Verse   Founded in 1912 by Harriet Monroe (1860–1936), the monthly magazine *Poetry* was one of the most important journals in the development of MODERNIST poetry and is still influential. Published in Chicago, and edited for a time by Ezra POUND, in its early years it published work by many of the most influential American poets, including Pound, T. S. ELIOT, Wallace STEVENS, H. D. (Hilda Doolittle) (1886–1961), William Carlos WILLIAMS, Marianne Moore (1887–1972), Robert FROST and Hart Crane (1899–1932). Some of the key poems of modernism were first published in *Poetry*, including Pound's 'In a Station of the Metro', Eliot's 'The Love Song of J. Alfred Prufrock' and (in a truncated version), Stevens's 'Sunday Morning'. Although the magazine had as one of its original aims the development of American poetry, it always had, and continues to have, an international outlook. The magazine also acts as an important review, and special issues devoted to IMAGISM (1913) and OBJECTIVISM (1931) were crucial in the definition of those movements.

Postmodernism   Variously defined, postmodernism can refer to a historical period that began in the 1940s, a style of literature, philosophy, art and architecture, or the situation of Western society in a late capitalist or post-capitalist age. The French theorist Jean-François Lyotard succinctly defined postmodernism as 'incredulity towards metanarratives'; that is, a scepticism towards the 'grand narratives' that seek to explain and plot human life and history. Literary postmodernism is generally characterized by features such as: a mixing of styles ('high' and low' for example) in the same text; discontinuity of tone, point of view, register and logical sequence; apparently random unexpected intrusions and disruptions in the text; a self-consciousness about language and literary technique, especially concerning the use of metaphor and symbol, and the use of self-referential tropes. Even though the writers most often associated with postmodernism may deal with serious themes, their work often has ABSURD, playful or comic aspects, and sometimes makes special use of parody and pastiche and of references to other texts and artefacts.

The American writers most typically termed postmodernist are Vladimir Nabokov (1899–1977), William S. Burroughs (1914–97), John Ashbery (b. 1927), Adrienne Rich (b. 1929), John Barth (b. 1930), Donald Barthelme (1931–89), Robert Coover (b. 1932), Richard Brautigan (1933–84), Thomas PYNCHON, James Tate (b. 1943), Leslie Marmon SILKO and Kathy Acker (1948–97).

Further reading

Paracriticisms (1975) by Ihab Hassan; *Postmodernism, or, The Cultural Logic of Late Capitalism* (1991) by Fredric Jameson; *The Modes of Modern Writing* (1977) by David Lodge; *The Postmodern Condition* (1979/1984) by Jean-François Lyotard, and *Postmodernist Fiction* (1987) by Brian McHale.

Pound, Ezra (Weston Loomis)   Perhaps the most influential poet and critic of the 20th century, whose work was crucial to the development of MODERNISM. Pound was born in 1885 in Hailey, Idaho, and brought up near Philadelphia, Pennsylvania. He attended the University of Pennsylvania, where he began a lifelong friendship with William Carlos WILLIAMS, and visited Europe on several occasions, developing a particular interest in the medieval troubadour tradition. After graduating from Hamilton College in New York State in 1905 Pound became a professor of romance languages at Wabash Presbyterian College in Crawfordsville, Indiana. He left after a minor scandal and travelled to Europe, publishing his first collection of poems, *A Lume Spento*, in Venice in 1908. In London Pound quickly became acquainted with major literary figures and published his second book of poems, *Personae*, in 1909. He played an increasingly important role in encouraging emerging talents, especially through his editorial positions on various journals, including POETRY, THE LITTLE REVIEW and THE DIAL. Although literature was his main focus, Pound was involved in all of the contemporary arts, and especially sculpture through his friendship with Henri Gaudier-Brzeska. Between 1912 and 1924, living in London and then Paris, Pound engaged in an enormous number of wide-ranging projects. He helped shape the work of important writers such as W. B. Yeats and James Joyce, encouraged many others, and worked closely with T. S. ELIOT on THE WASTE LAND. In this period he was closely involved in IMAGISM, published several more poetry collections (notably *Lustra*, 1916), wrote numerous critical essays and reviews and began his lifetime's work, THE CANTOS. He also developed what became a major interest in Chinese and Japanese poetry. In 1920 Pound published one of his major poems, 'Hugh Selwyn Mauberley', in which he examines what he sees as the role of the artist in modernity. Pound affirms that while the role of artists is to produce what is beautiful and lasting they must also be involved in the modern world as leaders and guides. In particular the poem looks back to the horror of WORLD WAR I and asserts that one of art's true functions is the prevention of such catastrophe. Although one of Pound's mottoes was 'make it new', his overall project was of invigorating a contemporary renaissance that would result in great art but which would also refresh and make the literature of the past contemporary; his vision was of an interconnected tradition of international writing.

From 1924 Pound lived in Rapallo, Italy. There he continued his considerable efforts on behalf of contemporary writers but he also worked in a more concentrated way on *The Cantos*. He also became increasingly concerned with economics and monetary reform, a concern that became obsessive and resulted in three books and numerous articles. He also supported the fascist leader Benito Mussolini, whom he saw as a kind of modern Renaissance prince who would forge a reformed society in which the artist would play a special role. Pound's increasingly hysterical criticism of usury, which he associated particularly with Jewish history and identity, led directly to a virulent anti-Semitism, which was expressed in radio broadcasts during WORLD WAR II. After the fall of Italy, Pound was arrested for treason in April 1945 by United States forces and imprisoned near Pisa for 6 months. There he wrote *The Pisan Cantos* (1948), containing some of his greatest poetry (the book was controversially awarded the 1949 BOLLINGEN PRIZE). When Pound was brought to the United States in 1946 he was declared insane and therefore mentally unfit to stand trial for treason. He was accordingly committed to St Elizabeth's in Washington, DC, a hospital for the criminally insane. There he continued to work and write, and he received many visitors; several poets have written movingly of visiting him there. In 1958, after the intervention of a group of writers led by Robert FROST, the charges of treason against Pound were dropped and he was allowed to return to Italy. He continued writing and working there, although only sporadically after 1960. He died in Venice in 1972.

Pound is an inescapable influence in the transformation and the direction of modern literature, although assessments of his own work will always be complicated by his extreme politics. While some critics have attempted to separate his aesthetics from his politics, this does a particular injustice to Pound himself, who considered the aesthetic to include a social purpose. At his finest Pound was one of the greatest lyric poets of the 20th century and among the most perceptive and forceful of critics.

The Collected Early Poems of Ezra Pound, edited by Michael King, was published in 1976, and a larger collected edition, *Personae*, in 1990. Pound's main prose works include *Gaudier-Brzeska: A Memoir* (1916), *ABC of Reading* (1934), *Make it New* (1934) and *Guide to Kulchur* (1938, 1952). There is much important writing in Pound's *Selected Essays* (1954), edited by T. S. Eliot (1954), *The Letters of Ezra Pound* (1950), edited by D. D. Paige, and *Selected Prose* (1973), edited by William Cookson. *The Cantos* were published in their final form in 1970.

Further reading

Ezra Pound: Tactics for Reading (1982), edited by Ian F. A. Bell; *A ZBC of Ezra Pound* (1971) by Christine Brook-Rose; *The Pound Era* (1971) by Hugh Kenner; *Ezra Pound: A Critical Anthology* (1970), edited by J. P. Sullivan, and *The Poetry of Ezra Pound* (1969) by Hugh Witemeyer. *Ezra Pound: The Last Rower* (1976) by C. David Heymann, *The Life of Ezra Pound* (1982) by Noel Stock, and *Ezra Pound: The Solitary Volcano* (1987) by John Tytell are valuable biographical studies.

Pragmatism   Philosophy in which the meaning of a concept is regarded as inseparable from its practical consequences, and in which a concept without practical consequences is considered meaningless and therefore unable to be categorized as true or false. Pragmatism is a notably American philosophy, having first been formulated by Charles Sanders Peirce (1839–1914), and then developed by William James (1842–1910) and John Dewey (1859–1952). Its most prominent contemporary exponent is Richard Rorty (b. 1931). Although there are areas of significant difference between these philosophers, it is generally true that pragmatism is a materialistic, anti-mystical and anti-metaphysical philosophy. It stresses, as Susan Haack has observed of James and Dewey, 'the concrete over the abstract, actual verification over potential verifiability, truths over Truth'. Pragmatism has been seen as typically American in its emphasis on the material, in the assessment of ideas according to their practical usefulness, and in its application to business and politics. It has exerted a powerful influence on many writers and is especially evident in the poetry of Robert Frost, Wallace Stevens and William Carlos Williams.

Further reading

'Pragmatism' by Susan Haack, in *The Blackwell Companion to Philosophy* (1996), edited by Nicholas Bunnin and E. P. Tsui-James; *Poetry and Pragmatism* (1992) by Richard Poirier, and *Consequences of Pragmatism* (1982) by Richard Rorty. William James's *Pragmatism* (1907) is a classic text.

Prairie   A considerable area of the United States, largely comprising what are now the states of Iowa, North Dakota, South Dakota, Minnesota, Nebraska and Kansas as well as parts of Missouri, Illinois, Ohio, Indiana, Wisconsin, Colorado and Wyoming. Originally grassland, and home to the buffalo that supported the way of life of the Plains Indians, the prairie was cultivated after the WESTWARD EXPANSION, and portioned and farmed as the West was opened up during 19th century. Settlement of the prairie resulted in the removal of the Plains Indians, not only by policies that led directly to their resettlement, but also by the whites' systematic destruction of the buffalo (virtually extinct by the 1880s), which was essential to the Indians' mode of existence.

The prairie is a typical setting of much WESTERN fiction, which often dramatizes competition over the land's ownership and future. Important prairie writing includes James Fenimore Cooper's novel *The Prairie* (1827), and the travel narratives *A Tour on the Prairies* (1835) by Washington Irving and *The Oregon Trail* (1847) by Francis Parkman (1823–93) (the prairie narrative was satirized by Edgar Allan Poe in *The Journal of Julius Rodman*, 1840). The prairie features prominently in the writings of Hamlin Garland (1860–1940), Laura Ingalls Wilder (1867–1957), Willa Cather, Carl Sandburg (1878–1967), Sinclair Lewis (1885–1951), and Marie Sandoz (1901–66), notably in *Old Jules* (1935).

Presbyterianism   Form of Protestant church organization, in which the church is governed by a committee comprising both ordained and lay elders, known as presbyters. Presbyterianism develops specifically from CALVINISM and effectively occupies a mid-position between the autonomy that CONGREGATIONALISM gives to individual congregations and the more hierarchical administration that characterizes the EPISCOPALIANS.

Presidents of the United States   After a popular vote every four years, the President is chosen by the Electoral College. Only U.S. citizens over the age of thirty-five who were born in the United States are eligible for the presidency, and (following the presidency of Franklin D. Roosevelt) no President may serve for more than two terms of office.

Presidents

1.	1789	George Washington	
2.	1797	John Adams	Federalist
3.	1801	Thomas Jefferson	Democratic-Republican
4.	1809	James Madison	Democratic-Republican
5.	1817	James Monroe	Democratic-Republican
6.	1825	John Quincy Adams	Democratic-Republican
7.	1829	Andrew Jackson	Democrat
8.	1837	Martin Van Buren	Democrat
9.	1841	William H. Harrison	Whig
10.	1841	John Tyler	Whig
11.	1845	James K. Polk	Democrat
12.	1849	Zachary Taylor	Whig
13.	1850	Millard Fillmore	Whig
14.	1853	Franklin Pierce	Democrat
15.	1857	James Buchanan	Democrat
16.	1861	Abraham Lincoln	Republican
17.	1865	Andrew Johnson	Republican
18.	1869	Ulysses S. Grant	Republican
19.	1877	Rutherford B. Hayes	Republican
20.	1881	James A. Garfield	Republican
21.	1881	Chester Arthur	Republican
22.	1885	Grover Cleveland	Democrat
23.	1889	Benjamin Harrison	Republican
24.	1893	Grover Cleveland	Democrat
25.	1897	William McKinley	Republican
26.	1901	Theodore Roosevelt	Republican
27.	1909	William H. Taft	Republican
28.	1913	Woodrow Wilson	Democrat
29.	1921	Warren G. Harding	Republican
30.	1923	Calvin Coolidge	Republican
31.	1929	Herbert Hoover	Republican
32.	1933	Franklin D. Roosevelt	Democrat
33.	1945	Harry S. Truman	Democrat
34.	1953	Dwight D. Eisenhower	Republican
35.	1961	John F. Kennedy	Democrat
36.	1963	Lyndon B. Johnson	Democrat
37.	1969	Richard M. Nixon	Republican
38.	1974	Gerald R. Ford	Republican
39.	1977	Jimmy Carter	Democrat
40.	1981	Ronald Reagan	Republican

41.	1989	George Bush	Republican
42.	1993	Bill Clinton	Democrat
43.	2001	George W. Bush	Republican

Progressivism Term used to describe a loose coalition of pressure groups that were active in the period 1890–1917 (sometimes called the 'Progressive Era'). Although it was never a single movement, progressivism generally advocated state intervention in social and economic affairs. It included various movements dedicated to enacting laws concerning TEMPERANCE, political corruption, child labour, women's SUFFRAGE and workers' rights. To some extent progressivism built on earlier populist movements, but it was never regionally or politically unified; some progressive groups were politically conservative while others were aligned with socialism. The presidency (1901–9) of Theodore Roosevelt (1858–1919) was especially associated with progressivism, during which various reforms were initiated. The Progressive Party, unofficially known as the Bull Moose Party, was founded in 1912, and was dissolved after unsuccessfully contesting the presidential election on Roosevelt's behalf. Two other shortlived 'Progressive' parties also fought elections, in 1924 and 1948.

Prohibition In 1919 Congress ratified the Eighteenth Amendment to the CONSTITUTION and passed the National Prohibition Act, widely known as the Volstead Act. The 'manufacture, sale or transportation of intoxicating liquors' became illegal from January 1920. The act was the culmination of a long campaign by various organizations that formed the TEMPERANCE MOVEMENT. It was not the first time that Prohibition had been enforced; since the mid-19th century individual states had made Prohibition laws, and during WORLD WAR I Prohibition had been introduced to preserve grain supplies. Federally enforced Prohibition after 1920, though, was on an unprecedented scale.

The enforcement of Prohibition and the consequent availability of alcohol varied considerably. Urban populations were supplied with alcohol either through bootlegging, that is, by smuggling, or through its illegal (and potentially dangerous) manufacture. Both activities were run by organized crime, and the bootlegger, the gangster and the racketeer were familiar 1920s characters. Often alcohol was openly on sale in 'speakeasies' (it is estimated that by 1929 in New York City there were twice as many speakeasies as there had been saloons before Prohibition). By the late 1920s Prohibition, which President Hoover had called 'a great social and economic experiment', was generally reckoned to have failed. It had criminalized what many had considered a normal activity, there had been many deaths from drinking illegally manufactured alcohol, and there had been such a growth of organized crime, gangsterism and police corruption that the very fabric of American society was threatened. It was repealed in 1933 after the ratification of the Twenty-first Amendment.

The gangster, the bootlegger and the racketeer became significant presences in American literature after the 1920s, and Prohibition forms the background to many works. At times it features prominently, as in THE GREAT GATSBY and in the writing of Damon Runyon (1884–1946) and John Dos Passos (1896–1970); elsewhere it is a more subtle presence. Certainly, much of the drinking that features in works set in the 1920s would have been illegal.

Further reading

The Great Illusion (1950) by Herbert Asbury; *The Long Thirst* (1975) by Thomas Coffey, and *Ardent Spirits* (1973) by John Kobler.

Proletarian literature   The conflation of class and race in the United States has tended to obscure a broad tradition of writing that focuses on the urban working class. Much modern AFRICAN AMERICAN and CHICANO literature, for instance, represents the dispossessed urban working poor and is part of a tradition of proletarian writing that begins in the 19th century. Particularly associated with REALISM, NATURALISM and MUCKRAKING, proletarian writing starts mainly with the New York stories of Stephen CRANE and is developed in the writing of Frank NORRIS, Theodore DREISER and Jack London (1876–1916), notably in *The People of the Abyss* (1903) and *The Iron Heel* (1908). Proletarian writing usually has the dual function of validating working-class lives and alerting the reader to unjust social conditions, while much of it also has a radical socialist or Marxist leaning. Twentieth century proletarian literature is especially associated with Upton Sinclair (1878–1968) and it develops notably during the DEPRESSION, with the work of John Dos Passos (1896–1970), John Steinbeck (1902–68), J. T. Farrell (1904–79), Clifford Odets (1906–63) and Richard WRIGHT. Between 1911 and 1948 the journal *Masses* (called *New Masses* after 1926) was strongly identified with proletarian writing.

Prose poem   Writing which is presented without the line-breaks characteristic of conventional poetry but which employs recognizable poetic techniques such as concentration of language, rhythmical effects and sustained imagery. With the notable exception of Edgar Allan POE's *Eureka* (1848), prose poems are usually compact, perhaps of a paragraph or so in length, and tend to have one thought or incident at their centre. The form has its origins in 19th century French literature, and was used influentially by Charles Baudelaire. Distinguished American practitioners of prose poems include Amy Lowell (1874–1925), Gertrude STEIN, T. S. ELIOT, Robert Bly (b. 1926), N. Scott Momaday (b. 1934), Charles Simic (b. 1938), Joy Harjo (b. 1951) and Maxine Chernoff (b. 1952). *Three Poems* (1972) by John ASHBERY and *The Burning Mystery of Anna in 1951* (1979) by Kenneth Koch (1925–2002) are long prose poems that extend the form's scope while exploring its paradoxical nature. The problematical genre of the prose poem was highlighted when Simic's 1990 collection of prose poems, *The World Doesn't End*, won the PULITZER PRIZE for poetry.

Further reading

The American Prose Poem (1998) by Michael Delville and *A Tradition of Subversion* (1992) by Margueritte S. Murphy.

Pulitzer Prizes Prestigious awards that have been presented annually since 1917. The prizes, which include a payment of $3,000 to each winner, were established in the will of the newspaper publisher Joseph Pulitzer (1847–1911) and are administered by Columbia University, New York. A panel of university-appointed judges determines the winners and these are announced each May. The number of categories has gradually grown since 1917.

There are twenty-one prizes in all, fourteen of which are related to journalism. The others, in the categories of fiction, drama, history, biography, poetry, non-fiction and music, are awarded for specific individual works rather than for an author's general achievement. Criteria for the prizes in drama, fiction and history include the specification that the work should preferably deal with an American theme, and the criteria for fiction, drama, biography, poetry and non-fiction and music specify that the work must be by an American author.

Pulp magazines Type of mass-circulation magazine especially associated with sensational fiction, and particularly with the DETECTIVE STORY, SCIENCE FICTION and mystery writing. Typically it contained serialized novels or short stories and was aimed at a masculine readership. The pulp magazine replaced the DIME NOVEL in the 1890s, mainly because of its considerably lower production and distribution costs. The process of cheaply turning wood pulp into paper had recently been developed, and, crucially, the pulp magazine qualified for lower postal rates than the dime novel. The first pulp magazine was *Argosy*, published in 1896 by Frank Munsey, and the pulps flourished until the 1930s when they were superseded by paperback books, 'pulp novels', the pictorial comic magazine, radio and film. Several famous detectives were staple pulp characters who survived into pulp novels and beyond. They include Mike Hammer, introduced by Mickey Spillane (b. 1918), Travis McGee, created by John D. McDonald (1916–86), and Perry Mason, the creation of Erle Stanley Gardner (1889–1970). Writers associated with the pulps include Raymond CHANDLER, Dashiell Hammett (1894–1961), Phyllis Ayame Whitney (b. 1903), Jim Thompson (1906–77) and Robert A. Heinlein (1907–88).

Puritan literature While PURITANISM is often thought of as mistrusting imaginative literature, there is a rich body of Puritan literature that includes sermons, meditations, journals, diaries, history and nature observation as well as poetry. Literature produced by the Puritans flourishes from about 1650 until about 1750, with a concentration in the period 1680–1740. It has also proved influential on the later development of American writing.

As is appropriate for a religious movement that concentrated so much on the word, the Puritans saw the sermon as their most important literary activity. But the intellectual scrutiny necessary for the sermon was also cultivated in other writing. In a real sense all Puritan literature is didactic, not only in being informed and justified by religious belief but also in its objective of teaching and fostering greater understanding of God. Thus, the activity of writing about history and natural history was religious in its avowed purpose of assisting in the discovery of God's pattern and design. The writing of history was held in especially high esteem, and *Magnalia Christi Americana* (1702) by Cotton Mather (1663–1728) is often considered the highest achievement of Puritan historiography. Furthermore, Puritan literature is characterized by its particular forms of belief. For example, the emphasis on the individual's need for rigorous self-examination led to a preference for writing that was an expression of personal sincerity, and hence to a concentration on the journal, the diary and personal meditation. The *Personal Narrative* (1765) of Jonathan Edwards (1703–58) is a major example of this style of Puritan self-representation, which has had a significant influence on the development of AUTOBIOGRAPHY in American literature. The CAPTIVITY NARRATIVE, such as that written by Mary Rowlandson (?1635–1711) is one embodiment of the Puritan precept of interpreting events in a religious manner. The emphasis on teaching moral understanding through literature resulted in the publication of the *NEW ENGLAND PRIMER*, one of the first examples of CHILDREN'S LITERATURE. Belief in the need for truth-telling, personal witness and sincerity led to distrust of prose fiction and there is scarcely any produced in Puritan times.

The Puritans endorsed what they called 'plain style', that is, clear writing in a style that does not distract from understanding. This preference is especially evident in *THE BAY PSALM BOOK*, and more generally in the Puritans' misgivings over language that was considered overly ornate. This distrust has often been used as evidence that the Puritans were against poetry. Certainly, they did not encourage poetry that was extravagant, with elaborate metaphors or conceits, because these were distractions from the poem's message, because elaboration might mean straying from God's word, and because the style suggested vanity on the part of the author. But poetry was valued because it was meditative and because it could express aspects of belief in a way that made them easy to memorize. The kind of poetry the Puritans preferred can be seen in the *New England Primer* and in *The Bay Psalm Book*, the preface to which states that 'God's altar needs not our polishings.' The most widely read poem in New England that originated from the Puritans was *The Day of Doom* (1662) by Michael Wigglesworth (1631–1705). This long poem is a narrative of the Puritan doctrines related to death and God's judgment. Although modern readers might question its value as poetry, its didacticism served an important function for its intended readers.

The Puritan poets that are most admired by modern readers are Edward Taylor (?1645–1729) and Anne BRADSTREET, neither of whom published poetry willingly during their lifetimes. Taylor's poetry, unpublished until 1939, is more elaborate than the plain style would permit. He wrote in the style of the METAPHYSICAL poets such as John Donne and although he fulfils the devotional and meditative prescription for poetry, his reticence concerning publication was perhaps understandable. Bradstreet's poetry is most appreciated by modern readers when it makes apparent her attempts to reconcile her beliefs with her situation as a woman.

Further reading

God's Altar: The World and the Flesh in Puritan Poetry (1978) by Robert Daly; 'New England Puritan Literature' by Emory Elliot, in *The Cambridge History of American Literature*, Volume I (1994), edited by Sacvan Bercovitch; *The Language of Puritan Feeling* (1980) by David Leverenz; *Fictions of the Feminine* (1988) by Margaret Olofson Thickstun, and *Puritan Poets and Poetics* (1985), edited by Peter White.

Puritanism   Although not exclusively American in origins or thought, Puritanism has strongly influenced the shaping of much that is characteristic about the United States and has significantly informed its literature.

The historical origins of Puritanism are in the English Reformation of the 16th century. The Puritans were originally part of the Protestant movement which separated from the Roman Catholic church mainly over what were considered its corrupt ritualism and its church structure, which was believed to be interfering with the mediation of God's word. However, the Puritans wished to go further than the Protestants in their 'purification' of the church, and dissented from Anglicanism at the end of the 16th century on account of what they saw as its maintenance of Roman Catholic practices. The Puritans were strongly influenced by CALVINISM, in particular by Calvin's ideal of founding a 'city of God' on earth, and by the tenets of his *Institutes of Christian Religion* (1536). A small group of extreme Puritans, known as separatists, who had left England for Holland, decided to leave Europe for the American colonies; they sailed on the *Mayflower* from England in 1620 and founded PLYMOUTH COLONY. A much larger group of Puritans left England in 1630 under the leadership of John Winthrop and founded the MASSACHUSETTS BAY COLONY. Centred on Boston, this colony became the major stronghold of Puritanism in English North America. Contrary to a widely held belief, Puritan emigrants were not UTOPIANS who believed in liberty and DEMOCRACY. Neither were they persecuted in Europe; they saw themselves as fleeing error and seeking a location where their beliefs could be practised without interference.

Puritanism had various branches and sects; this was indeed encouraged to some extent by CONGREGATIONALISM. Nevertheless, there were core beliefs that were commonly held. Deriving directly from the teachings of Calvin, there were four basic tenets of Puritanism: Total Depravity; Limited Atonement; Irresistible Grace and Predestination. Each derived from belief in the literal truth of the fall of Adam and Eve after they were tempted by the devil in the Garden of Eden. Belief in the fact of the fall was the basis of all Puritan thought. Puritans believed that with this fall came Total Depravity; that is, all nature and all humans were corrupted and incapable of perfection; 'In Adam's Fall / We sinned all', as the *NEW ENGLAND PRIMER* pithily expressed it.

Contrary to the belief that Christ's crucifixion had made redemption available to all, the Puritans believed in Limited Atonement; that is, only a minority, called the elect, were to be saved. The majority were damned, or reprobate. Furthermore, the doctrine of Irresistible Grace stated that the condition of being elect or reprobate was unalterable. As in the Calvinistic doctrine of Predestination, God had determined the course of human history since the beginning of time, and this included deciding who would be damned and who saved. Good works could not bring about salvation, although it was believed that individuals could show a readiness for grace by moral conduct.

Although the tenets of Irresistible Grace and Predestination may seem logically to lead to fatalism, they were in fact two of the most significant animating principles of Puritanism. It was the duty of all individuals to discover whether or not they were of the elect. Thus, the need for rigorous self-examination and a reading of reality for signs of God's purpose were key elements of Puritan thought. An individual's claim to be of the elect would be examined by church ministers and if accepted, permitted the individual special status in the community; for example, in most congregations only the so-called 'visible saints' could vote. A further significant aspect of Puritanism was the belief in individual covenant with God. As well as a private sense of mission and purpose, the Puritans had a strong belief in public mission. They characterized their emigration as an 'errand into the wilderness' and emphasized the need for communal unity.

Puritanism was a serious, sombre and even severe approach to life. The individual and communal commitment to duty was everywhere emphasized, and censure given to the frivolous and to anything that distracted from the mission of serving and glorifying God. Although it is sometimes crudely represented as a rigid belief system, Puritanism was a highly scholarly and intellectual movement, which encouraged serious enquiry into many disciplines and areas of knowledge. The universities of Harvard and Princeton were both founded under Puritan direction and Puritanism did much to develop the disciplines of natural science and history.

Eventually the influence of Puritanism in the colonies waned with the increased IMMIGRATION of non-Puritans, the variation of Puritan practice under the congregational system, the dispersal of the Puritan population with the acquisition of land, and the growing influence of the ENLIGHTENMENT. Certainly, by the time of the GREAT AWAKENING, the role of strict Puritanism in New England life had visibly decreased. Nevertheless, important elements of Puritan thought survived, and moreover have come to be considered crucial in the history of the United States. 'Without some understanding of Puritanism', wrote Perry Miller in 1956, 'there is no understanding of America.' A belief in public mission, a strong work ethic, a commitment to cultivating one's abilities, a questioning of institutions, an emphasis on individual worth, and even the primacy of capitalism are all American characteristics that have been seen to originate in Puritanism. Conversely, critics of Puritanism have seen it as a blight on American history and culture – 'blood poison' as Ezra POUND called it in a 1920 letter to William Carlos WILLIAMS. It has been held responsible for the American repression of sexuality, a fear of the body, a dualistic world view, the denigration of women and the cultivation of censoriousness.

In addition to the rich legacy of PURITAN LITERATURE, Puritanism profoundly affected many later American writers, including Nathaniel HAWTHORNE, Herman MELVILLE, Emily DICKINSON and T. S. ELIOT.

Further reading

The New England Mind: The Seventeenth Century (1939) and *Errand into the Wilderness* (1956) by Perry Miller remain leading books on Puritanism. Other recommended studies are *The American Puritan Imagination* (1974), edited by Sacvan Bercovitch; *The Puritan Origins of the American Self* (1975) by Sacvan Bercovitch; *Visible Saints: The History of a Puritan Idea* (1963) by Edmund S. Morgan; *Voices in the Wilderness* (1999) by Patricia Roberts-Miller, and *American Puritanism: Faith and Practice* (1970) by Darrett B. Rutman. *Puritans* (1998) by John Adair and *Colonial America* (1996) by Richard Middleton are useful histories.

Putnam's Monthly Magazine   As its complete title, *Putnam's Monthly Magazine of Literature, Science, and Art*, suggests, *Putnam's* was committed to development of national literature. Founded in 1853 in New York, it concentrated on the publication of American writing – in contrast to its competitor *HARPER'S MONTHLY MAGAZINE*, which also published British authors. *Putnam's* was a prestigious magazine, and paid its contributors well. They included James Fenimore COOPER, Henry Wadsworth Longfellow (1807–82), James Russell Lowell (1819–91), Henry David THOREAU and Herman MELVILLE. The magazine first published (anonymously) some of Melville's most important work: the short stories 'Bartleby' (1853) and *Benito Cereno* (1855) as well as the serialization of the novel *Israel Potter* (1855). *Putnam's* closed during the depression of 1857, though it was revived twice before merging with the *ATLANTIC MONTHLY*.

Pynchon, Thomas   Novelist, born in Long Island, New York, in 1937. Pynchon attended Cornell University and then worked at various jobs, including a spell as a technical writer at the Boeing Corporation in Seattle. In 1963 he published his first novel, *V.* Written in a pastiche of styles, its multilayered plot is mainly concerned with the search for a secret organization and for the truth it may reveal about historical interventions. The concern with secrecy, conspiracy and order continued in the shorter second novel, *The Crying of Lot 49* (1966). Skilfully blending low comedy, pastiche and tragedy, the novel explores the repressive nature of human systems by following the quest of Oedipa Maas to discover whether a series of apparent coincidences are actually events determined by a controlling figure, Pierce Inverarity. In ending indeterminately the novel celebrates the potentially anti-systemic nature of miracle and randomness. These two novels generated considerable critical attention, and Pynchon's third, *Gravity's Rainbow* (1973), was hailed as his major achievement. More sombre and APOCALYPTIC in tone than his other novels, it also involves a search, this time for a powerfully destructive rocket. Somewhat reclusive, Pynchon published nothing except for a collection of earlier stories, *Slow Learner* (1984), until his much-anticipated fourth novel *Vineland* (1990). Set in 1980s Northern California, it disappointed many of his readers by its retreat from the themes established in the earlier work. Similar disappointment followed the publication of the lengthy historical novel *Mason & Dixon* (1997) and critics have found it difficult to match the later novels with the earlier ones. Nevertheless Pynchon's enigmatic and engaging work makes him a considerable figure and an important voice.

Further reading

Thomas Pynchon's Narratives (2000) by Alan W. Brownlie; Signs and Symptoms (1983) by Peter L. Cooper; Thomas Pynchon (1990) by John Dugdale; Ideas of Order in the Novels of Thomas Pynchon (1983) by Molly Hite, and The Fictional Labyrinths of Thomas Pynchon (1988) by David Seed.

Quakers   Officially called the Society of Friends, the Quakers were formed in England during the mid 17th century and have been a significant presence in American history and culture. The Quakers reject forms of church hierarchy, priesthood and ritual, believing that God speaks directly to each individual and that everyone has an 'inward light' that manifests God's presence. They emphasize the need for plainness in speech and dress, and in their meetings people sit silently unless inspired by God to speak. Their belief that the inward light is common to all has led to toleration for others, and Quakers have long been associated with philanthropy, pacifism and social activism. Their ideals of good workmanship, industry and honesty have often made them successful in trades and industry.

The Quakers first came to the British colonies in North America in the 1650s. However, the PURITANS persecuted them as heretics; they could be banned from Puritan communities, whipped or fined, and between 1659 and 1661 four Quakers were hanged in Boston. Quaker communities developed, notably in Rhode Island, but it was the granting in 1681 of a royal charter to William Penn (1644–1718) that led to the Quakers flourishing in the colonies, since this permitted the founding of a Quaker colony (termed the 'Holy Experiment') in Pennsylvania. True to their beliefs the Quakers were prominent in establishing and honouring treaties with the Native Americans, in anti-SLAVERY movements, and in various philanthropic concerns and reform movements such as those devoted to TEMPERANCE and SUFFRAGE. The Quaker belief in inward light had some influence on the development of ROMANTICISM and TRANSCENDENTALISM.

Significant Quaker writings include *Some Fruits of Solitude* (1693) by William Penn, *Travels* (1791) by William Bartram (1739–1823) and the poetry of John Greenleaf Whittier (1807–92). Quaker beliefs had some influence on Walt WHITMAN, though he was not himself a Quaker, and Jean Toomer (1894–1967) became a Quaker leader. Quakers feature prominently in much American literature, notably in the *Autobiography* (1818, 1867) of Benjamin FRANKLIN, 'The Gentle Boy' (1832) by Nathaniel HAWTHORNE, and *MOBY-DICK* (1851) by Herman MELVILLE. The pacifism of the Quakers is often an issue in WESTERN writing, as in *Nick of the Woods* (1837) by Robert Montgomery Bird (1806–54).

Queer Theory   Term used to describe a variety of interdisciplinary approaches that originated in the 1980s. Building on elements of FEMINIST theory, and on Michel Foucault's theories of the social and linguistic construction of sexual identity, queer theory examines gay and lesbian writing, works to raise the profile of neglected gay and lesbian writers, and explores their encoding of sexuality. It has been contentious for several reasons, and even among its supporters some have objected to its use of the term 'queer'. Some have questioned its status as theory (preferring the term 'queer studies'), while others have complained that in privileging sexuality it neglects aspects of identity formulated by ethnicity and social and economic circumstances.

Further reading

Queer Studies (1996), edited by Brett Beemyn and Mickey Eliason; *Identity Poetics* (2001) by Linda Garber, and *Epistemology of the Closet* (1990) by Eve Kosofsky Sedgwick.

Ragtime   A variation of JAZZ, typically played on the solo piano, in which a strong marching rhythm is offset by syncopated melodic variations, often numerous and complex. Ragtime developed in the late 19th century from the 'cakewalk' style and is especially associated with Scott Joplin (1868–1917), who wrote many ragtime tunes, an instruction book titled *The School of Ragtime* (1909) and a ragtime opera, *Treemonisha* (1911). As in the case of jazz, writers have found narrative possibilities in ragtime's multilayered syncopations, notably E. L. Doctorow (b. 1931) in the novel *Ragtime* (1975).

Realism   Style of writing, usually prose, in which surface appearance is presented in an unembellished way. In contrast to ROMANCE or the FANTASTIC, the realist writer also seeks to represent experiences that are usual or typical rather than extraordinary or exotic. The realist novel emerged in France in the mid-19th century. In the United States it developed in the 1870s, to some extent growing out of the LOCAL COLOUR tradition, after romance had long been dominant. One of the first American realists, William Dean Howells (1837–1920), was soon followed by several other major figures, notably Frank Norris, Theodore Dreiser and Sinclair Lewis (1885–1951). For Norris, Dreiser and other NATURALIST writers, realism was the expression of a materialist philosophy, and the writer's duty was to represent the world in an objective and non-idealized manner. Realism became the dominant mode in fiction before being modified and imaginatively enlarged by MODERNIST writing during the 1920s.

Further reading

The Problem of American Realism (1997) by Michael Davitt Bell; American Realism (1972) edited by Jane Benaderte, and Documents of American Realism and Naturalism (1998), edited by Donald Pizer.

Reconstruction   The period after the Civil War during which the South was occupied by federal troops. After the war, the former Confederated States resisted the implementation of the Thirteenth Amendment, by which slavery had been abolished, and refused to ratify the Fourteenth Amendment, which guaranteed citizenship and the vote for ex-slaves. Under the 1867 Reconstruction Acts ten of the former rebel states (excluding Tennessee) were placed under military control and could not be readmitted to the Union unless they ratified the Fourteenth Amendment and adopted new state constitutions. Since ex-Confederates could neither vote nor hold political office, some African Americans were elected to state legislatures, and two were elected to the United States Senate. Resentful white Southerners often exaggerated African American political involvement during Reconstruction, and were also hostile to so-called 'carpetbaggers' (opportunistic Northern politicians in the South) and 'scalawags' (non-disfranchised white Southerners). In reaction, this period saw the formation of organizations such as the Ku Klux Klan and the Knights of the White Camelia. By 1870 all of the ex-rebel states had been readmitted to the Union, and by a series of legal and extra-legal measures many African Americans were gradually disfranchised by 1876. In 1877 the remaining federal troops left the South and Reconstruction was officially over.

The bitter divisions of Reconstruction are often represented in literature, notably in the pro-Klan novels of Thomas Dixon (1864–1946), especially *The Leopard's Spots* (1902) and *The Clansman* (1905), and also in *Up from Slavery* (1901) by Booker T. Washington (1856–1915), *Gone with the Wind* (1936) by Margaret Mitchell (1900–1949) and several works of William Faulkner, particularly *The Unvanquished* (1938).

Reform literature   The 1820s and 1830s saw a proliferation of reform movements, some growing out of anti-slavery sentiments. Mostly based in New England, and often with a religious background, groups were formed to agitate for TEMPERANCE, women's rights, prison reform and improvements in industrial conditions. Creative writing played an important role in the dissemination of reform ideas, and although often crude and moralistic, reform novels and plays provide an important background for many of the major writers of the 1840s and 1850s, as David S. Reynolds demonstrates in his study *Beneath the American Renaissance* (1988). Reynolds usefully divides reform literature into two types: the conventional, in which the 'rewards of virtue' are emphasized, and the subversive, in which the emphasis is on 'the grisly, sometimes perverse results of vice'. Conventional reform writing is often associated with the domestic novel in its praise of home. Ralph Waldo EMERSON, Edgar Allan POE, Nathaniel HAWTHORNE, Herman MELVILLE, Henry David THOREAU, Emily DICKINSON, and Walt WHITMAN all made significant creative use of reform themes and modes. Prominent BEST-SELLING authors associated with reform include Catharine Sedgwick (1789–1867), Timothy Shay Arthur (1809–85), Susan Warner (1819–85) and Maria Susanna Cummins (1827–66).

Regionalism   Literary movement that developed in the 1890s, in some respects growing out of the LOCAL COLOUR tradition. However, whereas local colourists were primarily descriptive of an area and its customs, regionalists were usually much more interested in exploring how a region had shaped the mentality and outlook of its inhabitants; in this regard regionalism sometimes shares characteristics of NATURALISM. Regionalism is especially associated with the Mid-West and later with the South, but it was also a feature of writing that originated in New England and in California – for example Robert FROST and Edward Arlington Robinson (1869–1935) are important New England regionalists, and Robinson Jeffers (1887–1962) and John Steinbeck (1902–68) are regionalists of California. Prominent Mid-Western regionalists include Hamlin Garland (1860–1940), Edgar Lee Masters (1869–1950), Willa CATHER, Sherwood Anderson (1876–1941), Carl Sandburg (1878–1967) and Sinclair Lewis (1885–1951), while Southern regionalists include Ellen Glasgow (1874–1945), William FAULKNER, Eudora Welty (1909–2001), Tennessee WILLIAMS, Carson McCullers (1917–67) and Flannery O'CONNOR.

Further reading

Regional Fictions (2001) by Stephanie Foote; *Breaking Boundaries* (1997), edited by Sherrie A. Inness and Diana Royer, and *Regions of Identity* (1999) by Kate McCullough.

Removal   The enforced removal in the 1830s of Native Americans to lands west of the Mississippi. As part of President Andrew Jackson's anti-Indian policy, the 1830 Indian Removal Act sanctioned white appropriation of desirable lands in the Southeast in exchange for undesirable prairie land in the West. It reneged on existing treaties guaranteeing Indian settlements, and the removals took place in defiance of a SUPREME COURT decision that upheld Indian rights. Although some tribes were resettled peacefully, the US Army enforced the removal of five tribes from the Southeast (Chickasaw,

Choctaw, Seminole, Cherokee and Creek). The removal of these so-called 'Five Civilized Tribes' was especially bitter, since they had done much to assimilate, adopting European styles of education and land cultivation; this was particularly true of the Cherokees. It is estimated that up to 100,000 Native Americans were forcibly removed and that approximately 25,000 died during the enforced treks. The journey of the Cherokees from Georgia to what is now Oklahoma in 1838–9 is known as the 'Trail of Tears'. Of the 15,000 who began the trail about 4,000 died. The Florida or Seminole Indians, led by Osceola, resisted removal and fought the second of the SEMINOLE WARS (1835–42).

The removals are frequently referred to in novels and poetry. In her critical study *Removals* (1991), Lucy Maddox examines the way the removals were mediated by 19th century writers. *Iron Cages* (1979) by Ronald T. Takaki provides a useful historical overview of the period.

Revolutionary War   Also known as the War of Independence, the Revolutionary War was fought between the colonials in North America and the British, and resulted in the United States achieving sovereignty.

A number of disagreements over various issues that had developed between the colonials and the British over the previous 15 years began to come to a head in 1775. In April of that year there were skirmishes at Lexington and Concord. These are usually taken as representing the start of the war, although it was by no means certain that independence was then an aspiration of the colonials. In June 1775 the Battle of Bunker Hill was fought in Boston. Although the British were victorious, the impressive display of the colonial forces encouraged revolutionary feeling. After these events Congress decided to raise an army (known as the Continental Army), and in August King George III declared that the colony was in a state of rebellion. On 2 July 1776 Congress, meeting in Philadelphia (then the colonial capital), voted for independence, and on 4 July it ratified the DECLARATION OF INDEPENDENCE.

George Washington (1732–99) commanded the Continental Army during the war. After initially mixed results there were two crucial turning points for the Americans. The first was the victory of General Horatio Gates over the British under General Burgoyne at Saratoga in October 1777. The second was Washington's being able to endure great hardship and keep the army together at Valley Forge during the winter of 1777–8. In June 1778 France formally entered the war in support of the Americans (although it had provided covert assistance prior to that). Spain followed in 1779, and the Netherlands in 1780. Although both the British and the Americans achieved significant victories in various campaigns by land and by sea, the war ended in Yorktown, Virginia, with the surrender of General Cornwallis to Washington on 19 October 1781. The Treaty of Paris (1783) concluded the war. By its terms Britain recognized the independence of the United States and its boundaries were formally agreed (one result of this was that Britain retained Canada).

As well as Washington, Gates and Benjamin FRANKLIN, notable figures on the American side in the war include Paul Revere (1735–1818), who made a celebrated ride from Charlestown to Lexington to bring news of British troop movements; John Paul Jones (1747–92), a privateer responsible for daring sea raids on the British, and Ethan Allen (1738–89), who commanded his own militia, the Green Mountain Boys, from Vermont. Benedict Arnold (1741–1801) was a successful general for the Americans who defected to the British.

The war and specific characters and incidents have been the subjects of numerous and varied literary works. These include the commemorative lyric poem 'Concord Hymn' (1836) by Ralph Waldo EMERSON (in which the fighting at Lexington is called 'the shot heard around the world'); the narrative poem 'Paul Revere's Ride' (1861) by Henry Wadsworth Longfellow (1807–82); the 'Revolutionary Romances', a series of seven novels dealing with the war in the South, by William Gilmore Simms (1806–70); several novels by James Fenimore COOPER, including *The Pilot* (1823), which is based on the adventures of John Paul Jones, and *Lionel Lincoln* (1825), set in Massachusetts at the start of the war. The novel *Israel Potter* (1855) by Herman MELVILLE is partly set during the war (and is dedicated to the monument commemorating the Battle of Bunker Hill).

Rich, Adrienne   Among the most widely published and significant of American FEMINIST poets. She was born in Baltimore, Maryland, in 1929 of a professional, partly Jewish background. Educated at Radcliffe College, she began her poetic career auspiciously when W. H. Auden selected her work for the Yale Younger Poets series, which published *A Change of World* in 1951. Praising these as poems that 'respect their elders ... and do not tell fibs' Auden laid the foundations for a critical reception of Rich's early work emphasizing its formal discipline and decorous mood. *The Diamond Cutters and Other Poems* (1955) confirms her facility for resolving poetic uncertainties through careful crafting of language, though the intensity of feeling that would mark her later poems is already evident. During this time Rich married and started a family. By *Snapshots of a Daughter-Law* (1963) she is beginning to favour free verse as a means of exploring emerging tensions; both formally and thematically she forsakes protective devices in order to confront the fragmentation associated with the modern sensibility. *Necessities of Life: Poems 1962–1965* followed in 1966 and *Selected Poems* a year later.

The close of the decade brought considerable social upheaval with protests against the VIETNAM WAR and an increasingly vocal women's liberation movement. Both developments affected Rich who, as a teacher of creative writing, was in a position to absorb these changes artistically and institutionally. Most notably, she began to question the literary tradition to which she belonged and to recognize that it caused her to falsify women's experience in her work. She aimed to draw the personal and the political together to form a new poetics of gender identity. After the death of her husband in

1970 she continued this transition, becoming a radical lesbian feminist and polemical poet and essayist who continues to publish prolifically.

From this period onward Rich's poetry is read within a radical feminist frame, with critics often drawing on her own prose writings to elucidate aspects of her politics and her art. Among the most significant of these writings are: *Of Woman Born: Motherhood as Experience and Institution* (1976); *On Lies, Secrets and Silence* (1980), and *What is Found There: Notebooks on Poetry and Politics* (1993). Important volumes of poetry include: *Diving into the Wreck: Poems 1971–1972* (1973); *The Dream of a Common Language: Poems 1974–1977* (1978), and *An Atlas of the Difficult World: Poems 1988–1991* (1991).

Further reading

Reading Adrienne Rich: Reviews and Re-Visions 1951–81 (1984), edited by Jane Roberta Cooper; *Stein, Bishop and Rich* (1997) by Margaret Dickie; *Adrienne Rich's Poetry and Prose* (1975/1993), edited by Barbara Charlesworth Gelpi and Albert Gelpi, and *The Aesthetics of Power* (1986) by Claire Keyes.

Romance   In American literature the romance is generally a fictional work dealing in a non-realistic way with unusual or fantastic events. Romance originated in the middle ages, but it was the 19th century historical romances of Walter Scott that formed the immediate basis for romance in America, where it became the dominant fictive form prior to the rise of REALISM. In its simplest sense, 'romance' may be used to distinguish a work of invention from a work that aims for historical accuracy. At its most complex, as in the work of Edgar Allan POE, Nathaniel HAWTHORNE and Herman MELVILLE, it is an introspective and highly self-conscious form, in which the nature of fiction and its relation to reality and to history may be examined. Commonly, a distinction is made between the romance and the novel, famously so by Hawthorne in his preface to *The House of the Seven Gables* (1851):

> When a writer calls his work a Romance, it need hardly be observed that he wishes to claim a certain latitude, both as to its fashion and material, which he would not have felt himself entitled to assume, had he professed to be writing a Novel. The latter form of composition is presumed to aim at a very minute fidelity, not merely to the possible, but to the probable and ordinary course of man's experience. The former – while, as a work of art, it must rigidly subject itself to laws, and while it sins unpardonably as so far as it may swerve aside from the truth of the human heart – has fairly a right to present that truth under circumstances, to a great extent, of the writer's own choosing or creation.

Further reading

Engendering Romance (1994) by Emily Budick; *The Development of American Romance* (1980) by Michael Davitt Bell; *The American Historical Romance* (1987) by George Dekker, and *The Theory of the American Romance* (1989) by William A. Ellis.

Romanticism A multifaceted movement in music, painting and literature that originated in Germany and Britain during the 18th century. Although it is notoriously impossible to define, romanticism is generally a reaction against rationalism and materialism. It can be broadly represented as a series of beliefs: in the primacy of the imagination rather than in a purely rational mode of apprehending and understanding reality; in the imagination's transformative power to invest reality with meaning; in the importance of individuality and personal freedom, and in the value of spontaneity and self-expression as opposed to artificiality and restraint. Commonly, there is also a PASTORAL element to romanticism, an exaltation of untamed nature and a consequent desire to find and express one's own individual nature. Other romantic characteristics include an admiration for the individuated hero who has broken from social restraints, and a representation of the poet as prophet or visionary. Although often represented as primarily an aesthetic movement, romanticism has important political, social and nationalistic dimensions. Its support for the ideals of DEMOCRACY and republicanism derives from a fundamental belief in human equality, while as an optimistic, UTOPIAN, philosophy, romanticism also envisions the perfectibility of the individual and of society through self-realization, progress and reform. In romantic thought there is often an idealization of primitive 'natural' societies, and antagonism towards what is perceived as repressive artificial civilization.

Romanticism is crucial to American culture, to the extent that the very creation of the United States has been considered an expression of romantic thought. It was the central movement of the AMERICAN RENAISSANCE, being most readily mediated through TRANSCENDENTALISM, and it continues to exert a profound influence on American thought and writing. In this respect the importance of Ralph Waldo EMERSON can hardly be exaggerated, since he both mediated European romantic thought and adapted it to the American intellectual situation. Romanticism perhaps has its fullest and least ambiguous expression in the work of Emerson, Henry David THOREAU and Walt WHITMAN, but it has been a central concern in the work of numerous writers, notably James Fenimore COOPER, William Cullen Bryant (1794–1878), Edgar Allan POE, Herman MELVILLE, Emily DICKINSON, Mark TWAIN, Kate CHOPIN, Wallace STEVENS, F. Scott FITZGERALD, Hart Crane (1899–1932), Vladimir Nabokov (1899–1977) and Sylvia PLATH.

Further reading

The Echoing Green (1984) by Carlos Baker; *American Romanticism and the Marketplace* (1985) by Michael T. Gilmore; *Romantic Revolutions* (1990), edited by Kenneth R. Johnston et al.; *American Romanticism*, two volumes (1987) by David Morse, and *Romantic Re-Vision* (1982) by Bryan J. Wolf.

Rosenberg case In 1951, during the 'Red scare', a New York Jewish couple, Julius and Ethel Rosenberg, were convicted of spying and passing information to the Russians. Despite serious and persistent doubts over their guilt and the nature of the secrets they supposedly passed on, they were executed in June 1953. The case is fictionalized in two important novels concerned with the period: *The Book of Daniel* (1971) by E. L. Doctorow (b. 1931) and *The Public Burning* (1976) by Robert Coover (b. 1932). The executions form a significant point of reference in Sylvia PLATH's novel *The Bell Jar* (1963).

Roth, Philip An important figure in the development of JEWISH AMERICAN LITERATURE, Roth was born in 1933 in Newark, New Jersey, and attended university at Bucknell and at Chicago, where he also lectured. Roth's first book, a collection of short fiction, *Goodbye Columbus* (1959), was critically well received, and he published his first novel, *Letting Go*, in 1962, followed by *When She Was Good* (1967). His ribald comic novel, *Portnoy's Complaint* (1969), examining the sexual frustration of the mother-dominated Alexander Portnoy, was a popular success. *The Ghost Writer* (1979) introduced a recurring figure in Roth's fiction, his alter ego Nathan Zuckerman, also the protagonist of *Zuckerman Unbound* (1981), *The Anatomy Lesson* (1983) (collected with 'The Prague Orgy' in *Zuckerman Bound*, 1985), and *The Counterlife* (1987). After publishing *Patrimony* (1991), a non-fictional account of his father's final illness and death, Roth published two significant novels, *Operation Shylock* (1993) and *Sabbath's Theater* (1995). These were followed by what many consider to be Roth's finest work: the novels *American Pastoral* (1997), *I Married a Communist* (1998) and *The Human Stain* (2000). In different ways each explores the effects of the COLD WAR on individuals and examines the nature of idealism, aspiration and commitment.

Critics have often considered Roth's work uneven, claiming that some of the novels are marred by a particular kind of self-absorption, and that some serious issues are caricatured or treated frivolously. At his best, though, especially in the later work, Roth's reflective seriousness and his graceful prose style make him a major writer.

Further reading

Understanding Philip Roth (1990) by Murray Baumgarten and Barbara Gottfried; *Philip Roth and the Jews* (1996) by Alan Cooper; *Philip Roth* (1982) by Hermione Lee, and *The Imagination in Transit* (1996) by Stephen Wade. Roth's *Reading Myself and Others* (1975) is a useful collection of interviews and essays.

Rough Riders Nickname of the First Regiment of US Volunteer Cavalry, a group frequently fictionalized in WESTERN writing. Commanded by Leonard Wood, the regiment was recruited in 1898 by Theodore Roosevelt (1858–1919) and is most associated with him. The volunteers came from various backgrounds, though they are usually represented as being COWBOYS. The regiment performed heroically in the SPANISH–AMERICAN WAR and their adventures generated significant publicity. The term 'rough rider' was in common usage prior to 1898, having been used by 'Buffalo Bill' Cody (1846–1917) in 1883 for his show, the 'Wild West & Congress of Rough Riders of the World'.

Sacco and Vanzetti case   Notorious case in which two Italian immigrants, Nicola Sacco and Bartolomeo Vanzetti, were executed for killing two men during a 1920 robbery in South Braintree, Massachusetts. Since Sacco and Vanzetti were labour organizers and known anarchists, their original conviction for the murders in 1921 led to accusations that they had been unfairly victimized and framed for the killings because of their political beliefs. In 1925 another man confessed to the murders, but in 1927 the Massachusetts Supreme Court upheld the original convictions. Despite international outrage and angry denunciations Sacco and Vanzetti were executed by electrocution in August 1927. In 1977 the governor of Massachusetts declared that they had been unfairly tried and that no 'stigma and disgrace' should be attached to their names.

Many writers participated in protests against the convictions of Sacco and Vanzetti, and the case stimulated a great deal of writing. Examples include: the poems 'Justice Denied in Massachusetts' by Edna St Vincent Millay (1892–1950) and 'Not Sacco and Vanzetti' by Countee Cullen (1903–46); the 'documentary' novel *Boston* (1928) by Upton Sinclair (1878–1968) and the verse drama *Winterset* (1935) by Maxwell Anderson (1888–1959). The case features prominently in *The Big Money* (1936) by John Dos Passos (1896–1970), *A Tattered Coat upon a Stick* (2000) by William Brennan and the memoir *The Never-Ending Wrong* (1977) by Katherine Anne Porter (1890–1980).

Salem witch trials   The trials took place in Salem, part of the MASSACHUSETTS BAY COLONY, between May and October 1692. After accusations of witchcraft in February 1692 made by a group of young girls a series of civic trials took place, which resulted in the indictment of almost 200 people. Fourteen women and five men were hanged as witches and one man was pressed to death, having refused to plead. (Two supposedly possessed dogs were also hanged.) Gradually public revulsion at the trials resulted in the court being dissolved. The remaining cases were heard in 1693 in a different court and there were no further convictions. The judicial participants in the trials did penance for their actions, and in 1711 all of the convictions were declared null and void, with compensation being awarded to the families of those who had been found guilty. The trials have held a significant place in American culture, often being represented as examples of mass hysteria or of the prejudices peculiar to the PURITANS, or as a defining moment in the formation of the American character. However, it is important to remember that at the time belief in the devil's working through witches was virtually unquestioned, and that trials and executions for witchcraft were common in Europe. Furthermore, the approach of the new century was widely believed to herald increased activity by the devil (see MILLENNIALISM).

In addition to numerous references to Salem in popular culture and in GOTHIC and HORROR writing, the trials have often been examined in key American texts. Nathaniel HAWTHORNE, whose ancestor John Hathorne was one of the Salem magistrates, wrote repeatedly of Puritanism as representing a guilty American past. Henry Wadsworth Longfellow (1807–82) described the trials in his 1868 poetic sequence 'The New England Tragedies' (Part III of *Christus: A Mystery*), while historical novels about Salem include the 1928 *A Mirror for Witches* by Esther Forbes (1891–1967). Plays about the trials include *Giles Covey, Yeoman* (1893) by Mary Wilkins Freeman (1852–1930). Although Arthur MILLER's celebrated drama *THE CRUCIBLE* (1953) is generally considered to be a play about McCARTHYISM, Miller intended an authentic rendering of the historical circumstances of Salem.

The most important contemporary account of the events at Salem is *The Wonders of the Invisible World* (1693) by Cotton Mather (1663–1728). The diary of Samuel Sewall (1652–1730), one of the trial judges, has been published but he writes very little about the trials. Historical studies include *Witchcraft at Salem* (1969) by Chadwick Hansen, *A Delusion of Satan* (1996) by Frances Hill and *Salem Story: Reading the Witch Trials of 1692* (1993) by Bernard Rosenthal. A useful selection of historical sources is available in *What Happened in Salem?* (1960), edited by David Levin.

Saturday Club   Name given in 1857 to a Boston group of writers and intellectuals that had started meeting for dinners as early as the 1840s. It came to be especially associated with the *ATLANTIC MONTHLY*, since many club members were contributors. Ralph Waldo EMERSON, James Russell Lowell (1819–91), Henry Wadsworth Longfellow (1807–82), Oliver Wendell Holmes (1809–94), Francis Parkman (1823–93) and Henry JAMES were among the club's members.

Saturday Evening Post   Weekly magazine founded in 1821 in Philadelphia. It had a long association with fiction, publishing work by distinguished contributors such as James Fenimore COOPER, Edgar Allan POE and Harriet Beecher STOWE. The magazine is most famous, however, for the work it published in the period 1899–1937, when edited by George Horace Lorimer (1867–1937). Under his editorship the *Post* became extremely popular, cultivating a middle-class, middlebrow readership, characterized in part by the illustrations of Norman Rockwell (1894–1978), who designed over 300 of its covers. The magazine was renowned for the extensive advertising it carried, and for high payments to contributors. Under the editorship of Lorimer its circulation reached 3 million, and it published fiction by many leading writers, including Stephen CRANE, Frank NORRIS, Theodore DREISER, Jack London (1876–1916), Willa CATHER, F. Scott FITZGERALD and Sinclair Lewis (1885–1951). After Lorimer's retirement the magazine declined and ceased publication in 1969, though it was revived in a modified form in 1971.

Schlemiel Someone who is clumsy, unlucky or stupid. The schlemiel is a recurring figure in Jewish American literature, appearing particularly in the work of Isaac Bashevis Singer (1904–91) and Bernard Malamud. The term is derived from the Yiddish 'shlemiel'.

Science fiction Term that covers a wide range of writing, varying greatly in quality, seriousness and subject. Historically, science fiction has strong affinities with romance, the fantastic, utopianism and horror, although it tends to be distinct from these in claiming at least some level of scientific plausibility. The term 'science fiction' was popularized by the editor Hugo Gernsback (1884–1967) in the 1920s.

Science fiction first developed as a variation on the fantastic in the early 19th century, and Mary Shelley's romance *Frankenstein* (1818) is usually considered the most influential early example of the genre. During the 19th century popular interest in scientific discovery coupled with an apparent decline in religious belief helped to create an audience for science fiction. In the United States, Edgar Allan Poe, Nathaniel Hawthorne and Fitz-James O'Brien (*c.* 1828–62) were significant early writers in the genre. Hawthorne was interested in what later became a typical science fiction theme, the ethical responsibilities of the scientist, whereas Poe often explored the contiguity between science and wonder. The utopian element of science fiction also developed in the 19th century. A considerable amount of science fiction overlaps with utopian and dystopian writing. Significant works in this hybrid form include *The Crater* (1848) by James Fenimore Cooper, *The Iron Heel* (1907) by Jack London (1876–1916), *Cat's Cradle* (1963) by Kurt Vonnegut (b. 1922), *The Dispossessed* (1974) by Ursula K. Le Guin (b. 1929) and *Woman on the Edge of Time* (1976) by Marge Piercy (b. 1936). Science fiction by women writers has been particularly connected to utopian and dystopian traditions.

Although science fiction maintained a profile in the early years of the 20th century, notably through the work of Edgar Rice Burroughs (1875–1950), it was later to flourish in two distinct periods. The first runs from the mid-1920s to 1940, when the genre's association with pulp fiction was most evident. Magazines such as *Amazing Stories* (1926), founded by Gernsback, and *Astounding Science Fiction* (1930), edited by John W. Campbell (1910–71), helped develop the entertaining short tale that has come to typify science fiction writing. The mass entertainment industries, radio and especially cinema, did much to popularize science fiction, and cinema remains vital to the genre. The second major period began in the 1950s, and has been considered a reaction to anxieties fuelled by the Cold War and a part of a revaluation of historical progress after World War II. In *Slaughterhouse-Five* (1969) Vonnegut writes that two of his war-scarred characters 'were trying to re-invent themselves and their universe.

Science fiction was a big help.' Science fiction became more serious in terms of the science that it utilized, and at its best became a significant method of social, moral and ethical enquiry. The genre, though, still proved capacious enough to include the superficial and the sensational and even, like the WESTERN, became strong enough to absorb its own parodies.

The new seriousness was evident in works that now form a canon of modern science fiction: *I, Robot* (1950) and the *Foundation* trilogy (1951–3) by Isaac Asimov (1920–92); *The Martian Chronicles* (1950) and *Fahrenheit 451* (1953) by Ray Bradbury (b. 1920); *Stranger in a Strange Land* (1961) by Robert A. Heinlein (1907–88); *A Canticle for Lebowitz* (1960) by Walter M. Miller (1922–96); *Dune* (1965) by Frank Herbert (1920–86); *I Have No Mouth and I Must Scream* (1967) by Harlan Ellison (b. 1934); *Do Androids Dream of Electric Sheep?* (1968; filmed as *Blade Runner*, 1982) by Philip K. Dick (1928–82); *The Left Hand of Darkness* (1969) by Ursula K. Le Guin, and *The Female Man* (1975) by Joanna Russ (b. 1937). Since 1950 science fiction became more 'mainstream' than ever before – a fact apparent in the way that it was used by novelists not otherwise associated with it. Examples include E. L. Doctorow (b. 1931) in *Big as Life* (1966), Thomas PYNCHON in *Gravity's Rainbow* (1973) and Gore Vidal (b. 1925) in *Kalki* (1978).

Still, and perhaps increasingly, a vital genre, contemporary science fiction builds on a now established tradition while incorporating and evaluating rapid technological development. An important innovation in the genre has been the development of 'cyberpunk' writing; the term was first used by Bruce Bethke in 1983 and subsequently applied to a new kind of anti-hero. After his influential novel *Neuromancer* (1984), cyber writing was associated especially with William Gibson (b. 1948). Cyber is concerned with a variety of themes, such as the extension of human sensibility through technology, the process of dehumanization by technocracy, and the conflation of image and reality in a computer age.

Further reading

Future Perfect (1966) by H. Bruce Franklin; Feminism and Science Fiction (1989) by Sarah Lefanu; A New Species: Gender and Science in Science Fiction (1993) by Robin Roberts; Alien Encounters (1981) by Mark Rose, and Fiction 2000: Cyberpunk and the Future of Narrative (1992), edited by George Slusser and Tom Shippey.

Scientific racism   Historically, various attempts have been made to establish a racial hierarchy or to explain racial differences in terms of inherent or 'essential' attributes. From the late 18th century onwards, 'scientific' attempts influenced racial discourse in the United States.

Supposedly scientific racial theories have involved studying skull sizes and facial type (notably in the 1830s as a defence of racialized SLAVERY) to demonstrate the inferior intelligence of the black; polygenesis, that is, the belief that whites, blacks and Native Americans are distinct species with separate origins; the theory that environmental factors determine racial character, and the model of a racial hierarchy, in which the races are all of the same species but the Caucasian is the perfect type whereas the other two races (Ethiopian and Mongol) are degenerate. Though gradually discredited over time, such theories are essentialist or hereditarian, in their assumption that a person's race determines character, and that racial types are genetically fixed. Both essentialism and hereditarianism are still extant. The publication in 1994 of *The Bell Curve: Intelligence and Class Structure in American Life* by Richard Herrnstein and Charles Murray was proof to many of the continued survival of scientific racism.

Much writing by African Americans refutes the claims of scientific racism. The very existence of the SLAVE NARRATIVE demonstrated the slave's full humanity, and some of the narratives, specifically *NARRATIVE OF THE LIFE OF FREDERICK DOUGLASS*, refute essentialism by demonstrating the process by which the slave is manufactured. Important essays challenging scientific racism include DOUGLASS's 'The Claims of the Negro Ethnologically Considered' (1854), and 'The Conservation of Races' (1897) by W. E. B. DU BOIS. The measuring of slave features to demonstrate animal characteristics is a key episode in Toni MORRISON's *BELOVED*.

Further reading

Racial Theories by Michael Banton (1998); A Question of Character (2000) by Cathy Boeckmann, and Race: The History of an Idea in America by Thomas F. Gossett (1963, 1997).

Scopes trial In 1925 high-school teacher John T. Scopes was convicted and fined $100 in Dayton, Tennessee, for teaching the evolution theories of Charles Darwin, in violation of a newly passed Tennessee law. The trial attracted much attention in the United States and the conviction was seen as a victory for FUNDAMENTALIST literal interpretations of the Bible. The conviction stimulated much Northern ridicule of the 'backward' and uncultured South, which in turn precipitated defence of the region from groups such as the AGRARIANS. Tennessee's law against teaching evolution was repealed in 1967. The trial is depicted in the play *Inherit the Wind* (1955) by Jerome Lawrence (b. 1915) and Robert E. Lee (1918–94).

Scottsboro case A significant incident of injustice which alerted many to the extent of racial inequality and disfranchisement within the United States. The case began in 1931 after two white women accused nine young black men of rape, alleged to have taken place on a train passing through Alabama. The trial took place in Scottsboro, Alabama, and in spite of medical testimony that no rape had been committed, the all-white jury convicted the 'Scottsboro Boys' and all except the youngest of the nine (who was 12 years old) were sentenced to death. Various groups took up their cause and in 1932 the SUPREME COURT overturned the convictions. However, in a retrial (during which one of the women recanted her testimony), one of the re-convicted men was again sentenced to death. The Supreme Court overturned this conviction in

1935, on the grounds that blacks had been systematically excluded from jury service. A series of retrials followed, and although charges were dropped against five of the defendants, four received life sentences. Three of the four were released in the 1940s and the fourth escaped to Michigan, which refused to deport him to Alabama. In 1976 the governor of Alabama granted a full pardon to the last known survivor of the nine.

The Scottsboro case has been the central focus of many literary works, including poetry by Countee Cullen (1903–46) and by Muriel Rukeyser (1913–80), the play *Scottsboro Limited* (1932) by Langston Hughes, and the documentary novel *Hear that Train Blow!* (1970) by Kelly Covin (1923–91).

Scribner's Magazine Periodical published monthly between 1887 and 1939, the successor to *Scribner's Monthly*. The magazine was important in publishing the work of some major American authors, whose novels were also published by Scribner's under the ownership of the second Charles Scribner (1854–1930). These included Henry JAMES, Edith Wharton (1862–1937), Stephen CRANE, F. Scott FITZGERALD, Ernest HEMINGWAY and Thomas Wolfe (1900–38).

Secession The right of individual states to secede from the Union was long assumed to exist, as part of the social contract by which the United States was brought into existence. Although threatened, notably by South Carolina during the NULLIFICATION crisis of 1832–3 and by some Southern states during the period prior to the CIVIL WAR, it was not an actuality until eleven of the slave-holding states withdrew from the Union. The first to secede was South Carolina in December 1860, followed by Mississippi, Florida, Alabama, Georgia, Louisiana and Texas in subsequent months. These states formed the CONFEDERATED STATES OF AMERICA, and after the Civil War started in April 1861, the states of Virginia, North Carolina, Arkansas and Tennessee also seceded from the Union and joined the Confederacy. Abraham Lincoln always claimed that the Civil War started from the need to preserve the Union against the secessionists rather than the desire to abolish SLAVERY.

Segregation The separation of people on the basis of their perceived racial identity, especially through the provision of distinct public institutions or facilities, in order to maintain and enforce inequalities between the races. There are two kinds of racial segregation: *de jure*, in which laws exist to keep the races apart, and *de facto*, where there may be no laws but there may be other factors (economic, for example) that effectively segregate communities, creating different areas for whites and for blacks.

So-called JIM CROW LAWS, intended to separate whites from non-whites and thereby help to maintain the superior social status of whites, were passed by states in the South during the 1880s, were validated by the 1896 PLESSY V. FERGUSON case and were in force until the 1950s. Thus after RECONSTRUCTION until the 1950s, racial segregation existed in schools, public transportation, places of employment and public spaces as well as in sports, recreation and entertainment. The practice of segregation was declared unconstitutional in public schools by the Brown v. Board of Education of Topeka ruling of 1954. The civil rights movement was active in challenging segregation practices through occupation (integration) of public spaces, and the 1964 Civil Rights Act out-lawed racial discrimination in employment, voting and the use of public facilities. It is often pointed out however that the end of *de jure* racial segregation has by no means ended *de facto* segregation.

Taking the lead of Ralph Ellison, literary scholars have examined what he called segregation 'of the word'. In his 1953 essay 'Twentieth Century Fiction and the Black Mask of Humanity' Ellison located forms of stereotyping of the black in novels by whites, which he equated with intellectual segregation. For example, a non-white character may speak in fractured English whereas the white character does not; or a register may be appropriate to non-whites that is inappropriate to whites.

Self-reliance   Title of an essay by Ralph Waldo Emerson, collected in his first series of *Essays* (1841). The term is often used to describe a set of ideals related to the American character (and especially associated with manhood): independence of thought and action; nonconformity; belief in self-worth and trust in one's own judgment.

Seminole Wars   There were three distinct wars between the United States and the Seminole Indians in Florida. The first (1817–18) started after attempts to capture African American slaves who had taken refuge with the Seminoles in Florida, which was owned at that time by the Spanish. The second war (1835–42) was the most serious. It resulted from Seminole resistance to the policy of removal, under which they were to be forced to leave their lands in Florida in exchange for territory west of the Mississippi river. Led by Osceola, the Seminoles fought with guerrilla tactics and inflicted heavy casualties on the Union forces before surrendering. By the time the war ended it had cost the United States $50 million and up to 2,000 soldiers had been killed. Of the approximately 5,000 Seminoles in Florida at the start of the war only 600 were left after it, the rest having either been killed or relocated. The third war (1855–8) enacted the policy of rounding up and removing any resisting Seminoles from Florida.

Seneca Falls Convention   Held in Seneca Falls, New York, in July 1848, the conven-tion was the first women's rights convention to be held in the United States. It was organized by Elizabeth Cady Stanton (1815–1902) and Lucretia Mott (1793–1880) after they had been excluded from the World Anti-Slavery Convention in London in 1840 because of their gender. The convention passed a series of resolutions involving women's rights, including a statement on the right to the vote. It also passed the 'Declaration of Sentiments'. Written by Stanton, the declaration was modelled on the Declaration of Independence. Stating, 'The history of mankind is a history of repeated injuries and usurpations on the part of man toward woman, having in direct object the establishment of an absolute tyranny over her', the declaration details American women's legal injustices.

Although the support for voting rights was controversial, the convention was instrumental in instituting the agitation for women's SUFFRAGE, granted in 1920 with the passing of the Nineteenth Amendment.

Sewanee Review   Distinguished quarterly journal of criticism and creative writing, published at the University of the South in Sewanee, Tennessee. The review was founded in 1892, and sought to encourage writing about the South. It flourished especially during and after the editorship of Allen Tate (1899–1979), between 1944 and 1946, when it was associated with NEW CRITICISM.

Sharecropping   System of working the land that operated in the South from the 1870s until the 1930s. In the system the tenant worked a plot of land for the owner, producing a crop (usually cotton). The tenant was granted the use of a cabin and a mule as well as the tools and seed needed to raise the crop. When the crop was sold the tenant received an agreed proportion of the money raised, usually about half, and the remainder went to the landowner. Sharecropping developed after the CIVIL WAR because of the lack of cash capital. The system caused many problems. It tied tenants to the land with no incentive to improve it; it encouraged the cultivation of cotton rather than of other crops that were less damaging to the soil, and it kept the share-cropper in a constant state of powerlessness in relation to the landowner. To many, sharecropping seemed to be another form of SLAVERY, especially as agriculture was seriously depressed in the 1870s. Up until 1900 most of the sharecroppers were black, but with the GREAT MIGRATION this changed and whites were in the majority. Sharecropping, along with similar systems such as share renting and the crop-lien system, features prominently in much Southern writing, and notably in the work of William FAULKNER and the early fiction of Richard WRIGHT.

Short story   Although originating in France and Germany at the end of the 18th century, the short story was developed by American writers to the extent that it is often considered a pre-eminently American genre.

There is no easy definition of the short story. Length may vary considerably, and the differences between a short story, a tale and a sketch have often been indistinct. Also, many of the short story's supposedly defining features have been contradicted by the immense variety of stories. The reasons given for the development of the short story in the United States have also been varied. It has been argued that the short story is most often produced in a ruptured society or a society in rapid transition; a stable society produces novels rather than short stories. As Raymond CARVER asserted in his essay 'Fires' (1983), the novelist 'needs a world that makes sense'. This theory is largely supported by reference to when and where the American short story flourished: 1830–60; 1870–90, in the late 20th century and during the SOUTHERN RENAISSANCE. The Irish writer Frank O'Connor famously claimed that the short story was 'remote from the community' and belonged mainly to 'submerged population groups'. This too has been borne out to some degree, perhaps because of the longer survival of ORAL TRADITIONS within such groups. Certainly, some of the finest contemporary short stories are by African Americans such as John Edgar Wideman (b. 1941) and Alice WALKER, and by Native Americans such as Leslie Marmon SILKO. Another theory explaining the American development of the short story has been the COPYRIGHT situation in the early 19th century. The uncertainties of copyright meant that authors were not necessarily guaranteed royalties on sales of novels, whereas they were paid for short fiction in weekly and monthly magazines. Since the 1830s there were a large number of these, some paying handsome fees. Writers often made considerably more money from short fiction than from novels, and this remained so until well into the 20th century.

The work of Washington IRVING, Edgar Allan POE and Nathaniel HAWTHORNE in the 1830s and 1840s was crucial to the aesthetic development of the short story, and Poe's 1842 review of Hawthorne's *Twice-Told Tales* is frequently cited as the most influential early statement on the aesthetics of the short story. Poe claimed that symmetry and unity characterized the short story, and that everything in it should contribute to a 'unique and single effect'. With little variation this has remained as true for Poe as it has been for major short-story writers such as Herman MELVILLE, Stephen CRANE, Kate CHOPIN, Jack London (1876–1916), Edith Wharton (1862–1937), Henry JAMES, Ernest HEMINGWAY, William FAULKNER, Eudora Welty (1909–2001), Flannery O'CONNOR, James Thurber (1894–1961), Carver and Walker. An important development since Poe's time, however, has been the short-story cycle or sequence. This may involve a series of stories connected thematically or geographically, or by recurring characters. In its overall effects, the cycle may be comparable to a novel, even though the short stories may be autonomous. Prominent cycles include *Winesburg, Ohio* (1919) by Sherwood Anderson (1876–1941); Hemingway's *In Our Time* (1925); Faulkner's *The Unvanquished* (1938) and *Go Down, Moses* (1942); Richard WRIGHT's *Uncle Tom's Children* (1940); *Love Medicine* (1984, 1993) by Louise Erdrich (b. 1954), and *Close Range* (1999) by Annie Proulx (b. 1935).

Further reading

Modern American Short Story Sequences (1995), edited by J. Gerald Kennedy; *The Culture and Commerce of the American Short Story* (1993) by Andrew Levy; *Short Story Theories* (1976), edited by Charles E. May; *The Contemporary American Short Story Cycle* (2001) by James Nagel; *The Development of the American Short Story* (1970) by Frederick Lewis Pattee, and *The American Short Story* (1964) by William Peden.

Signifying   Form of African American verbal play, consisting of elaborate or exaggerated response to a statement by another. Signifying is improvisational and creative; it may consist of exaggeration, innuendo and parody and is similar to 'playing the dozens' or 'specifying' in that it may be, and may be intended to be, unintelligible to a listener from outside the African American community. In *The Signifying Monkey* (1988) Henry Louis Gates, Jr argues that signifying provides a model for African American literary traditions, in that texts may be considered to be elaborately signifying other texts.

Silko, Leslie Marmon SHORT-STORY writer, novelist and poet, a major figure of contemporary NATIVE AMERICAN LITERATURE. Silko was born in Albuquerque, New Mexico, in 1948, and was raised on a Laguna Pueblo reservation. In 1968 she graduated from the University of New Mexico, and after publishing fiction and poetry, she brought out her first collection, *Laguna Woman*, in 1974. It was with the powerful novel *Ceremony* (1977) that Silko won major recognition. In it she explores the psychic damage to Tayo, a VETERAN of WORLD WAR II, and how a measure of healing is attained through his acceptance of Laguna myths and rituals. Silko, who characteristically explores the fluidity of genre boundaries, uses a non-linear narrative in *Ceremony*, partly as an attempt to amalgamate aspects of an ORAL TRADITION with the contemporary novel. This technique was extended further in the brilliantly crafted *Storyteller* (1981), a polyvalent text that includes photographs, short stories, poems and Laguna legends. The resultant collage effects embody the work's major theme: the responsibility of a storyteller to adapt and find relevant purpose in ancient stories, not only to keep alive an otherwise forgotten amalgamation of legend and history, but also to recognize the stories as a source of strength and endurance in the 20th century. Silko has developed this idea in other works, particularly in her novels *The Almanac of the Dead* (1991) and *The Gardens in the Dunes* (1999) and her collection of essays, *Yellow Woman* (1996). The essays reflect her abiding concern with the threatened environment, and this is further evident in the moving selection of letters between Silko and the poet James Wright (1927–80) published as *The Delicacy and Strength of Lace* (1986). The letters also meditate on the writer's responsibility towards language.

Further reading

Conversations with Leslie Marmon Silko (2000), edited by Ellen L. Arnold; *Leslie Marmon Silko* (1999), edited by Louise K. Barnett; *Leslie Marmon Silko: A Study of the Short Fiction* (1998) by Helen Jaskoski, and *Leslie Marmon Silko* (1997) by Gregory Salyer.

Slave narrative The individual's testimony of experiencing SLAVERY is often considered the first distinctively American literary genre and forms an important foundation for AFRICAN AMERICAN LITERATURE.

In the period 1760–1865 about seventy testimonial narratives by fugitive or former slaves were published. Prominent among these are *The Interesting Narrative of Olaudah Equiano* (1789) by Olaudah Equiano (?1745–97), Frederick DOUGLASS's

Narrative of the Life of Frederick Douglass, An American Slave (1845) and *Incidents in the Life of a Slave Girl* (1861) by Harriet Jacobs. The slave narrative in the ABOLITION period was a stylized form written for a definite end, in which the generic rather than the individual nature of the slave's experience would be emphasized. Narratives tended to mark the stages of the slave's move from slavery to freedom (though not beyond), marked by transitions such as the realization of what slavery meant after a period of innocence, the decision to escape and then the episode of escape. The slave narrative is by no means an 'unvarnished tale'. In some regards the slave narrative was a religious narrative, since its movement from innocence to freedom reflected a Christian journey from innocence to fall to redemption. Narratives also emphasized the cruelty of slavery, the brutalization of the slave, the disruption of the family unit and the moral contamination of slavery for both slave and master. In addition to the persuasive element of the narrative's content, the very existence of an authenticated narrative served as proof of the slave's intelligence and full humanity at a time when these were sometimes disputed.

After emancipation, slave narratives were memoirs of slavery, often more directly concerned with assimilation into society. In this respect they are similar to the SUCCESS NARRATIVE in charting the individual's progress from slavery to freedom and fulfilment; the most renowned example of this type of narrative is *Up from Slavery* (1901) by Booker T. Washington (1856–1915). In the 1930s the FEDERAL WRITERS' PROJECT commissioned the transcription of oral testimonies from more than 2,500 former slaves (they were published in eighteen volumes in 1978).

During the antebellum period there were many fictional works that made use of the slave narrative. In addition to novels by African Americans, such as *Clotel* (1853) by William Wells Brown (?1814–84) and *Our Nig* (1859) by Harriet Wilson (?1828–?63), there were slavery novels by whites which utilized the slave narrative, Harriet Beecher Stowe's *Uncle Tom's Cabin* (1852) being a notable example. More recently, African American novelists have used aspects of the slave narrative to explore either the continuing legacy of slavery or the failure of assimilation. These include Richard Wright in *Black Boy* (1945), Ralph Ellison in *Invisible Man* (1952), Malcolm X (1925–65) and Alex Haley (1921–92) in *The Autobiography of Malcolm X* (1964), Ishmael Reed (b. 1938) in *Flight to Canada* (1976), Charles Johnson (b. 1948) in *Oxherding Tale* (1982) and *Middle Passage* (1990) and Toni Morrison in *Beloved*. The recent so-called 'neo-slave narratives' often have the function of articulating what was left silent, perhaps through self-censorship, in the classic narratives. Thus, Morrison has said that in writing *Beloved* her job was 'to rip that veil drawn over "proceedings too terrible to relate"'.

Further reading

The Slave's Narrative (1985), edited by Charles T. Davis and Henry Louis Gates, Jr (1985); Witnessing Slavery (1979, 1994) by Frances E. Foster; Neo-Slave Narratives (1999) by Ashraf H. A. Rushdy, and The Slave Narrative and its Place in American History (1988) by Marion Wilson Starling.

Slave trade   The demand for labour in the American colonies led to the importation of indentured workers from Europe and the introduction of SLAVERY, with slaves brought from the Western coast of Africa. Slave trade between Europe and Africa had existed since the 15th century, and the first Africans were brought to Virginia in 1619. In Britain and in America the QUAKERS initiated opposition to the international slave trade at the end of the 17th century, and the United States CONSTITUTION, ratified in 1788, declared that the slave trade with Africa would end within 20 years. The British abolished slave trading to British colonies in 1807 and in 1808 the United States Congress outlawed the importation of African slaves. By then, approximately 650,000 living Africans had been brought to what became the United States. Some illegal international trading occurred after 1808, and the domestic slave trade continued. It is estimated that when slavery ended in 1865, over 99 per cent of the 4 million slaves had been born in the United States.

Slavery   Although a constant presence in human history, slavery in the United States refers to the bonded servitude of Africans and those of African descent that existed for over 200 years. Attempts by early colonizers in the 16th century to enslave the native population proved unsuccessful and African slaves were consequently imported. African slave labour was of crucial importance to the economic development of the United States. Slavery was abolished by the ratification of THIRTEENTH AMENDMENT in 1865.

Estimates of the numbers of slaves brought from Africa vary widely, though it is believed that between 10 and 11 million living slaves arrived in the Americas from Africa; large numbers died during the transatlantic 'middle passage' (the mortality rate for both slaves and crew in the middle passage has been estimated at between 5 and 20 per cent). Of the number brought to the American continent, mainly from West Africa, up to 650,000 were brought to lands that eventually became the United States. The importation of African slaves was made illegal in 1808, although the domestic trading of slaves continued.

In the colonies and later in the United States, slavery was distinguished from other forms of bonded labour by being for the life of the individual, by being hereditary and, eventually, by being based upon racial identification. The hereditary aspect of slavery in the United States was crucial in increasing the numbers of slaves. Slavery followed the condition of the mother; that is, if a person's mother was a slave, then that person was also a slave, the status and race of the father being irrelevant. The slave population in the United States grew from around 875,000 in 1800 to around 4 million in 1860 (when the total US population was 32 million). The racialization of slavery was gradual, though it was accelerated by the attacks on slavery as the ABOLITION movement developed, and by the SCIENTIFIC RACISM of the 1820s.

Between 1777 and 1804 slavery was abolished in all of the states north of Maryland. It was maintained in the South primarily because of the heavy labour requirement of an agrarian society, in particular for the crops, including cotton, that were produced in the plantation system (by 1850 nearly two-thirds of slaves on plantations were employed in the production of cotton). However, slavery varied greatly; as well as the plantations many slaves were held on small farms or in domestic service, and in the 1850s about half of slaveholders held no more than five slaves each.

Even in the colonial period there had always been some opposition to slavery, particularly from the QUAKERS, but this opposition grew in the early 1800s, leading to the ABOLITION movement and ultimately to the EMANCIPATION PROCLAMATION in 1863, during the CIVIL WAR. The existence of slavery as the DECLARATION OF INDEPENDENCE was ratified has been seen as especially ironic, destroying the optimistic assertion of liberty in that document. In a speech of 1852, called 'What to the Slave is the Fourth of July?', Frederick DOUGLASS declared that to the slave 'your celebration is a sham; your boasted liberty, an unholy license; your national greatness, swelling vanity . . . your sermons and thanksgivings, with all your religious parade . . . are . . . mere bombast, fraud, deception, impiety and hypocrisy – a thin veil to cover up crimes which would disgrace a nation of savages'. In his poem 'Misgivings' Herman MELVILLE wrote of America as 'the world's fairest hope linked with man's foulest crime'.

Literature about slavery is among the most powerful and vivid of all American writing. This literature can be classified into three groups: first, the testimonial writing by former slaves, such as the SLAVE NARRATIVE; second, the literature about slavery by non-enslaved whites and blacks, such as pro- and anti-slavery fiction and non-fiction, oratory, pamphlets and poetry; and, third, post-emancipation imaginative versions of slavery.

The first two categories are deeply embedded in the discourse about slavery prior to 1865. The slave narratives provided valuable testimony that could be used by abolitionists, but they might also directly challenge the pseudo-scientific racism that developed early in the nineteenth century, which sought to dehumanize the non-white. The literature of personal witness to slavery includes the work of Phillis WHEATLEY, Olaudah Equiano (?1745–97), Harriet JACOBS, William Wells Brown (?1814–84) and Frederick Douglass. The vast amount of fiction about slavery includes the 1859 novel *Our Nig* by Harriet Wilson (?1828–?63) and *Uncle Tom's Cabin* (1852) by Harriet Beecher STOWE, which is probably the most politically influential American novel ever written, as well as the pro-Southern work of William Gilmore Simms (1806–70). *The Slave* (1836) by Richard Hildreth (1807–65) is often considered the first anti-slavery novel. Anti-slavery poetry was comparatively uncommon, but the works of John Greenleaf Whittier (1807–92), James M. Whitfield (1822–71), Frances E. W. Harper (1825–1911) and James Russell Lowell (1819–91) are significant. The slavery debate occasioned vast amounts of polemical books, addresses, lectures and pamphlets, including the influential works *Appeal . . . to the Coloured Citizens of the World* (1828) by David Walker (1785–1830) and *An Appeal in Favor of that Class of Americans Called Africans* (1833) by Lydia Maria Child (1802–80), as well as writing by William Ellery

Channing (1780–1842), Maria W. Stewart (1803–79), William Lloyd Garrison (1805–79), Sarah Moore Grimké (1792–1873), Angelina Emily Grimké Weld (1805–79), Ralph Waldo Emerson and Henry David Thoreau.

Since emancipation, slavery has been written about as a means of understanding later race relations in the United States, and it has been a subject of much contention. For a period during Reconstruction the paternalistic view of slavery was maintained, and this led directly to its romantic representation in the 1936 novel *Gone with the Wind* by Margaret Mitchell (1900–49). Other writers, including Mark Twain, wrote of it in ways that indicated how far it was a deeply disturbing fact of history. In the 20th century, slavery was often examined in terms of the psychological damage inflicted on the dehistoricized and almost dehumanized slave and in terms of its effects on black identity. Slavery is an element in much important fiction, including novels by William Faulkner and Toni Morrison, often examined in terms of necessarily confronting a fractured American history and a lacerating present.

Further reading

For historical accounts of slavery see: *The Slave Community* (1979) by John W. Blassingame; *Roll, Jordan, Roll* (1974) by Eugene D. Genovese, and *American Slavery* (1993) by Peter Kolchin. Studies of literature and slavery include: *Postslavery Literatures in the Americas* (2000) by George B. Handley; *Figures in Black* (1987) by Henry Louis Gates, Jr, and *Slavery and the Literary Imagination* (1989) edited by Deborah E. McDowell and Arnold Rampersad.

The Smart Set   Monthly literary magazine published in New York. It was founded in 1890 by William D'Alton Mann, but it was under the joint editorship (1914–23) of H. L. Mencken (1880–1856) and George Jean Nathan (1882–1958) that it flourished. Sophisticated, witty and trendsetting, it published work by many international writers associated with modernism, as well as significant work by American authors, including Eugene O'Neill and F. Scott Fitzgerald. It ceased publication in 1930.

Social Darwinism   The application to human society of Charles Darwin's theory of natural selection, that is, that competition for resources ensures the evolution of the species, since only those best adapted to the demands of the environment will survive. The British philosopher Herbert Spencer (1820–1903), who coined the term 'survival of the fittest', propounded this doctrine, and it was spread enthusiastically in the United States by the sociologist William Graham Sumner (1840–1910). It was especially influential during the period 1890–1920, when it seemed an apt explanation of how society functioned at a time of rapid urbanization, evident urban poverty, the first wave of American plutocrats and the rise of monopolizing big business. Social Darwinism was used to explain the inevitability of poverty (the poor were ill-adapted for survival) and the emergence of the millionaire (the strong individual). It was consequently cited in support of laissez-faire economics and government non-intervention in monopolies and mergers. The doctrine also had a racial dimension, since it supported the dominance of the supposed evolutionarily advanced races, especially the Anglo-Saxon.

Social Darwinist ideas were taken up by novelists, and often used in association with NATURALISM. They play an important part in the new urban REALISM of the 1890s. The fiction of Frank NORRIS, Theodore DREISER and Jack London (1876–1916), is imbued with Social Darwinist thought, as is, to a lesser extent, the early work of Stephen CRANE.

Social mobility The movement of an individual or a group in a hierarchically structured society, usually in terms of occupation. Social mobility may be measured within the lifetime of an individual or between generations, and may be used to determine the life opportunities that a specific society affords. American culture has a core belief in the possibility of upward social mobility for individuals and groups, and this is expressed in the concept of the AMERICAN DREAM and repeatedly endorsed in literature concerned with IMMIGRATION. The movement of Jewish Americans from immigrant status in the mid 19th century into the professional classes after 1945 is an example of group upward mobility, whereas the upward mobility of the individual is typically the subject of the SUCCESS NARRATIVE. While it is extremely difficult to make accurate assessments of social mobility, evidence indicates that the degree of social mobility in the United States differs little from that of other industrialized societies.

The Sound and the Fury Novel by William FAULKNER, written in 1928 and published in 1929. Set mostly in Mississippi, the novel is in four parts, each using a different narrator with a distinct style, and centred on a particular day: respectively, 7 April 1928, 2 June 1910, 6 April 1928 and 8 April 1928. Each of the first three parts is narrated by one of three Compson brothers, Benjy, Quentin and Jason, while the fourth has an omniscient narrator. To a large extent each brother's narration centres on his relation with his absent sister, Candace (known as Caddy), whose illegitimate daughter, Quentin, is living in the Compson home in the novel's present, 1928. Part of the novel's greatness is in its stylistic complexity, as Faulkner develops a language appropriate to the mind and character of each brother. This style is demanding and sometimes opaque in the first two sections, where the solipsistic natures of the mentally retarded Benjy and the sensitive, suicidal Quentin are explored through STREAM OF CONSCIOUSNESS impressionistic narratives that make oblique or threaten to excise reference to objective external reality. Jason's narrative is more engaged with the external world, reflecting his cunning, materialistic nature, and allowing the representation of his misogynistic, psychopathic world view. The final narrative, centred to some extent on the Compsons' African American servant Dilsey and her family, offers an objective counterpoint to and perspective on the white family. After 1946 the novel included an appendix, which Faulkner described as 'the key to the whole book'. The

Compson children appear in the short stories 'That Evening Sun' (1931) and 'A Justice' (1931); Quentin is a major presence in *Absalom, Absalom!* (1936), and Jason features in *The Mansion* (1959).

The Sound and the Fury explores a wide range of themes by focusing on the Compson family. These include the absence of love, the tyranny of time, and the burden of the Southern past and its codes that define and determine behaviour. Unable to control, accommodate or imitate Caddy's life-affirming vital passion, the Compson family is declining into moral torpor and emotional paralysis.

Further reading

The Most Splendid Failure (1976) by André Bleikasten; *The Sound and the Fury: A Critical Casebook* (1982), edited by André Bleikasten; *Twentieth Century Interpretations of The Sound and the Fury* (1968), edited by Michael H. Cowan; *Faulkner's Rhetoric of Loss* (1983) by Gail L. Mortimer, and *The Novels of William Faulkner* (1959) by Olga W. Vickery. David Minter has edited the useful Norton Critical Edition of the novel (1976).

Southern Gothic   Twentieth century variation of GOTHIC literature, making use of Southern settings and concerns. Southern Gothic usually involves grotesque or lurid situations, and often wavers between the tragic and the comic. Sometimes the term is extended to include the work of Edgar Allan POE, but more usually it refers to a group of writers working from the 1940s onwards. These include William FAULKNER, Eudora Welty (1909–2001), Tennessee WILLIAMS, Carson McCullers (1917–67), Truman Capote (1924–84) and Flannery O'CONNOR. Southern Gothic has been considered as an oblique confrontation of the disruptions of Southern history.

Southern literature   Writing about the South may usefully be divided into five distinct periods: Colonial (before 1800); Antebellum (1800–60); post-CIVIL WAR (1865–1920); SOUTHERN RENAISSANCE (1929–55), and the New South (1955 onwards). In each period, but especially from 1800 onwards, emphasis has been placed on the South as a region with its own distinct history and identity.

There is a notable lack of imaginative literature produced in the South before 1800, a fact that has prompted much comment. It has been argued that oratory, historiography and politics rather than fiction, drama and poetry engaged the creative and intellectual energies of Southerners. Certainly, the non-fictive writings of Thomas Jefferson (1743–1826) often display a creativity lacking in poetry by Southerners, imitative as it is of English models. However, increasing attacks on the South over the issue of SLAVERY galvanized Southern writing at the start of the 19th century. The PLANTATION NOVELS by writers such as Sarah J. Hale (1788–1879), John Pendleton Kennedy (1795–1870) and William Gilmore Simms (1806–70) placed emphasis on the South as a different kind of society than that of the North, and laid the basis for the nostalgia of post-war plantation literature. Theirs is the version of the 'Old South' that becomes familiar in the 20th century, a South of leisure, grace and aristocratic chivalry. This was however also the period of the SLAVE NARRATIVE, offering a corrosively different version of the Southern society of farmers and planters.

After the Civil War there was a notable hiatus in Southern literature, although a series of novels written during RECONSTRUCTION, notably those by Thomas Dixon (1864–1946), engaged with the Southern past in particular ways. The idea of a stately, dignified society lost with the war gathered momentum among whites, and is one of the ideas behind the Southern Renaissance, at least insofar as this was shaped by the influence of the AGRARIANS. The GREAT MIGRATION of blacks from the South did much to diminish black voices in Southern writing, although the work of Zora Neale HURSTON is a notable exception, as, later, is the early work of Richard WRIGHT. William FAULKNER is both the major writer of the renaissance and the writer who did most to articulate distinctively Southern themes in the 20th century. To a large extent he defines modern Southern literature, with its preoccupation with the lurid, the grotesque, with forms of ROMANCE and, above all, with the tragic sense of a Southern past that is simultaneously legacy, burden and curse. Faulkner was deeply ambivalent towards the South: he understood its faults and self-delusions from within, yet never lived elsewhere for any appreciable length of time, and the South and its history constantly formed the focus for his finest fiction. In Faulkner's work the Southern past is both shameful and ennobling, the origin of the problems of the modern South. Faulkner's ambivalence becomes so problematic that it can only be dealt with by detached irony, such as that displayed by his character Gavin Stevens, especially in *Intruder in the Dust* (1948). The alternative, experienced by Quentin Compson in *The Sound and the Fury* (1929) and *Absalom, Absalom!* (1936), is lacerating pain leading to suicide. The sense of a fractured past contributed to the dominance of the SOUTHERN GOTHIC in the work of writers such as Flannery O'CONNOR, Eudora Welty (1909–2001) and Carson McCullers (1917–67). Confronting it led also to the fullest restoration of the myth of the Old South in *Gone With the Wind* (1936) by Margaret Mitchell (1900–49). Much of the appeal of this myth, even in the hands of sophisticated writers such as Allen Tate (1899–1979) and Robert Penn Warren (1905–89), had to do with a sense that the modern South was becoming or was in danger of becoming an industrial, mechanized pastless society indistinguishable from the North.

Faulkner's influence might have proved difficult to evade for the Southern writers who emerged after the 1950s. However, the changes that took place in the South have lessened that influence. Rural poverty, racial segregation and a strong class hierarchy were primary elements of the society providing the setting for Faulkner's work. Since the 1960s the CIVIL RIGHTS MOVEMENT, heavy financial investment and technological innovation have helped transform the South considerably, to the extent that questions that were so pressing for Faulkner have been less urgent for recent writers. Literature of the 'New South' displays more variety than ever before, to the extent that some critics have even wondered whether there is now a 'Southern Literature' at all. A strong sense of history remains, as in the work of Margaret Walker (1915–98), and so too does a strongly religious element, evident in the novels of Walker Percy (1916–90). But writers such as Alice WALKER (notably in *Meridian*, 1976), Ellen Gilchrist (b. 1935) and Bobbie Ann Mason (b. 1940) have written about the South in ways that seek to connect the past with a clear sense of a future. What was often considered the theme of Southern literature, the relation between past and present, has become less prominent, and notably less tragic.

Further reading

Twentieth Century Southern Literature (1997) by J. A. Bryant; 'After the Southern Renascence' by John Burt, in *The Cambridge History of American Literature*, Volume VII (1999), edited by Sacvan Bercovitch; *The Literature of Memory* (1977) by Richard Gray; *The South in American Literature* (1954) by J. B. Hubbell, and *The History of Southern Literature* (1985), edited by Louis D. Rubin et al.

Southern Renaissance Term used to describe the remarkable flourishing of SOUTHERN LITERATURE, especially in fiction and poetry, during the period 1929–55. Its origins have been seen in the writings of the FUGITIVES and the AGRARIANS, but it was particularly with the work of William FAULKNER that a true 'renaissance' developed. Prominent writers of the Southern Renaissance include Thomas Wolfe (1900–38), Robert Penn Warren (1905–89), Eudora Welty (1909–2001), Tennessee WILLIAMS, Carson McCullers (1917–67) and Flannery O'CONNOR.

Further reading

Renaissance in the South (1963) by John M. Bradbury and *A Southern Renaissance* (1980) by Richard H. King.

Southern Review Published between 1935 and 1942 from Baton Rouge, Louisiana, and relaunched in 1965, *Southern Review* was an influential quarterly, publishing criticism, fiction and poetry. Under the editorship of Robert Penn Warren (1905–89) and Cleanth Brooks (1906–94) it was especially associated with NEW CRITICISM and was significant in the development of the SOUTHERN RENAISSANCE. There were two earlier journals called *The Southern Review*, both aspiring to cultivate Southern writing and culture. The first was published from Charleston, South Carolina (1828–32), and the second from Baltimore, Maryland (1867–79).

Spanish–American War Conflict fought in 1898 between Spain and the United States which resulted in Spain losing its possessions in the Americas and in the United States emerging as a world power.

The origins of the war were in Cuba's struggle for independence from Spain, which began in 1895. Although the United States was officially neutral, there was much public support for the Cubans and illicit gun running to arm the rebels. (Stephen CRANE was shipwrecked in 1897 while reporting on this activity, and the experience forms the basis for his 1898 story 'The Open Boat'.) The United States sent a battleship, the *Maine*, to Cuba to protect its citizens, but the ship was sunk in February 1898 with the loss of 260 men. This occasioned the declaration of war between the two powers. The United States had a relatively easy victory, with casualties totalling approximately 6,000 men, mostly through disease. (Secretary of State John Hay called it 'a splendid little war'.) The Treaty of Paris officially ended the conflict in December 1898. Under the treaty's terms Spain relinquished its possession of Cuba and ceded Guam and Puerto Rico to the United States. It also agreed to sell the Philippines to the United States for $20 million.

The war is often seen as an important turning point in United States history, representing the ending of one empire and the beginning of another, and the start of the 'American century'. The expansionist policy evident particularly in the purchase of the Philippines was attacked by many writers, notably Mark Twain and Hamlin Garland (1860–1940). The story 'Editha' (1907) by William Dean Howells (1837–1920) is critical of the mentality that he saw driving the conflict. Sherwood Anderson (1876–1941), Carl Sandburg (1878–1967) and the underage Damon Runyon (1884–1946) fought in the war. Crane and Frank Norris reported on it from Cuba. The thriller *Cuba Libre* (1998) by Elmore Leonard (b. 1925) is set in Cuba during the war.

Spirituals   A vital element of the African American cultural tradition, spirituals were performed since the earliest period of SLAVERY and are very much bound up with the slave's need for expression and hope. While religious, the spirituals were performed at work as well as in church. The religious centre of the songs often includes the aspiration to freedom from enslavement, using either the Old Testament parallel of the enslaved Israelites looking forward to freedom from bondage in the Promised Land, or the New Testament concept of a heaven that means freedom and rest from labour. Usually the spiritual interwove a solo and a choral element, the so-called 'call and response' tradition that originated in West and Central Africa. While they were often uplifting and part of a communal identity, the tragic element of the songs was also evident, especially to insiders. In his NARRATIVE OF THE LIFE OF FREDERICK DOUGLASS, DOUGLASS cautioned against the appearance of happiness that slave singing produced; 'slaves sing most when they are most unhappy,' he wrote, and 'every tone was a testimony against slavery, and a prayer to God for deliverance from chains. The hearing of those wild notes always depressed my spirit ... to those songs I traced my first glimmering conception of the dehumanizing character of slavery.' W. E. B. Du Bois wrote movingly of the spirituals in *The Souls of Black Folk* (1903), calling them 'The Sorrow Songs' and declaring that they were 'the sole American music' and 'the most beautiful expression of human experience ... the singular spiritual heritage of the nation and the greatest gift of the Negro people'.

After emancipation, spirituals were collected in *Slave Songs of the United States* (1867), edited by William Francis Allen (1830–89). Performances of the songs became popular from the 1880s onwards and they became internationally known through the work of the Fisk University Jubilee Singers, the singers Paul Robeson, Marian Anderson and others. The spiritual played an important part in the development of BLUES and JAZZ, and many authors, including William FAULKNER and James BALDWIN, have used songs for titles of creative works.

Sports literature   Literary representation of sports is ancient, having its roots in the Homeric epics. To use the broadest definition of 'sport', which includes hunting, fishing and gambling as well as organized spectator sports, there is a considerable American tradition of sports writing. Sports have formed the subject for adventure stories, DIME NOVELS, serious fiction, light verse and poetry, and sports literature encompasses a wide range of themes and concepts. These include sport as a metaphor for American life, celebration of the body, examination of masculinity, of success, of the aftermath of success, of the nature and uses of violence, the representation of racial integration and the nature of the hero. Sport has been seen as answering a need for ritual in secular American life, as a form of PASTORAL, and, especially for the male writer, as a significant point of contact between father and son. Sports, and individual sporting heroes, have occupied a special place in AFRICAN AMERICAN LITERATURE, with the boxers Joe Louis and Muhammad Ali, the baseball player Jackie Robinson and the basketball player Michael Jordan being represented as champions whose achievements are realizations of African American aspirations and potential.

In 18th and 19th century American literature sport was mostly represented by hunting, fishing and some horseracing, and this representation continued well into the 20th century by writers such as William FAULKNER and Ernest HEMINGWAY. Athletic prowess as an expression of individualistic manly heroism was also an important feature in FRONTIER, WESTERN and COWBOY literature, but the figure of the athlete as hero really develops in the 19th century in CHILDREN'S LITERATURE and in the dime novel, where Frank Merriwell, created by William G. ('Gilbert') Patten (1866–1945) was a popular figure. Towards the end of the 19th century competitive sport was examined by NATURALISTIC writers as a trope for American life, especially in works by Jack London (1876–1916) and Frank NORRIS, and they also established another key element of American sports literature: sport as a physical and moral testing of the individual character. With the increasing popularity of team sports, football and baseball start to be treated in adult literature from the 1920s, notably in the work of Ring Lardner (1885–1933), and various professional sports are significantly represented in works by Damon Runyon (1884–1946), Eugene O'NEILL, Hemingway, F. Scott FITZGERALD and Thomas Wolfe (1900–38). More recently, sport has been an important feature in the fiction of Bernard MALAMUD, Norman Mailer (b. 1923), William Kennedy (b. 1928), Robert Coover (b. 1932), John Updike (b. 1932), Don DeLILLO, Philip ROTH and Annie Proulx (b. 1935), and in poetry by Marianne Moore (1887–1972), Randall Jarrell (1914–65), James Dickey (1923–97), Kenneth Koch (1925–2002), James Wright (1927–80) and

Donald Hall (b. 1928). There is a rich body of non-fictional works on particular sports, notably by writers such as A. J. Liebling (1904–63) on boxing and Roger Angell (b. 1920) on baseball.

Significant individual works include: Malamud's *The Natural* (1952); Coover's *Universal Baseball Association* (1968); *The Dream Team* (1973) by Joe McGinniss (b. 1939); DeLillo's *End Zone* (1972); Kenneth Koch's comic long poem *Ko; or, a Season on Earth* (1960); *Everybody's All-American* (1981) by Frank Deford (b. 1938); Donald Hall's *Fathers Playing Catch with Sons* (1985); *The Sportswriter* (1987) by Richard Ford (b. 1944); *On Boxing* (1987) by Joyce Carol Oates (b. 1938), and Annie Proulx's *Close Range* (1999).

Further reading

Laurel and Thorn: The Athlete in American Literature (1988) by Robert J. Higgs; Dreaming of Heroes (1982) and Sporting with the Gods (1991) by Michael Oriard, and The Sporting Myth and the American Experience (1975) by Wiley Lee Umphlett.

Stamp Act   Passed in 1765, the act marked an innovation in the British system of raising revenue in the American colonies. To help offset the costs of the most recent of the French and Indian Wars, a tax was applied to all legal papers, newspapers, pamphlets and various other documents, in line with the laws then operating in Britain. (The papers had to bear a revenue stamp indicating that the tax had been paid.) This measure introduced direct taxation from Britain and was enacted without the consent of the colonies. There was fierce and occasionally violent opposition to the act, and a special colonial convention (the 'Stamp Act Congress') was held in New York to appeal against it. Opposition damaged transatlantic trade and led to the repeal of the act in 1766. However, Parliament then passed the Declaratory Act, which asserted the right of the British to raise direct taxes on the colonies (an assertion that justified the 1767 Townshend Acts). The Stamp Act was a significant factor in the gradual development of American opposition to the British rule of the colonies, and gave rise to the slogan 'no taxation without representation'.

Stein, Gertrude   Influential writer whose demanding work challenges conventional generic boundaries. Stein was born in Allegheny City, Pennsylvania, in 1874, where her father was a businessman. She spent much of her childhood in Austria and France as well as Oakland, California, before attending what is now Radcliffe College. There she studied philosophy, which included courses in psychology taught by William James (1842–1910), and she researched the anatomy of the brain at the Johns Hopkins Medical School. Stein's inherited wealth gave her considerable independence, and in 1902 she moved to London with her brother Leo before settling in Paris. From 1910 until her death in 1946 she lived mainly in Paris with her lover Alice B. Toklas (1877–1967). There she became a prominent figure in intellectual and artistic circles, a friend of leading avant-garde painters such as Pablo Picasso and Henri Matisse and of important literary figures. She had an especially profound influence on expatriate American writers in Paris, and on what she called the 'LOST GENERATION', which included Ernest HEMINGWAY and F. Scott FITZGERALD. Stein's own writing was frequently experimental and sometimes opaque, resulting from her attempt to work with language in the ways that contemporary painters were working with paint. Her prose is characterized by fragmentation, repetition and rhythm. For Stein language was a material and visible medium, and part of her greatness lay in her ability to represent and communicate complex and demanding concepts in simple language. She was one of the first writers fully to embrace modernity and to declare the 19th century dead. Although still relatively unassimilated into the American literary canon, her work remains fresh and challenging and offers sophisticated rewards to the dedicated reader.

Stein's publications include *Three Lives* (1909), focused on the lives of three working-class women, *Tender Buttons* (1914), *Geography and Plays* (1922), the lengthy *The Making of Americans* (1925), *Lucy Church Amiably* (1927), THE AUTOBIOGRAPHY OF ALICE B. TOKLAS (1933), *The Geographical History of America* (1936), *Everybody's Autobiography* (1937), *Wars I Have Seen* (1945) and *Brewsie and Willie* (1946), based on contact with American soldiers who visited her in Paris. Several collections of her essays and lectures are helpful in explaining her ideas of literature and composition, especially 'Composition as Explanation' (1926), *Lectures in America* (1935) and *Narration* (1935). She also wrote two opera librettos: *Four Saints in Three Acts* (1934) and, her final work, *The Mother of Us All* (1947).

Further reading

Gertrude Stein in Pieces (1970) by Richard Bridgman; A Primer for the Gradual Understanding of Gertrude Stein (1971) by Robert B. Haas; Critical Essays on Gertrude Stein (1986), edited by Michael J. Hoffman, and Reading Gertrude Stein (1990) by Lisa Ruddick. Biographical studies include Charmed Circle (1974) by James R. Mellow and Favored Strangers (1995) by Linda Wagner-Martin.

Stevens, Wallace   One of the most important American poets, Stevens was born in Reading, Pennsylvania, in 1879. He attended Harvard University and worked as a journalist before beginning a legal career. A specialist in insurance law, he worked from 1916 for the Hartford Accident and Indemnity Company in Hartford, Connecticut, and was the company's vice-president from 1934 until his death in 1955.

Stevens's first book, *Harmonium* (1923), is one of American poetry's defining works. In it he began to interrogate what would be his major theme, the relation between imagination and reality. Stevens typically wrote in stately, dignified blank verse, although he also expressed his playful, whimsical side in many exuberant lyrics. His other collections were: *Ideas of Order* (1935); *The Man with the Blue Guitar* (1937); *Parts of a World* (1942); *Transport to Summer* (1947), and *The Auroras of Autumn* (1950). His *Collected Poems* was published in 1954, supplemented by *Opus Posthumous* (1957, revised 1989). He also published a collection of prose pieces, *The*

Necessary Angel (1951). Stevens's meditative long poems represent some of his finest and most profound work, notably 'The Comedian as the Letter C' (1923), 'The Man with the Blue Guitar' (1937), 'Notes Towards a Supreme Fiction' (1942), 'Esthétique du Mal' (1947) and 'An Ordinary Evening in New Haven' (1950).

Stevens wrote, 'The great poems of heaven and hell have been written and the great poem of earth remains to be written.' After the achievements of Dante and Milton, he thus expressed an aspiration for modern, post-Christian poetry celebrating material reality, unmediated by dream or despair. However, Stevens was engaged in a restless dialectic, torn between a ROMANTIC desire to celebrate the imagination's power, and an attempt to engage, however imperfectly, with 'things as they are'. He considered the imagination to be a force enriching reality, without which reality is unrealized, unpalatable and impoverished. 'We have it,' he wrote, 'because we do not have enough without it.' However, he also expressed the opposing belief, 'bare earth is best,' claiming that the poet's chief responsibility is in the attempt to apprehend and represent reality as it is. The imagination, the human perception of reality itself, is inevitably and tragically false in representing reality, since it necessarily transforms and abstracts. In Stevens's dialectic there is an attempt to find a mode in which the imagination enriches but remains responsible to reality. This mode is partly expressed in his concept of the 'fiction'. Myths that once provided satisfactory explanations of the world no longer suffice, because timeless, unchanging truths do not exist. We must give credence instead to fictions, which are only temporarily true and must change, but which will temporarily satisfy our human needs. Stevens is a poet of immense subtlety, whose poetry can be challenging and difficult but also richly rewarding.

Further reading

Wallace Stevens: A Mythology of Self (1985) by Milton J. Bates; *Wallace Stevens: The Poems of Our Climate* (1977) by Harold Bloom; *Wallace Stevens: The Poetics of Modernism* (1985), edited by Albert Gelpi; *Wallace Stevens and the Seasons* (2001) by George S. Lensing; *The Long Poems of Wallace Stevens* (1985) by Rajeev S. Patke; *The Clairvoyant Eye* (1965) by Joseph N. Riddel, and *Words Chosen Out of Desire* (1984) by Helen Vendler.

Stonewall riots   Series of riots that took place in June 1969 in Greenwich Village, New York City, after a police raid on a gay bar, The Stonewall Inn. There had already been a series of raids on the bar, but on this occasion the crowd resisted the police. The riots initiated a new era of gay activism and gay pride and Stonewall is considered a major landmark for gay and lesbian writing. The riots are described in *The Beautiful Room is Empty* (1988) by Edmund White (b. 1940).

Stowe, Harriet Beecher   Novelist best known for her anti-SLAVERY novel *Uncle Tom's Cabin* (1852). Harriet Beecher was born in 1811 in Litchfield, Connecticut, into a distinguished and strongly Calvinist family; her father was the renowned minister Lyman Beecher. She was a pupil at her sister's school, at which she later taught, in

Hartford, Connecticut, and in Cincinnati, Ohio. In 1836 she married a clergyman, Calvin Ellis Stowe. She visited Kentucky before living in Maine, where she began writing *Uncle Tom's Cabin*, her first novel, in 1850. This was followed by the factual *A Key to Uncle Tom's Cabin* (1853) in which Stowe presented documentary material to support her representation of slavery. Her second novel, *Dred: A Tale of the Great Dismal Swamp* (1856), was based on NAT TURNER'S REVOLT. The enormous success of *Uncle Tom's Cabin* made Stowe an international celebrity. Her later novels and short stories are primarily regional and in the domestic tradition. They include the satirical *The Minister's Wooing* (1859) and *Oldtown Folks* (1869). She also published the controversial *Lady Byron Vindicated* (1870), in which she detailed the infidelities of Lord Byron and stated that he had committed incest. Stowe lived partly in New England and partly on a Florida plantation. She died in Hartford in 1896.

Critical opinion of Stowe has been sharply divided. The importance of her first novels to the ABOLITIONIST movement is undeniable, but their influential representation of African Americans been considered unfortunately stereotypical. The later work has been considered conservative by some because of its representation of women in the domestic sphere, while others have praised its attention to realist detail and have considered Stowe an important precursor of later women writers, especially those of the LOCAL COLOUR tradition.

Further reading

Critical Essays on Harriet Beecher Stowe (1980), edited by Elizabeth Ammons; Harriet Beecher Stowe (1994) by Joan D. Hedrick; The Beechers (1981) by Milton Rugoff, and Harriet Beecher Stowe: The Known and the Unknown (1965) by Edward Wagenknecht.

Stream of consciousness Term used originally by William James (1842–1910) in *The Principles of Psychology* (1890) to describe the individual's thought processes. James represented personal consciousness as continually changing, and the thought process as not necessarily rational in its shifts. In literary criticism 'stream of consciousness' describes a narrative technique in which a character's thoughts are presented without intervention or comment by the narrator, and in which there may be no apparent logical sequence to them. Although some pre-20th century novelists had experimented with narrative techniques similar to stream of consciousness, it was especially associated with MODERNISM through the influence of James Joyce's *Ulysses* (1922). The finest American example of the technique is in the first three parts of *THE SOUND AND THE FURY* (1929) by William FAULKNER. The technique may be very demanding for the reader, who must follow a character's non-logical thought processes and often has to guess at the significance of particular images or ideas.

Success narrative Prose writing, usually AUTOBIOGRAPHICAL and told in the first person, which traces a character's rise in the world, usually as an endorsement of the AMERICAN DREAM. There are many models for the success narrative, one of the originals being Benjamin FRANKLIN's *Autobiography* (1818, 1867). The novels of Horatio ALGER are influential models of the fictional success narrative. Often considered a specifically male form, the narrative usually includes a series of conventional gestures, such as concentration on the decision to leave home, a consideration of the alternative life the protagonist might have otherwise led, and a contrast of two points in the protagonist's life, usually involving revisiting as a success a location associated with failure or poverty. As well as being endorsed by writers, the narrative's trajectory of success and fulfilment has often been the target of satire or critical evaluation.

Further reading

Failure and Success in America (1978) by Martha Banta and *The Great White Way* (1993) by Phillipa Kafka.

Suffrage movement   In the mid 19th century various organizations were formed to campaign for the right of free women to vote. Before the CIVIL WAR these were usually part of the anti-SLAVERY movement, but after the 1848 SENECA FALLS CONVENTION, under the guidance of Lucretia Mott (1793–1880) and Elizabeth Cady Stanton (1815–1902), the focus began to be more exclusively on women's rights. After the war the campaign intensified, with the founding in 1866 of the American Equal Rights Association. However, in 1869 differences over support for the suffrage for African American men led to its being split, into the American Woman Suffrage Association, led by Lucy Stone (1818–93), and the more radical women-only National Woman Suffrage Association, led by Stanton and Susan B. Anthony (1820–1906). In 1890 the associations were reunited as the National American Woman Suffrage Association. By the 1890s various states, beginning with Wyoming (1890), had begun to allow women to vote, but to include all states an amendment to the CONSTITUTION was needed. Attempts in 1878 and 1914 failed, but after WORLD WAR I suffrage was supported by the main political parties and accordingly the constitutional amendment permitting women's suffrage was passed by June 1919. In August 1920 the required number of states had ratified it and the Nineteenth Amendment to the Constitution was declared. It declares, 'The right of citizens of the United States to vote shall not be denied or abridged by the United States or by any State on account of sex.'

Several prominent writers, notably Charlotte Perkins Gilman (1860–1935), were involved in the suffrage movement, and *On to Victory* (1987), edited by Bettina Friedl, is an important collection of suffragist plays. The history of the movement is told in the compendious six-volume *History of Woman Suffrage* (1881–1922).

Supreme Court of the United States   The Supreme Court was instituted under the third article of the CONSTITUTION in 1787. It is empowered to act in a variety of cases and to review acts of Congress and treaties, but its major responsibility is upholding and interpreting the Constitution. Prior to 1869 its size varied, but since then it has comprised eight justices and one chief justice. All are appointed for life, although they can be impeached or dismissed for misconduct. When a place becomes vacant, the president proposes a nominee whose appointment must be ratified by the Senate. The court deals mainly with cases that have been appealed from a state supreme court or federal court when a constitutional question is involved; the court is obliged to handle appealed cases, whereas its scrutiny of others is discretionary. Decisions by the court do not have to be unanimous, and when a majority verdict is reached it is customary for dissenting justices to publish their opinion.

T

Talented tenth   The term used by W. E. B. Du Bois to signify his vision for the development and full acceptance of blacks into American society. Although Du Bois first uses the phrase 'talented tenth' in a 1903 essay with that title, the concept behind it was consistently represented in his essays, particularly those in *The Souls of Black Folk* (1903). Du Bois proposed that each black community should select the top 10 per cent of its young people and focus its resources on their development as professionals. In this way, Du Bois argued, black doctors, lawyers, teachers and ministers would assist the progress of the entire community. The economic and intellectual opportunities for all blacks would improve with the creation of a black professional class. In 'The Talented Tenth' he asked

> Can the masses of the Negro people be in any possible way more quickly
> raised than by the effort and example of this aristocracy of talent and
> character? Was there ever a nation on God's fair earth civilized from the
> bottom upward? Never; it is, ever was and ever will be from the top downward
> that culture filters. The Talented Tenth rises and pulls all that are worth the
> saving up to their vantage ground.

The talented tenth idea was specifically in opposition to the then influential ideas of Booker T. Washington (1856–1915), who wanted blacks to develop 'usable skills' and work their way up into full assimilation into American society. Du Bois foresaw that this emphasis on non-professional labour as appropriate to blacks would result in them being a permanent underclass in the United States and his talented tenth was developed as a necessary alternative. The 'object of all true education', Du Bois wrote, 'is not to make men carpenters, it is to make carpenters men.'

Tall tale   Literary style, derived from ORAL TRADITIONS and especially associated with the FRONTIER, in which the narrative involves exaggerated or impossible feats. There are several varieties of tall tale. Those that concern legendary figures such as Paul Bunyan and Johnny Appleseed echo European narratives explaining the shaping of the landscape. Others may be exaggerations for primarily comic purposes, while there is a large series of tall tales regarding the adventures of DIME NOVEL heroes such as Calamity Jane and Buffalo Bill. Washington IRVING, Augustus Longstreet (1790–1870), George W. Harris (1814–69), Thomas B. Thorpe (1815–78), Mark TWAIN, Ambrose Bierce (1842–?1914) and William FAULKNER all made significant use of the tall tale, while several contemporary writers, such as Sherman Alexie (b. 1966), have used it as a form of parable.

Tammany Hall   Term used to describe the executive of the Democratic Party in New York City. Taking its name from a Delaware chief (he is fictionalized in James Fenimore COOPER's *The Last of the Mohicans* (1826)), Tammany was founded in 1789 as an anti-FEDERALIST organization, in opposition to the limitation of the franchise. It evolved into an association concerned with welfare and after 1817 became especially associated with Catholic Irish immigrants and then with the Democratic Party. As a party machine its name became synonymous with a combination of corruption, coercion and strategic benevolence. Its power decreased considerably after the 1930s, as the NEW DEAL provided some measure of social security.

Tammany is depicted in a wide range of novels set in New York, notably *Legs* (1975) and *Billy Phelan's Greatest Game* (1978) by William Kennedy (b. 1928), *Billy Bathgate* (1989) by E. L. Doctorow (b. 1931) and *What I Lived For* (1994) by Joyce Carol Oates (b. 1938).

Taylorization   Term applied to a system of mass production based on the principles of 'scientific management' developed by Frederick Winslow Taylor (1856–1915). In the 1880s Taylor introduced time and motion studies in order to maximize the efficiency of the factory worker. His methods concentrated on the elimination of superfluous motion and on the congruence of worker and machine. Taylorization was much resisted by workers who felt increasingly unfulfilled in the jobs they performed. In her book *Taylored Lives: Narrative Productions in the Age of Taylor, Veblen and Ford* (1993), Martha Banta explores the literary depiction of mass production.

Teapot Dome scandal   Scandal involving the administration of President Warren Harding. In 1922 it was revealed that the secretary for the interior, Albert B. Fall, had secretly and fraudulently leased US Navy oil reserves in Teapot Dome, Wyoming, to an oil company in return for money and gifts. He had also done the same with another company for reserves in Elk Hills, California. Fall and other members of the administration were convicted of fraud and some were imprisoned. The term 'teapot dome' came to refer to any government corruption. The scandal is the subject of the novel *Oil!* (1927) by Upton Sinclair (1878–1968).

Temperance movement   Various movements dedicated either to the PROHIBITION or moderation of alcohol consumption and availability were founded in the early 19th century, notably the American Temperance Society in 1826. By the 1830s over a million people had joined temperance societies, many of which were affiliated to Protestant churches, and temperance was the leading REFORM movement. In the 1870s a series of women-led temperance marches became known as the 'woman's crusade', and women came to play significant roles in the temperance movement, reflecting concern over the effects of alcohol on domestic life. Two major temperance organizations were the Woman's Christian Temperance Union, founded in 1874, and the Anti-Saloon League, formed in 1895. Famous temperance campaigners include Martha McClellan Brown (1838–1916), Frances Willard (1839–98), Frances E. W. Harper (1825–1911) and Carrie Nation (1846–1911), renowned for physical attacks on saloons wielding a hatchet. Since temperance came to be seen as a woman's movement, it was accordingly regarded as an attack on manhood. Historians have also noted the promotion of Protestantism and the racial stereotyping in temperance thought. The temperance campaign led to the institution of Prohibition in 1919, and although this was a failure, temperance movements continued, notably with the National Temperance League, founded in 1950.

There was a huge amount of temperance literature produced between 1829 and 1918. Mostly this comprised sermons, fiction, essays and verse, often circulated as pamphlets or tracts, and there were many popular novels devoted to the subject. Temperance fiction sometimes combined the moralistic with the sensationally lurid, and some temperance literature, such as the novel *Ten Nights in a Barroom and What I Saw There* (1854) by Timothy Shay Arthur (1809–85), dramatized by William W. Pratt, was phenomenally popular. Various writers, notably Edgar Allan POE, Herman MELVILLE (who refused 'to believe in a Temperance Heaven') and Stephen CRANE, made significant creative use of temperance discourse. Early in his career Walt WHITMAN wrote a temperance novel, *Franklin Evans* (1842), and the autobiographical *John Barleycorn* (1913) by Jack London (1876–1916) was taken up as a temperance text.

Further reading

Symbolic Crusade (1963) by Joseph Gusfield; Well-tempered Women (1998) by Carol Mattingly; Stephen Crane's Blue Badge of Courage (2000) by George Monteiro; The Serpent in the Cup (1997), edited by David S. Reynolds and Debra J. Rosenthal, and Beneath the American Renaissance (1988) by David S. Reynolds.

Termination   Government policy regarding Native Americans, the results of which frequently form a significant background to contemporary Native American writing. Termination became official policy in 1953 with the passing of House Concurrent Resolution 108. Tribes could choose to renounce the special status accorded by federal statutes; they would become subject to state laws, and allotted reservation land would lose its status and could be sold to non-Indians. The policy was intended to facilitate

Native American assimilation into mainstream American culture and society, and around 100 tribes and bands were terminated. However, termination caused severe problems. Much Indian land was sold and thousands of Indians were relocated to urban environments. In the 1960s the policy was abolished (it was officially repudiated in 1988), and many terminated tribes have since regained federal recognition.

Theatre Guild   Founded by Lawrence Langner (1890–1962) in New York in 1918, the guild was committed to the production of artistic, non-commercial plays, being financed by member subscription rather than dependent on audiences for income. While its productions included classic and new European plays (notably those of George Bernard Shaw), it was a significant catalyst in the development of the American theatre. After 1928 the plays of Eugene O'NEILL were especially associated with the guild.

Thirteen Colonies   The British colonies in North America that were in existence at the time of the DECLARATION OF INDEPENDENCE and which became the original states of the new Union. They were, in order of their founding: Virginia (1607), Massachusetts (1620/1628), New Hampshire (1623), Maryland (1634), Connecticut (1635), Rhode Island (1636), Delaware (1638), North Carolina (1663), South Carolina (1663), New Jersey (1664), New York (1664) (1613 as New Netherland), Pennsylvania (1681) and Georgia (1733). Although the preamble to the declaration states that it is 'The Unanimous Declaration of the Thirteen United States of America', only twelve of the thirteen had voted for it by 4 July; New York abstained and did not ratify it until 15 July.

Thirteenth Amendment   The amendment to the CONSTITUTION that ended chattel SLAVERY, whose end had already been signalled by the 1863 EMANCIPATION PROCLAMATION. Ratified in December 1865, the amendment states that 'neither slavery nor involuntary servitude, except as a punishment for crime whereof the party shall have been duly convicted, shall exist within the United States, or any place subject to their jurisdiction'. John Greenleaf Whittier (1807–92) wrote the poem 'Laus Deo!' to commemorate the amendment's ratification.

Thoreau, Henry David   Essayist and poet, one of the most important of the writers associated with TRANSCENDENTALISM. Thoreau was born in 1817 in Concord, Massachusetts. He attended Harvard University (1833–37), and was in the audience when Ralph Waldo EMERSON delivered his 'AMERICAN SCHOLAR' address there in 1837. After university he tried school teaching, among other occupations, but dedicated himself to writing poetry and essays, some of which were published in THE DIAL. He was strongly influenced by Emerson, in whose home he lived for two years (1841–43). In 1845 Thoreau built a hut by Walden Pond outside Concord and lived there until

1847 as an experiment in self-sufficiency. The now classic book WALDEN, OR LIFE IN THE WOODS (1854) is an analytical account of the experience. He later supported himself as a surveyor and was active in ABOLITIONISM. He was imprisoned for one night, having refused to pay his poll tax in protest against SLAVERY and the MEXICAN WAR. Important essays include 'Resistance to Civil Government' (1849), 'Slavery in Massachusetts' (1854) and 'Walking' (1862). He died in Concord of tuberculosis in 1862.

Thoreau's reputation as a major writer developed only after his death. Apart from his poetry and essays, he produced only two books in his lifetime, *Walden* and the privately printed *A Week on the Concord and Merrimack Rivers* (1849). Neither book sold well. During his life Thoreau was known as a disciple of Emerson and had a reputation as a local eccentric. Now his concerns seem proleptically modern. He was an individualist who resisted an identity shaped by what he termed 'the mass of men'. He was a pragmatic transcendentalist, and something of an ascetic protesting against what we would now think of as mass consumer culture, and his belief in peaceful civil protest was taken up in the CIVIL RIGHTS MOVEMENT. His nature writing has had a significant influence, both in terms of its acute observation of the local and the immediate and in its concern with the overall environment. Above all he tried to see life simply and to write lucidly of what he saw, in praise of a life of 'simplicity, independence, magnanimity, and trust' as he called it in *Walden*.

Further reading

Henry David Thoreau (1987), edited by Harold Bloom; *The Environmental Imagination* (1995) by Lawrence Buell; *The Days of Henry Thoreau* (1965) by Walter Harding, and *Henry Thoreau: A Life of the Mind* (1986) by Robert D. Richardson.

Till, Emmett Till was a 14-year-old black youth visiting Money, Mississippi, from Chicago in August 1955 who was kidnapped and murdered for speaking 'familiarly' to a white woman in a store. The murder, and the subsequent acquittal of the two white men accused of it, caused much outrage, which helped to fuel the CIVIL RIGHTS MOVEMENT.

Writers have frequently referred to the murder. It appears prominently in the play *Blues for Mister Charlie* (1964) by James BALDWIN, in Toni MORRISON's novel *Song of Solomon* (1977) and in her unpublished 1985 play *Dreaming Emmett*. Ishmael Reed (b. 1938) uses the Till case to satirize FEMINIST thought in *Reckless Eyeballing* (1986). Anne Moody (b. 1940) writes of it as her awakening to racial realities in *Coming of Age in Mississippi* (1968), and it is also the subject of the novel *Wolf Whistle* (1993) by Lewis Nordan (b. 1939). In two linked poems, 'A Bronzeville Mother Loiters in Mississippi. Meanwhile a Mississippi Mother Burns Bacon' and 'The Last Quatrain of the Ballad of Emmett Till' (1960), Gwendolyn BROOKS deconstructs the BALLAD form in a corrosive analysis of the sexual and racial myths behind the killing. 'Emmett Till' (1990) by Wanda Coleman (b. 1946) is another powerful poem on the murder. *A Death in the Delta* (1991) by Stephen J. Whitfield is an account of the murder and its aftermath.

Tin Pan Alley   Term used since the 1880s to denote popular music, especially the popular song. The name supposedly refers to the constant noise of pianos being played in the area of New York City around 28ᵗʰ Street, off 5ᵗʰ Avenue and Broadway, and then more generally the area around Broadway, the location of many music publishers, songwriters and arrangers. The works of Jerome Kern (1885–1945), Irving Berlin (1888–1989), Cole Porter (1891–1964) and George Gershwin (1898–1937) are considered to represent the golden age of Tin Pan Alley in the 1930s and 1940s, their songs often having witty, original and elegant lyrics.

Further reading

The Poets of Tin Pan Alley (1990) by Philip Furia; *Word Crazy* (1991) by Thomas S. Hischak, and *Tin Pan Alley* (1982) by John Shepherd.

Townshend Acts   Four acts passed by the British government in 1767 as part of its policy on the American colonies. The acts, which replaced the STAMP ACT, were sponsored by the chancellor of the exchequer, Charles Townshend. They allowed for: the suspension of the New York assembly; the imposition of taxes on various imports (including tea) for the purpose of raising revenue; the increase of the power of customs inspectors, and the importation of tea into the colonies free of British taxes. Together, the acts were intended both to generate tax and to curb the growing autonomy of the colonies. However, they caused widespread resentment and civil disorder and contributed greatly to anti-British feeling. The agitation that they aroused led directly to the 'Boston Massacre' of March 1770, in which five colonials were killed by British troops. This and other incidents led to the Townshend Acts being repealed in the following month. However, the duty on tea remained and was combined with the granting of a virtual monopoly to the East India Company of tea imports. The Boston Tea Party (December 1773) was part of a concerted protest against this situation. *Letters from a Farmer in Pennsylvania* (1768) by John Dickinson (1732–1808) offered a legal argument for resisting the acts.

Transcendental Club   Name given to a group of intellectuals that met occasionally, sometimes at the home of Ralph Waldo EMERSON, between 1836 and 1840. The meetings involved informal debates on set topics. The group included Bronson Alcott (1799–1888), George Ripley (1802–80), Margaret Fuller (1810–50), Theodore Parker (1810–60), Nathaniel HAWTHORNE and Henry David THOREAU. It was closely associated with TRANSCENDENTALISM and with the publication of *THE DIAL*. Its members referred to the group as 'the Symposium' or 'Hedge's Club' (because of the presence of Frederic Henry Hedge).

Transcendentalism   Literary, religious and philosophical movement originating in New England in the mid-1830s and remaining influential until the 1860s. The philosophy behind transcendentalism was an eclectic mix of English ROMANTICISM (especially as mediated by William Wordsworth, Samuel Taylor Coleridge and Thomas Carlyle), anti-rationality, anti-PURITANISM, the mysticism of Emanuel Swedenborg, and aspects of Eastern philosophies. The term transcendentalism, which was actually coined by those who ridiculed the movement for its dreamy abstractions, derives from the German philosopher Immanuel Kant, who wrote of the need to transcend reason alone for a true understanding of reality.

The central beliefs of transcendentalism were in unity between nature and God, the presence of God in each individual, and the potential perfectibility of humans. These core beliefs generated others, particularly in individualism and in the SELF-RELIANCE extolled by Ralph Waldo EMERSON, who wrote that 'nothing is at last sacred but the integrity of your own mind'. Although transcendentalism was criticized for its supposed otherworldliness, it did have a strong practical element, evident in the formation of the UTOPIAN community of BROOK FARM, in its anti-institutionalism and in the dedication of many of its members to social reform.

Writers who were either transcendentalists or were closely associated with the movement include Bronson Alcott (1799–1888), Emerson, Margaret Fuller (1810–50) and Henry David THOREAU. Key transcendentalist works include Emerson's essays, especially 'Nature' (1836), 'THE AMERICAN SCHOLAR' (1837), 'The Over-Soul' (1841) and 'Self-Reliance' (1841), and Thoreau's WALDEN (1854). THE DIAL was the journal produced by the group. The influence of transcendentalism was such that it touched even those writers such as Edgar Allan POE, Nathaniel HAWTHORNE, Herman MELVILLE and Emily DICKINSON who were uneasy about it or who rejected it outright.

Further reading

The Transcendentalist Constant (1980) by Roger Asselineau; Literary Transcendentalism (1973) by Lawrence Buell; The New England Transcendentalists and 'The Dial' (1980) by Joel Myerson, and 'The Transcendentalists' by Barbara Packer in The Cambridge History of American Literature, Volume II (1995), edited by Sacvan Bercovitch. Transcendentalism: A Reader (2000), edited by Joel Myerson, is an important anthology.

Trickster   Figure that appears in hundreds of stories of the ORAL TRADITION and which is used in various ways by many American writers, especially those within the NATIVE AMERICAN and AFRICAN AMERICAN traditions. Trickster is generally amoral, a protean figure, able to assume different shapes and forms, and he may be a creator or destroyer, young or old (he is sometimes called 'Old Man'), hero or mischief-maker, scapegoat or God. The kinds of tale told about trickster vary enormously: some have a religious dimension, some are concerned with the creation of the world or the origins of certain foods, animals and plants, while others are mainly for amusement. In the Native American traditions, certain tricksters are associated with specific regions: Coyote is the trickster for the American Indians of the Central Plains, California and the Southwest; Nanabozho (or Great Hare or Master Rabbit) for those of Eastern North America, and Raven (and sometimes Mink or Blue Jay) for those of the Pacific Northwest. Especially in their adaptation in America, African traditions often involve trickster cunningly outwitting a powerful antagonist. The main African tricksters are Monkey and Hare, who is later transformed into Brer Rabbit (sometimes by being conflated with Nanabozho). There are particular cycles of stories for Coyote and for Raven.

Many modern and contemporary writers have made use of the trickster figure, notably Ralph ELLISON, Toni MORRISON, Gerald Vizenor (b. 1934), Ishmael Reed (b. 1938), Leslie Marmon SILKO and Louise Erdrich (b. 1954).

Further reading

Trickster Makes this World (1998) by Lewis Hyde; The Trickster in African American Women's Literature (1998) by Isiah Lavender; Native American Renaissance (1983) by Kenneth Lincoln, and The Trickster of Liberty (1988) by Gerald Vizenor.

Tuskegee Institute   Founded by Booker T. Washington (1856–1915) in 1881, the black college Tuskegee Normal and Industrial Institute in Alabama embodied Washington's belief in the importance of vocational and practical education for blacks. Though influential, his belief in 'usable skills' as a means of assimilation and elevation was much criticized by other African American leaders, including W. E. B. Du Bois, who developed the alternative concept of the TALENTED TENTH. Washington was the principal of Tuskegee until his death. In the 1920s the college broadened away from vocational education towards higher education, began to award degrees, and was renamed Tuskegee Institute (1937) and then Tuskegee University (1985).

Ralph ELLISON studied music at Tuskegee (1933–6) and the college in his novel INVISIBLE MAN is an imaginative version of the institute. Through his relation to the college and its principal, Bledsoe, Ellison's protagonist gradually recognizes and rejects its accommodationist ethos. In the novel the statue of the founder refers to the campus's monument to Washington, which depicts him lifting the 'veil of ignorance' from the head of a young black.

Twain, Mark   Pseudonym of Samuel Langhorne Clemens. Clemens was born in Florida, Missouri, in 1835 and grew up in the nearby river-town of Hannibal. After the death of his father in 1847 Clemens held a variety of jobs before becoming an apprentice printer at the age of 13. He left Hannibal in 1853 and worked as a compositor on several newspapers, while also contributing humorous sketches. He trained as a Mississippi river boat pilot, receiving his full licence in 1859 (the experiences are nostalgically recalled in *Life on the Mississippi* (1883)). At the outbreak of the CIVIL WAR in 1861 Clemens briefly joined the Confederate forces, but then moved with his brother Orion to Nevada, becoming a mining speculator. Although unsuccessful at this, he started writing sketches and short fiction more regularly, and it was at this time (1863) he began using the pseudonym 'Mark Twain'. His stories and sketches in the TALL TALE tradition proved popular, and in 1867 he was commissioned as a sketch-writer on a journey to Europe and the Holy Land. His often-irreverent sketches, published in book form as *The Innocents Abroad* (1869), were also extremely popular. Clemens married Olivia Langdon in 1870 and settled in Hartford, Connecticut. The couple had three daughters, two of whom predeceased Clemens. *Roughing It* (1872), an account of his experiences in the West, and *The Gilded Age* (1873), a novel co-written with Charles Dudley Warner (1829–1900), combined with his lectures and sketches to give Clemens an international reputation.

Although his great comic talent was rarely absent from his writing, Clemens gradually became more serious, darkly satirical and pessimistic. The contrast between *The Adventures of Tom Sawyer* (1876) and THE ADVENTURES OF HUCKLEBERRY FINN (1884) is indicative of this change, with the later novel exploring aspects of cruelty, inhumanity and loneliness that were largely absent from Tom Sawyer's PASTORAL world. Clemens's dark and increasingly APOCALYPTIC vision continued with *A Connecticut Yankee in King Arthur's Court* (1889), a dark satire of the idealization of Arthurian England and the technology of the modern age. Ironically, Clemens's own interest in technological innovation led to financial difficulties and to bankruptcy in 1894 after he invested heavily in a typesetting machine invented by James W. Paige. Clemens and his family moved to Europe and he undertook a strenuous lecture tour to repay creditors. Publications during this period include *Pudd'nhead Wilson* (1894) and *Personal Recollections of Joan of Arc* (1895). *Pudd'nhead Wilson* is one of Clemens's most important works, a mordantly comic story satirizing the ONE-DROP RULE and the belief in innate characteristics determined by race.

Income from lectures and his novels made Clemens solvent, and he returned to the United States in 1900. Increasingly he spoke out on public issues, including the Belgian atrocities in the Congo, the operation of LYNCH LAW in the United States, and the American purchase of the Philippines after the SPANISH–AMERICAN WAR. He became an international public figure, receiving many awards and honorary degrees. Although of mixed quality, his fiction after 1900 is particularly nihilistic, attacking humanity's self-delusion. *The Mysterious Stranger*, not fully published until 1969, is a classic of this period. The Clemens family returned to Europe in 1903, settling near Florence. There, Olivia died in 1904. Clemens died in Redding, Connecticut, in 1910.

Clemens has been among the most popular, influential and critically acclaimed of all American authors. Although his work is uneven in quality, at its best it shows him as a conscientious, careful artist. Believing in DEMOCRACY and the need for honesty and moral integrity, he was at his most scathing when he saw these aspirations being distorted or destroyed by pretension, hypocrisy or injustice. His most enduring and influential achievements are his incorporation of a frontier ORAL TRADITION into a series of major works of art, and his serious use of the American vernacular.

Further reading

For biographies, see *Mr Clemens and Mark Twain* (1966) by Justin Kaplan and *The Authentic Mark Twain* (1984) by Everett Emerson. Critical studies include *The Man Who Was Mark Twain* (1991) by Guy Cardwell; *Dark Twins: Imposture and Identity in Mark Twain's America* (1989) by Susan Gillman; *Mark Twain: The Development of a Writer* (1962) by Henry Nash Smith, and *Mark Twain: A Collection of Critical Essays* (1994), edited by Eric J. Sundquist.

Underground Railroad   An informal and irregular system through which assistance was given to slaves escaping from SLAVERY. It was far less organized than is often suggested (and has even been considered legendary). The railroad existed since the 1820s, and involved a system of 'lines', 'conductors' and safe houses or 'stations' to facilitate a slave's journey to the free states or to Canada. Both whites and blacks assisted in the system, the most famous 'conductor' being the ex-slave Harriet Tubman (?1820–1913), who helped over 200 slaves to escape, and the militant white ABOLITIONIST John Brown (1800–59). Harriet Beecher STOWE also had contact with the Underground Railroad, referring to it in *Uncle Tom's Cabin* (1852). The railroad is significant in the novels *BELOVED* by Toni MORRISON and *Dessa Rose* (1986) by Sherley Anne Williams (b. 1944).

Union Magazine of Literature and Art   Monthly magazine first published in New York from 1847, and edited at first by Caroline Stansbury Kirkland (1801–64). It published contributions by Kirkland, William Gilmore Simms (1806–70), Henry Wadsworth Longfellow (1807–82), Edgar Allan POE and Henry David THOREAU. Under the ownership of John Sartain, it was known after 1848 as *Sartain's Union Magazine*, and it ceased publication in 1852.

Unitarianism   Religious movement that originated in England in the 17th century and developed in North America in particular ways. The Unitarian movement existed within CONGREGATIONALISM, and grew particularly influential after the GREAT AWAKENING and during the ENLIGHTENMENT. Rejecting the Trinitarian doctrine that God is a being comprising God the Father, Jesus Christ and the Holy Spirit, Unitarians affirmed that God was a single entity. Their most enduring and influential characteristics have been their liberalism, their rational enquiry into scripture and their work for social reform. The modern phase of Unitarianism began with William Ellery Channing

(1780–1842), especially with his 1819 sermon 'Unitarian Christianity' in which he stated the need for a complete split between Unitarians and the Congregationalists. Unitarianism played an important part in the development of TRANSCENDENTALISM, although transcendentalism led to a significant split among Unitarians. (Ralph Waldo EMERSON had been a Unitarian minister before rejecting the movement in favour of transcendentalism.) During the late 19th and 20th centuries the Unitarians merged more closely with humanism and increasingly emphasized the necessity of rational scientific enquiry as a dimension of religious belief.

Utopia   Fictional work in which an alternative ideal society is presented. The originating work of the tradition is Sir Thomas More's *Utopia* (1516), the title of which is a pun; derived from the Greek, 'utopia' means both somewhere non-existent (u-topia) and somewhere desirable (eu-topia). In the style of More, many utopian works are written as travel narratives, where the utopian society's traditions and manners are explained to visitors. The genre has strong links to SCIENCE FICTION, since many utopias are imagined as possible futures. Some utopias represent genuine affirmative social aspirations, while others are primarily criticisms of contemporary society.

American literature has a considerable history of utopian writing. Many utopias, including More's, were actually set in an imagined America or 'new world', and during the colonial period both visitors and emigrants frequently represented America in utopian terms. The sense of America as utopian possibility has long persisted, and may be seen in the continuing affirmation of the AMERICAN DREAM. There is a notable utopian strain in much American writing that is not strictly in the utopian tradition. This belief in American perfectibility is evident in influential writing by J. Hector St John De Crèvecoeur (1735–1813), Thomas Jefferson (1743–1826), Ralph Waldo EMERSON, Henry David THOREAU and Walt WHITMAN.

Americans have often taken a pragmatic view of utopia. This has been amply evident not only in the PURITAN attempt to found a theocracy, and similar attempts by many religious groups, but also in the many communities created during the interest in FOURIERISM, and in the formation of 'Bellamy societies' after the publication of the influential utopian novel *Looking Backward: 2000–1887* (1888) by Edward Bellamy (1850–98). A similar sense of utopia as realistic possibility is evident in socialist utopias, such as *A Traveller from Altruria* (1894), *Through the Eye of the Needle* (1907) by William Dean Howells (1837–1920) and *The Iron Heel* (1908) by Jack London (1876–1916). Each of these was in some measure born out of PROGRESSIVISM and was published during the most intense period of utopian writing, 1888–1919.

Utopias written by American women have played an important role in the shaping and dissemination of FEMINIST thought. Between the mid 19th century and the end of the 20th it has been estimated that over 200 utopian works by American women were published, and the 1970s saw a new resurgence of the form. Prominent women's utopian texts include *Herland* (1915) by Charlotte Perkins Gilman (1860–1935), *The*

Dispossessed (1974) and *Always Coming Home* (1985) by Ursula Le Guin (b. 1929), *Woman on the Edge of Time* (1976) by Marge Piercy (b. 1936), *The Female Man* (1974) by Joanna Russ (b. 1937) and *The Wanderground* (1979) by Sally Miller Gearhart (b. 1931). In contrast to male utopias, those written by women tend more directly to reflect contemporary social injustices and commonly involve an alternative to patriarchal society. It is worth noting that although there is often an overlap between feminism and science fiction in contemporary women's utopian writing, there are utopian elements in non-science fiction feminist texts, such as Alice WALKER's *The Color Purple* (1982).

An anti-utopian tradition has existed alongside utopian writing, offsetting its optimistic sense of future possibility. James Fenimore COOPER's *The Crater* (1847) is part of this tradition, and there are anti-utopian elements in writing by Edgar Allan POE, Nathaniel HAWTHORNE and Herman MELVILLE. The GOTHIC tradition in itself may be seen to undermine utopia's ROMANTIC affirmation. There has also been a tradition of dystopian writing, in which the imagined alternative future is repressive and usually totalitarian. Fully realized dystopias, as in *Bend Sinister* (1947) by Vladimir Nabokov (1899–1977) or *Fahrenheit 451* (1953) by Ray Bradbury (b. 1920), tend to be specifically an imagined projection of trends in contemporary society. Some utopian novels, for example *The Iron Heel* and *Woman on the Edge of Time*, include a dystopian vision regarding the suppression of freedom and the concentration of power into the hands of a few.

Further reading

Partial Visions: Feminism and Utopia in the 1970s (1991) by Angelica Bammer; *Narrating Utopia* (1999) by Chris Ferns; *Daring to Dream: Utopian Stories by U. S. Women (1836–1919)* (1984) by Carol Farley Kessler; *Demand the Impossible: Science Fiction and the Utopian Imagination* (1986) by Tom Moylan, and *America as Utopia* (1981), edited by Kenneth M. Roemer.

Vaudeville   Type of stage entertainment popular from the early 20th century until the 1930s, when it was largely replaced by radio and the motion picture. Vaudeville descended directly from BURLESQUE and the MINSTREL SHOW, and though less stylized, usually consisted of a variety of dramatic sketches, songs, acrobatic acts, magicians and comic turns, with a tendency towards the risqué. Notable performers included Fred Stone (1873–1959) and Eva Tanguay (1878–1947), as well as many who later made the transition to radio or film. Edward Franklin Albee (1857–1930), the adoptive grandfather of the playwright Edward Albee (b. 1928), was one of vaude-ville's most powerful impresarios. The term vaudeville derives from the 18th century French phrase 'vau de ville' or 'vau de vire', referring to a type of topical song associated with the Vire Valley.

Veteran figure   Broadly, depiction of the war veteran in American literature has developed from the representation of a hero to that of someone socially displaced and psychologically damaged by war. It should also be noted that in AFRICAN AMERICAN LITERATURE the representation of veterans of WORLD WAR I and WORLD WAR II is of important figures in the movement towards social justice and civil rights.

The veterans of America's colonial wars and of the REVOLUTIONARY WAR were commonly regarded as shapers of the United States, although – as in Herman MELVILLE's historical novel *Israel Potter* (1855) – this depiction often involved a sense of injustice at the nation's neglect of the veteran. To some degree the figure of the heroic veteran continues after the CIVIL WAR, notably in Southern representations, but also, for example, in the early novels of Henry JAMES, which suggest that the character qualities formed by the war are helpful to social and economic success. Although anticipated to some extent by Stephen CRANE's representation of the veteran, the figure of the displaced and damaged veteran begins after World War I, and can be seen in works by John Dos Passos (1896–1970), F. Scott FITZGERALD, William FAULKNER (notably *Soldier's Pay*, 1926) and Ernest HEMINGWAY (especially *The Sun Also Rises*, 1926). This representation continues after World War II, and is exacerbated to some degree, as in the fiction of Kurt Vonnegut (b. 1922), by the war's appalling atrocities. Significantly, both N. Scott Momaday (b. 1934) in *House Made of Dawn* (1968) and Leslie Marmon SILKO in *Ceremony* (1977), showed World War II veterans of Native American descent undergoing rituals of healing after being psychologically wounded by the war. The theme of the veteran's difficulties in adjusting to post-war life is common in literature after the VIETNAM WAR, and the maladjusted, psychologically disturbed veteran suffering from post-traumatic stress disorder is a staple of cinematic representation of the war. Prominent literary representations of the Vietnam veteran include *Sticks and Bones* (1972) by David Rabe (b. 1940), *Born on the Fourth of July* (1976) by Ron Kovic (b. 1946), *In Country* (1985) by Bobbie Ann Mason (b. 1940), *Marking Time* (1986) by W. D. Ehrhart, *The Things They Carried* (1990) by Tim O'Brien (b. 1946), and short stories by Raymond CARVER.

Further reading

Shook Over Hell (1997) by Eric T. Dean; No Victory Parades (1971) by Murray Polner, and The Wages of War (1989) by Richard Severo and Lewis Milford.

Vietnam War   Following the 1954 withdrawal of the French from their former colony Vietnam, the country was divided into three states, Cambodia, Laos and Vietnam. Vietnam itself became partitioned along the 17th parallel, into North and South, and war between the two started in 1955. From 1954 the United States had provided financial support for South Vietnam, primarily to prevent it from coming under control of the communist North, and as the war developed the US provided 'military advisers'. By 1962 these were authorized by President Kennedy to fight if necessary. In August 1964, after the North Vietnamese had attacked an American warship, the Tonkin Gulf Resolution enabled President Johnson to participate fully in the war. American involvement was considerable, and by 1967 there were over half a million US military personnel in Vietnam, many of them draftees. The main American military strategies were the bombing of North Vietnam and the suppression of Viet Cong forces. However, opposition to the war grew in the United States from 1965, due to the lack of military success, the heavy American casualties, the unpopularity of the draft system, a series of atrocities, and criticism of American military tactics (especially the heavy bombing of North Vietnam and attacks on undefended villages). This opposition intensified after the 1968 Northern Tet offensive, which indicated to many Americans that the war could never be won. The withdrawal of American troops began in 1969 and was completed after a ceasefire was agreed in January 1973. The Vietnam War is the longest in American history. Approximately 58,000 Americans were killed, and over 300,000 wounded. The financial cost has been estimated at over $140 billion.

There is a significant body of writing on the war. This can be broadly divided into three types: works dealing with the first-hand experiences of the war in Vietnam; works focusing on the return of the war VETERAN, and those concerned with the war years in the United States. Works concentrating on the war in Vietnam include: *The Basic Training of Pavlo Hummel* (1969) and *Streamers* (1975) by David Rabe (b. 1940); *Dispatches* (1977) by Michael Herr (b. 1940); *A Rumor of War* (1977) by Philip Caputo (b. 1941), and *If I Die in a Combat Zone* (1973), *Going After Cacciato* (1978) and *The Things They Carried* (1990) by Tim O'Brien (b. 1946). The returning Vietnam veteran appears in numerous literary works, often represented as maladjusted or requiring a particular kind of adjustment to American life. The war as experienced in the United States, and the anti-war movement, appear in many works, notably *The Armies of the Night* (1969) by Norman Mailer (b. 1923), and there is a rich body of anti-war poetry that includes works by Denise Levertov (1923–97), Robert Bly (b. 1926), Robert Creeley (b. 1926) and Adrienne RICH. Distinguished journalism about the war includes pieces by Mary McCarthy (1912–89), Tom Wolfe (b. 1931), Joan Didion (b. 1934) and Seymour M. Hersh (b. 1937).

Further reading

The Wars we Took to Vietnam (1996) by Milton J. Bates; Re-Writing America (1991) by Philip D. Beidler; Fourteen Landing Zones (1991), edited by Philip K. Jason; Acts and Shadows (2000) by Philip K. Jason; Friendly Fire (2000) by Katherine Kinney, and Out of the Vietnam Vortex (1974) by James F. Mersmann. Reporting Vietnam (1998), edited by Milton J. Bates et al., is a useful selection of war journalism. Histories of the war include America in Vietnam (1978) by Guenter Lewy and America's Longest War (1996) by George C. Herring.

Violet Quill   Small group of gay writers that was formed in the 1970s to help in the development of gay writing. The members were Christopher Cox, Robert Ferro (1941–88), Michael Grumley, Andrew Holleran (b. 1943), Felice Picano (b. 1944), Edmund White (b. 1940), and George Whitmore (1945–88). The group broke up in the early 1980s. *The Violet Quill Reader* (1994), edited by David Bergman, gives an account of the group, and Picano's novel *The Book of Lies* (1999) provides a fictionalized version.

Vorticism   Artistic movement within MODERNISM whose name derived from the term 'vortex', used by Ezra POUND to denote the energy of an art-work. In 1914 Pound redefined IMAGISM to emphasize the dynamic nature of the image as 'a radiant node or cluster ... what I can, and must perforce, call a VORTEX, from which, and through which, and into which ideas are constantly rushing'. Vorticism was an attempt to stimulate all of the arts, particularly painting, and it was influential from about 1912 to 1920. The American-born London-based novelist and painter Wyndham Lewis (1882–1957) was the movement's leading figure, and he and Pound edited the short-lived magazine BLAST: *Review of the Great English Vortex* (1914–15).

Wagon trails   Series of trails that started to operate in the 1820s and continued to be used throughout the 19ᵗʰ century. Usually the trails were used by migrants in wagon trains consisting of up to 100 horse-drawn covered wagons familiarly known as 'prairie schooners'. This form of collective migration was preferred because of the increased security it offered in arduous and possibly hostile areas. Particular routes developed, notably the Oregon trail, the Overland trail and the Santa Fe trail, all of which started at Independence, Missouri. The Oregon trail was the first of these routes, covering almost 2,000 miles from Independence to Oregon. It was first used in the 1820s and was especially popular during the migrations of the 1840s. The Overland trail diverged from the Oregon trail to terminate in California. This was the trail used during the California GOLD RUSH. The Santa Fe trail terminated in New Mexico and was especially important as a trade route. Eventually the building of the transcontinental railways made the trails redundant. The experiences of the wagon trains and of the individual trails are recorded in much writing by and about pioneers.

Walden, or Life in the Woods   Series of connected essays by Henry David THOREAU, published in 1854. Together they form an AUTOBIOGRAPHICAL narrative, both explanatory and interrogative, concerning his experience of building a hut by Walden Pond outside of Concord, Massachusetts, and living there for 2 years (1845–7). Thoreau presents his experience as an experiment: 'I went to the woods because I wished to live deliberately, to front only the essential facts of life, and see if I could not learn what it had to teach, and not, when I came to die, discover that I had not lived. . . . I wanted to live deep and suck out all the marrow of life.'

   Walden is an extraordinary but highly successful mixture of styles. It is a spiritual autobiography, a manual for living, an analysis of the meaning of labour and a criticism of consumerist society. It is an examination of nature and of modern society, in which humans have 'no time to be anything but a machine'. It is a record of intense involvement with the sounds and phenomena of the woods that also includes awareness that this environment is being invaded and is under threat. It is anti-institutional and individualistic, urging the reader to 'Simplify, simplify'. Its tones are carefully modulated, moving smoothly between the lyrical, the comic, the scholarly, the scientific, the angry, the delighted and the outraged.

   In addition to the fresh relevance *Walden* has had for different generations in the United States, it has been one of the most internationally admired of all American books. It has had a significant influence on subsequent nature writing.

Further reading

The Roots of Walden (1990) by Gordon V. Boudreau; *Critical Essays on Thoreau's Walden* (1988), edited by Joel Myerson, and *New Essays on Walden* (1992), edited by Robert F. Sayre.

Walker, Alice   Popular and critically acclaimed African American novelist, poet and essayist. Walker was born in 1944 in Eatonton, Georgia, to SHARECROPPING parents. After attending Spelman College in Atlanta and Sarah Lawrence College in New York she became active in the CIVIL RIGHTS MOVEMENT, often referred to in her writing. Walker published her first book of poems, *Once*, in 1968 and her first novel, *The Third Life of Grange Copeland*, in 1970. *Meridian* (1976) followed, but it was *The Color Purple* (1982), the first novel by an African American woman to win the PULITZER PRIZE, which brought her acclaim and a mass audience. Her later novels are *The Temple of My Familiar* (1989), *Possessing the Secret of Joy* (1992) and the AUTOBIOGRAPHICAL *The Way Forward is with a Broken Heart* (2001). Walker's poems were collected as *Her Blue Body Everything We Know* in 1991. Her first collection of essays, *In Search of Our Mothers' Gardens*, was published in 1983, and *The Complete Stories* in 1994.

   In her early novels and short stories particularly, Walker demonstrates a sophisticated management of narrative technique, especially in the fragmented narrative of *Meridian* and the EPISTOLARY style of *The Color Purple*. Thematically her work is united by the project of raising the visibility of black women. Walker has long been critical of the invisibility of black working women, whether in novels, literary history, the civil rights movement, black nationalism, rock and roll or white middle-class FEMINISM. In all of the genres in which she works she has placed the experiences of black women at the centre. Thus in her classic 1974 essay 'In Search of Our Mothers' Gardens' she praised the artistic creativity evident in domestic skills that were generally unvalued. She has engaged with what was once a neglected tradition of African American women's writing, evident especially in her work on Zora Neale HURSTON. She has used the term 'womanist' in an attempt to enlarge the class and race limitations of 'feminist'. At times Walker's privileging of black female experience has been controversial; *The Color Purple* especially was seen as an attack on black men.

Further reading

Useful critical works include *Alice Walker: Critical Perspectives Past and Present* (1993), edited by Henry Louis Gates, Jr, and K. A. Appiah; *The Other Side of the Story* (1989) by Molly Hite, and *Alice Walker* (2000) by Maria Lauret.

Wall Street   Street in Manhattan, New York City, which since the 1850s has been the financial centre of the United States. The area in and around Wall Street houses some of the world's most powerful financial institutions, including the New York Stock Exchange, the American Stock Exchange, the Federal Reserve Bank, and the headquarters of numerous commodity, brokerage and insurance companies. The street itself was named after a barrier erected by the Dutch in 1653 to repel an English attack. Wall Street appears in numerous literary works, including 'Bartleby the Scrivener' (1853) by Herman MELVILLE, *The Big Money* (1936) by John Dos Passos (1896–1970) and *The Bonfire of the Vanities* (1987) by Tom Wolfe (b. 1930). Its manipulation of markets was a target of MUCKRAKING enquiries. The Wall Street crash of 1929 heralded the DEPRESSION.

War of Independence   See REVOLUTIONARY WAR.

War of 1812   War fought between the United States and Britain. The dispute arose from the ongoing Napoleonic war between the British and the French. Although the United States was neutral, the British blockade of French ports disrupted American trade, and the British interfered with American shipping and would press-gang American sailors. Another contributory grievance was the covert British support for the Shawnee rising under Tecumseh. President Madison declared war in June 1812.

Neither side gained a clear ascendancy. The Americans won a celebrated naval victory with the frigate *Constitution*, and a significant land battle in New Orleans, but their invasions of Canada failed. The British made several raids on American cities, including one on Washington DC during which they burnt the Capitol and the White House. The war was ended with the Treaty of Ghent in December 1814. Under the treaty's terms, the boundaries between the United States and Canada remained as they had been prior to 1812. The conclusion of the Napoleonic war nullified the issue of interference with American shipping.

Although the war had not been popular among Americans (the New England states even considered SECESSION), the avoidance of defeat intensified American patriotism and introduced a new self-confidence. James Fenimore COOPER claimed that the war destroyed American 'mental bondage' to Britain. The American national anthem, the anti-British 'Star-Spangled Banner', grew out of this war and is an expression of this new confidence. Written by Francis Scott Key (1779–1843), it commemorates the halting of the British forces in 1814 before they could reach Baltimore. The 1830 poem 'Old Ironsides' by Oliver Wendell Holmes (1809–94) recalls the victory of the *Constitution*.

The Waste Land   One of the most considerable works of the 20th century, T. S. ELIOT's poem was edited by Ezra POUND and first published in 1922. Central to MODERNISM, *The Waste Land* is a discontinuous, sharply fragmented, densely allusive and highly concentrated poem in five sections. Though lacking a readily apparent surface narrative, the poem has a deep structure that affords some unity. This underlying structure alludes to Arthurian romances involving the search for the Holy Grail and the story of a wounded, impotent king ruling over a barren land. The king's sacrifice and subsequent rebirth will result in the kingdom becoming fertile once again. Eliot creatively uses the links between this story, seasonal vegetation rituals, and the fact that some of these rituals underlie some key elements of Christian belief. Ultimately he makes the myth of the wounded king relevant to a search for meaning and purpose in what he sees as a fragmented, inchoate and spiritually desolate modern world. Various languages, language registers, poetic styles and scraps of literary allusion demonstrate Eliot's sense of contemporary confusion and lack of purpose.

In some respects *The Waste Land* is a highly paradoxical poem. While it insists on the power and continuing relevance of ancient myth in contemporary society, it also explores the obscuring and denigration of myth. The work's exciting modernist techniques, such as the use of collage and a variety of voices, may suggest an embrace of modernity, but this is at odds with the sense of loss and despair that it asserts as characteristic of the modern age. Also, while Eliot's contemporaries acclaimed the poem as a public document that characterized a generation, it is at the same time a deeply private and individual poem.

Further reading

He Do the Police in Different Voices (1986) by Calvin Bedient; *The Waste Land: A Facsimile and Transcript of the Original Drafts* (1971), edited by Valerie Eliot; *T. S. Eliot's 'The Waste Land'* (1994) by Gareth Reeves, and *The Waste Land, by T. S. Eliot* (1983) by Grover Smith.

Watergate   Popular name for the scandal that led to the only ever resignation of the president of the United States. In June 1972 the headquarters of the Democratic Party in the Watergate Complex in Washington, DC, were burgled and wiretapped, and seven men were consequently tried for the offence. Although the re-elected Republican president Richard Milhous Nixon and his staff strenuously denied persistent allegations that the White House administration had been involved in the burglary and were attempting to conceal this, a Senate Committee was convened to investigate the affair. The committee demanded that the president hand over nine audiotapes of meetings with his advisers, and after a bitter legal battle seven of these were eventually released, with a conspicuous eighteen-and-a-half minute gap in one of them. Further tapes and transcripts apparently confirmed the alleged involvement and cover-up. Acting on a recommendation from the House Judiciary Committee, the House of Representatives prepared to impeach President Nixon, and he resigned on 9 August 1974. Nixon's successor, Gerald Ford, pardoned him of all federal offences that he might have committed while in office.

Watergate is often regarded as a transforming moment in American attitudes to its political administration, not only because of the original crime and cover-up but also for what the tapes revealed about the nature of the Nixon presidency. The scandal also led to various terms entering the American language. These include: the practice of adding the suffix '-gate' to the key word in any scandal; the term 'deep throat', meaning a secret informer, and the phrase 'expletive deleted', which was frequently used on the transcripts of the White House tapes.

The Way to Rainy Mountain   Novel by N. Scott Momaday (b. 1934). First published in 1969, it is one of the key texts of NATIVE AMERICAN LITERATURE. Momaday makes use of the techniques of European American MODERNIST writing as well as Kiowa ORAL TRADITIONS. *The Way to Rainy Mountain* is made up of twenty-four numbered sections, each of which is divided into three parts. The sections explore a variety of themes, including Kiowa culture and history, the contact with Europeans, and the tenuous survival of the nation after the contact. However, the three sections affirm in different ways a connecting spirit. The three parts of each section are seemingly discrete narratives involving, respectively, mythic, historically objective and personal approaches to events. Ostensibly this division echoes a modernist emphasis on the loss of the past and on the fragmentary nature of contemporary experience. However, through the subtle connections that Momaday makes between each of the three parts, the overall effect is that of drawing together the apparently disparate ways of viewing reality and hence imaginatively affirming forms of continuity. In this respect, *The Way to Rainy Mountain* is very much concerned with enduring and with continuing through means of cultural adaptation. Its success as a narrative derives from Momaday's bicultural adaptation of an oral tradition to an allusive modernist idiom, and from the way that this technique is intimately related to the theme of adaptability to change.

Further reading

N. *Scott Momaday* (1985) by Matthias Schubnell and *Ancestral Voice: Conversations with N. Scott Momaday* (1989) by Charles L. Woodward.

Weathermen   White left-wing terrorist group also known as the 'Weather Underground'. The group was formed in 1969 as a militant faction of the 'Students for a Democratic Society' that had developed in opposition to the Vietnam War. The Weathermen planted bombs at various corporation headquarters, government buildings, university campuses and private homes (including that of the father of the poet James Merrill (1926–95)). The group was disbanded in the mid-1970s. The name 'Weathermen' was taken from the 1967 song 'Subterranean Homesick Blues' by Bob Dylan (b. 1941).

Western   As distinct from any writing generally set in the West, the Western is, broadly, any literary work set on the FRONTIER that involves conflict between groups over the future ownership or usage of the land. The conflict may involve settlers and Native Americans, homesteaders and ranchers, or lawful community builders and lawless destroyers, but it is typically concerned with the land. Westerns also frequently explore the nature of individual heroism and of manliness, with the frontier being represented as a space where manhood can be fully expressed beyond the domesticating influence of women. Westerns usually endorse the FRONTIER THESIS in representing the frontier as a shaping force for the American character, and although ostensibly concerned with the future of West and the formation of community, they are often nostalgic over the transformation of the wilderness. Some of the most influential Westerns have been very much concerned with questions of justice, race relations and the future of the United States. As a literary, cinematic and televisual form, the Western has been extremely popular around the world. It has also been a remarkably durable form, being regularly updated and transformed, and it has readily absorbed parody at the same time as it has resisted historical correction to its mythic representation of the West.

The Western has its origins in the fiction of James Fenimore COOPER, particularly his LEATHER-STOCKING TALES (1823–41), and Cooper's self-reliant independent frontiersman Natty Bumppo is the model for hundreds of Western heroes. The development of the DIME NOVEL started the first major period of the Western from around 1860; it was to flourish again from 1940. Some of the most important defining works of the Western are *The Virginian* (1902) by Owen Wister (1860–1938); *Riders of the Purple Sage* (1912), *Light of the Western Stars* (1913) and *The Vanishing American* (1925) by Zane Grey (1872–1939), and *The Wind* (1925) by Dorothy Scarborough (1878–1935). The revival of the Western in the 1940s saw the emergence of new classic Westerns, especially *The Ox-Bow Incident* (1940) by Walter van Tilburg Clark (1909–71); *Shane* (1949) by Jack Schaefer (1907–91), and *Hondo* (1953) by Louis L'Amour (1908–88), while there were also several revisionist Westerns, such as *Welcome to Hard Times* (1960) by E. L. Doctorow (b. 1931) and *Little Big Man* (1964) by Thomas Berger (b. 1924). Other popular Western writers include Max Brand (1892–1944) and Larry McMurtry (b. 1936).

Further reading

Adventure, Mystery and Romance (1976) and The Six-Gun Mystique (1971) by John G. Cawelti; Plotting the 'Golden West' (1981) by Stephen Fender; The Western: A Collection of Critical Essays (1979), edited by James K. Folsom; Reading the West (1996), edited by Michael Kowalewski, and West of Everything (1992) by Jane Tompkins.

Westward expansion   A series of movements from the late 18ᵗʰ to the late 19ᵗʰ century saw the continental United States develop from being a set of eastern seaboard colonies to a nation occupying much of the North American continent to the Pacific. It also saw the displacement of the Plains Indians, because of territorial annexation and the slaughter of the buffalo on which their lifestyle largely depended. The land was procured by various means. A great deal was bought, through agreements with Native Americans, by the Louisiana Purchase and by the 1867 treaty with Russia that led to the acquisition of Alaska. Land was also annexed from Native Americans, Britain and Mexico after territorial conflicts, especially bloody in the case of the Indians. The settling of the western lands was hastened by the gold rushes, and facilitated by the Homestead Act and the building of the railroads (the first transcontinental line was completed in 1869). The ideology of manifest destiny was important in justifying territorial annexation and occupation. The extent of western expansion is evident from the white population growth and the rapid assimilation of states into the union. In the period 1860–1900 the total white population of the states of Kansas, Nebraska, Iowa, Minnesota and North and South Dakota grew from 1 million to 7 million. States that became part of the Union during the period 1836–1912 were Arkansas (1836), Michigan (1837), Florida, Texas (both 1845), Iowa (1846), Wisconsin (1848), California (1850), Minnesota (1858), Oregon (1859), Kansas (1861), Nevada (1864), Nebraska (1867), Colorado (1876), North Dakota, South Dakota, Montana, Washington (all 1889), Idaho, Wyoming (both 1890), Utah (1896), Oklahoma (1907) and New Mexico and Arizona (both 1912).

Wheatley, Phillis   African American poet (?1753–84). Wheatley was born in West Africa, brought to America as a slave in 1761 and bought by John and Susannah Wheatley in Boston. Her African name is unknown; her first name derives from the name of the slave ship in which she was brought to America and, as was customary, her surname was that of her owners. Unusually, Wheatley was provided with an informal education, and published her first poem in 1767. She came to England in 1773 and was represented as a prodigy. A book of thirty-eight poems, titled *Poems on Various Subjects, Religious and Moral by Phillis Wheatley, Negro Servant to Mr John*

Wheatley, of Boston, in New England, was published in London later that year and made Wheatley famous. On her return to Boston, she was freed from SLAVERY. She married in 1778 and although she wrote more poetry a second book never appeared.

While recognized as a significant figure in American literary history, being the first African American to publish a book, Wheatley is also controversial. At a time when humanity itself was defined by the capacity for reason, her poetry provided significant proof of the capacity of the African for the mastery of language and higher thought, and hence lent weight to the ABOLITIONIST cause through its implicit refutation of the brutishness of the slave. However, the conventional pieties of the poems and their reliance on a European model have led to them being considered fundamentally assimilationist. For example, in the poem 'On Being Brought from Africa to America' Wheatley suggests that blacks may be 'refin'd' into Christianity and that it was 'mercy' which brought her from a 'pagan' land and into Christian belief.

Further reading

Written by Herself: Literary Production by African American Women, 1746–1892 (1993) by Frances Smith Foster; *The Poems of Phillis Wheatley* (1989), edited by Julian D. Mason, and *Critical Essays on Phillis Wheatley* (1982), edited by William H. Robinson.

Whig Party   The party was formally founded in 1834, although there had been an informal grouping since the 1820s, formed in opposition to the policies of President Andrew Jackson. The Whigs took their name from the British parliamentary party that was more radical and progressive than their rivals the Tories. In spite of political successes in the 1840s the Whigs were divided and eventually disappeared because of the SLAVERY issue in the 1850s. Anti-slavery Whigs, known as 'conscience Whigs', joined the FREE SOIL PARTY and later, guided by sectional interests, the Republican Party. The so-called 'cotton Whigs', who were not opposed to slavery, joined the Democratic Party.

Whitman, Walt   One of the most considerable and influential of American poets, whose lifetime work LEAVES OF GRASS (1855–92) was crucial in the shaping of a distinctive American poetry.

Whitman was born on Long Island, New York, in 1819 and grew up in Brooklyn. His father was a carpenter and builder. Leaving school at the age of 12, Whitman worked as a printer and a schoolteacher before becoming a newspaper editor, assuming editorship of the *Brooklyn Daily Eagle* in 1846. He published a TEMPERANCE novel, *Franklin Evans*, in 1842. Whitman was dismissed from the *Eagle* in 1848 because of his allegiance to the FREE SOIL PARTY. He travelled south to work in New Orleans for 3 months, a period often referred to in his poetry. Returning to New York via the West, Whitman worked at various jobs and developed an interest in PHRENOLOGY. The first, anonymous, version of *Leaves of Grass*, consisting of twelve poems and a preface, was published in 1855 at Whitman's expense. Although the book was poorly received, Ralph Waldo EMERSON wrote Whitman an enthusiastic letter that was included in the enlarged second edition (1856), in which Whitman's name appeared on the title page. Although the book still sold poorly, a third edition appeared in 1860.

During the CIVIL WAR Whitman was a wound-dresser in Washington; the experience and the war mark a significant stage of development in his poetry, evident in *Drum-Taps* (1865). After the war Whitman held several government jobs, and his poetry started to attract favourable attention. The fourth edition of *Leaves of Grass* was published in 1867, and in 1868 a selection of his work was published in England. This selection stimulated special interest in Whitman, partly because of his apparently frank presentation of his homosexuality and because his work seemed the embodiment of the DEMOCRATIC American spirit. Whitman was partly paralysed after a stroke in 1873. After a visit to the West he retired to Camden, New Jersey. In 1888 he published *The Complete Poems and Prose*, and two further editions of *Leaves of Grass* followed; the final one, the so-called 'death-bed' edition, appeared posthumously. Whitman died in Camden in 1892.

Whitman adopted for his poetry the persona of 'one of the roughs' – a boisterous optimistic lover of freedom and democracy asserting the oneness of humanity and nature, celebrating his body's sensuality and affirming the republic's possibilities. Certainly the content and style of his poetry reflect this persona, evident in the Emersonian attitude to nature, the mysticism, the FREE VERSE based on speech rhythms, the use of American idiom and the ample catalogues. The persona stimulated the acclaim Whitman received from abroad; at home it led to charges of obscenity. But in some respects Whitman's careful cultivation of this persona has obscured his special qualities as a poet: a genuine sensitivity, the often-delicate use of language and the meticulous yet unobtrusive structuring of the longer poems. He thought carefully about how to represent democratic ideals of inclusiveness and equality in poetry, not only in terms of subject but also aesthetically. The adopted persona has also tended to conceal the doubting, melancholic aspects of Whitman, the recurrent brooding sense of failure in his poetry, his occasional bitterness and the harsh criticism of his country's failure to live up to its stated ideals. Although easily represented as a life-affirming writer, he wrote frequently and movingly about death, especially after the Civil War. While the poetry affirms homosexual love in ways that have been of great importance to many of his readers, Whitman himself was evasive and reserved on the subject. For all of his self-declared simplicity Whitman is a complex and multifaceted poet who profoundly influenced the subsequent direction of American poetry.

Further reading

Whitman the Political Poet (1989) by Betsy Erkkila; *The Cambridge Companion to Walt Whitman* (1995), edited by Ezra Greenspan; *The Continuing Presence of Walt Whitman* (1992), edited by Robert K. Martin; *Walt Whitman's Poetry: A Psychological Journey* (1968) by Edwin H. Miller; *Walt Whitman: A Critical Anthology* (1969), edited by Francis Murphy, and *The Lunar Light of Whitman's Poetry* (1987) by M. Wynn

Thomas. *The Solitary Singer* (1955, 1985) by Gay Wilson Allen and *Walt Whitman: The Song of Himself* (1999) by Jerome Loving are recommended critical biographies.

Williams, Tennessee One of the major American dramatists, Williams was born in Columbus, Mississippi, in 1911 (originally his name was Thomas Lanier Williams). He attended the University of Missouri and Washington University but graduated from the University of Iowa, in 1938. His first dramatic success was in the one-act plays of *American Blues* (1939), and his first major play was *The Glass Menagerie* (1944). In it Williams explored what would be a recurrent theme: the way in which frustrated and damaged characters construct an imaginative world in which they can perform, and the way in which this performance further removes them from reality. This theme continues in his masterpiece, *A Streetcar Named Desire* (1947). There, the world of the self-deluding former Southern belle Blanche Du Bois is damaged by the brutally realistic attitudes of her brother-in-law, Stanley Kowalski. A major film was made of *Streetcar*, and this was also true of *Cat on a Hot Tin Roof* (1955) and *The Night of the Iguana* (1961), although Williams was unhappy with the results. Williams often dealt with taboo or extreme subjects, linked by some critics to his own intense feelings of insecurity and, as a homosexual, his sense of being an outsider; he said he wrote because he 'found life unsatisfactory'. His other significant plays are *Suddenly Last Summer* (1958) and *Sweet Bird of Youth* (1959). He also published two novels, several collections of short stories and an autobiography (*Memoirs*, 1975), and wrote several works for HOLLYWOOD, notably *Baby Doll* (1956). From the 1960s, though, Williams's work was poorly received, and he began to suffer from ill-health, mainly brought on by alcoholism and other addictions, and from depression. He died in New York in 1983.

Further reading

Tennessee Williams (2000), edited by Harold Bloom; *Understanding Tennessee Williams* (1995) by Alice Griffin, and *Tennessee Williams' Plays* (1987) by Judith J. Thompson. *Tennessee Williams* (1993) by Ronald Hayman and *A Kindness of Strangers* (1985) by Donald Spoto are critical biographies.

Williams, William Carlos Poet and fiction-writer, born in Rutherford, New Jersey, in 1883 to a father of English origin and a mother of Basque ancestry. Williams studied medicine at the University of Pennsylvania, where he met Ezra POUND, who became a lifelong friend and correspondent, although the two disagreed on many issues. After studying at Leipzig, Williams returned to Rutherford and worked there as a doctor for the rest of his life. He died in 1963. For much of his life his poetry was neglected, although from the late 1940s he was increasingly recognized as a major poet and his work has been tremendously influential in the development of American poetry since the 1950s.

Williams began publishing poetry in 1909 but it was with *Al Que Quiere!* (1917) that he began to demonstrate a distinctive style, which emerged fully in *Spring and All* (1923). One of the major poetry collections of the 20th century, *Spring and All* is a sequence of exploratory prose and poetry, including the much-anthologized small part of section XXII, usually titled 'The Red Wheelbarrow'. Although his poetry shares some of IMAGISM's characteristics, Williams was closer to OBJECTIVISM in seeking to represent material objects without transforming them into symbols. Instead of ascribing to the imagination a ROMANTIC, transformative power, he saw it as permitting a clearer perception of the world as it is. As he wrote in *Spring and All*, 'To refine, to clarify, to intensify that eternal moment in which we alone live there is but a single force – the imagination.' His celebration of concrete reality, and his refutation of the symbolic and the mythic, is strongly linked to his lifelong interest in contemporary painting, and his poem usually titled 'By the Road to the Contagious Hospital' notably embodies this ideal. To some extent a political ideology functions in Williams's poetic. In seeking to make poetry out of the commonplace, he was both expressing a belief in the availability of anything to form a poem's subject and validating the common everyday world. Like WHITMAN, Williams was also deeply self-conscious about being an American and an American poet. His classic study *In the American Grain* (1925) explores incidents and characters of American history as markers in a process of American self-realization. However, Williams was also a poet who changed and who celebrated the human capacity for change, even if this meant self-contradiction. For all of his antipathy towards MODERNIST myth-making, his EPIC poem *Paterson* (1946–58) fits readily into that convention. Sometimes considered his masterpiece, it expresses the importance of concrete locality as a container of human history, myth and desire. Also his prose fiction, unjustly neglected, explores a wide range of ideas and beliefs. Much of his fiction is rooted in his experiences as a doctor working among the poor and the marginalized.

Williams's other major books are: the poetry collections *Kora in Hell* (1920), *The Wedge* (1944) and *Pictures from Brueghel* (1962); the novel trilogy *White Mule* (1937), *In the Money* (1940) and *The Build-Up* (1952); the short-story collections *The Knife of the Times* (1932) and *The Farmers' Daughters* (1951); the essays in *The Great American Novel* (1923) and *I Wanted to Write a Poem* (1958), and his *Autobiography* (1951). Williams's *Collected Poems* was published in two volumes in 1987, edited by A. Walton Litz and Christopher MacGowan.

Further reading

William Carlos Williams and Transcendentalism (1992) by Ron Callan; *The Revolution in the Visual Arts and the Poetry of William Carlos Williams* (1994) by Peter Halter; *A Homemade World* (1975) by Hugh Kenner; *Poets of Reality* (1965) by J. Hillis Miller; *Critical Essays on William Carlos Williams* (1966), edited by J. Hillis Miller; *The Inverted Bell* (1974) by Joseph N. Riddel, and the biography *William Carlos Williams: A New World Naked* (1981) by Paul Mariani.

Wilson, August Dramatist whose work focuses on the 20th century experiences of African Americans. Wilson was born in 1945 in Pittsburgh and left school at 15 (he has said that he then spent 5 years educating himself in the public library). During the

1960s he became involved with the Black Arts Movement, and in 1968 he founded Black Horizons Theatre in Pittsburgh. After moving to St Paul, Minnesota, in 1978, Wilson achieved popular and critical acclaim in 1984 with the play *Ma Rainey's Black Bottom*. Set in the 1920s, the play explores the relation between a black blues singer and her white manager. In 1985 *Fences*, which focused on the relationship between a father and son in the 1950s, also received acclaim. Wilson's other plays are *Joe Turner's Come and Gone* (1988), *The Piano Lesson* (1990), *Two Trains Running* (1992) and *Seven Guitars* (1996). Overall, his plays form a cycle in which Wilson examines African American experiences in relation to a specific period, from around 1911 (*Joe Turner's Come and Gone*) to the late 1960s/early 1970s (*Seven Guitars*). His plays are characterized by an interest in music and a strong use of African American vernacular.

Further reading

August Wilson: A Casebook (1994), edited by Marilyn Elkins; *May all your Fences have Gates* (1994), edited by Alan Nadel; *August Wilson and the African American Odyssey* (1995) by Kim Pereira; *The Dramatic Vision of August Wilson* (1995) by Sandra Shannon, and *August Wilson* (1999) by Peter Wolfe.

The Woman Warrior: Memoirs of a Girlhood Among Ghosts Autobiographical memoir in five parts by Maxine Hong Kingston, published in 1976. This highly acclaimed book is considered an influential autobiography and is of great importance to the development and wider acceptance of Asian American literature.

The work's main focus is on the experiences of two generations of Chinese: the parental generation who emigrate to the United States, and their American-born children. Both generations confront wounding disruptions. The parents experience a searing discontinuity between their Chinese and their American lives, and an irreparable sense of loss since the China that they left has vanished after the communist revolution. The children are psychologically torn between allegiance to their parents' mysterious recalcitrance over assimilation and the demands on them to conform to white ('ghost') American culture. The narrator's sense of displacement is deepened by her recognition that traditional Chinese society was deeply anti-female. Although *The Woman Warrior* explores disruption and crisis, it is also concerned with asserting imaginative continuity. This is achieved most notably through the narrator's creative adaptation of the Chinese myth of the warrior girl Fa Mu Lan to her own American circumstances. While it is classed as non-fiction *The Woman Warrior* crosses many genre boundaries in its celebration of the power of imaginative writing to restore lost continuities. As the narrator writes of interacting with one of her mother's stories, 'The beginning is hers, the ending, mine.'

Further reading

Fictions in Autobiography (1985) by Paul John Eakin; *Framing the Margins* (1994) by Phillip Brian Harper; *Approaches to Teaching Kingston's The Woman Warrior* (1991), edited by Shirley Geok-lin Lim, and *Maxine Hong Kingston's The Woman Warrior: A Casebook* (1999), edited by Sau-ling Cynthia Wong.

Woman's Home Companion   Monthly magazine aimed at a female readership, originally founded in 1873 as *Home Companion*. Published in New York City, it featured articles on domestic matters and under the editorship of Gertrude B. Lane, from 1911 to 1940, it also published some important fiction by women writers, notably Willa CATHER. The magazine ceased publication in 1957.

World War I   Also known as the Great War, the war began in Europe in August 1914 and the United States entered the conflict on the side of the Allies in April 1917, primarily because of German attacks on American shipping. Five million American men either volunteered for service or were conscripted. The American navy played a prominent role in the war and, after March 1918, over 2 million men were in Europe as part of the American Expeditionary Force under the command of General John J. Pershing. The AEF fought with distinction on the French western front, gaining a significant victory at Saint-Mihiel. American economic contribution to the allies, estimated at over $7 billion, was also crucial to the war effort. The war ended in November 1918 and was formally concluded with the 1919 Treaty of Versailles. The United States did not ratify the treaty, and made its own peace treaty with Germany in 1921. The number of American war dead is estimated at 116,000, 59,000 of whom died of disease. The total number of war dead is calculated at over 8.5 million soldiers and up to 13 million civilians.

American writing was profoundly affected by the war. The unprecedented number of dead, and the overall scale of its horrors and atrocities, seemed to represent an end to historical progress and to threaten civilization itself. A consequent mood of futility and despair is present in some of MODERNISM's key texts, notably T. S. ELIOT's *THE WASTE LAND* and Ezra POUND's 'Hugh Selwyn Mauberley' (1920), and the concept of a LOST GENERATION pervades much post-war writing. American writers involved in the war in Europe include Ernest HEMINGWAY, who was wounded while a volunteer ambulance-driver in Italy, John Dos Passos (1896–1970) and e. e. cummings (1894–1962), who were ambulance corps volunteers in France, where cummings was imprisoned. William FAULKNER and F. Scott FITZGERALD joined the armed forces but did not go to Europe. Gertrude STEIN and Edith Wharton (1862–1937) both spent the war in France, and Wharton wrote several propaganda works.

The war features as a significant point of reference in a large number of texts. Works dealing directly with the war and its aftermath include *Three Soldiers* (1921) by Dos Passos, cummings's *The Enormous Room* (1922), Hemingway's *In Our Time* (1925) and *A Farewell to Arms* (1929), and Faulkner's *Soldier's Pay* (1926) and *A Fable* (1954).

Further reading

World War I and the American Novel (1967) by Stanley Cooperman; *Exile's Return* (1934, 1951) by Malcolm Cowley; *Over There: The United States in the Great War* (1999) by Byron Farwell; *Partisans and Poets* (1997) by Mark W. Van Wienen, and *America's Great War* (2000) by Robert H. Zieger.

World War II   The United States entered the war, which had begun in 1939, after the bombing of the US Pacific fleet by the Japanese at Pearl Harbor, Hawaii, on 7 December 1941. Before then the US had supported the Allies by various means, notably by providing credit through the 'Lend–Lease' programme. The war was fought mainly in two theatres: in Europe, where the US joined the allied forces against Italy and Germany, and in the Pacific, against Japan. The US forces established a powerful presence in Britain, and under the command of General Eisenhower were heavily engaged in the invasions of Sicily and Italy in 1943 and of France on 'D-Day', 6 June 1944. The war in Europe ended on 8 May 1945 with the surrender of Germany. On the Pacific front heavy American casualties were incurred in the capture of islands such as Iwo Jima and Okinawa. The war in the Pacific ended with the Japanese surrender on 14 August 1945 after the dropping of atom bombs on Hiroshima (6 August) and Nagasaki (8 August). During the war over 15 million American men and women served in the armed services. Total American war casualties are estimated at 292,000, 6,000 of whom were civilians. Estimates of the total number of war dead range from 35 to 60 million, including up to 6 million people killed in the Holocaust.

The war represented a profound turning point in American history. The development of the atomic bomb instituted the nuclear age, and the Cold War began after the ending of the wartime alliance with the Soviet Union. Revelations of the concentration camps and the horrors of the Holocaust proved deeply shocking. Within the US the war resulted in better social opportunities for African Americans and hastened the end of racial segregation.

Many American writers served in the war overseas, including Karl Shapiro (1913–2000), Herman Wouk (b. 1915), J. D. Salinger (b. 1919), James Jones (1921–77), Kurt Vonnegut (b. 1922), Norman Mailer (b. 1923), Anthony Hecht (b. 1923) and Joseph Heller (1923–99). Their experiences resulted in many works directly concerned with the war, notably Mailer's *The Naked and the Dead* (1948); Jones's three novels *From Here to Eternity* (1951), *Pistol* (1959) and *The Thin Red Line* (1962); Vonnegut's *Slaughterhouse-Five* (1969); Heller's *Catch-22* (1961); Wouk's *The Winds of War* (1971) and *War and Remembrance* (1978), and Shapiro's *V-Letter and Other Poems* (1944). Other significant war writing includes *Wars I Have Seen* (1945) by Gertrude Stein; *The Moon is Down* (1942) by John Steinbeck (1902–68); *Into the Valley* (1943), *Hiroshima* (1946) and *A Bell for Adano* (1944) by John Hersey (1914–93), and *Losses* (1948) by Randall Jarrell (1914–65). There was much distinguished journalism and reportage of the war, by writers such as Steinbeck, Hersey, Ernie Pyle (1900–45), J. Saunders Redding (1906–88), Martha Gellhorn (1908–98), Edward R. Murrow (1908–65), and celebrated photographs by Margaret Bourke-White (1904–71). The internment of over 100,000 Japanese Americans during the war is explored in works such as *Nisei Daughter* (1953) by Monica Sone (b. 1919) and *No-No Boy* (1957) by John Okada (1924–71).

Further reading

Writing After War (1994) by John Limon; The United States and World War II (1992) by Robert James Maddox; Literatures of Memory (2000) by Peter Middleton; A Gulf so Deeply Cut: American Women Poets and the Second World War (1991) by Susan M. Schweik; Double Victory (2000) by Ronald T. Takaki, and American Novels of the Second World War (1969) by Joseph J. Waldmeir. Reporting World War II (2 vols, 1995), edited by Samuel Hynes et al., is a useful collection of journalism.

Wright, Richard   An influential African American novelist, Wright was born in 1908 in rural Mississippi. After an unstable childhood he moved to Memphis and later to Chicago, where he worked for the FEDERAL WRITERS' PROJECT and joined the Communist Party. He moved to New York in 1937. Wright broke with communism in 1944 and in 1947 he moved to Paris, where he developed an interest in EXISTENTIALISM. He died in Paris in 1960.

Wright helped to initiate the protest movement in African American writing, using REALISM and often exploring hitherto taboo subjects to attack social and racial injustice. His Marxist-influenced 1937 essay 'Blueprint for Negro Writing' defined tasks for the black writer, including those of raising the consciousness of other blacks and of providing a guide for 'daily living'. His first collection of stories, *Uncle Tom's Children* (1938), and the best-selling *NATIVE SON* (1940) followed the essay's tenets. His political leanings prompted investigation into him by the FBI. Wright's AUTOBIOGRAPHY *Black Boy* (1945) is a powerful account of his childhood and his eventual move from the South. (*American Hunger*, originally the second part of *Black Boy* but unpublished in 1945, was fully published in 1977.) Wright's last major novel was *The Outsider* (1953), often considered the first existential work by an American.

Wright's critical reception has been mixed. While the stark realism and clear message of his work have often been acclaimed, its crudeness and propagandist stance have also been noted. Importantly, though, the BLACK ARTS MOVEMENT made Wright into an indispensable precursor of militant writing.

Further reading

Native Son: The Emergence of a New Black Hero (1991) by Robert Butler; The Critical Response to Richard Wright (1995) edited by Robert Butler; Richard Wright: Critical Perspectives Past and Present (1993) edited by Henry Louis Gates, Jr, and K. A. Appiah; Richard Wright and Racial Discourse (1996) by Yoshinobu Hakutani; Richard Wright's Art of Tragedy (1986) by Joyce Ann Joyce, and the critical biography Richard Wright (2001) by Hazel Rowley.

Yankee   Term used since the 1770s to describe any inhabitant of the colonies, but which has been used more specifically since the CIVIL WAR to describe a New Englander. The term connotes ingenuity, trading ability, invention, shrewdness, cunning, taciturnity and technological skill, as embodied for instance in the character Hank Morgan in Mark TWAIN's novel *A Connecticut Yankee in King Arthur's Court* (1889). This characteristic Yankee figure has a long literary history, appearing in works by Royall Tyler (1757–1826), Seba Smith (1792–1868), Washington IRVING, Henry David THOREAU and James Russell Lowell (1819–91). The origin of 'Yankee' is unknown; the most widely accepted suggestion is that it derives from the Dutch 'Janke' for 'Johnny'. 'Yankee Doodle', by Richard Shuckburgh, was a popular song during the REVOLUTIONARY WAR.

Yellow journalism   Term used to describe the sensationalist journalism that developed during the newspaper circulation wars in New York during the 1890s. The competition was primarily between the New York *World*, published by Joseph Pulitzer, and the New York *Journal* owned by William Randolph Hearst. Yellow journalism was characterized by strong headlines, illustrations, patriotic editorials, comic strips, and enquiry into the scandalous and the sensational. It also had a moral crusading element that proved important to the development of MUCKRAKING.

The term 'yellow press' derives from a character, the 'Yellow Kid', drawn by Richard F. Outcault for his popular coloured comic strip 'Hogan's Alley'. First published by the *World*, 'Hogan's Alley' was taken over by the *Journal*, though the *World* maintained a version of the strip drawn by another cartoonist. The strip's popularity laid the foundation for the modern newspaper comic strip.

Young America   Loose grouping of writers in New York in the 1840s. The Young Americans tried to encourage the development of a nationalist, specifically American, literature, and were opposed to the Anglophile writers associated with the *KNICKERBOCKER MAGAZINE*. They also campaigned for an international law on COPYRIGHT in order to assist the development of American literature. The group was particularly associated with the weekly review *Literary World* (1847–53), edited by Evert Duyckinck (1816–78) and his brother George (1823–63). The Young Americans included William Gilmore Simms (1806–70), Edgar Allan POE and Herman MELVILLE. Melville expressed his Young America sentiments for the *Literary World* in the 1850 essay 'Hawthorne and His Mosses', in which he wrote, 'let America first praise mediocrity even, in her own children, before she praises . . . the best excellence in the children of any other land'. Melville later satirized Young America in his 1852 novel *Pierre*.

Bibliography

This bibliography provides full details of works recommended in relevant individual entries, and also includes works that were especially helpful in the preparation of the Glossary.

Aaron, Daniel (1973) *The unwritten war: American writers and the Civil War*, New York and London: Oxford University Press.

Abrams, Ann (1999) *The pilgrims and Pocahontas: rival myths of American origin*, Boulder, CO: Westview Press.

Ackroyd, Peter (1984) *T. S. Eliot: a life*, London: Hamish Hamilton.

Acocella, Joan (2000) *Willa Cather and the politics of criticism*, Lincoln: University of Nebraska Press.

Adair, John (1998) *Puritans: religion and politics in seventeenth century England and America*, Stroud: Sutton Publishing.

Adams, David K. and Minnen, Cornelis A. van (eds) (1994) *Reflections on American exceptionalism*, Keele: Ryburn.

Adams, James T. (1931) *The epic of America*, Boston: Little, Brown; London: Routledge.

Aderman, Ralph M. (ed.) (1990) *Critical essays on Washington Irving*, Boston: G. K. Hall.

Ahnebrink, Lars (1961) *The beginnings of naturalism in American fiction*, Cambridge, MA: Harvard University Press.

Allen, Elizabeth (1984) *A woman's place in the novels of Henry James*, London: Macmillan.

Allen, Gay Wilson (1955, 1985) *The solitary singer: a critical biography of Walt Whitman*, New York: Macmillan.

Allen, Gay Wilson (1975) *The new Walt Whitman handbook*, New York: New York University Press.

Allen, Paula Gunn (1986) *The sacred hoop: recovering the feminine in American Indian traditions*, Boston: Beacon Press.

Allen, Paula Gunn (ed.) (1989) *Spider Woman's granddaughters: traditional tales and contemporary writing by Native American women*, New York: Fawcett Columbine.

Allmendinger, Blake (1992) *The cowboy: representations of labor in an American work culture*, New York: Oxford University Press.

Alter, Iska (1981) *The good man's dilemma: social criticism in the fiction of Bernard Malamud*, New York: AMS Press.

Alter, Robert (1977) *Defenses of the imagination: Jewish writers and modern historical crisis*, Philadelphia: Jewish Publication Society of America.

Altieri, Charles (1979), *Enlarging the temple: new directions in American poetry during the 1960s*, Lewisburg, PA: Bucknell University Press.

Altieri, Charles (1984), *Self and sensibility in contemporary American poetry*, Cambridge and New York: Cambridge University Press.

Ammons, Elizabeth (ed.) (1980) *Critical essays on Harriet Beecher Stowe*, Boston: G. K. Hall.

Anders, John P. (1999) *Willa Cather's sexual aesthetics and the male homosexual literary tradition*, Lincoln: University of Nebraska Press.

Andrews, Bruce and Bernstein, Charles (eds) (1984) *The L=A=N=G=U=A=G=E book*, Carbondale: Southern Illinois University Press.

Andrews, William L. (1986) *To tell a free story: the first century of Afro-American auto-biography, 1760–1865*, Urbana: University of Illinois Press.

Andrews, William L. (ed.) (1991) *Critical essays on Frederick Douglass*, Boston: G. K. Hall.

Andrews, William L., Foster, Frances Smith and Harris, Trudier (eds) (1997) *The Oxford companion to African American literature*, New York: Oxford University Press.

Anzaldúa, Gloria (ed.) (1990) *Making face, making soul = Haciendo caras: creative and critical perspectives by feminists*, San Francisco: Aunt Lute Foundation Books.

Arac, Jonathan (1997) *Huckleberry Finn as idol and target: the functions of criticism in our time*, Madison: University of Wisconsin Press.

Arnold, Ellen L. (ed.) (2000) *Conversations with Leslie Marmon Silko*, Jackson: University Press of Mississippi.

Asbury, Herbert (1950) *The great illusion: an informal history of prohibition*, Garden City, NY: Doubleday.

Asselineau, Roger (1980) *The transcendentalist constant in American literature*, New York: New York University Press.

Atlas, James (2000) *Saul Bellow: a biography*, New York: Random House.

Axelrod, Alan (1983) *Charles Brockden Brown: an American tale*, Austin: University of Texas Press.

Axelrod, Steven Gould (1978) *Robert Lowell: life and art*, Princeton: Princeton University Press.

Axelrod, Steven Gould (1990) *Sylvia Plath: the wound and the cure of words*, Baltimore: Johns Hopkins University Press.

Axelrod, Steven Gould (ed.) (1999) *The critical response to Robert Lowell*, Westport, CT: Greenwood Press.

Axelsson, Arne (1990) *Restrained response: American novels of the Cold War and Korea, 1945–1962*, New York: Greenwood Press.

Ayers, Edward L. (1984) *Vengeance and justice: crime and punishment in the 19th-century American South*, New York: Oxford University Press.

Baker, Carlos (1969) *Ernest Hemingway: a life story*, New York: Scribner.

Baker, Carlos (1984) *The echoing green: romanticism, modernism, and the phenomena of transference in poetry*, Princeton: Princeton University Press.

Baker, Houston A. Jr (1980) *The journey back: issues in Black literature and criticism*, Chicago: University of Chicago Press.

Baker, Houston A. Jr (1984) *Blues, ideology, and Afro-American literature: a vernacular theory*, Chicago: University of Chicago Press.

Baker, Houston A. Jr (1987) *Modernism and the Harlem renaissance*, Chicago: University of Chicago Press.

Baker, Peter (1991) *Obdurate brilliance: exteriority and the modern long poem*, Gainesville: University Press of Florida.

Baldwin, James, *The price of the ticket: collected nonfiction, 1948–1985*, New York: St Martin's Press.

Bammer, Angelica (1991) *Partial visions: feminism and utopianism in the 1970s*, London: Routledge.

Banta, Martha (1978) *Failure and success in America: a literary debate*, Princeton: Princeton University Press.

Banta, Martha (1987) *Imaging American women: idea and ideals in cultural history*, New York: Columbia University Press.

Banta, Martha (1993) *Taylored lives: narrative productions in the age of Taylor, Veblen, and Ford*, Chicago: University of Chicago Press.

Banton, Michael (1998) *Racial theories*, Cambridge: Cambridge University Press.

Barlow, Judith E. (1985) *Final acts: the creation of three late O'Neill plays*, Athens: University of Georgia Press.

Barlow, William (1989) *'Looking up at down': the emergence of blues culture*, Philadelphia: Temple University Press.

Barnard, Rita (1995) *The Great Depression and the culture of abundance: Kenneth Fearing, Nathanael West, and mass culture in the 1930s*, Cambridge and New York: Cambridge University Press.

Barnett, Louise K. (ed.) (1999) *Leslie Marmon Silko: a collection of critical essays*, Albuquerque: University of New Mexico Press.

Barr, Marleen S. (1987) *Alien to femininity: speculative fiction and feminist theory*, New York: Greenwood Press.

Bates, Milton J. (1985) *Wallace Stevens: a mythology of self*, Berkeley: University of California Press.

Bates, Milton J. (1996) *The wars we took to Vietnam: cultural conflict and storytelling*, Berkeley: University of California Press.

249

Bates, Milton J. (chief ed.) (1998) *Reporting Vietnam*, 2 vols, New York: Library of America.

Baudrillard, Jean (1988) *America*, translated by Chris Turner, London and New York: Verso.

Baumgarten, Murray and Gottfried, Barbara (1990) *Understanding Philip Roth*, Columbia, SC: University of South Carolina Press.

Baym, Nina (general ed.) (1998) *The Norton anthology of American literature*, 5th edn, 2 vols, New York and London: W. W. Norton.

Bean, Anne Marie, Hatch, James V. and McNamara, Brooks (1996) *Inside the minstrel mask: readings in nineteenth-century blackface minstrelsy*, Hanover, NH: University Press of New England.

Beaver, Harold (1985) *The great American masquerade*, London: Vision; Totowa, NJ: Barnes and Noble.

Beck, Charlotte H. (2001) *The fugitive legacy: a critical history*, Baton Rouge: Louisiana State University Press.

Bedient, Calvin (1986) *He do the police in different voices: The Waste Land and its protagonist*, Chicago: University of Chicago Press.

Beemyn, Brett and Eliason, Mickey (eds) (1996) *Queer studies: a lesbian, gay, bisexual, and transgender anthology*, New York: New York University Press.

Beidler, Philip D. (1991) *Re-writing America: Vietnam authors in their generation*, Athens: University of Georgia Press.

Bell, Ian F. A. (ed.) (1982) *Ezra Pound: tactics for reading*, London: Vision Press.

Bell, Michael Davitt (1980) *The development of American romance: the sacrifice of relation*, Chicago: University of Chicago Press.

Bell, Michael Davitt (1997) *The problem of American realism: studies in the cultural history of a literary idea*, Chicago: University of Chicago Press.

Bell, Millicent (1993) *New essays on Hawthorne's major tales*, Cambridge and New York: Cambridge University Press.

Bell, Vereen (1983) *Robert Lowell: nihilist as hero*, Cambridge, MA: Harvard University Press.

Belsey, Catherine and Moore, Jane (eds) (1989) *The feminist reader: essays in gender and the politics of literary criticism*, Oxford: Blackwell.

Benaderte, Jane (ed.) (1972) *American Realism*, New York: Putnam.

Bennett, Paula (ed.) (1998) *Nineteenth-century American women poets: an anthology*, Oxford and Malden, MA: Blackwell.

Benston, Kimberly W. (ed.) (1978) *Imamu Amiri Baraka (Leroi Jones): a collection of critical essays*, Englewood Cliffs, NJ: Prentice-Hall.

Benston, Kimberley W. (ed.) (1987) *Speaking for you: the vision of Ralph Ellison*, Washington, DC: Howard University Press.

Benston, Kimberley W. (2000) *Performing blackness: enactments of African-American modernism*, London: Routledge.

Bercovitch, Sacvan (1975) *The Puritan origins of the American self*, New Haven: Yale University Press.

Bercovitch, Sacvan (1978) *The American jeremiad*, Madison: University of Wisconsin Press.

Bercovitch, Sacvan (1986) *Reconstructing American literary history*, Cambridge, MA: Harvard University Press.

Bercovitch, Sacvan (1993) *The rites of assent: transformations in the symbolic construction of America*, New York and London: Routledge.

Bercovitch, Sacvan (ed.) (1974) *The American Puritan imagination: essays in revaluation*, London and New York: Cambridge University Press.

Bercovitch, Sacvan (ed.) (1986) *Ideology and classic American literature*, Cambridge and New York: Cambridge University Press.

Bercovitch, Sacvan (general ed.) (1994–99) *The Cambridge history of American literature*: volume 1 (1994), *1590–1820*; vol. 2 (1995), *Prose writing, 1820–1865*; vol. 7 (1999), *Prose writing, 1940–1990*; vol. 8 (1996), *Poetry and criticism, 1940–1995*, Cambridge and New York: Cambridge University Press.

Berger, Alan (1985) *Crisis and covenant: the Holocaust in American Jewish fiction*, Albany: State University of New York Press.

Berger, Alan L. (1997) *Children of Job: American second-generation witnesses to the Holocaust*, Albany: State University of New York Press.

Berger, James (1999) *After the end: representations of post-apocalypse*, Minneapolis: University of Minnesota Press.

Bergman, David (ed.) (1994) *The violet quill reader: the emergence of gay writing after Stonewall*, New York: St Martin's Press.

Bergon, Frank (1975) *Stephen Crane's artistry*, New York: Columbia University Press.

Bhatia, Santosh K. (1985) *Arthur Miller: social drama as tragedy*, New Delhi: Arnold-Heinemann.

Bigsby, Christopher (1985) *David Mamet*, London and New York: Methuen.

Bigsby, Christopher (ed.) (1997) *The Cambridge companion to Arthur Miller*, Cambridge and New York: Cambridge University Press.

Black, Stephen (1999) *Eugene O'Neill: beyond mourning and tragedy*, New Haven: Yale University Press.

Blassingame, John W. (1979) *The slave community: plantation life in the antebellum South*, New York: Oxford University Press.

Blau, Herbert (1987) '*The eye of prey': subversions of the postmodern*, Bloomington: Indiana University Press.

Bleikasten, André (1976) *The most splendid failure: Faulkner's The Sound and the Fury*, Bloomington: Indiana University Press.

Bleikasten, André (1990) *The ink of melancholy: Faulkner's novels from The Sound and the Fury to Light in August*, Bloomington: Indiana University Press.

Bleikasten, André (ed.) (1982) *William Faulkner's The Sound and the Fury: a critical casebook*, New York: Garland.

Bloom, Harold (1977) *Wallace Stevens: the poems of our climate*, Ithaca, NY: Cornell University Press.

Bloom, Harold (ed.) (1985) *John Ashbery*, New York: Chelsea House.

Bloom, Harold (ed.) (1986) *Ralph Ellison*, New York: Chelsea House.

Bloom, Harold (ed.) (1986) *Robert Frost*, New York: Chelsea House.

Bloom, Harold (ed.) (1986) *Zora Neale Hurston*, New York: Chelsea House.

Bloom, Harold (ed.) (1987) *Henry David Thoreau*, New York: Chelsea House.

Bloom, Harold (ed.) (1987) *Richard Wright*, New York: Chelsea House.

Bloom, Harold (ed.) (1988) *Frederick Douglass' Narrative*, New York: Chelsea House.

Bloom, Harold (ed.) (1990) *Toni Morrison*, New York: Chelsea House.

Bloom, Harold (ed.) (2000) *Tennessee Williams*, New York: Chelsea House.

Blotner, Joseph L. (1974) *Faulkner: a biography*, New York: Random House.

Boeckmann, Cathy (2000) *A question of character: scientific racism and the genres of American fiction, 1892–1912*, Tuscaloosa: University of Alabama Press.

Bogard, Travis (1987) *Contour in time: the plays of Eugene O'Neill*, New York: Oxford University Press.

Bolden, B. J. (1999) *Urban rage in Bronzeville: social commentary in the poetry of Gwendolyn Brooks, 1945–1960*, Chicago: Third World Press.

Booker, M. Keith (2001) *Monsters, mushroom clouds, and the Cold War: American science fiction and the roots of postmodernism, 1946–1964*, Westport, CT: Greenwood Press.

Boren, Lynda S. and deSaussure Davis, Sara (eds) (1992) *Kate Chopin reconsidered: beyond the Bayou*, Baton Rouge: Louisiana State University Press.

Boudreau, Gordon V. (1990) *The roots of Walden and the tree of life*, Nashville: Vanderbilt University Press.

Bradbury, John M. (1963) *Renaissance in the South: a critical history of the literature, 1920–1960*, Chapel Hill: University of North Carolina Press.

Bradbury, Malcolm (1992) *The modern American novel*, Oxford and New York: Oxford University Press.

Branch, Taylor (1988) *Parting the waters: America in the King years, 1954–63*, New York: Simon and Schuster.

Breslin, James E. (1986) 'Gertrude Stein and the Problems of Autobiography', reprinted in Hoffman, Michael J. (ed.), *Critical essays on Gertrude Stein*, Boston: G. K. Hall, 149–159.

Breslin, Paul (1987) *The psycho-political muse: American poetry since the fifties*, Chicago: University of Chicago Press.

Bridgman, Richard (1970) *Gertrude Stein in pieces*, New York: Oxford University Press.

Brinkmeyer, Robert (1989) *The art and vision of Flannery O'Connor*, Baton Rouge: Louisiana State University Press.

Britzolakis, Christina (1999) *Sylvia Plath and the theatre of mourning*, Oxford and New York: Oxford University Press.

Brodtkorb, Paul (1965) *Ishmael's white world; a phenomenological reading of Moby-Dick*, New Haven: Yale University Press.

Brooker, Jewel Spears (1994) *Mastery and escape: T. S. Eliot and the dialectic of modernism*, Amherst: University of Massachusetts Press.

Brook-Rose, Christine (1971) *A ZBC of Ezra Pound*, London: Faber and Faber.

Brooks, Cleanth (1978) *William Faulkner: toward Yoknapatawpha and beyond*, New Haven: Yale University Press.

Browder, Laura (2000) *Slippery characters: ethnic impersonators and American identities*, Chapel Hill: University of North Carolina Press.

Brown, Bill (ed.) (1997) *Reading the West: an anthology of dime westerns*, Boston: Bedford Books.

Brownlie, Alan W. (2000) *Thomas Pynchon's narratives: subjectivity and problems of knowing*, New York: Peter Lang.

Bruccoli, Matthew J. (1981) *Some sort of epic grandeur: the life of F. Scott Fitzgerald*, New York: Harcourt Brace Jovanovich; London: Cardinal Books.

Bruccoli, Matthew (ed.) (1985) *New essays on The Great Gatsby*, Cambridge and New York: Cambridge University Press, 1985.

Bruce-Novoa, Juan (1980) *Chicano authors:inquiry by interviews*, Austin: University of Texas Press.

Bruffee, Kenneth A. (1983) *Elegiac romance: cultural change and loss of the hero in modern fiction*, Ithaca, NY: Cornell University Press.

Brunner, Edward (2001) *Cold War poetry*, Urbana: University of Illinois Press.

Brunvand, Jan Harold (ed.) (1979) *Readings in American folklore*, New York: Norton.

Bryant, J. A. (1997) *Twentieth century Southern literature*, Lexington: University Press of Kentucky.

Bryant, John (ed.) (1986) *A companion to Melville studies*, New York: Greenwood Press.

Budick, Emily (1994) *Engendering romance: women writers and the Hawthorne tradition, 1850–1990*, New Haven: Yale University Press.

Buell, Lawrence (1973) *Literary transcendentalism: style and vision in the American Renaissance*, Ithaca, NY: Cornell University Press.

Buell, Lawrence (1993) *Ralph Waldo Emerson: a collection of critical essays*, Englewood Cliffs, NJ: Prentice-Hall.

Buell, Lawrence (1995) *The environmental imagination: Thoreau, nature writing, and the formation of American culture*, Cambridge, MA: Belknap Press of Harvard University Press.

Bundtzen, Lynda K. (1983) *Plath's incarnations: woman and the creative process*, Ann Arbor: University of Michigan Press.

Burt, John (1999) 'After the Southern Renascence', in Bercovitch, Sacvan (general ed.), *The Cambridge history of American literature*, vol. 7, *Prose writing, 1940–1990*, Cambridge and New York: Cambridge University Press, 311–424.

Bush, Ronald (1976) *The genesis of Ezra Pound's Cantos*, Princeton: Princeton University Press.

Bush, Ronald (1984) *T. S. Eliot: a study in character and style*, New York: Oxford University Press.

Butler, Robert (1991) *Native Son: the emergence of a new Black hero*, Boston: Twayne.

Butler, Robert (ed.) (1995) *The critical response to Richard Wright*, Westport, CT: Greenwood Press.

Byerman, Keith E. (1994) *Seizing the word: history, art, and self in the work of W. E. B. DuBois*, Athens: University of Georgia Press.

Calderón, Héctor and Saldívar, José David (eds) (1991) *Criticism in the borderlands: studies in Chicano literature, culture, and ideology*, Durham, NC: Duke University Press.

Callahan, John F. (1972) *The illusions of a nation: myth and history in the novels of F. Scott Fitzgerald*, Urbana: University of Illinois Press.

Callan, Ron (1992) *William Carlos Williams and transcendentalism: fitting the crab in a box*, Basingstoke: Macmillan.

Cameron, Kelly (1994) *Henry James and masculinity: the man at the margins*, Basingstoke: Macmillan.

Camfield, Gregg (1997) *Necessary madness: the humor of domesticity in nineteenth-century American literature*, New York: Oxford University Press.

Campbell, James (1991) *Talking at the gates: a life of James Baldwin*, London and Boston: Faber.

Campbell, James (1999) *This is the Beat generation: New York, San Francisco, Paris*, London: Secker and Warburg.

Cardwell, Guy (1991) *The man who was Mark Twain: images and ideologies*, New Haven: Yale University Press.

Carson, Neil (1982) *Arthur Miller*, New York: Grove Press.

Cawelti, John G. (1971) *The six-gun mystique*, Bowling Green, OH: Bowling Green University Popular Press.

Cawelti, John G. (1976) *Adventure, mystery, and romance: formula stories as art and popular culture*, Chicago and London: University of Chicago Press.

Champion, Laurie (ed.) (1991) *The critical response to Mark Twain's Huckleberry Finn*, New York: Greenwood Press.

Charters, Ann (ed.) (2001) *Beat down to your soul: what was the Beat generation?*, New York: Penguin Books.

Cheung, King-Kok (1993) *Articulate silences: Hisaye Yamamoto, Maxine Hong Kingston, Joy Kogawa*, Ithaca, NY: Cornell University Press.

Cheung, King-Kok (ed.) (1997) *An interethnic companion to Asian American literature*, New York: Cambridge University Press.

Chipman, Bruce L. (1999) *Into America's dream-dump: a postmodern study of the Hollywood novel*, Lanham, MD: University Press of America.

Christian, Barbara (1985) *Black feminist criticism: perspectives on black women writers*, New York: Pergamon Press.

Civello, Paul (1994) *American literary naturalism and its twentieth-century transformations: Frank Norris, Ernest Hemingway, Don DeLillo*, Athens: University of Georgia Press.

Clark, Robert (ed.) (1985) *James Fenimore Cooper: new critical essays*, London: Vision Press.

Clayton, John Jacob (1979) *Saul Bellow: in defense of man*, Bloomington: Indiana University Press.

Coffey, Thomas (1975) *The long thirst: prohibition in America, 1920–1933*, New York: Norton.

Cohen, Sarah Blacher (ed.) (1978) *Comic relief: humor in contemporary American literature*, Urbana: University of Illinois Press.

Colacurcio, Michael J. (1984) *The province of piety: moral history in Hawthorne's early tales*, Cambridge, MA: Harvard University Press.

Collins, Lucy (2001) 'Confessionalism', in Roberts, Neil (ed.), *A companion to twentieth century poetry*, Oxford and Malden, MA: Blackwell, 197–208.

Commager, Henry Steele (1978) *The empire of reason: how Europe imagined and America realized the Enlightenment*, Garden City, NY: Anchor Press/Doubleday.

Conkin, Paul K. (1988) *The Southern Agrarians*, Knoxville: University of Tennessee Press.

Conner, Marc C. (ed.) (2000) *The aesthetics of Toni Morrison: speaking the unspeakable*, Jackson: University Press of Mississippi.

Cooper, Alan (1996) *Philip Roth and the Jews*, Albany: State University of New York Press.

Cooper, Jane Roberta (ed.) (1984) *Reading Adrienne Rich: reviews and re-visions, 1951–81*, Ann Arbor: University of Michigan Press.

Cooper, Peter L. (1983) *Signs and symptoms: Thomas Pynchon and the contemporary world*, Berkeley: University of California Press.

Cooperman, Stanley (1967) *World War I and the American novel*, Baltimore: Johns Hopkins Press.

Costello, Bonnie (1991) *Elizabeth Bishop: questions of mastery*, Cambridge, MA: Harvard University Press.

Cowan, Louise (1959) *The Fugitive group: a literary history*, Baton Rouge: Louisiana State University Press.

Cowan, Michael H. (ed.) (1968) *Twentieth century interpretations of The Sound and the Fury: a collection of critical essays*, Englewood Cliffs, NJ: Prentice-Hall.

Cowell, Pattie and Stanford, Ann (eds) (1983) *Critical essays on Anne Bradstreet*, Boston: G. K. Hall.

Cowley, Malcolm (1934, 1951) *Exile's return: a literary odyssey of the 1920s*, New York: Viking Press.

Cronin, Gloria L. (2001) *A room of his own: in search of the feminine in the novels of Saul Bellow*, Syracuse, NY: Syracuse University Press.

Crowley, John W. (1994) *The white logic: alcoholism and gender in American modernist fiction*, Amherst: University of Massachusetts Press.

Cunliffe, Marcus (1986) *The literature of the United States*, 4th edn, Harmondsworth and New York: Penguin Books.

Currie, Mark (ed.) (1995) *Metafiction*, London: Longman.

Daly, Robert (1978) *God's altar: the world and the flesh in Puritan poetry*, Berkeley: University of California Press.

Dardis, Tom (1989) *The thirsty muse: alcohol and the American writer*, New York: Ticknor and Fields.

Davidson, Cathy N. and Wagner-Martin, Linda (general eds) (1995) *The Oxford companion to women's writing in the United States*, New York: Oxford University Press.

Davis, Charles T. and Gates, Henry Louis Jr (eds) (1985) *The slave's narrative*, Oxford and New York: Oxford University Press.

Davis, Philip (1995) *Experimental essays on the novels of Bernard Malamud: Malamud's people*, Lampeter: Mellen.

Dayan, Joan (1987) *Fables of mind: an inquiry into Poe's fiction*, New York: Oxford University Press.

Dean, Anne (1990) *David Mamet: language as dramatic action*, Rutherford: Fairleigh Dickinson; London: Associated University Presses.

Dean, Eric T. (1997) *Shook over hell: post-traumatic stress, Vietnam, and the Civil War*, Cambridge, MA: Harvard University Press.

Dekker, George (1967) *James Fenimore Cooper: the American Scott*, New York: Barnes and Noble.

Dekker, George (1987) *The American historical romance*, Cambridge and New York: Cambridge University Press.

Denis Donoghue (1966) *Connoisseurs of chaos: ideas of order in modern American poetry*, London: Faber.

Denis Donoghue (1987) *Reading America: essays on American literature*, New York: Knopf/Random House.

Denis Donoghue (2000) *Words alone: the poet T.S. Eliot*, New Haven: Yale University Press.

Denning, Michael (1998) *Mechanic accents: dime novels and working-class culture in America*, London: Verso.

Denning, Michael (1996) *The cultural front: the laboring of American culture in the twentieth-century*, London and New York: Verso.

Dickie, Margaret (1986) *On the modernist long poem*, Iowa City: University of Iowa Press.

Dickie, Margaret (1997) *Stein, Bishop and Rich: lyrics of love, war and place*, Chapel Hill: University of North Carolina Press.

Dillingham, William B. (1969) *Frank Norris: instinct and art*, Lincoln: University of Nebraska Press.

Dillingham, William B. (1986) *Melville's later novels*, Athens: University of Georgia Press.

Docherty, Brian (ed.) (1990) *American horror fiction: from Brockden Brown to Stephen King*, Basingstoke: Macmillan.

Dollard, John (1937) *Caste and class in a Southern town*, New Haven: Yale University Press.

Dooley, Patrick K. (1993) *The pluralistic philosophy of Stephen Crane*, Urbana: University of Illinois Press.

Doren, Carl Van (1938) *Benjamin Franklin*, Garden City, NY: Garden City Publishing.

Dryden, Edgar A. (1968) *Melville's thematics of form: the great art of telling the truth*, Baltimore: Johns Hopkins University Press.

Duberman, Martin (1972) *Black Mountain: an exploration in community*, New York: Dutton.

Dudden, Arthur Power and Briggs, Peter M. (eds) (1987) *American humor*, New York and Oxford: Oxford University Press.

Dugdale, John (1990) *Thomas Pynchon: allusive parables of power*, London: Macmillan.

DuPlessis, Rachel Blau and Quartermain, Peter (eds) (1999) *The objectivist nexus: essays in cultural poetics*, Tuscaloosa: University of Alabama Press.

Eagleton, Terry (1993) *Literary theory: an introduction*, Minneapolis: University of Minnesota Press.

Eakin, Paul John (1985) *Fictions in autobiography: studies in the art of self-invention*, Princeton: Princeton University Press.

Eakin, Paul John (1999) *How our lives become stories: making selves*, Ithaca, NY and London: Cornell University Press.

Eastman, Barbara (1979) *Ezra Pound's Cantos: the story of the text 1948–1975*, Orono, ME: National Poetry Foundation/University of Maine.

Edel, Leon (1953–72) *Henry James*, 5 vols, Philadelphia: Lippincott.

Edel, Leon (1977) *Henry James*, 2 vols, Harmondsworth: Penguin.

Edel, Leon (1985) *Henry James: a life*, New York: Harper & Row.

Eliot, Valerie (ed.) (1971) *The Waste Land: a facsimile and transcript of the original drafts including the annotations of Ezra Pound*, London: Faber.

Elkins, Marilyn (ed.) (1994) *August Wilson: a casebook*, New York: Garland.

Elliott, Emory (1988) (general ed.) *Columbia literary history of the United States*, New York: Columbia University Press.

Elliot, Emory (1994) 'New England Puritan literature', in Bercovitch, Sacvan (general ed.), *The Cambridge history of American literature*, vol. 1, *1590–1820*, Cambridge and New York: Cambridge University Press, 169–306.

Ellis, William A. (1989) *The theory of the American romance: an ideology in American intellectual history*, Ann Arbor: UMI Research Press.

Ellison, Ralph (1964) *Shadow and act*, New York: Random House.

Ellison, Ralph (1986) *Going to the territory*, New York: Random House.

Emerson, Everett (1984) *The authentic Mark Twain: a literary biography of Samuel L. Clemens*, Philadelphia: University of Pennsylvania Press.

Erkkila, Betsy (1989) *Whitman the political poet*, New York: Oxford University Press.

Eysteinsson, Ástráður, (1990) *The concept of modernism*, Ithaca, NY: Cornell University Press.

Farwell, Byron (1999) *Over there: the United States in the Great War, 1917–1918*, New York: Norton.

Fearnow, Mark (1997) *The American stage and the Great Depression: a cultural history of the grotesque*, Cambridge and New York: Cambridge University Press.

Feidelson, Charles Jr (1953) *Symbolism and American literature*, Chicago: University of Chicago Press.

Feirstein, Frederick (ed.) (1989) *Expansive poetry: essays on the new narrative and the new formalism*, Santa Cruz, CA: Story Line Press.

Fender, Stephen (1981) *Plotting the 'Golden West': American literature and the rhetoric of the California Trail*, Cambridge: Cambridge University Press.

Ferguson, Robert A. (1997), *The American Enlightenment 1750–1820*, Cambridge, MA and London: Harvard University Press; reprinted from Bercovitch, Sacvan (general ed.), *The Cambridge history of American literature*, vol. 1, *1590–1820*, Cambridge and New York: Cambridge University Press, 345–537.

Ferns, Chris (1999) *Narrating Utopia: ideology, gender, form in utopian literature*, Liverpool: Liverpool University Press.

Ferraro, Thomas J. (1993) *Ethnic passages: literary immigrants in twentieth-century America*, Chicago: University of Chicago Press.

Ferres, John H. (ed.) (1972) *Twentieth century interpretations of The Crucible: a collection of critical essays*, Englewood Cliffs, NJ: Prentice-Hall.

Fiedler, Leslie (1960) *Love and death in the American novel*, New York: Stein and Day.

Fiedler, Leslie (1969) *The return of the vanishing American*, New York: Stein and Day.

Fiedler, Leslie (1978) *Freaks: myths and images of the secret self*, New York: Simon and Schuster.

Fiedler, Leslie (1980) *The inadvertent epic: from Uncle Tom's Cabin to Roots*, New York: Simon and Schuster.

Fields, Wayne (ed.) (1979) *James Fenimore Cooper: a collection of critical essays*, Englewood Cliffs, NJ; London: Prentice-Hall.

Finkelstein, Norman (2001) *Not one of them in place: modern poetry and Jewish American identity*, Albany: State University of New York Press.

Finnegan, Ruth (1992) *Oral poetry: its nature, significance, and social context*, Bloomington: Indiana University Press.

Fisher, Philip (ed.) (1991) *The new American studies: essays from Representations*, Berkeley: Oxford University Press.

Fisher, Philip (1999) *Still the new world: American literature in a culture of creative destruction*, Cambridge, MA: Harvard University Press.

Fitzgerald, Sally (ed.) (1979) *The habit of being: letters of Flannery O'Connor*, New York: Farrar, Straus, and Giroux.

Flanzbaum, Hilene (ed.) (1999) *The Americanization of the Holocaust*, Baltimore: Johns Hopkins University Press.

Fleischner, Jennifer (1996) *Mastering slavery: memory, family, and identity in women's slave narratives*, New York: New York University Press.

Flory, Wendy Stallard (1980) *Ezra Pound and the Cantos: a record of struggle*, New Haven: Yale University Press.

Floyd, Virginia (1985) *The Plays of Eugene O'Neill: a new assessment*, New York: Ungar.

Foley, John M. (ed.) (1986) *Oral tradition in literature: interpretation in context*, Columbia: University of Missouri Press.

Folsom, James K. (ed.) (1979) *The Western: a collection of critical essays*, Englewood Cliffs, NJ: Prentice-Hall.

Foote, Stephanie (2001) *Regional fictions: culture and identity in nineteenth-century American literature*, Madison: University of Wisconsin Press.

Ford, Boris (ed.) (1986) *American literature*, New Pelican guide to English literature, vol. 9, Harmondsworth: Penguin.

Foster, Edward Halsey (1995) *Understanding the Black Mountain poets*, Columbia SC: University of South Carolina Press.

Foster, Frances E. (1979, 1994) *Witnessing slavery: the development of ante-bellum slave narratives*, Westport, CT: Greenwood Press.

Foster, Frances Smith (1993) *Written by herself: literary production by African American women, 1746–1892*, Bloomington: Indiana University Press.

Foster, Shirley and Simons, Judy (1995) *What Katy read: feminist re-readings of 'classic' stories for girls*, Iowa City: University of Iowa Press.

Frank, Frederick S. (1990), *Through the pale door: a guide to and through the American gothic*, New York: Greenwood Press.

Franklin, H. Bruce (1963) *The wake of the gods: Melville's mythology*, Stanford: Stanford University Press.

Franklin, H. Bruce (1966) *Future perfect: American science fiction of the nineteenth century*, New York: Oxford University Press.

Franklin, H. Bruce (1989) *Prison literature in America: the victim as criminal and artist*, New York: Oxford University Press.

Fried, Marlene Gerber (ed.) (1990) *From abortion to reproductive freedom: transforming a movement*, Boston: South End Press.

Friedl, Bettina (ed.) (1987) *On to victory: propaganda plays of the woman suffrage movement*, Boston: Northeastern University Press.

Fuchs, Daniel (1984) *Saul Bellow: vision and revision*, Durham, NC: Duke University Press.

Fuchs, Elinor (1996) *The death of character: perspectives on theater after modernism*, Bloomington: Indiana University Press.

Fulop, Timothy Earl and Raboteau, Albert J. (eds) (1997) *African-American religion: interpretive essays in history and culture*, New York and London: Routledge.

Furia, Philip (1990) *The poets of Tin Pan Alley: a history of America's great lyricists*, New York: Oxford University Press.

Furman, Jan (1996) *Toni Morrison's fiction*, Columbia, SC: University of South Carolina Press.

Fussell, Edwin S. (1965) *Frontier: American literature and the American West*, Princeton: Princeton University Press.

Gallagher, Catherine and Greenblatt, Stephen (2000) *Practicing New Historicism*, Chicago: University of Chicago Press.

Galloway, David (1981) *The absurd hero in American fiction: Updike, Styron, Bellow, Salinger*, Austin: University of Texas Press.

Garber, Linda (2001) *Identity poetics: race, class, and the lesbian-feminist roots of queer theory*, New York: Columbia University Press.

Gardner, Thomas (1989) *Discovering ourselves in Whitman: the contemporary American long poem*, Urbana: University of Illinois Press.

Garfield, Deborah M. and Zafar, Rafia (eds) (1996) *Harriet Jacobs and Incidents in the Life of a Slave Girl*, Cambridge and New York: Cambridge University Press.

Gates, Henry Louis Jr (ed.) (1984) *Black literature and literary theory*, New York: Methuen.

Gates, Henry Louis Jr (1987) *Figures in Black: words, signs, and the 'racial' self*, New York: Oxford University Press.

Gates, Henry Louis Jr (1988) *The signifying monkey: a theory of Afro-American literary criticism*, New York: Oxford University Press.

Gates, Henry Louis Jr and Appiah, K. A. (eds) (1993) *Toni Morrison: critical perspectives past and present*, New York: Amistad.

Gates, Henry Louis Jr and Appiah, K. A. (eds) (1993) *Alice Walker: critical perspectives past and present*, New York: Amistad.

Gates, Henry Louis Jr and Appiah, K. A. (eds) (1993) *Richard Wright: critical perspectives past and present*, New York: Amistad.

Gates, Henry Louis Jr and McKay, Nellie Y. (general eds) (1997) *The Norton anthology of African American literature*, New York: Norton.

Gelb, Arthur and Gelb, Barbara (2000) *O'Neill: life with Monte Cristo*, New York: Applause.

Gelpi, Albert (1975) *The tenth muse: the psyche of the American poet*, Cambridge MA: Harvard University Press.

Gelpi, Albert (1987) *A coherent splendor: the American poetic renaissance, 1910–1950*, Cambridge and New York: Cambridge University Press.

Gelpi, Albert (ed.) (1985) *Wallace Stevens: the poetics of modernism*, Cambridge and New York: Cambridge University Press.

Gelpi, Barbara Charlesworth and Gelpi, Albert (eds) (1975/1993) *Adrienne Rich's poetry and prose: poems, prose, reviews, and criticism*, New York: Norton.

Genovese, Eugene D. (1974) *Roll, Jordan, roll: the world the slaves made*, New York: Pantheon Books.

Gentry, Marshall Bruce and Stull, William L. (eds) (1990) *Conversations with Raymond Carver*, Jackson: University Press of Mississippi.

Gerber, Philip (1992) *Theodore Dreiser revisited*, New York: Twayne.

Gery, John (1996) *Nuclear annihilation and contemporary American poetry: ways of nothingness*, Gainesville: University Press of Florida.

Giannone, Richard (1989) *Flannery O'Connor and the mystery of love*, Urbana: University of Illinois Press.

Gifford, Terry (1999) *Pastoral*, London: Routledge, 1999.

Gilbert, James B. (1981) *Another chance: postwar America, 1945–1985*, Chicago: Dorsey Press.

Gilbert, Sandra and Gubar, Susan (1979) *The madwoman in the attic: the woman writer and the nineteenth-century literary imagination*, New Haven: Yale University Press.

Gillis, Chester (1999) *Roman Catholicism in America*, New York and Chichester: Columbia University Press.

Gillman, Susan (1989) *Dark twins: imposture and identity in Mark Twain's America*, Chicago: University of Chicago Press.

Gilmore, Michael T. (ed.) (1977) *Twentieth century interpretations of Moby-Dick: a collection of critical essays*, Englewood Cliffs, NJ: Prentice-Hall.

Gilmore, Michael T. (1985) *American romanticism and the marketplace*, Chicago: University of Chicago Press.

Gilmore, Thomas B. (1987) *Equivocal spirits: alcoholism and drinking in twentieth-century literature*, Chapel Hill: University of North Carolina Press.

Ginsberg, Elaine K. (ed.) (1996) *Passing and the fictions of identity*, Durham, NC: Duke University Press.

Ginsburg, Faye D. (1998) *Contested lives: the abortion debate in an American community*, Berkeley: University of California Press.

Glenday, Michael K. (1991) *Saul Bellow and the decline of humanism*, Basingstoke: Macmillan.

Goddu, Teresa A. (1997) *Gothic America: narrative, history, and nation*, New York: Columbia University Press.

Gogol, Miriam (ed.) (1995) *Theodore Dreiser: beyond naturalism*, New York: New York University Press.

Goldensohn, Lorrie (1992) *Elizabeth Bishop: the biography of a poetry*, New York: Columbia University Press.

Goldstein, Laurence (1994) *The American poet at the movies: a critical history*, Ann Arbor: University of Michigan Press.

Gordon, Lyndall (1977) *Eliot's early years*, Oxford and New York: Oxford University Press.

Gordon, Lyndall (1988) *Eliot's new life*, London: Vintage.

Gordon, Lyndall (1999) *T. S. Eliot: an imperfect life*, London: Vintage.

Gosselin, Adrienne Johnson (ed.) (1999) *Multicultural detective fiction: murder from the 'other' side*, New York: Garland.

Gossett, Thomas F. (1963, 1997) *Race: the history of an idea in America*, New York and Oxford: Oxford University Press.

Graham, Don (ed.) (1980) *Critical essays on Frank Norris*, Boston: G. K. Hall.

Granger, Bruce Ingham (1964) *Benjamin Franklin: an American man of letters*, Ithaca, NY: Cornell University Press.

Gray, Richard J. (1977) *The literature of memory: modern writers of the American South*, London: Edward Arnold; Baltimore: Johns Hopkins University Press.

Gray, Richard J. (1990) *American poetry of the twentieth century*, London: Longman.

Gray, Richard J. (1994) *The life of William Faulkner: a critical biography*, Oxford and Cambridge, MA: Blackwell.

Greenspan, Ezra (1983) *The schlemiel comes to America*, Metuchen, NJ: Scarecrow Press.

Greenspan, Ezra (ed.) (1995) *The Cambridge companion to Walt Whitman*, Cambridge and New York: Cambridge University Press.

Griffin, Alice (1995) *Understanding Tennessee Williams*, Columbia, SC: University of South Carolina Press.

Gross, Louis (1989) *Redefining the American Gothic: from Wieland to Day of the Dead*, Ann Arbor: University of Michigan Research Press.

Gusfield, Joseph (1963) *Symbolic crusade: status politics and the American temperance movement*, Urbana: University of Illinois Press.

Guttmann, Allen (1971) *The Jewish writer in America: assimilation and the crisis of identity*, New York: Oxford University Press.

Haack, Susan (1996), 'Pragmatism', in Bunnin, Nicholas and Tsui-James, E. P. (eds), *The Blackwell Companion to Philosophy*, Oxford and Cambridge, MA: Blackwell Reference, 643–661.

Haas, Robert B. (1971) *A primer for the gradual understanding of Gertrude Stein*, Los Angeles: Black Sparrow Press.

Habegger, Alfred (1989) *Henry James and the 'woman business'*, Cambridge and New York: Cambridge University Press.

Hadley, Tessa (2002) *Henry James and the imagination of pleasure*, Cambridge and New York: Cambridge University Press.

Hakutani, Yoshinobu (1996) *Richard Wright and racial discourse*, Columbia: University of Missouri Press.

Halliburton, David (1989) *The color of the sky: a study of Stephen Crane*, Cambridge and New York: Cambridge University Press.

Halter, Peter (1994) *The revolution in the visual arts and the poetry of William Carlos Williams*, Cambridge and New York: Cambridge University Press.

Halttunen, Karen (1982) *Confidence men and painted women: a study of middle-class culture in America, 1830–1870*, New Haven: Yale University Press.

Hamilton, Ian (1982) *Robert Lowell: a biography*, New York: Random House.

Hamilton, Ian (1990) *Writers in Hollywood 1915–1951*, London: Heinemann.

Hammond, Jeffrey A. (2000) *The American Puritan elegy: a literary and cultural study*, Cambridge and New York: Cambridge University Press.

Handley, George B. (2000) *Postslavery literatures in the Americas: family portraits in Black and White*, Charlottesville: University Press of Virginia.

Hansen, Chadwick (1969) *Witchcraft at Salem*, New York: Braziller.

Harding, Walter (1965) *The days of Henry Thoreau*, New York: Knopf.

Harper, Phillip Brian (1994) *Framing the margins: the social logic of postmodern culture*, New York: Oxford University Press.

Harris-Lopez, Trudier (1984) *Exorcising blackness: historical and literary lynching and burning rituals*, Bloomington: Indiana University Press.

Hart, James D. (1983) *The Oxford companion to American literature*, 5th edn., New York: Oxford University Press.

Hart, James D. (1995) *The Oxford companion to American literature*, 6th edn., revised by Phillip W. Leininger, New York: Oxford University Press.

Harter Deborah A. (1996) *Bodies in pieces: fantastic narrative and the poetics of the fragment*, Stanford: Stanford University Press.

Hartley, George (1989) *Textual politics and the Language poets*, Bloomington: Indiana University Press.

Harvard, William C. and Sullivan, Walter (eds) (1982) *A band of prophets: the Vanderbilt Agrarians after fifty years*, Baton Rouge: Louisiana State University Press.

Hassan, Ihab (1975) *Paracriticisms: seven speculations of the times*, Urbana: University of Illinois Press.

Hauck, Richard (1971) *A cheerful nihilism: confidence and 'the absurd' in American humorous fiction*, Bloomington: Indiana University Press.

Hay, Samuel A. (1994) *African American theatre: a historical and critical analysis*, Cambridge and New York: Cambridge University Press.

Hayman, Ronald (1993) *Tennessee Williams: everyone else is an audience*, New Haven: Yale University Press.

Hedrick, Joan D. (1994) *Harriet Beecher Stowe: a life*, New York: Oxford University Press.

Hemenway, Robert E. (1977) *Zora Neale Hurston: a literary biography*, Urbana: University of Illinois Press.

Herd, David (2000) *John Ashbery and American poetry*, Manchester: Manchester University Press; New York: Palgrave.

Herring, George C. (1996) *America's longest war: the United States and Vietnam, 1950–1975*, New York: McGraw-Hill.

Herrnstein, Richard and Murray, Charles (1994) *The bell curve: intelligence and class structure in American life*, New York: Free Press.

Herron, Don (1991) *Reign of fear: the fiction and films of Stephen King*, London: Pan Books.

Heymann, C. David (1976) *Ezra Pound, the last rower: a political profile*, New York: Viking Press.

Higgins, Brian and Parker, Hershel (eds) (1992) *Critical essays on Herman Melville's Moby-Dick*, New York: G. K. Hall.

Higgs, Robert J. (1988) *Laurel and thorn: the athlete in American literature*, Lexington: University Press of Kentucky.

Hill, Frances (1996) *A delusion of Satan: the full story of the Salem witch trials*, London: Hamish Hamilton.

Hill, Patricia Liggins (general ed.) (1998) *Call and response: the Riverside anthology of the African American literary tradition*, Boston: Houghton Mifflin.

Hindus, Milton (ed.) (1955) *Leaves of Grass: one hundred years after*, Stanford: Stanford University Press.

Hischak, Thomas S. (1991) *Word crazy: Broadway lyricists from Cohan to Sondheim*, New York: Praeger.

Hite, Molly (1983) *Ideas of order in the novels of Thomas Pynchon*, Columbus: Ohio State University Press.

Hite, Molly (1989) *The other side of the story: structures and strategies of contemporary feminist narrative*, Ithaca, NY: Cornell University Press.

Hochman, Barbara (1988) *The art of Frank Norris, storyteller*, Columbia: University of Missouri Press.

Hochschild, Jennifer L. (1995) *Facing up to the American dream: race, class, and the soul of the nation*, Princeton: Princeton University Press.

Hoffman, Daniel (1972) *Poe Poe Poe Poe Poe Poe Poe*, Garden City, NY: Doubleday.

Hoffman, Daniel (ed.) (1979) *Harvard guide to contemporary American writing*, Cambridge, MA: Belknap Press of Harvard University Press.

Hoffman, Michael J. (ed.) (1986) *Critical essays on Gertrude Stein*, Boston: G. K. Hall.

Holloway, Karla F. C. (1987) *The character of the word: the texts of Zora Neale Hurston*, New York: Greenwood Press.

hooks, bell (1981) *Ain't I a woman: black women and feminism*, Boston: South End Press.

hooks, bell (1984) *Feminist theory from margin to center*, Boston: South End Press.

House, Kay S. (1965) *Cooper's Americans*, Columbus: Ohio State University Press.

Howard, Lillie P. (1980) *Zora Neale Hurston*, Boston: Twayne.

Howard, Richard (1970) *Alone with America: the art of poetry in the United States since 1950*, New York: Atheneum; London: Thames and Hudson.

Huang, Nian-Sheng (1994) *Benjamin Franklin in American thought and culture, 1790–1990*, Philadelphia: American Philosophical Society.

Hubbell, J. B. (1954) *The South in American literature, 1607–1900*, Durham, NC: Duke University Press.

Hudson, Arthur Palmer (1974) 'Folklore' in Spiller, Robert E. (general ed.), *The literary history of the United States*, New York: Macmillan, 703–727.

Huerta, Jorge (1982) *Chicano theatre: themes and forms*, Ypsilanti, MI: Bilingual Press.

Hull, Gloria (1987) *Color, sex, and poetry: three women writers of the Harlem Renaissance*, Bloomington: Indiana University Press.

Hume, Kathryn (1984) *Fantasy and mimesis: responses to reality in Western literature*, London and New York: Methuen.

Hunt, Peter (1991) *Criticism, theory and children's literature*, Oxford: Blackwell.

Hutchinson, George (1995) *The Harlem Renaissance in Black and White*, Cambridge, MA and London: Belknap Press of Harvard University Press.

Hyde, Lewis (1998) *Trickster makes this world: mischief, myth, and art*, New York: Farrar, Straus, and Giroux.

Hyde, Lewis (ed.) (1980) *On the poetry of Allen Ginsberg*, Ann Arbor: University of Michigan Press.

Hynes, Samuel (general ed.) (1995) *Reporting World War II*, 2 vols, New York: Library of America.

Inness, Sherrie A. and Royer, Diana (eds) (1997) *Breaking boundaries: new perspectives on women's regional writing*, Iowa City: University of Iowa Press.

Irwin, W. R. (1976) *The game of the impossible: a rhetoric of fantasy*, Urbana: University of Illinois Press.

Jablon, Madelyn (1997) *Black metafiction: self-consciousness in African American literature*, Iowa City: University of Iowa Press.

Jackson, Rosemary (1981) *Fantasy: the literature of subversion*, London and New York: Methuen.

Jameson, Fredric (1991) *Postmodernism, or, the cultural logic of late capitalism*, Durham, NC: Duke University Press.

Jancovich, Mark (1993) *The cultural politics of the New Criticism*, Cambridge and New York: Cambridge University Press.

Jancovitch, Mark (1992) *Horror*, London: Batsford.

Jarman, Mark and David Mason (eds) (1996) *Rebel angels: 25 poets of the new formalism*, Brownsville, OR: Story Line Press.

Jaskoski, Helen (ed.) (1996) *Early Native American writing: new critical essays*, Cambridge: Cambridge University Press.

Jaskoski, Helen (1998) *Leslie Marmon Silko: a study of the short fiction*, New York: Twayne; London: Prentice-Hall International.

Jason, Philip K. (ed.) (1991) *Fourteen landing zones: approaches to Vietnam War literature*, Iowa City: University of Iowa Press.

Jason, Philip K (2000) *Acts and shadows: the Vietnam War in American literary culture*, Lanham, MD: Rowman and Littlefield.

Johnston, Kenneth R. et al (eds) (1990) *Romantic revolutions: criticism and theory*, Bloomington: Indiana University Press.

Jolly, Roslyn (1993) *Henry James: history, narrative, fiction*, Oxford and New York: Clarendon Press.

Jones, Gayl (1991) *Liberating voices: oral tradition in African American literature*, Cambridge, MA: Harvard University Press.

Jones, LeRoi (Baraka) (1963, 1995) *Blues people: Negro music in White America*, New York: Morrow.

Jones, Maldwyn A. (1995) *The limits of liberty: American history 1607–1992*, Oxford and New York: Oxford University Press.

Joyce, Joyce Ann (1986) *Richard Wright's art of tragedy*, Iowa City: University of Iowa Press.

Juhasz, Suzanne (1983) *The undiscovered continent: Emily Dickinson and the space of the mind*, Bloomington: Indiana University Press.

Juhasz, Suzanne (ed.) (1983) *Feminist critics read Emily Dickinson*, Bloomington: Indiana University Press.

Kafka, Phillipa (1993) *The great white way: African American women writers and American success mythologies*, New York: Garland.

Kalstone, David (1989) *Becoming a poet: Elizabeth Bishop with Marianne Moore and Robert Lowell*, ed. Robert Hemenway, New York: Farrar, Straus, Giroux.

Kane, Leslie (1999) *Weasels and wisemen: ethics and ethnicity in the work of David Mamet*, New York: St Martin's Press.

Kane, Leslie (ed.) (2001) *David Mamet in conversation*, Ann Arbor: University of Michigan Press.

Kaplan, Justin (1966) *Mr Clemens and Mark Twain: a biography*, New York: Simon and Schuster.

Karcher, Carolyn L. (1980) *Shadow over the Promised Land: slavery, race, and violence in Melville's America*, Baton Rouge: Louisiana State University Press.

Kawash, Samira (1997) *Dislocating the color line: identity, hybridity, and singularity in African-American narrative*, Stanford: Stanford University Press.

Kazin, Alfred (1956) *On native grounds: an interpretation of modern American prose literature*, Garden City, NY: Doubleday.

Kearns, George (1989) *Ezra Pound: The Cantos*, Cambridge: Cambridge University Press.

Keller, Karl (1979) *The only kangaroo among the beauty: Emily Dickinson and America*, Baltimore: Johns Hopkins University Press.

Kellner, Bruce (ed.) (1984) *Harlem Renaissance: a historical dictionary for the era*, Westport, CT: Greenwood Press.

Kelly, William P. (1983) *Plotting America's past: Fenimore Cooper and The Leatherstocking Tales*, Carbondale: Southern Illinois University Press.

Kennedy, J. Gerald (ed.) (1995) *Modern American short story sequences: composite fictions and fictive communities*, Cambridge and New York: Cambridge University Press.

Kennedy, J. Gerald and Weissberg, Liliane (eds) (2001) *Romancing the shadow: Poe and race*, Oxford and New York: Oxford University Press.

Kenner, Hugh (1959) *The invisible poet: T.S. Eliot*, London: W. H. Allen.

Kenner, Hugh (1971) *The Pound Era*, London: Faber; Berkeley: University of California Press.

Kenner, Hugh (1975) *A homemade world: the American modernist writers*, New York: Knopf; London: Boyars.

Kent, George E. (1990) *A life of Gwendolyn Brooks*, Lexington: University Press of Kentucky.

Keohane, Nannerl O., Rosaldo, Michelle Z. and Gelpi, Barbara C. (eds) (1981) *Feminist theory: a critique of ideology*, Chicago: University of Chicago Press.

Kessler, Carol Farley (1984) *Daring to dream: Utopian stories by United States women, 1836–1919*, Boston: Pandora Press.

Kessler, Edward (1986) *Flannery O'Connor and the language of apocalypse*, Princeton: Princeton University Press.

Keyes, Claire (1986) *The aesthetics of power: the poetry of Adrienne Rich*, Athens: University of Georgia Press.

Kilcup, Karen L. (ed.) (1997) *Nineteenth-century American women writers: an anthology*, Oxford and Malden, MA: Blackwell.

Kilcup, Karen L. (ed.) (1999) *Soft canons: American women writers and masculine tradition*, Iowa City: University of Iowa Press.

Kilcup, Karen L. (ed.) (2000) *Native American women's writing, c.1800–1924: an anthology*, Oxford and Malden, MA: Blackwell.

Kim, Elaine (1982) *Asian American literature: an introduction to the writings and their social context*, Philadelphia: Temple University Press.

King, Desmond S. (2000) *Making Americans: immigration, race, and the origins of the diverse democracy*, Cambridge, MA: Harvard University Press.

King, Richard H. (1980) *A Southern Renaissance: the cultural awakening of the American South, 1930–1955*, New York: Oxford University Press.

King, Stephen (1981) *Danse macabre*, New York: Everest House.

Kinnamon, Keneth (1997) *Critical essays on Richard Wright's Native Son*, New York: Twayne; London: Prentice-Hall International.

Kinney, Katherine (2000) *Friendly fire: American images of the Vietnam War*, Oxford and New York: Oxford University Press.

Klein, Kathleen Gregory (1988) *The woman detective: gender and genre*, Urbana: University of Illinois Press.

Klein, Marcus (1981) *Foreigners: the making of American literature 1900–1940*, Chicago: University of Chicago Press.

Kobler, John (1973) *Ardent spirits: the rise and fall of Prohibition*, New York: Putnam.

Kolchin, Peter (1993) *American slavery, 1619–1877*, New York: Hill and Wang; Harmondsworth: Penguin.

Kolodny, Annette (1975) *The lay of the land: metaphor as experience and history in American life and letters*, Chapel Hill: University of North Carolina Press.

Kowalewski, Michael (ed.) (1996) *Reading the West: new essays on the literature of the American West*, Cambridge and New York: Cambridge University Press.

Kramer, Jane (1969) *Paterfamilias: Allen Ginsberg in America*, London: Gollancz.

Kremer, S. Lillian (1989) *Witness through the imagination: Jewish-American Holocaust literature*, Detroit: Wayne State University Press.

Kroeber, Karl (1992) *Retelling/ rereading: the fate of storytelling in modern times*, New Brunswick, NJ: Rutgers University Press.

Krupat, Arnold (1989) *The voice in the margin: Native American literature and the canon*, Berkeley: University of California Press.

Lauret, Maria (2000) *Alice Walker*, Basingstoke: Macmillan; New York: St Martin's Press.

Lauter, Paul (1991) *Canons and contexts*, New York and Oxford: Oxford University Press.

Lauter, Paul (general ed.) (2002) *The Heath anthology of American literature*, 4ᵗʰ edn, 2 vols, Lexington, MA: Heath.

Lavender, Isiah (1998) *The trickster in African American women's literature: slavery to the contemporary age*, thesis, Baton Rouge: Louisiana State University.

Lawrence, D. H. (1923) *Studies in classic American literature*, New York: Thomas Seltzer.

Lawson, Bill E. and Frank M. Kirkland (eds) (1999) *Frederick Douglass: a critical reader*, Oxford and Malden, MA: Blackwell Publishers.

Leach, Douglas E. (1966) *Flintlock and tomahawk: New England in King Philip's War*, New York: Macmillan.

Lee, A. Robert (ed.) (1996) *The Beat Generation writers*, London: Pluto Press.

Lee, Brian (1986) *American fiction 1865–1940*, London: Longman.

Lee, Hermione (1982) *Philip Roth*, London and New York: Methuen.

Lee, Hermione (1989) *Willa Cather: a life saved up*, London: Virago.

Leeming, David Adams (1994) *James Baldwin: a biography*, New York: Knopf.

Leeming, David and Jake Page (eds) (1999) *Myths, legends, and folktales of America*, New York and Oxford: Oxford University Press.

Lefanu, Sarah (1989) *Feminism and Science Fiction*, Bloomington: Indiana University Press.

Lehan, Richard D. (1966) *F. Scott Fitzgerald and the craft of fiction*, Carbondale and London: Southern Illinois University Press.

Lehman, David (ed.) (1980) *Beyond amazement: new essays on John Ashbery*, Ithaca, NY: Cornell University Press.

Lensing, George S. (2001) *Wallace Stevens and the seasons*, Baton Rouge: Louisiana State University Press.

Lentricchia, Frank (ed.) (1991) *Introducing Don DeLillo*, Durham, NC and London: Duke University Press.

Lenz, William E. (1985) *Fast talk and flush times: the confidence man as a literary convention*, Columbia: University of Missouri Press.

Leonard, James S., Tenney, Thomas A. and Davis, Thadious M. (eds) (1992) *Satire or evasion? Black perspectives on Huckleberry Finn*, Durham, NC: Duke University Press.

Leverenz, David (1980) *The language of Puritan feeling: an exploration in literature, psychology, and social history*, New Brunswick, NJ: Rutgers University Press.

Levin, David (ed.) (1960) *What happened in Salem? Documents pertaining to the 17th-century witchcraft trials*, New York: Twayne.

Levy, Andrew (1993) *The culture and commerce of the American short story*, Cambridge and New York: Cambridge University Press.

Lewecki, Zbigniew, *The bang and the whimper: apocalypse and entropy in American literature* (1984) Westport, CT: Greenwood Press.

Lewis, David Levering (1989) *When Harlem was in vogue*, New York: Knopf.

Lewis, David Levering (1993) *W. E. B. Du Bois: biography of a race, 1868–1919*, New York: Henry Holt.

Lewis, R. W. B. (1955) *The American Adam: innocence, tragedy, and tradition in the nineteenth century*, Chicago: University of Chicago Press.

Lewis, R. W. B. (1965) *Trials of the Word: essays in American literature and the humanistic tradition*, New Haven: Yale University Press.

Lewy, Guenter (1978) *America in Vietnam*, New York: Oxford University Press.

Leyda, Jay (1969) *The Melville log: a documentary life of Herman Melville, 1819–1891*, 2 vols, New York: Gordian Press.

Lhamon, W. T. (1998) *Raising Cane: blackface performance from Jim Crow to Hip Hop*, Cambridge, MA: Harvard University Press.

Li, David Leiwei (1998) *Imagining the nation: Asian American literature and cultural consent*, Stanford: Stanford University Press.

Lim, Shirley Geok-lin (ed.) (1991) *Approaches to teaching Kingston's The Woman Warrior*, New York: Modern Language Association of America.

Limon, John (1994) *Writing after war: American war fiction from realism to post-modernism*, New York: Oxford University Press.

Lincoln, Kenneth (1983) *Native American renaissance*, Berkeley: University of California Press.

Lindberg, Gary (1981) *The confidence man in American literature*, New York: Oxford University Press.

Lindemann, Marilee (1999) *Willa Cather: Queering America*, New York: Columbia University Press.

Lingeman, Richard (1986) *Theodore Dreiser: at the gates of the city, 1871–1907*, New York: Putnam.

Lingeman, Richard (1990) *Theodore Dreiser: an American journey, 1908–1945*, New York: Putnam.

Lipset, Seymour Martin (1996) *American exceptionalism: a double-edged sword*, New York: Norton.

Lockridge, Ernest (ed.) (1968) *Twentieth century interpretations of The Great Gatsby: a collection of critical essays*, Englewood Cliffs, NJ: Prentice-Hall.

Lodge, David (1977) *The modes of modern writing: metaphor, metonymy, and the typology of modern literature*, London: Edward Arnold; Ithaca, NY: Cornell University Press.

Long, Robert Emmet (1990) *James Fenimore Cooper*, New York: Continuum.

Loving, Jerome (1999) *Walt Whitman: the song of himself*, Berkeley: University of California Press.

Lowell, Robert (1987) *The Collected Prose*, London: Faber; New York: Farrar, Straus, Giroux.

Lynn, Kenneth S. (1987) *Hemingway*, New York: Simon and Schuster.

Lyotard, Jean-François (1979/1984) *The postmodern condition: a report on knowledge*, translated by Geoff Bennington and Brian Massumi, Minneapolis: University of Minnesota Press.

Ma, Sheng-Mei (1998) *Immigrant subjectivities in Asian American and Asian diaspora literatures*, Albany: State University of New York Press.

MacAndrew, Elizabeth (1979) *The Gothic tradition in fiction*, New York: Columbia University Press.

MacKinnon, Catharine A. (1987) *Feminism unmodified: discourses on life and law*, Cambridge, MA: Harvard University Press.

MacLeod, Anne (1994) *American childhood: essays on children's literature of the nineteenth and twentieth centuries*, Athens: University of Georgia Press.

MacShane, Frank (1976) *The life of Raymond Chandler*, New York: E. P. Dutton.

Maddox, Lucy (1991) *Removals: nineteenth-century American literature and the politics of Indian affairs*, New York: Oxford University Press.

Maddox, Robert James (1992) *The United States and World War Two*, Boulder, CO: Westview Press.

Madsen, Deborah L. (1998) *American exceptionalism*, Edinburgh: Edinburgh University Press; Jackson: University Press of Mississippi.

Magistrale, Tony (ed.) (1992) *The dark descent: essays defining Stephen King's horrorscape*, New York: Greenwood Press.

Makin, Peter (1985) *Pound's Cantos*, London and Boston: George Allen and Unwin.

Malin, Irving (1962) *New American Gothic*, Carbondale: Southern Illinois University Press.

Manheim, Michael (1982) *Eugene O'Neill's new language of kinship*, Syracuse, NY: Syracuse University Press.

Marcus, Jane (1988) *Art and anger: reading like a woman*, Columbus: Miami University/Ohio State University Press.

Mariani, Paul (1981) *William Carlos Williams: a new world naked*, New York: McGraw-Hill.

Martin, Robert K. (ed.) (1992) *The continuing presence of Walt Whitman: the life after the life*, Iowa City: University of Iowa Press.

Martin, Robert K. and Eric Savoy (eds) (1998) *American Gothic: new interventions in a national narrative*, Iowa City: University of Iowa Press.

Martínez, Julio A. and Francisco A. Lomelí (eds) (1989) *Chicano literature: a reference guide*, Westport, CT: Greenwood Press.

Marx, Leo (1964) *The Machine in the garden: technology and the pastoral ideal in America*, New York: Oxford University Press.

Matterson, Stephen (1990) *The Great Gatsby*, Basingstoke: Macmillan.

Matterson, Stephen (2001) 'Robert Lowell: *Life Studies*', in Roberts, Neil (ed.), *A companion to twentieth century poetry*, Oxford and Malden, MA: Blackwell, 481–490.

Matthiessen, F. O. (1941) *American renaissance: art and expression in the age of Emerson and Whitman*, London and New York: Oxford University Press.

Mattingly, Carol (1998) *Well-tempered women: nineteenth-century temperance rhetoric*, Carbondale: Southern Illinois University Press.

May, Charles E. (ed.) (1976) *Short story theories*, Athens: Ohio University Press.

May, Henry (1976) *The Enlightenment in America*, New York: Oxford University Press.

McCaffery, Larry (1982) *The metafictional muse: the works of Robert Coover, Donald Barthelme, and William H. Gass*, Pittsburgh: University of Pittsburgh Press.

McClatchy, J. D. (ed.) (1988) *Poets on painters: essays on the art of painting by twentieth-century poets*, Berkeley: University of California Press.

McClatchy, J. D. (1989) *White paper: on contemporary American poetry*, New York: Columbia University Press.

McCullough, Kate (1999) *Regions of identity: the construction of America in women's fiction, 1885–1914*, Stanford: Stanford University Press.

McDowell, Deborah E. and Arnold Rampersad (eds) (1989) *Slavery and the literary imagination*, Baltimore: Johns Hopkins University Press.

McFeely, William S. (1991) *Frederick Douglass*, New York: Norton.

McGowan, Philip (2001) *American carnival: seeing and reading American culture*, Westport, CT: Greenwood Press.

McHale, Brian (1987) *Postmodernist fiction*, London and New York: Methuen.

McPherson, James M. (1975) *The Abolitionist legacy: from Reconstruction to the NAACP*, Princeton: Princeton University Press.

McPherson, James M. (1989) *Battle cry of freedom: the Civil War era*, New York: Oxford University Press.

McSweeney, Kerry (1988) *Invisible Man: race and identity*, Boston: Twayne.

McWilliams, John P. (1989) *The American epic: transforming a genre, 1770–1860*, Cambridge and New York: Cambridge University Press.

Mellow, James R. (1974) *Charmed circle: Gertrude Stein and company*, New York: Praeger.

Mersmann, James F. (1974) *Out of the Vietnam vortex: a study of poets and poetry against the war*, Lawrence: University Press of Kansas.

Messent, Peter B. (1992) *Ernest Hemingway*, Basingstoke: Macmillan; New York: St Martin's Press.

Michael Delville (1998) *The American prose poem: poetic form and the boundaries of genre*, Gainesville: University Press of Florida.

Middleton, David L. (ed.) (2000) *Toni Morrison's fiction: contemporary criticism*, New York: Garland.

Middleton, Peter (2000) *Literatures of memory: history, time and space in postwar writing*, Manchester and New York: Manchester University Press.

271

Middleton, Richard (1996) *Colonial America: a history, 1565–1776*, Oxford and Malden, MA: Blackwell.

Miles, Barry (ed.) (1986) *Allen Ginsberg, Howl: Original Draft Facsimile*, New York: Harper & Row.

Miles, Barry (1989) *Ginsberg: a biography*, London and New York: Viking.

Miller, Arthur (2000) *The Crucible in History and Other Essays*, London: Methuen.

Miller, Cristanne (1987) *Emily Dickinson: a poet's grammar*, Cambridge, MA: Harvard University Press.

Miller, Edwin Haviland (1968) *Walt Whitman's poetry: a psychological journey*, New York: New York University Press.

Miller, Edwin Haviland (1991) *Salem is my dwelling-place: a life of Nathaniel Hawthorne*, Iowa City: University of Iowa Press.

Miller, J. Hillis (1965) *Poets of reality: six twentieth-century writers*, Cambridge, MA: Belknap Press of Harvard University Press.

Miller, J. Hillis (ed.) (1966) *Critical essays on William Carlos Williams*, Englewood Cliffs, NJ: Prentice-Hall.

Miller, James E. (1957) *A critical guide to Leaves of Grass*, Chicago: University of Chicago Press.

Miller, James E. (1967) *F. Scott Fitzgerald: his art and his technique*, New York: New York University Press.

Miller, James E. Jr (1979) *The American quest for a supreme fiction: Whitman's legacy in the personal epic*, Chicago: University of Chicago Press.

Miller, Perry (1939) *The New England mind: the seventeenth century*, New York: Macmillan.

Miller, Perry (1956) *Errand into the wilderness*, Cambridge, MA: Belknap Press of Harvard University Press.

Millgate, Michael (1966) *The achievement of William Faulkner*, London: Constable; New York: Random House.

Millier, Brett C. (1993) *Elizabeth Bishop: life and the memory of it*, Berkeley: University of California Press.

Minter, David (ed.) (1976) *The Sound and the Fury: an authoritative text, backgrounds and contexts, criticism*, New York: Norton.

Mitchell, Domhnall (2000) *Emily Dickinson: monarch of perception*, Amherst: University of Massachusetts Press.

Mitchell, Juliet and Oakley, Ann (eds) (1986) *What is feminism?*, New York: Pantheon Books.

Mitchell, Lee Clark (1989) *Determined fictions: American literary naturalism*, New York: Columbia University Press.

Mogen, David, Busby, Mark and Bryant, Paul (eds) (1989) *The frontier experience and the American dream: essays on American literature*, College Station: Texas A&M University Press.

Moi, Toril (1985) *Sexual/Textual Politics: feminist literary theory*, London and New York: Methuen.

Monteiro, George (2000) *Stephen Crane's blue badge of courage*, Baton Rouge: Louisiana State University Press.

Moody, David A. (1994) *Thomas Stearns Eliot, poet*, Cambridge and New York: Cambridge University Press.

Moorton, Richard F., Jr (ed.) (1991) *Eugene O'Neill's century: centennial views on America's foremost tragic dramatist*, New York: Greenwood Press.

Mootry, Maria K. and Smith, Gary (eds) (1987) *A life distilled: Gwendolyn Brooks, her poetry and fiction*, Urbana: University of Illinois Press.

Moreland, Richard, (1990) *Faulkner and modernism: rereading and rewriting*, Madison: University of Wisconsin Press.

Morgan, Edmund S. (1963) *Visible saints: the history of a Puritan idea*, New York: New York University Press.

Morse, David, (1987) *American romanticism*, 2 vols, Basingstoke: Macmillan.

Mortimer, Gail L. (1983) *Faulkner's rhetoric of loss: a study in perception and meaning*, Austin: University of Texas Press.

Most, Glenn W. and Stowe, William W. (eds) (1983) *The poetics of murder: detective fiction and literary theory*, San Diego, CA: Harcourt Brace Jovanovich.

Motley, Warren (1987) *The American Abraham: James Fenimore Cooper and the frontier patriarch*, Cambridge and New York: Cambridge University Press.

Mottram, Eric (1972) *Allen Ginsberg in the sixties*, Brighton: Unicorn.

Moylan, Tom (1986) *Demand the impossible: science fiction and the utopian imagination*, London and New York: Methuen.

Muller, Gilbert H. (1999) *New strangers in paradise: the immigrant experience and contemporary American fiction*, Lexington: University Press of Kentucky.

Murphy, Francis (ed.) (1969) *Walt Whitman: a critical anthology*, Harmondsworth: Penguin.

Murphy, Margueritte S. (1992) *A tradition of subversion: the prose poem in English from Wilde to Ashbery*, Amherst: University of Massachusetts Press.

Murray, Albert (1976) *Stomping the Blues*, New York: McGraw-Hill.

Murray, David (1991) *Forked tongues: speech, writing and representation in North American Indian texts*, London: Pinter.

Murray, David (2000) *Indian giving: economies of power in Indian-white exchanges*, Amherst: University of Massachusetts Press.

Myerson, Joel (1980) *The New England transcendentalists and The Dial: a history of the magazine and its contributors*, Rutherford: Fairleigh Dickinson University Press.

Myerson, Joel (ed.) (1988) *Critical essays on Henry David Thoreau's Walden*, Boston: G. K. Hall.

Myerson, Joel (ed.) (2000) *Transcendentalism: a reader*, New York and Oxford: Oxford University Press.

Nackenoff, Carol (1994) *The fictional republic: Horatio Alger and American political discourse*, New York: Oxford University Press.

Nadel, Alan (1988) *Invisible criticism: Ralph Ellison and the American canon*, Iowa City: University of Iowa Press.

Nadel, Alan (ed.) (1994) *May all your fences have gates: essays on the drama of August Wilson*, Iowa City: University of Iowa Press.

Nagel, James (2001) *The contemporary American short story cycle: the ethnic resonance of genre*, Baton Rouge: Louisiana State University Press.

Nash, Gerald D. (1992) *The crucial era: the Great Depression and World War II, 1929–1945*, New York: St Martin's Press.

Nelson, Cary (1981) *Our last first poets: vision and history in contemporary American poetry*, Urbana: University of Illinois Press.

Nelson, Cary (1989) *Repression and recovery: modern American poetry and the politics of cultural memory, 1910–1945*, Madison: University of Wisconsin Press.

Nesset, Kirk (1995) *The stories of Raymond Carver: a critical study*, Athens: Ohio University Press.

Neuman, Shirley and Nadel, Ira (eds) (1988) *Gertrude Stein and the making of literature*, Boston: Northeastern University Press.

Newman, Charles (ed.) (1970) *The art of Sylvia Plath: a symposium*, Bloomington: Indiana University Press.

Newman, Judie (1984) *Saul Bellow and history*, Basingstoke: Macmillan.

Nicholls, Peter (1995) *Modernisms: a literary guide*, Berkeley: University of California Press.

Noll, Mark A. (1992) *A history of Christianity in the United States and Canada*, Grand Rapids, MI and London: W. B. Eerdmans.

Novick, Peter (1999) *The Holocaust in American life*, Boston: Houghton Mifflin.

O'Brien, Sharon (1987) *Willa Cather: the emerging voice*, New York: Oxford University Press.

O'Meally, Robert G. (ed.) (1988) *New essays on Invisible Man*, Cambridge and New York: Cambridge University Press.

Ogren, Kathy J. (1989) *The jazz revolution: twenties America and the meaning of jazz*, New York: Oxford University Press.

Oliver, Paul (1960, 1990) *Blues fell this morning: meaning in the blues*, Cambridge and New York: Cambridge University Press.

Olney, James (ed.) (1988) *Studies in autobiography*, New York: Oxford University Press.

Ong, Walter (1982) *Orality and literacy: the technologizing of the word*, London and New York: Methuen.

Oriard, Michael (1982) *Dreaming of heroes: American sports fiction, 1868–1980*, Chicago: Nelson-Hall.

Oriard, Michael (1991) *Sporting with the gods: the rhetoric of play and game in American culture*, Cambridge and New York: Cambridge University Press.

Osteen, Mark (2000) *American magic and dread: Don DeLillo's dialogue with culture*, Philadelphia: University of Pennsylvania Press.

Oster, Judith (1992) *Toward Robert Frost: the reader and the poet*, Athens: University of Georgia Press.

Packer, Barbara (1995) 'The Transcendentalists', in Bercovitch, Sacvan (general ed.), *The Cambridge history of American literature*, vol. 2, *Prose writing, 1820–1865*, Cambridge and New York: Cambridge University Press, 329–604.

Panish, Jon (1997), *The color of jazz: race and representation in postwar American culture*, Jackson: University Press of Mississippi.

Parish, Peter J. (1975) *The American Civil War*, New York: Holmes and Meier.

Parish, Peter J. (1989) *Slavery: history and historians*, New York: Harper & Row.

Parker, Hershel (1996) *Herman Melville: a biography, 1819–1851*, Baltimore: Johns Hopkins University Press.

Patell, Cyrus R. K. (1999) 'Emergent literatures', in Bercovitch, Sacvan (general ed.), *The Cambridge history of American literature*, vol. 7, *Prose writing, 1940–1990*, Cambridge and New York: Cambridge University Press, 539–716.

Patke, Rajeev S. (1985) *The long poems of Wallace Stevens: an interpretative study*, Cambridge and New York: Cambridge University Press.

Pattee, Frederick Lewis (1970) *The development of the American short story: an historical survey*, New York and London: Harper & Brothers.

Paul, Sherman (1978) *Olson's push: origin, Black Mountain, and recent American poetry*, Baton Rouge: Louisiana State University Press.

Peabody, Richard (ed.) (1997) *A different beat: writings by women of the Beat generation*, London and New York: Serpent's Tail.

Peach, Linden (2000) *Toni Morrison*, Basingstoke: Macmillan; New York: St Martin's Press.

Pearce, Roy Harvey (1961) *The continuity of American poetry*, Princeton: Princeton University Press.

Peden, William (1964) *The American short story: front line in the national defense of literature*, Boston: Houghton Mifflin.

Pereira, Kim (1995) *August Wilson and the African American odyssey*, Urbana: University of Illinois Press.

Perloff, Marjorie (1985) *The dance of the intellect: studies in the poetry of the Pound tradition*, Cambridge and New York: Cambridge University Press.

Perloff, Marjorie (1990) *Poetic license: essays on modernist and postmodernist lyric*, Evanston, IL: Northwestern University Press.

Perloff, Marjorie (1991) *Radical artifice: writing poetry in the age of media*, Chicago: University of Chicago Press.

Perloff, Marjorie (2002) *21st-century modernism: the 'new' poetics*, Oxford and Malden, MA: Blackwell.

Perry, Lewis and Fellman, Michael (eds) (1979) *Anti-slavery reconsidered: new perspectives on the abolitionists*, Baton Rouge: Louisiana State University Press.

Peterson, Carla L. (1995) *Doers of the word: African-American women speakers and writers in the North, 1830–1880*, New York: Oxford University Press.

Pfister, Joel (1995) *Staging depth: Eugene O'Neill and the politics of psychological discourse*, Chapel Hill: University of North Carolina Press.

Pinsker, Stanford (1992) *Jewish American fiction, 1917–1987*, New York: Twayne.

Pinsky, Robert (1976) *The situation of poetry: contemporary poetry and its traditions*, Princeton: Princeton University Press.

Pizer, Donald (1976) *The novels of Theodore Dreiser: a critical study*, Minneapolis: University of Minnesota Press.

Pizer, Donald (1993) *The theory and practice of American literary naturalism*, Carbondale: Southern Illinois University Press.

Pizer, Donald (ed.) (1998) *Documents of American realism and naturalism*, Carbondale: Southern Illinois University Press.

Plant, Deborah G. (1995) *Every tub must sit on its own bottom: the philosophy and politics of Zora Neale Hurston*, Urbana: University of Illinois Press.

Plasa, Carl (ed.) (1998) *Toni Morrison, Beloved*, Duxford: Icon.

Poirier, Richard (1977, 1990) *Robert Frost, the work of knowing*, New York: Oxford University Press.

Poirier, Richard (1985) *A world elsewhere: the place of style in American literature*, Madison: University of Wisconsin Press.

Poirier, Richard (1992) *Poetry and pragmatism*, Cambridge, MA: Harvard University Press.

Pollack, Vivian R. (1984) *Dickinson: the anxiety of gender*, Ithaca, NY: Cornell University Press.

Polner, Murray (1971) *No victory parades: the return of the Vietnam veteran*, New York: Holt, Rinehart and Winston; London: Orbach and Chambers.

Polsky, Ned (1967) *Hustlers, beats, and others*, Chicago: Aldine.

Porte, Joel (ed.) (1982) *Emerson in his journals*, Cambridge, MA: Belknap Press of Harvard University Press.

Porter, David (1978) *Emerson and literary change*, Cambridge, MA: Harvard University Press.

Porter, Horace A. (1989) *Stealing the fire: the art and protest of James Baldwin*, Middletown, CT: Wesleyan University Press.

Potter, David M. and Fehrenbacher, Don E. (1976) *The impending crisis 1848–1861*, New York: Harper & Row.

Powell, Richard J. (1989) *The blues aesthetic: black culture and modernism*, Washington, DC: Washington Project for the Arts.

Pratt, Louis H. (1978) *James Baldwin*, Boston: Twayne.

Preminger, Alex and Brogan, T. V. F. (eds) (1996) *The new Princeton encyclopedia of poetry and poetics*, New York: MJF Books.

Price, Jonathan (ed.) (1972) *Critics on Robert Lowell: readings in literary criticism*, Coral Gables, FL: University of Miami Press; London: Allen and Unwin.

Pritchard, William H. (1984) *Frost: a literary life reconsidered*, New York: Oxford University Press.

Przybylowicz, Donna (1985) *Desire and repression: the dialectic of self and other in the late works of Henry James*, University, AL: University of Alabama Press.

Punter, David (1996) *The literature of terror: a history of gothic fictions from 1765 to the present day*, 2 vols, London and New York: Longman.

Quinn, Justin (2002) *Gathered beneath the storm: Wallace Stevens, nature and community*, Dublin: University College Dublin Press.

Railton, Stephen (1978) *Fenimore Cooper: a study of his life and imagination*, Princeton: Princeton University Press.

Rainey, Lawrence S. (1991) *Ezra Pound and the monument of culture: text, history, and the Malatesta cantos*, Chicago: University of Chicago Press.

Rainey, Lawrence S. (1998) *Institutions of modernism: literary elites and public culture*, New Haven: Yale University Press.

Rampersad, Arnold (1976, 1990) *The art and imagination of W. E. B. Du Bois*, Cambridge, MA: Harvard University Press.

Rans, Geoffrey (1991) *Cooper's Leather-Stocking novels: a secular reading*, Chapel Hill: University of North Carolina Press.

Reeves, Gareth (1994) *T. S. Eliot's The Waste Land*, London and New York: Harvester Wheatsheaf.

Reeves, Thomas (ed.) (1978) *McCarthyism*, Malabar, FL: Krieger.

Reynolds, David S. (1988) *Beneath the American renaissance: the subversive imagination in the age of Emerson and Melville*, New York: Knopf.

Reynolds, David S. and Rosenthal, Debra J. (eds) (1997) *The serpent in the cup: temperance in American literature*, Amherst: University of Massachusetts Press.

Reynolds, Guy (1996) *Willa Cather in context: progress, race, empire*, Basingstoke: Macmillan; New York: St Martin's Press.

Richardson, Mark (1997) *The ordeal of Robert Frost: the poet and his poetics*, Urbana: University of Illinois Press.

Richardson, Robert D. (1986) *Henry Thoreau: a life of the mind*, Berkeley: University of California Press.

Richardson, Robert D. (1995) *Emerson: the mind on fire, a biography*, Berkeley: University of California Press.

Riddel, Joseph N. (1965) *The clairvoyant eye: the poetry and poetics of Wallace Stevens*, Baton Rouge: Louisiana State University Press.

Riddel, Joseph N. (1974) *The inverted bell: modernism and the counterpoetics of William Carlos Williams*, Baton Rouge: Louisiana State University Press.

Ringe, Donald (1982) *American Gothic: imagination and reason in nineteenth-century fiction*, Lexington: University Press of Kentucky.

Robbins, Ruth (2000) *Literary feminisms*, New York: St Martin's Press.

Roberts, Diane (1994) *Faulkner and Southern womanhood*, Athens: University of Georgia Press.

Roberts, Robin (1993) *A new species: gender and science in science fiction*, Urbana: University of Illinois Press.

Roberts-Miller, Patricia (1999) *Voices in the wilderness: public discourse and the paradox of Puritan rhetoric*, Tuscaloosa: University of Alabama Press.

Robinson, Marc (1994) *The other American drama*, Cambridge and New York: Cambridge University Press.

Robinson, William H. (ed.) (1982) *Critical essays on Phillis Wheatley*, Boston: G. K. Hall.

Rodriguez, Barbara (1999) *Autobiographical inscriptions: form, personhood, and the American woman writer of color*, New York: Oxford University Press.

Roemer, Kenneth M. (ed.) (1981) *America as Utopia*, New York: Franklin.

Rogin, Michael Paul (1983) *Subversive genealogy: the politics and art of Herman Melville*, New York: Knopf.

Rorty, Richard (1982) *Consequences of pragmatism*, Minneapolis: University of Minnesota Press.

Rose, Jacqueline (1991) *The haunting of Sylvia Plath*, Cambridge, MA: Harvard University Press.

Rose, Mark (1981) *Alien encounters: anatomy of science fiction*, Cambridge, MA: Harvard University Press.

Rosenheim, Shawn and Rachman, Stephen (eds) (1995) *The American face of Edgar Allan Poe*, Baltimore: Johns Hopkins University Press.

Rosenmeier, Rosamond (1991) *Anne Bradstreet revisited*, Boston: Twayne.

Rosenthal, Bernard (1993) *Salem story: reading the Witch Trials of 1692*, Cambridge and New York: Cambridge University Press.

Rosenthal, Bernard (ed.) (1981) *Critical essays on Charles Brockden Brown*, Boston: G. K. Hall.

Rosenthal, M. L. (1967) *The new poets: American and British poetry since World War II*, New York: Oxford University Press.

Roth, Martin (1976) *Comedy and America: the lost world of Washington Irving*, Port Washington, NY: Kennikat Press.

Roth, Philip (1975) *Reading myself and others*, New York: Farrar, Straus, and Giroux.

Rovit, Earl (1963, 1986) *Ernest Hemingway*, Boston: Twayne.

Rowley, Hazel (2001) *Richard Wright: the life and times*, New York: Henry Holt.

Rubin, Louis D. (ed.) (1974) *The comic imagination in American literature*, Washington, DC: Voice of America.

Rubin, Louis D. (general ed.) (1985) *The history of Southern literature*, Baton Rouge: Louisiana State University Press.

Rubin-Dorsky, Jeffrey (1988) *Adrift in the Old World: the psychological pilgrimage of Washington Irving*, Chicago: University of Chicago Press.

Ruddick, Lisa (1990) *Reading Gertrude Stein: body, text, gnosis*, Ithaca, NY: Cornell University Press.

Rugoff, Milton (1981) *The Beechers: an American family in the nineteenth century*, New York: Harper & Row.

Ruland, Richard and Bradbury, Malcolm (1991) *From Puritanism to postmodernism: a history of American literature*, New York: Viking.

Runyon, Randolph (1992) *Reading Raymond Carver*, Syracuse, NY: Syracuse University Press.

Ruppersburg, Hugh and Engles, Tim (eds) (2000) *Critical essays on Don DeLillo*, New York: G. K. Hall.

Rushdy, Ashraf H. A. (1999) *Neo-Slave narratives: studies in the social logic of a literary form*, New York: Oxford University Press.

Rutman, Darrett B. (1970) *American Puritanism: faith and practice*, Philadelphia: Lippincott.

Saldívar, Ramón (1990) *Chicano narrative: the dialectics of difference*, Madison: University of Wisconsin Press.

Saldívar-Hull, Sonia (2000) *Feminism on the border: Chicana gender politics and literature*, Berkeley: University of California Press.

Salyer, Gregory (1997) *Leslie Marmon Silko*, New York: Twayne; London: Prentice-Hall International.

Salzberg, Joel (ed.) (1987) *Critical essays on Bernard Malamud*, Boston: G. K. Hall.

Sawyer, Andy and Seed, David (eds) (2000) *Speaking science fiction: dialogues and interpretations*, Liverpool: Liverpool University Press.

Sayre, Robert F. (1992) *New essays on Walden*, Cambridge and New York: Cambridge University Press.

Scharnhorst, Gary and Bales, Jack (1985) *The lost life of Horatio Alger Jr*, Bloomington: Indiana University Press.

Schaub, Thomas H. (1991) *American fiction in the Cold War*, Madison: University of Wisconsin Press.

Scheese, Don (1996) *Nature writing: the pastoral impulse in America*, New York: Twayne; London: Prentice-Hall International.

Schrecker, Ellen (1998) *Many are the crimes: McCarthyism in America*, Boston: Little, Brown.

Schubnell, Matthias (1985) *N. Scott Momaday: the cultural and literary background*, Norman: University of Oklahoma Press.

Schwartz, Lloyd and Estess, Sybil P. (eds) (1983) *Elizabeth Bishop and her art*, Ann Arbor: University of Michigan Press.

Schweik, Susan M. (1991) *A gulf so deeply cut: American women poets and the Second World War*, Madison: University of Wisconsin Press.

Sedgwick, Eve Kosofsky (1990) *Epistemology of the closet*, Berkeley: University of California Press.

Seed, David (1988) *The fictional labyrinths of Thomas Pynchon*, Basingstoke: Macmillan; Iowa City: University of Iowa Press.

Seed, David (1999) *American science fiction and the Cold War: literature and film*, Edinburgh: Edinburgh University Press.

Seed, David (ed.) (2000) *Imagining apocalypse: studies in cultural crisis*, Basingstoke: Macmillan; New York: St Martin's Press.

Serafin, Steven R. (general ed.) (1999) *Encyclopedia of American literature*, New York: Continuum.

Severo, Richard and Milford, Lewis (1989) *The wages of war: when America's soldiers came home – from Valley Forge to Vietnam*, New York: Simon and Schuster.

Sewall, Richard B. (1974) *The life of Emily Dickinson*, 2 vols, New York: Farrar, Straus and Giroux.

Seyersted, Per (1969) *Kate Chopin: a critical biography*, Oslo: Universitetsforlaget; Baton Rouge: Louisiana State University Press.

Shannon, Sandra (1995) *The dramatic vision of August Wilson*, Washington, DC: Howard University Press.

Shaw, Harry B. (1980) *Gwendolyn Brooks*, Boston: Twayne.

Shechner, Mark (1990) *The conversion of the Jews and other essays*, Basingstoke: Macmillan; New York: St Martin's Press.

Shepherd, John (1982) *Tin Pan Alley*, London and Boston: Routledge and Kegan Paul.

Shoptaw, John (1994) *On the outside looking out: John Ashbery's poetry*, Cambridge, MA: Harvard University Press.

Showalter, Elaine (1977) *A literature of their own: British women novelists from Brontë to Lessing*, Princeton: Princeton University Press.

Silliman, Ron (1987) *The new sentence*, New York: Roof.

Silverman, Kenneth (1991) *Edgar A. Poe: mournful and never-ending remembrance*, New York: HarperCollins.

Simmons, Diane (1999) *Maxine Hong Kingston*, New York: Twayne.

Skandera-Trombley, Laura E. (ed.) (1998) *Critical essays on Maxine Hong Kingston*, New York: G. K. Hall; London: Prentice-Hall International.

Skenazy, Paul and Martin, Tera (eds) (1998) *Conversations with Maxine Hong Kingston*, Jackson: University Press of Mississippi.

Slater, Philip Eliot (1990) *The pursuit of loneliness: American culture at the breaking point*, 3rd edn., Boston: Beacon Press.

Slide, Anthony (1995) *The Hollywood novel: a critical guide*, Jefferson, NC and London: McFarland and Co.

Slotkin, Richard (1973) *Regeneration through violence: the mythology of the American frontier, 1600–1860*, Middletown, CT: Wesleyan University Press.

Slotkin, Richard (1992) *Gunfighter nation: the myth of the frontier in twentieth-century America*, New York: Atheneum/Maxwell Macmillan International.

Slotkin, Richard and Folsom, James (1978) *So dreadfull a judgement: Puritan responses to King Philip's War, 1676-1677*, Middletown, CT: Wesleyan University Press.

Slusser, George and Shippey, Tom (eds) (1992) *Fiction 2000: cyberpunk and the future of narrative*, Athens: University of Georgia Press.

Smith, Grover (1983) *The Waste Land, by T. S. Eliot*, London and Boston: Allen and Unwin.

Smith, Henry Nash (1950) *Virgin land: the American West as symbol and myth*, Cambridge, MA: Harvard University Press.

Smith, Henry Nash (1962) *Mark Twain: the development of a writer*, Cambridge, MA: Belknap Press of Harvard University Press.

Smith, Martha Nell (1992) *Rowing in Eden: rereading Emily Dickinson*, Austin: University of Texas Press.

Smith, Stan (1982) *Inviolable voice: history and twentieth-century poetry*, Dublin: Gill and Macmillan; Atlantic Highlands, NJ: Humanities Press.

Sollors, Werner (1978) *Amiri Baraka/LeRoi Jones: the quest for a 'populist modernism'*, New York: Columbia University Press.

Sollors, Werner (1997) *Neither black nor white yet both: thematic explorations of interracial literature*, New York: Oxford University Press.

Sollors, Werner (ed.) (1998) *Multilingual America: transnationalism, ethnicity, and the languages of American literature*, New York: New York University Press.

Sollors, Werner and Deidrich, Maria (eds) (1994) *The Black Columbiad: defining moments in African American literature and culture*, Cambridge, MA and London: Harvard University Press.

Spatz, Thomas (1969) *Hollywood in fiction: some versions of the American myth*, The Hague: Mouton.

Speir, Jerry (1981) *Raymond Chandler*, New York: Ungar.

Spiller, Robert E. (general ed.) (1974) *The literary history of the United States*, 4th edn., New York: Macmillan.

Spoto, Donald (1985) *A kindness of strangers: the life of Tennessee Williams*, Boston: Little, Brown.

Stallman, R. W. (1968) *Stephen Crane: a biography*, New York: Braziller.

Stanford, Ann (1974) *Anne Bradstreet the worldly Puritan: an introduction to her poetry*, New York: Franklin.

Stanley, David and Thatcher, Elaine (eds) (2000) *Cowboy poets and cowboy poetry*, Urbana: University of Illinois Press.

Stanley, Liz (1992) *The auto/biographical I: the theory and practice of feminist auto/biography*, Manchester and New York: Manchester University Press.

Starling, Marion Wilson (1988) *The slave narrative: its place in American history*, Boston: G. K. Hall.

Stephenson, Gregory (1990) *The daybreak boys: essays on the literature of the Beat generation*, Carbondale: Southern Illinois University Press.

Stevenson, Anne (1989) *Bitter fame: a life of Sylvia Plath*, London and New York, Viking.

Stock, Noel (1982) *The life of Ezra Pound*, San Francisco: North Point Press.

Stouck, David (1975) *Willa Cather's imagination*, Lincoln: University of Nebraska Press.

Sullivan, J. P. (ed.) (1970) *Ezra Pound: a critical anthology*, Harmondsworth: Penguin.

Sullivan, Larry E. and Sherman, Lydia Cushman (eds) (1996) *Pioneers, passionate ladies, and private eyes: dime novels, series books, and paperbacks*, New York: Haworth Press.

Summers, Anthony (1980, 1998) *Not in your lifetime*, New York: Marlowe.

Sundquist, Eric J. (1983) *Faulkner: the house divided*, Baltimore: Johns Hopkins University Press.

Sundquist, Eric J. (ed.) (1990) *Frederick Douglass: new literary and historical essays*, Cambridge and New York: Cambridge University Press.

Sundquist, Eric J. (1993) *To wake the nations: race in the making of American literature*, Cambridge, MA: Belknap Press of Harvard University Press.

Sundquist, Eric J. (ed.) (1994) *Mark Twain: a collection of critical essays*, Englewood Cliffs, NJ: Prentice-Hall.

Swann, Charles (1991) *Nathaniel Hawthorne: tradition and revolution*, Cambridge and New York: Cambridge University Press.

Takaki, Ronald T. (1990) *Iron cages: race and culture in nineteenth-century America*, New York: Knopf.

Takaki, Ronald T. (1993) *A different mirror: a history of multicultural America*, Boston: Little, Brown.

Takaki, Ronald T. (1998) *A larger memory: a history of our diversity with voices*, Boston: Little, Brown.

Takaki, Ronald T. (2000) *Double victory: a multicultural history of America in World War II*, Boston: Little, Brown.

Tanner, Tony (1965) *The reign of wonder: naivety and reality in American literature*, Cambridge: Cambridge University Press.

Tanner, Tony (1971) *City of words: American fiction, 1950–1970*, London: Cape.

Tanner, Tony (1987) *Scenes of nature, signs of men*, Cambridge and New York: Cambridge University Press.

Tanner, Tony (2000) *The American mystery: American literature from Emerson to DeLillo*, Cambridge and New York: Cambridge University Press.

Taylor, Gordon O. (1983) *Studies in modern American autobiography*, London: Macmillan.

Taylor-Guthrie, Danille (1994) *Conversations with Toni Morrison*, Jackson: University Press of Mississippi.

Terrell, Carroll (1980, 1984) *A companion to the Cantos of Ezra Pound*, Berkeley: University of California Press.

Thickstun, Margaret Olofson (1988) *Fictions of the feminine: Puritan doctrine and the representation of women*, Ithaca, NY: Cornell University Press.

Thomas, Dwight and Jackson, David K. (1987) *The Poe log*, Boston: G. K. Hall.

Thomas, M. Wynn (1987) *The lunar light of Whitman's poetry*, Cambridge, MA: Harvard University Press.

Thompson, Judith J. (1987) *Tennessee Williams' plays: memory, myth, and symbol*, New York: Lang.

Tilton, Robert S. (1994) *Pocahontas: the evolution of an American narrative*, Cambridge and New York: Cambridge University Press.

Tompkins, Jane (1985) *Sensational designs: the cultural work of American fiction, 1790–1860*, New York: Oxford University Press.

Tompkins, Jane (1992) *West of everything: the inner life of westerns*, New York: Oxford University Press.

Toth, Emily (1990) *Kate Chopin*, New York: Morrow.

Turner, Arlin (1980) *Nathaniel Hawthorne: a biography*, New York: Oxford University Press.

Tytell, John (1987) *Ezra Pound: the solitary volcano*, New York: Anchor; London: Bloomsbury.

Umphlett, Wiley Lee (1975) *The sporting myth and the American experience: studies in contemporary fiction*, Lewisburg, PA: Bucknell University Press.

Umphlett, Wiley Lee (ed.) (1991), *The achievement of American sport literature: a critical appraisal*, Rutherford, NJ: Fairleigh Dickinson University Press; London: Associated University Presses.

Underwood, Tim, and Miller, Chuck (eds) (1982) *Fear itself: the horror fiction of Stephen King*, San Francisco: Underwood-Miller.

Underwood, Tim, and Miller, Chuck (eds) (1986) *Kingdom of fear: the world of Stephen King*, New York: New American Library.

Underwood, Tim, and Miller, Chuck (eds) (1988) *Bare bones: conversations on terror with Stephen King*, New York: Warner Books.

Updike, John (1999) *More matter: essays and criticism*, New York: Knopf/Random House; London: Hamish Hamilton.

Vaughan, Alden T. and Clark, Edward W. (eds) (1981) *Puritans among the Indians: accounts of captivity and redemption, 1676–1724*, Cambridge, MA: Belknap Press.

Veeser, H. Aram (ed.) (1989) *The New Historicism*, New York: Routledge.

Veeser, H. Aram (ed.) (1994) *The New Historicism reader*, New York: Routledge.

Vendler, Helen (1969) *On extended wings: Wallace Stevens' longer poems*, Cambridge, MA: Harvard University Press.

Vendler, Helen (1980) *Part of nature, part of us: modern American poets*, Cambridge, MA: Harvard University Press.

Vendler, Helen (1984) *Wallace Stevens: words chosen out of desire*, Knoxville: University of Tennessee Press.

Vendler, Helen (1988) *The music of what happens: poems, poets, critics*, Cambridge, MA: Harvard University Press.

Vendler, Helen (1995) *The given and the made: strategies of poetic redefinition*, Cambridge, MA: Harvard University Press.

Vickery, Olga W. (1959) *The novels of William Faulkner: a critical interpretation*, Baton Rouge: Louisiana State University Press.

Vidal, Gore (1993) *United States: essays 1952–1992*, New York: Random House.

Vincent, Howard P. (1948) *The trying-out of Moby-Dick*, Boston: Houghton Mifflin.

Vizenor, Gerald (1988) *The trickster of liberty: tribal heirs to a wild baronage*, Minneapolis: University of Minnesota Press.

Vizenor, Gerald (1994) *Manifest manners: postindian warriors of survivance*, Hanover: University Press of New England.

Wade, Stephen (1996) *The imagination in transit: the fiction of Philip Roth*, Sheffield: Sheffield Academic Press.

Wade, Stephen (1999) *Jewish American literature since 1945: an introduction*, Edinburgh: Edinburgh University Press.

Wadlington, Warwick (1975) *The confidence game in American literature*, Princeton and London: Princeton University Press.

Wagenknecht, Edward (1965) *Harriet Beecher Stowe: the known and the unknown*, New York: Oxford University Press.

Waggoner, Hyatt (1955) *Hawthorne, a critical study*, Cambridge, MA: Belknap Press of Harvard University Press.

Wagner, Linda (ed.) (1984) *Critical essays on Sylvia Plath*, Boston: G. K. Hall.

Wagner-Martin, Linda (1987) *Sylvia Plath: a biography*, New York: Simon and Schuster.

Wagner-Martin, Linda (ed.) (1987) *Ernest Hemingway: six decades of criticism*, East Lansing: Michigan State University Press.

Wagner-Martin, Linda (1995) *Favored strangers: Gertrude Stein and her family*, New Brunswick, NJ: Rutgers University Press.

Wald, Gayle (2000) *Crossing the line: racial passing in twentieth-century U.S.*, Durham, NC: Duke University Press.

Waldmeir, Joseph J. (1969) *American novels of the Second World War*, The Hague and Paris: Mouton.

Walker, Jeffrey (1989) *Bardic ethos and the American epic poem: Whitman, Pound, Crane, Williams, Olson*, Baton Rouge: Louisiana State University Press.

Walker, Nancy A. (1988) *A very serious thing: women's humor and American culture*, Minneapolis: University of Minnesota Press.

Wall, Cheryl A. (1995) *Women of the Harlem Renaissance*, Bloomington: Indiana University Press.

Watts, Jerry Gafio (1994) *Heroism and the black intellectual: Ralph Ellison, politics, and Afro-American intellectual life*, Chapel Hill: University of North Carolina Press.

Watts, Jerry Gafio (2001) *Amiri Baraka: the politics and art of a Black intellectual*, New York: New York University Press.

Watts, Steven (1994) *The romance of real life: Charles Brockden Brown and the origins of American culture*, Baltimore: Johns Hopkins University Press.

Waugh, Patricia (1984) *Metafiction: the theory and practice of self-conscious fiction*, London and New York: Methuen.

Way, Brian (1980) *F. Scott Fitzgerald and the art of social fiction*, London: Edward Arnold.

Welland, Dennis (1983) *Miller, the playwright*, London and New York: Methuen.

Wellek, René (1986) *A history of modern criticism: 1750–1950*; vol. 6, *American criticism*, New Haven: Yale University Press.

West, Mark I. (1988) *Trust your children: voices against censorship in children's literature*, New York: Neal-Schuman Publishers.

Westerkamp, Marilyn J. (1999) *Women and religion in early America, 1600–1850*, London: Routledge.

Westling, Louise H. (1996) *The green breast of the new world: landscape, gender, and American fiction*, Athens: University of Georgia Press.

White, Peter (ed.) (1985) *Puritan poets and poetics: seventeenth-century American poetry in theory and practice*, University Park: Pennsylvania State University Press.

Whitfield, Stephen J. (1991) *A death in the Delta: the story of Emmett Till*, Baltimore: Johns Hopkins University Press.

Wienen, Mark W. Van (1997) *Partisans and poets: the political work of American poetry in the Great War*, Cambridge and New York: Cambridge University Press.

Wiget, Andrew (1985) *Native American literature*, Boston: Twayne.

Will, Barbara (2000) *Gertrude Stein, modernism, and the problem of 'genius'*, Edinburgh: Edinburgh University Press.

Willett, Ralph (1996) *The naked city: urban crime fiction in the USA*, Manchester: Manchester University Press.

Williams, Merle A. (1993) *Henry James and the philosophical novel: being and seeing*, New York: Cambridge University Press.

Williams, Wirt (1982) *The tragic art of Ernest Hemingway*, Baton Rouge: Louisiana State University Press.

Williamson, Joel (1980) *New people: miscegenation and mulattoes in the United States*, New York: Free Press.

Williamson, Joel (1993) *William Faulkner and Southern history*, New York: Oxford University Press.

Wilmeth, Don B. and Bigsby, Christopher (eds) *The Cambridge history of American theatre*, 3 vols, Cambridge and New York: Cambridge University Press.

Wilson, Edmund (1962) *Patriotic gore: studies in the literature of the American Civil War*, New York: Oxford University Press.

Wilt, Judith (1990) *Abortion, choice, and contemporary fiction: the armageddon of the maternal instinct*, Chicago: University of Chicago Press.

Winks, Robin W. (ed.) (1988) *Detective fiction: a collection of critical essays*, Woodstock, VT: Countryman Press.

Winters, Yvor (1947) *In defense of reason*, New York: Swallow/Morrow.

Witemeyer, Hugh (1969) *The poetry of Ezra Pound: forms and renewal, 1908–1920*, Berkeley: University of California Press.

Witemeyer, Hugh (ed.) (1997) *The future of modernism*, Ann Arbor: University of Michigan Press.

Wittke, Carl (1930) *Tambo and Bones: a history of the American minstrel stage*, Durham, NC: Duke University Press.

Wolf, Bryan J. (1982) *Romantic re-vision: culture and consciousness in nineteenth-century American painting and literature*, Chicago: University of Chicago Press.

Wolfe, Peter (1985) *Something more than night: the case of Raymond Chandler*, Bowling Green, OH: Bowling Green State University Popular Press.

Wolfe, Peter (1999) *August Wilson*, New York: Twayne.

Wong, Sau-ling Cynthia (ed.) (1999) *Maxine Hong Kingston's The Woman Warrior: a casebook*, New York: Oxford University Press.

Wong, Shawn (ed.) (1996) *Asian American literature: a brief introduction and anthology*, Berkeley: HarperCollins College.

Woodard, Charles L. (1989) *Ancestral voice: conversations with N. Scott Momaday*, Lincoln: University of Nebraska Press.

Yellin, Jean Fagan (1994) *The Abolitionist sisterhood: women's political culture in antebellum America*, Ithaca, NY: Cornell University Press.

Yellin, Jean Fagan (ed.) (1987) *Incidents in the Life of a Slave Girl: written by herself*, Cambridge, MA: Harvard University Press.

Yenser, Stephen (1975) *Circle to circle: the poetry of Robert Lowell*, Berkeley: University of California Press.

Zamora, Lois Parkinson (1989) *Writing the Apocalypse: historical vision in contemporary U.S. and Latin American fiction*, Cambridge and New York: Cambridge University Press.

Zeiger, Melissa F. (1997) *Beyond consolation: death, sexuality, and the changing shapes of elegy*, Ithaca, NY: Cornell University Press.

Zelizer, Barbie (1992) *Covering the body: the Kennedy assassination, the media, and the shaping of collective memory*, Chicago: University of Chicago Press.

Zieger, Robert H. (2000) *America's Great War: World War I and the American experience*, Lanham, MD: Rowman and Littlefield.

Zoellner, Robert (1973) *The salt-sea mastodon: a reading of Moby-Dick*, Berkeley: University of California Press.

Index of writers and works

'A' 127
ABC of Reading 73, 173
Absalom, Absalom! 47, 78, 207, 208
'Absolution' 9
Acker, Kathy, 171
Acosta, Oscar Zeta 42
Actual, The 24
Adams, Andy 54
Adams Cantos 36
Adams, Henry 18, 47, 60, 90, 158
Adams, James Barton 54
Addams, Charles 156
Adding Machine, The 77
Adventures of Augie March, The 24
Adventures of Huckleberry Finn, The 4–5, 43, 94, 104, 166, 225
Adventures of Tom Sawyer, The 4, 43, 225
After the Fall 138
Aiken Conrad 79, 125
Al Que Quiere! 240
Albee, Edward 3, 76, 228
Alcott, Bronson 63, 222, 223
Alcott, Louisa May 43, 47, 64
Aldrich, Thomas Bailey 43
Alexander's Bridge 38
Alexie, Sherman 83, 105, 131, 151, 218
Alger, Horatio 8–9, 10, 26, 216
Algren, Nelson 61, 79
Alhambra, The 109
All God's Chillun Got Wings 96, 161
All I asking for is my Body 17
All My Sons 138
All of Us 38
All the Sad Young Men 82
Allen, Paula Gunn 83, 151
Allen, William Francis 210
Allen, Woody 105, 116
Almanac of the Dead 151, 201
Always Coming Home 228

Ambassadors, The 112
America is in the Heart 18
American Blues 240
American Buffalo 131
American Claimant, The 50
American Clock, The 138–9
American Hunger 245
American Indian Legends 150
American Pastoral 165, 191
American Scene, The 112
'American Scholar, The' 11–12, 220, 223
American Tabloid 57, 118, 157
American Tragedy, An 67, 152, 153, 157
American, The 111
Americana 59
Anatomy Lesson, The 191
Anaya, Rudolfo A. 41
And the Stars were Shining 15
Anderson, Edward 163
Anderson, Maxwell 192
Anderson, Regina M. 76
Anderson, Sherwood 126, 153, 186, 200, 210
Andrews, Bruce 122
Angel City 100
Angell, Roger 212
Angelou, Maya 19
Anna Christie 161
Annie Allen 33
Another Country 20
Antin, Mary 115
Anzaldúa, Gloria 42
Apess, William 119, 149–50
Appeal . . . to the Coloured Citizens of the World 204
Appeal in Favor of that Class of Americans Called Africans, An 204
April Galleons 15
Archbishop's Ceiling, The 138
Argall 169
Ariel 14–15

Index of writers and works

Armies of the Night, The 230
Army Life in a Black Regiment 47
'Art of Fiction, The' 112
Arthur Mervyn 34
Arthur, Timothy Shay 8, 186, 219
As I Lay Dying 78
Ashbery, John 15–16, 156, 157, 171, 177
Ashley, Carlos 54
Asimov, Isaac 195
Assistant, The 131
Asylum, The 93
At Fault 44
At Home and Abroad 166
An Atlas of the Difficult World: Poems 1988–1991
    189
Auroras of Autumn, The 213
Auster, Paul 115, 139
Autobiography (William Carlos Williams) 241
Autobiography of a Brown Buffalo, The 42
Autobiography of Alice B. Toklas, The 19, **20**, 213
Autobiography of an Ex-Colored Man, The 164
Autobiography of Benjamin Franklin 19, 85, 86, 184,
    216
Autobiography of LeRoi Jones/Amiri Baraka 22
Autobiography of Malcolm X 19, 202
Awakening, The 44–5, 62, 153
Awkward Age, The 112

Babbit, Irving 156
Babbitt, Natalie 43
Baby Doll 240
Babysitter's Club novels 43–4
Baldwin, James 6, 14, **20–1**, 31, 46, 71, 76, 114,
    140–1, 156, 211, 221
Ballad of the Sad Café 21
Banks, Russell 117
Baraka, Imamu Amiri 6, 14, **21–2**, 29, 31, 76, 114
Barker, James Nelson 169
Barlow, Joel 50, 74, 127
Barnes, Djuna 8
Barnum, Phineas T. 22, 50
Barth, John 3, 75, 76, 77, 104, 136, 171
Barthelme, Donald 3, 77, 136, 156, 171
'Bartleby the Scrivener' 107, 135, 182, 233
Bartram, William 165, 183
Basic Training of Pavlo Hummel, The 220
Battle-Pieces and Aspects of the War 47, 135
Baum, Frank L. 43, 77
Bay Psalm Book 22, 179
Bayou Folk 44
Beautiful and Damned, The 81
Beautiful Room is Empty, The 214
Bech at Bay 157

Beet Queen, The 151
Bell for Adano, A 244
Bell Jar, The 167, 191
Bellamy, Edward 227
Bellarosa Connection, The 24
Bellow, Saul 24–5, 48, 76, 79, 100, 104, 115, 157, 163
Beloved **25**, 146, 196, 202, 226
Ben Hur 26
Benchley, Robert 104
Bend Sinister 228
Benét, Stephen Vincent 21, 47, 117
Benito Cereno 107, 135, 182
Bennett, Gwendolyn 97
Berger, Thomas 237
Berlin, Irving 104, 222
Bernstein, Charles 122
Berryman, John 8, 32, 49, 69, 74, 100, 104, 118, 127,
    129, 139
Bethke, Bruce 195
Beyond the Horizon 161
Bierce, Ambrose 47, 93, 102, 104, 218
Big as Life 195
Big Money, The 192, 233
Big Nowhere, The 100
Big Roundup, The 54
Big Sleep, The 39
'Big Two-Hearted River' 99
Biglow Papers, The 137
Billings, Josh 55, 104
Billy Bathgate 218
Billy Budd 135
Billy Phelan's Greatest Game 218
Bingo Palace, The 151
Bird, Robert Montgomery 184
Bishop, Elizabeth 28–9, 69, 125, 157
'Black Arts Movement, The' 29
Black Boy 19, 202, 245
'Black Boy Looks at the White Boy, The' 76
'Black Cat, The' 170
Black Dahlia, The 100, 157
Black Elk Speaks 150
Black Music 21
Black Riders, The 55
Bless Me, Ultima 42
Blithedale Romance, The 33, 98
Bloch, Robert 102
Block, Lawrence 62
Blonde 157
Blue Dahlia, The 39
'Blue Hotel, The' 56
Blue Light 101
'Blueprint for Negro Writing' 245
Blues for Mister Charlie 221

Blues People 21
Bluest Eye, The 146
Blume, Judy 43
Bly, Robert 177, 230
Body Artist, The 59
Bogan, Louise 137
Bombeck, Erma 104
Bonfire of the Vanities, The 233
Bonnin, Gertrude (Zitkala-Ša) 19, 150
Bontemps, Arna 56, 83, 97
Book of Daniel, The 191
Book of Lies, The 231
Borderlands/La Frontera 42
Born on the Fourth of July 229
Boston 192
Bostonians, The 111, 112
Boy's Will, A 88
Boyle, T. Coraghessan 104
Bracebridge Hall 109
Brackett, Leigh 14
Bradbury, Ray 77, 195, 228
Bradford, William 168
Bradstreet, Anne 32–3, 69, 127, 179
Brand, Max 54, 237
Brautigan, Richard 171
Bread Givers 19, 107, 115
Brennan, William, 192
Brewsie and Willie 213
Bridge, The 74, 127, 169
Brisbane, Albert 84
Broken Glass 101, 139
Bronzeville Boys and Girls 34
'Bronzeville Mother Loiters in Mississippi, A.
    Meanwhile a Mississippi Mother Burns Bacon'
    21, 221
Brooks, Cleanth 7, 209
Brooks, Gwendolyn 3, 6, 21, **33–4**, 46, 125, 154, 221
Brown, Charles Brockden 34, 93, 102
Brown, Sterling A. 5
Brown, Wesley 140
Brown, William Wells 2, 164, 202, 204
Bryant, William Cullen 93, 103, 121, 158, 190
Buck, Pearl 157
Build-Up, The 241
Bukowski, Charles 100
Bulosan, Carlos 18
Buntline, Ned 64
Burnett, Frances Hodgson 43
Burning Mystery of Anna in 1951, The 177
Burroughs, Edgar Rice 194
Burroughs, William 23, 90, 171
'By the Road to the Contagious Hospital' 241
By-Line 99

Byrd, William 103

Cable, George Washington 56, 126, 166
Cage, John 139
Cahan, Abraham 107, 114–15
Cain, James M. 62
Call if You Need Me 38
Call it Sleep 115
Call of the Wild 92, 153
Can You Hear, Bird 15
Cane 97
Cannibal Galaxy, The 101
Canticle for Lebowitz, A 14, 195
Cantos, The 36–7, 73, 74, 127, 172, 173
Capote, Truman 8, 26, 157, 207
Captain Smith and Princess Pocahontas 169
Caputo, Philip 230
Carrie 119
Carruth, Hayden 8
Carver, Raymond 8, **37–8**, 65, 139, 200, 229
Castillo, Ana 42, 75
Cat on a Hot Tin Roof 240
Cat's Cradle 194
Catch-22 244
Catcher in the Rye, The 43
Cathedral 38
Cather, Willa 26, **38–9**, 87, 134, 165, 174, 186, 193,
    243
Cattle Brands 54
Ceremony 151, 201, 229
Chandler, Raymond 8, **39**, 62, 99, 178
Change of World, A 188
'Change the Joke and Slip the Yoke' 140
Changing Light at Sandover, The 14, 69
Channing, William Ellery 204–5
'Charlie Christian Story, The' 113
Charlotte Temple 26
Chavéz, Denise 41
Cheever, John 8, 79, 104, 157
Chernoff, Maxine 177
Chesnutt, Charles W. 5, 104, 164
Child, Lydia Maria 2, 111, 116, 204
'Children of the Poor, The' 34
Chimera 136
Chin, Frank 16–17
China Men 44, 120
Chinese History Cantos 36
Chittenden, Lawrence 54
Chopin, Kate 18, **44–5**, 56, 62, 126, 153, 164, 190,
    200
Christine 119
Christus: A Mystery 193
Chronicle of the Conquest of Granada, A 109

Index of writers and works

Chu, Louis 17
Cisneros, Sandra 42
'Civil Disobedience' See 'Resistance to Civil
    Government'
'Claims of the Negro Ethnologically Considered,
    The' 196
Clampitt, Amy 69, 157
Clansman, The 121, 185
Clarel 127, 135
Clark, Charles Badger 54
Clark, Walter Van Tilburg 130, 236
'Clean Well-Lighted Place, A' 99
Cleaver, Eldridge 6, 29
Clifton, Lucille 29
Climbing Jacob's Ladder 76
Close Range 54, 200, 212
Clotel; or The President's Daughter 164, 202
Cloudsplitter 117
Cocktail Party, The 70
Cody, William F. 64, 191
Cogewea, The Half-Blood 150
Cold Spring, A 28
Coleman, Wanda 221
Collected Early Poems (Ezra Pound)
Collected Essays (Ellison) 70–71
Collected Poems (Ginsberg) 91
Collected Poems (Plath) 167
Collected Poems (Stevens) 213
Collected Poems (Williams) 241
Collected Prose (Bishop) 28
Collected Prose (Lowell) 129
Color Purple, The 75, 228, 232, 233
Colored Museum, The 139
Colossus, The 167
Columbiad, The 51, 74
Columbus 109
'Comedian as the Letter C, The' 214
Coming of Age in Mississippi 46, 221
Companions of Columbus, The 109
Complete Poems and Prose, The (Whitman) 239
Complete Poems, The (Bishop) 28
Complete Stories, The (Walker) 232
'Composition as Explanation' 213
'Concord Hymn' 188
Conduct of Life, The 72
Confessions of Nat Turner to the Public, The 148
Confessions of Nat Turner, The 148–149
Confidence-Man, The 22, 50, 135
Connecticut Yankee in King Arthur's Court, A 225,
    246
Connelly, Michael 62
Conquest of Canaan 51, 74
'Conservation of Races, The' 196

Cook, Ebenezer 103
Cooke, John Esten 169
Cool Million, A 9
'Cool Tombs' 169
Coolidge, Susan 43
Cooper, James Fenimore 4, 11, 26, 37, 42, **52–3**, 60,
    64, 74, 87, 103, 119, 121, 122–3, 129, 141, 163,
    174, 182, 188, 190, 193, 194, 218, 228, 234, 236
Coover, Robert 3, 48, 77, 136, 171, 191, 211, 212
Cornwell, Patricia 62
Corso, Gregory 23
Coryell, John Russell 61, 64
Cosmopolitan Greetings 91
Counterlife, The 191
Couples 57, 118
Courtship of Miles Standish, The 168
Covin, Kelly 197
Cowboy Poetry: A Gathering 54
Cowboy Songs 54
Cox, Christopher 231
Crack-Up, The 8
Crane, Hart 74, 99, 126, 127, 169, 171, 190
Crane, Stephen 47, **55–6**, 86, 95, 107, 111, 139,
    152–3, 177, 193, 197, 200, 206, 209–10, 219,
    229
Crater, The 52, 194, 228
Crawford, F. Marion 102
Creeley, Robert 30, 139, 230
Cross, Amanda 62
Crossing the Water 167
Crucible, The 56–7, 134, 138, 193
Crying of Lot 49, The 136, 182
Cryptogram, The 131
Cuba Libre 210
Cullen, Countee 5, 6, 56, 83, 95, 97, 192, 197
cummings, e. e. 243
Cummins, Maria Susanna 26, 186
'Custom-House, The' 98

Daisy Miller 111
Dangling Man 24, 76
Dannay, Frederic 62
Danse Macabre 119
Dark Half, The 119
Darkness in Saint Louis Bearheart 151
Darktown Strutters 140
Davidson, Donald 7, 89
Davis, Angela 29
Davis, John 169
Davis, Rebecca Harding 18
Dawn 67
Day by Day 129
Day of Doom, The 13, 26, 102, 127, 179

Day of the Locust, The 99
De Crèvecouer, J. Hector St John 2, 134, 165, 227
De Forest, John William 47
De Tocqueville, Alexis 60, 75, 107
Dead Lecturer, The 21
Dead Zone, The 119
Dean's December, The 24
Death Comes for the Archbishop 38
Death in the Afternoon 99
Death of a Salesman 138
Death of Jim Loney, The 151
Declaration of Independence 58, 72, 85, 204
Declaration of Sentiments 198–9
Deer Park, The 100
Deerslayer, The 123
Deford, Frank 212
Delicacy and Strength of Lace, The 201
DeLillo, Don 48, **59**, 118, 211, 212
Democracy (Adams) 60, 90
Democracy (Didion) 60
Democracy in America 60, **60**, 75
Des Imagistes 106
Desire Under the Elms 161
Desperation 119
Dessa Rose 226
Diamond Cutters and Other Poems, The 188
Dick, Philip K. 195
Dickey, James 95, 211
Dickinson, Emily 11, 12, **62–3**, 93, 103, 181, 186, 190, 223
Dickinson, John 222
'Diddling Considered as One of the Exact Sciences' 50
Didion, Joan 3, 60, 99, 230
Disenchanted, The 99
Dispatches 230
Dispossessed, The (Le Guin) 194, 227–8
Diving into the Wreck: Poems 1971–1972 189
'Divinity School Address, The' 12
Dixon, Thomas 121, 185, 208
Do Androids Dream of Electric Sheep? 195
Doctorow, E. L. 19, 26, 48, 61, 92, 115, 157, 184, 191, 196, 218, 237
Dodge, Mary Mapes 43
Dolores Claiborne 119
Dolphin, The 129
Donleavy, J. P. 104
Doolittle, Hilda (H. D.) 86, 106, 144, 171
Dos Passos, John 61, 73, 108, 176, 177, 192, 229, 233, 243
Double Dream of Spring, The 15
Double Indemnity 39
Douglas, Lloyd C. 26

Douglass, Frederick 2, 58, **66**, 117, 125, 130, 147–148, 195, 201–2, 204, 210
Dove, Rita 6, 170
Draft of XVI Cantos, A 36
Dream of a Common Language: Poems 1974–1977, The 189
Dream Songs, The 69, 74, 127, 139
Dream Team, The 212
Dreamcatcher 119
Dreaming Emmett 221
Dred: A Tale of the Great Dismal Swamp 2, 148, 215
Dreiser, Theodore 40, **67**, 99, 152, 153, 157, 177, 185, 193, 206
Drinking Life, A 8
Drum-Taps 47, 239
Dubin's Lives 131
DuBois, W. E. B. 5, 56, 65, **68**, 71, 117, 147, 196, 210, 217, 224
Duck Variations 131
Dunbar, Alice Nelson 56
Dunbar, Paul Lawrence 5
Duncan, Robert 30
Dune 195
Dunne, Finley Peter 104
Dust Tracks on a Road 19, 105
Duston, Hannah 37
Dutch 158
Dutchman 21, 22
Duyckinck, Evert 246
Duyckinck, George 246
Dwight, Timothy 50, 51, 74
Dylan, Bob 14, 21, 46, 57, 163, 236

Earthsea Quartet 43
Eastman, Charles Alexander 150
Eat a Bowl of Tea 17
Edgar Huntly 34
'Editha' 210
Education of Henry Adams, The 47
Edwards, Jonathan 13, 19, 94, 179
'Efforts of Affection' 28
Eggers, Dave 19
Ehrhart, W. D. 229
Elijah Visible 101
Eliot, T. S. 63, **69–70**, 77, 86, 94, 107, 126, 128, 137, 143, 144, 156, 157, 171, 172, 177, 181, 234, 243
Ellis, Edward S. 64
Ellison, Harlan 195
Ellison, Ralph 6, 9, 14, 26, 31, **70–1**, 76, 79, 83, 95, 108–109, 113, 114, 140, 141, 164, 198, 202, 224
Ellroy, James 57, 62, 100, 118, 157
Elsie Venner 33

Emerson, Ralph Waldo 4, 10, 11, 18, 33, 63, **71–2**,
    75, 76, 89, 91, 98, 116–17, 124, 130, 137, 158,
    186, 188, 190, 193, 198, 205, 220, 222, 223, 227,
    239
'Emmett Till' 221
Emperor Jones, The 96, 161
End of the Road, The 76
End Zone 59, 212
Enormous Room, The 243
Epic of the Wheat 158
Equiano, Olaudah 5, 201, 204
Erdrich, Louise 11, 83, 131, 151, 200, 224
Essays (Emerson) 72
Estampas del valle 41–2
'Esthétique du Mal' 214
'Ethics of Living Jim Crow, an Autobiographical
    Sketch, The' 116
Eulogy on King Philip 119, 150
Eureka 170, 177
Europeans, The 111
Everybody's All-American 212
Everybody's Autobiography 213
'Everybody's Protest Novel' 20
Everything that Rises Must Converge 160
Executioner's Song, The 157

Fable, A 78, 243
'Facts in the case of M Valdemar, The' 136
Fahrenheit 451 195, 228
'Faithful Narrative of the Surprising Work of God,
    A' 94
Fall of America: Poems of These States, The 91
'Fall of the House of Usher, The' 166, 170
Family Reunion, The 70
Fanshawe 97
Farewell to Arms, A 98, 243
Farewell, My Lovely 39
Farmers' Daughters, The 241
Farrell, J. T. 61, 177
Fathers Playing Catch with Sons 212
Faulkner, William 3, 4, 8, 25, 37, 47, 50, 59, 61, 62,
    77, **77–9**, 93, 99, 102, 122, 144, 146, 157, 163,
    164, 165, 185, 186, 199, 200, 205, 206–7, 207,
    208, 209, 211, 215, 218, 229, 243
Fauset, Jessie Redmon 97
Fear of Flying 80
Federalist Papers, The 51
Female Man, The 195, 228
Feminine Mystique, The 80
Fences 7, 242
'Fenimore Cooper's Literary Offences' 53
Ferlinghetti, Lawrence 23, 102
Fern, Fanny 104

Ferro, Robert 231
Fifth Chinese Daughter 17, 107
Financier, The 67
Fire Next Time, The 21, 71, 156
'Fires' 199
Fireside Travels 81
Firestarter 119
First Settlers of Virginia, The 169
Fisher, Vardis 65
Fitzgerald, F. Scott 4, 8, 9, **81–2**, 94–95, 98, 99, 100,
    114, 128, 144, 154, 165, 190, 193, 197, 205, 211,
    213, 229, 243
Fitzgerald, Zelda 81–82
Fixer, The 131
Flags in the Dust 78
Fletcher, Curly 54
Fletcher, John Gould 7
Flight to Canada 202
Floating Opera, The 76
Flow Chart 15
Focus 138
For Lizzie and Harriet 129
For the Union Dead 129
'For the Union Dead' 69
42ⁿᵈ Parallel, The 108
For Whom the Bell Tolls 99
Forbes, Esther 43, 193
Ford, Richard 65, 126, 139, 212
Formal Elegy 118
Foundation 195
Four Quartets 70
Four Saints in Three Acts 213
France and England in North America 87
'Frankie and Johnny' 21
Franklin Evans 219, 238
Franklin, Benjamin 2, 10, 19, 58, 73, **85–6**, 103, 184,
    188, 216
Franny and Zooey 156
Freeman, Mary Wilkins 126, 193
French, Marilyn 80
Freneau, Philip 93
Friedan, Betty 80
From Here to Eternity 244
From Sand Creek 151
From the Deep Woods to Civilization 150
From the Mixed-Up Files of Mrs. Basil E. Frankweiler
    43
Frost, Robert, 26, 28, 86, **88–9**, 125, 127, 143, 144,
    171, 173, 174, 186
Fuller, Margaret 33, 62–3, 80, 222, 223

Gallagher, Tess 38
Gallery of Women, A 67

Garden of Eden, The 99
Gardens in the Dunes, The 201
Gardner, Erle Stanley 62, 178
Garland, Hamlin 87, 126, 174, 186, 210
Garrison, William Lloyd 1, 125, 205
Gass, William 139
Gaudier-Brzeska: A Memoir 173
Gearhart, Sally Miller 228
Geisel, Theodor (Dr Seuss) 43
Gellhorn, Martha 244
General History of Virginia, New England and the Summer Isles, The 113, 168
'Genius', The 67
'Gentle Boy, The' 184
Geographical History of America, The 213
Geography and Plays 213
Geography III 28
Geronimo: His Own Story 150
Gershwin, George 222
Gershwin, Ira 104
Get Shorty 100
Ghost Writer, The 191
Gibson, William 195
'Gift Outright, The' 88
Gilbert, Fabiola Cabeza de Baca 41
Gilchrist, Ellen 209
Gilded Age, The 50, 90, 225
Giles Covey, Yeoman 193
Gilman, Charlotte Perkins 77, 80, 93, 216, 227
Ginsberg Allen 23, 49, 69, 86, **90–1**, 102, 115
Gioia, Dana 155
Giovanni, Nikki 6, 29
Giovanni's Room 20
Girls on the Run 15
Glasgow, Ellen 186
Glass Menagerie, The 240
Glengarry Glen Ross 131
Go 23
Go Down, Moses 78, 200
Go Tell it on the Mountain 20
God's Mercy Surmounting Man's Cruelty 37
Godfather, The 26
Going After Cacciato 230
Going to the Territory 70
Gold, Michael 115
Golden Bowl, The 112
Goldman, Emma 12, 126
Gone to Soldiers 101
Gone with the Wind 26, 47, 122, 166, 185, 205, 208
Good Man is Hard to Find, A 160
Goodbye Columbus 191
Goodman, Paul 12
Graham, Jorie 69, 157

Grapes of Wrath, The 61, 73
Gravity's Rainbow 182, 195
Gray, Thomas R. 148
Great American Novel, The 241
Great Gatsby, The 9, 81–2, **94–5**, 165, 176
Great Jones Street 59
Green Hills of Africa 99
Green, Anna Katharine 61
Gregory, Dick 46, 104–105
Grey, Zane 26, 54, 145, 236
Grimké, Sarah Moore 2, 80, 205
Grisham, John 26
Grumley, Michael 231
Guide to Kulchur 173
Guterson, David 126
Guthrie, Woody 21
Guy Domville 112

Hagedorn, Jessica 18
Hairy Ape, The 161
Hale, Lucretia 43
Hale, Sarah J. 91, 166, 207
Haley, Alex 6, 19, 202
Haliburton, T. C. 103
Hall, Donald 212
Hamilton, Alexander 51, 79
Hamilton, Virginia 43
'Hamlet and His Problems' 70
Hamlet, The 50, 78
Hammett, Dashiell 62, 178
Hammill, Pete 8
Hans Brinker 43
Hansberry, Lorraine 6
Hanson, Elizabeth 37
'Hard Rain's A-Gonna Fall, A' 57
Harjo, Joy 151, 177
Harmonium 213
Harper, Frances E. W. 2, 164, 204, 219
Harper, Michael 6
Harris, George W. 103–104, 218
Harris, Joel Chandler 43, 166
Harris, Mark 74
Harte, Bret 18, 92, 104, 126, 166
Haunting of Hill House, The 93
Hawthorne (James) 112
'Hawthorne and His Mosses' 98, 246
Hawthorne, Nathaniel 4, 11, 33, 34, 93, **97–8**, 102, 103, 107, 121, 130, 135, 136, 142, 181, 184, 186, 189, 193, 194, 200, 222, 223, 228
Hay, John 166
Hear that Train Blow 197
Heart's Needle 49
Heartbreaking Work of Staggering Genius, A 19

Hecht, Anthony 69, 125, 244
Heinlein, Robert A. 178, 195
Hejinian, Lyn 122
Heller, Joseph 3, 26, 104, 115, 116, 244
Hellman, Lillian 115
Hemingway, Ernest 3, 4, 8, 26, 38, 65, **98–9,**
    127–128, 139, 143, 144, 153, 157, 165, 197, 200,
    211, 213, 229, 243
Henderson the Rain King 24
Henry, Patrick 51
Henry. O. 8
Henson, Lance 151
Her Blue Body Everything We Know 232
Herbert, Frank 195
Herland 227
'Heroic Slave, The' 66
Herr, Michael 230
Herrick, Robert 146
Hersey, John 156, 157, 244
Hersh, Seymour M. 230
Herzog 24
Higginson, Thomas Wentworth 18, 47, 148
High Window, The 39
Hildreth, Richard 204
Hill, Joe 118
Himes, Chester B. 62, 141
Hinojosa, Rolando 41
Hiroshima 156, 157, 244
Historie of Travaile into Virginia Britannia, The 168
History 127, 129
History of New York by Diedrich Knickerbocker, A
    109
History of Plymouth Plantation 168
Hogan, Linda 151
Holleran, Andrew 231
Holley, Marietta 104
Hollywood 100
Hollywood Nocturnes 100
Holmes, John Clellon 23
Holmes, Oliver Wendell 12, 18, 33, 81, 193, 234
Holocaust 101
Homage to Mistress Bradstreet 32
Homicide 132
Hondo 236
hooks, bell 7, 81
Hotel Lautréamont 15
House Behind the Cedars, The 164
House Made of Dawn 151, 229
House of Games 50, 131
House of the Seven Gables 98, 189
House on Mango Street, The 42
Houseboat Days 15
'How it Feels to be Colored Me' 105

Howe, Susan 122
Howells, William Dean 18, 90, 97, 153, 184, 210,
    227
Howl and Other Poems 90
'Howl' 90, **102–3**
'Hugh Selwyn Mauberley' 172, 243
Hughes, Langston 5, 6, 31, 56, 86, 96–7, 104, 105,
    164, 197
Human Stain, The 164, 191
Humboldt's Gift 24
Humiliations Followed by Deliverances 37
Humishuma/Christine Quintasket/Mourning Dove
    150
Hunger of Memory 42
Hungry Hearts 115
Hurston, Zora Neale 5, 19, 31, 79, 83, 97, 104, **105,**
    162, 164, 208, 233
Hutchinson, Anne 12–13

I Don't Need You Any More 139
I Have a Dream 45, 118
I Have No Mouth and I Must Scream 195
I Know Why the Caged Bird Sings 19
I Love Myself When I am Laughing 105
I Married a Communist 134, 191
I Wanted to Write a Poem 241
I, Robot 195
I'll Take my Stand 7
Iceman Cometh, The 161
'Ichabod' 48
Ideas of Order 213
Idiots First 131
If He Hollers Let Him Go 141
If I Die in a Combat Zone 230
Imitations 129
'Imp of the Perverse, The' 166
Imported Bridegroom and Other Stories of the New
    York Ghetto, The 114
'In A Station of the Metro' 106, 171
In Cold Blood 157
In Country 229
In His Steps 26
In Our Time 98, 200, 243
In Search of Our Mothers' Gardens 232, 233
In the American Grain 241
In the Money 241
In the Spirit of Crazy Horse 11
Incident at Vichy 138
Incidents in the Life of a Slave Girl 37, 90, 110–11,
    117, 148, 202
Indian Boyhood 150
'Indian Burying Ground, The' 93
Indian Killer 151

Indian Princess, The 169
Ingraham, Prentiss 64
Inherit the Wind 196
Innocents Abroad, The 104, 225
Insomnia 119
Interesting Narrative of Olaudah Equiano, The 201
Into the Valley 244
Intruder in the Dust 59, 62, 78, 164, 208
Invisible Man 9, 31, 70, 71, 76, 83, 95, **108–9**, 141,
    202, 224
Iola Leroy 164
Iron Heel, The 177, 194, 227, 228
Irving, John 104
Irving, Washington 26, 53, 93, 103, **109–10**, 121,
    174, 200, 218, 246
Islands in the Stream 99
Islas, Arturo 42
Israel Potter 182, 188, 229
It 119
Ivory Tower, The 112

Jackson, Charles 8
Jackson, Shirley 93, 102, 104, 156
Jacobs, Harriet 2, 37, 90, **110–11**, 117, 148, 202,
    204
James, Alice 111
James, Henry 4, 18, 19, 22, 93, 97, 102, 107, **111–12**,
    144, 154, 158, 193, 197, 200
James, William 111, 173, 215
Jarrell, Randall 49, 100, 125, 163, 211, 244
Jay, John 79
Jazz 146
Jeffers, Robinson 186
Jefferson, Thomas 10, 51, 58, 73, 140, 142, 165, 207,
    227
Jennie Gerhardt 67
Jewett, Sarah Orne 18, 126
Jews Without Money 115
Joe Turner's Come and Gone 242
John Barleycorn 8, 219
'John Brown of Osawatomie' 117
'John Brown' 117
John Brown's Body 47, 117
Johnny Panic and the Bible of Dreams 167
Johnson, Charles R. 141, 164, 202
Johnson, Helene 97
Johnson, James Weldon 5, 97, 164
Johnson, Susannah 37
Jonah's Gourd Vine 105
Jones, James 26, 244
Jong, Erica 80, 115
Jordan, June 6, 29
Journal of Arthur Gordon Pym, The 170

Journal of Julius Rodman, The 174
Journals of Sylvia Plath, The 67
Joy Luck Club, The 17
Judson, Edward Z. C. 64
Juneteenth 71, 164
Jungle, The 13, 146
'Justice Denied in Massachusetts' 192
'Justice, A' 207

Kaddish and other Poems 91
'Kaddish' 69, 91
Kalki 195
Kees, Weldon 79
Keillor, Garrison 104, 165
Kemble, Fanny 166
Kennedy, Adrienne 76
Kennedy, John Pendleton 166, 207
Kennedy, Robert F. 57
Kennedy, William 61, 211, 218
Kern, Jerome 222
Kerouac, Jack 23, 90, 163
Key to Uncle Tom's Cabin, A 2, 215
Key, Francis Scott 234
Kilmer, Joyce 137
Kincaid, Jamaica 6
King, Grace Elizabeth 56
King, Martin Luther Jr 45, 118
King, Stephen 14, 26, 93, 102, **119**
'Kingfishers, The' 30
Kingston, Maxine Hong 17, 19, 44, 107, **120**, 162,
    242
Kirkland, Caroline Stansbury 226
Kiskaddon, Bruce 54
Knife of the Times, The 241
Knight, Etheridge 6, 29
Ko; or, a Season on Earth 212
Koch, Kenneth 156, 177, 211, 212
Konigsburg, E. L. 43
Kopit, Arthur 3, 100
Kora in Hell 241
Kovic, Ron 229
Krumgold, Joseph 43
Kunitz, Stanley 170

L. A. Confidential 100
L'Amour, Louis 26, 54, 236
Lady Byron Vindicated 215
Lady in the Lake, The 39
Laguna Woman 201
Lamplighter, The 26
Land of Unlikeness 128
Lanier, Sidney 47
Lardner, Ring 104, 211

Larsen, Nella 5, 95, 97, 164
'Last Days of John Brown, The' 117
Last of the Menu Girls, The 41
Last of the Mohicans, The 37, 87, 123, 141, 218
'Last Quatrain of the Ballad of Emmett Till, The'
   21, 221
Last Tycoon, The 82, 89
Last Yankee, The 139
'Laus Deo!' 220
Lawrence, Jerome 196
Lazarus, Emma 114
Le Guin, Ursula 43, 77, 194, 195, 228
Leather-Stocking Tales 42, 52, 64, 74, 87, **122–3**,
   236
Leavenworth Case, The 61
Leaves of Grass 73, **123–4**, 127, 238–239
Lectures in America 213
Lee, Li-Young 17
Lee, Manfred B. 62
Lee, Robert E. 196
Left Hand of Darkness, The 195
'Legend of Sleepy Hollow, The' 109
Legs 218
Leithauser, Brad 155
Leonard, Elmore 62, 100, 210
Leopard's Spots, The 121, 185
LeRoi Jones, Everett: see Baraka, Imamu Amiri
Letter from Birmingham Jail 118
Letters (Barth) 75
Letters from a Farmer in Pennsylvania 222
Letters from an American Farmer 2, 165
Letters Home 167
Letters of Ezra Pound, The 173
Letters on the Equality of the Sexes 80
Letting Go 191
Levertov, Denise 30, 230
Levitation: Five Fictions 101
Lewis, Sinclair 87, 153, 157, 174, 185, 186 193
Lewis, Wyndham 231
Libra 59, 118
Liebling, A. J. 212
Life and Adventures of Joaquin Murieta, The 150
Life and Times of Frederick Douglass 66
Life in the Iron Mills 18,
Life in the Theatre, A 131
Life of Black Hawk, The 150
Life of George Washington 109
Life of Phineas T. Barnum 22, 50
Life on the Mississippi 224
Life Studies 49, 69, **125**, 128–9
'Ligeia' 170
Light in August 78, 122, 164
Light of the Western Stars 54, 236

Lindsay, Vachel 169
Lionel Lincoln 129, 188
'Literati of New York City' 121
Little Big Man 237
Little House on the Prairie series 43, 101
Little Lord Fauntleroy 43
Little Princess, A 43
Little Sister, The 39, 100
Little Women 43, 47
Locke, Alain 96
Log of a Cowboy, The 54
London, Jack 8, 92, 153, 177, 193, 194, 200, 206,
   211, 219, 227
Long Day's Journey Into Night 8, **126–7**, 161
Long Goodbye, The 39
Long Tomorrow, The 14
Longfellow, Henry Wadsworth 18, 21, 33, 47, 74, 81,
   91, 121, 127, 158, 168, 182, 188, 193, 226
Longstreet, Augustus 103, 218
Looking Backward: 2000–1887 227
Loos, Anita 104
Lord Weary's Castle 128
Lorde, Audre 7, 81
Losses 244
Lost in the Funhouse 136
Lost Lady, A 38
Lost Weekend, The 8
Lost World, The 100
'Lottery, The' 156
Love in the Ruins 14
Love Medicine 11, 151, 200
'Love Song of J. Alfred Prufrock, The' 70, 171
Lovecraft, H. P. 93, 102
Lowell, Amy 86, 106, 107, 125, 128, 177
Lowell, James Russell 18, 33, 47, 81, 103, 127, 128,
   137, 158, 182, 193, 204, 246
Lowell, Robert 14, 28, 49, 69, 125, 127, **128–9**, 163
Lucy Church Amiably, 188–9, 213
Lucy Gayheart 38
Lume Spento, A 172
Lustra 172

M'Fingal, A Modern Epic 51
Ma Rainey's Black Bottom 242
MacDonald, Betty 104
MacDonald, Dwight 163
Madhubuti, Haki R. 29
Madison, James 51, 79
Maggie, A Girl of the Streets 55, 56, 152–3
Magic Barrel, The 131
Magnalia Christi Americana 179
Mailer, Norman 26, 76, 100, 115, 118, 157, 163, 211,
   230, 244

Make it New 173
Making Face/Making Soul 42
Making of Americans, The 213
Malaeska: The Indian Wife of the White Hunter 64
Malamud, Bernard 100, 105, 115, **131**, 194, 211, 212
Malatesta Cantos 36
Mamet, David 50, 99, 115, **131–2**
'Man Who Was Almost A Man, The' 95
'Man with the Blue Guitar, The' 214
Man with the Blue Guitar, The 213
Mansion, The 50, 78, 207
Mao II 59
Marble Faun, The (Faulkner) 78
Marble Faun, The (Hawthorne) 98
Mardi 58, 134–5
Marking Time 229
Marquis, Don 104
Martian Chronicles, The 195
Martin, Ann M. 44
Mason & Dixon 182
Mason, Bobbie Ann 157, 208, 229
Masters, Edgar Lee 186
Mather, Cotton 32, 37, 179, 193
Matthiessen, Peter 11, 163
Maud Martha 34
Maum Guinea, and Her Plantation 'Children' 64
Maximus Poems, The 74, 127
May-Day 72
McBain, Ed 62
McCarthy, Mary 3, 230
McCullers, Carson 21, 186, 207, 208, 209
McDonald, John D. 178
McGinnins, Joe 212
McKay, Claude 5, 79, 97
McMurtry, Larry 237
McNickle, D'Arcy 150
McTeague 153, 158
Means, Russell 11
'Meditations' (Bradstreet) 32
Melville, Herman 4, 11, 12, 14, 22, 26, 37, 47, 50, 58,
    90, 97, 98, 103, 107, 117, 127, **134–6**, 137, 165,
    181, 182, 184, 186, 188, 189, 190, 200, 204, 219,
    223, 228, 229, 233, 246
Memoirs (Tennessee Williams) 240
Memoirs of Carwin the Biloquist 34
Memory of Two Mondays, A 138
Mencken, H. L. 104, 205
Meridian 46, 118, 141, 209, 232
Merrill, James 14, 69, 77, 127, 236
'Mesmeric Revelation' 136
Michener, James 26
Middle Passage 202
Middle Years, The 112

Migrant Souls 42
Mila 18 100
Millay, Edna St Vincent 192
Miller, Arthur 56, 57, 61, 77, 100, 101, 115, 134,
    138–9, 193
Miller, Walter M. 14, 195
Millett, Kate 80
Milosz, Czeslaw 157
Mind Breaths 91
Minister's Wooing, The 215
Mirror for Witches, A 193
Misery 119
Misfits, The 138
'Misgivings' 204
Miss Ravenel's Conversion from Secession to Loyalty
    47
Mitchell, Isaac 93
Mitchell, Margaret 26, 47, 122, 166, 185, 205, 208
Mixquiahuala Letters, The 75
Moby-Dick 53, 73, 98, 135, **142–3**, 184
Momaday, N. Scott 83, 151, 162, 177, 229, 235–6
Monroe, Harriet 171
Moody, Anne 46, 221
Moon is Down, The 244
Moore, Marianne 28, 63, 144, 171, 211
Moraga, Cherríe 41, 42
More, Paul Elmer 156
Mori, Toshio 17
Morris, Edmund 158
Morrison, Toni 6, 25, 26, 31, 83, 114, 131, **145–6**,
    157, 162, 164, 196, 202, 205, 221, 224, 226
Mosley, Walter 62
Mosquitoes 78
Mother of Us All, The 213
Mothers: An American Saga of Courage, The 65
Mountain Interval 88
Mourning Becomes Electra 161
Mourning Dove/Humishuma/Christine Quintasket
    150
Moveable Feast, A 99
Moviegoer, The 76
Mr Sammler's Planet 24
Mules and Men 83, 105
Murayama, Milton 17
Murder in the Cathedral 70
'Murders in the Rue Morgue, The' 61, 170
Murray, Albert 114
Murrow, Edward R. 244
Music: Reflections on Jazz and Blues, The 21–2
My Ántonia 38
My Bondage and My Freedom 66
My Lady Pokahontas 169
Myra Breckinridge 100

Mysterious Stranger, The 225
'Mystery of Marie Rogêt, The' 170

Nabokov, Vladimir 19, 26, 104, 136, 156, 163, 171, 190, 228
Naked and the Dead, The 244
Names, The 59
Narration 213
'Narrative of a Noble Deliverance from Captivity' 37
Narrative of the Captivity of . . . Mary Rowlandson 37
Narrative of the Captivity of Mrs Johnson, A 37
Narrative of the Life of Frederick Douglass 66, **147–8**, 196, 201–2, 210
Nash, Ogden 104
'Nat Turner's Insurrection' 148
Nathan, George Jean 205
Native Son 6, 20, 141, **151–2**, 245
Natural, The 131, 212
Nature 72, 223
Naylor, Gloria 3, 6
Neal, Larry 29
Near the Ocean 129
Necessary Angel, The 213–14
Necessities of Life: Poems 1962–1965 188
Needful Things 119
'Negro Artist and the Racial Mountain, The' 6
Nemerov, Howard 170
Nest of Ninnies, A 16
Neuromancer 195
Never-Ending Wrong, The 192
'New Colossus, The' 114
New Cowboy Poetry 54
New England Primer 26, 43, **155**, 179
'New England Tragedies, The' 193
New Hampshire 88
New Negro, The 96
New World, The: An Epic Poem 74
Nick Carter stories 61, 64
Nick of the Woods 184
Niedecker, Lorine 159
Nigger 46
Nigger Heaven 96
Night in Acadie, A 44
Night of the Iguana, The 240
Night Shift 119
Nisei Daughter 17, 107, 244
No-No Boy 17, 107, 244
Nordan Lewis 221
Norris, Frank 13, 134, 153, **158**, 177, 185, 193, 206, 210, 211
North and South 28

North of Boston 88
Northwood 166
'Not Sacco and Vanzetti' 192
Not Under Forty 39
Notebook 129
Notebook 1967–68 129
Notes of a Son and Brother 112
Notes on the State of Virginia 140, 165
'Notes Towards a Supreme Fiction' 214
'Novel with a Purpose', The' 158

O Pioneers! 38
O'Brien, Fitz-James 47, 194
O'Brien, Tim 139, 229, 230
O'Connor, Flannery 160, 186, 200, 207, 208, 209
O'Hara, Frank 156
O'Hara, John 8, 157
O'Neill, Eugene 8, 77, 96, 126–127, 157, **161–2**, 205, 211 220
O'Rourke, P. J. 104
O'Ruddy, The 55
Oakes, Urian 69
Oates, Joyce Carol 93, 102, 157, 163, 212, 218
Obscure Destinies 38
Occom, Samson 149
Octopus, The 13, 153, 158
'Ode to the Confederate Dead' 47, 69
Odets, Clifford 61, 177
Of Woman Born: Motherhood as Experience and Institution 189
Oil! 218
Okada, John 17, 107, 244
Old Glory, The 129
'Old Ironsides' 234
Old Jules 174
Old Man and the Sea, The 99
Olds, Sharon 69
Oldtown Folks 215
Oleanna 131
Olsen, Tillie 61, 115
Olson, Charles 29, 74, 127
Omoo 134
'On Being Brought from Africa to America' 238
On Boxing 212
On Lies, Secrets and Silence 189
On the Road 23, 163
On the Slave Trade 2
Once 232
One Art 28
One of Ours 38
'Open Boat, The' 55, 56, 209
Operation Shylock 191
Oppen, George 159

Opus Posthumus 213
'Ordinary Evening in New Haven, An' 214
Oregon Trail, The 174
Ormond 34
Ortiz, Simon 151
Oswald's Tale 118, 157
Other Traditions 15–16
'Our Mother Pocahontas' 169
Our Nig 202, 204
Outcry, The 112
Outsider, The 76, 245
'Over-Soul, The' 223
Owen, Robert Dale 169
Ox-Bow Incident, The 130, 236
Oxherding Tale 141, 164, 202
Ozick, Cynthia 101, 115

Paine, Thomas 73
Paley, Grace 115
Paradise 146
Paredes, Américo 41
Paretsky, Sara 62
Parker, Dorothy 8, 99, 104, 156–7
Parker, Theodore 222
Parkman, Francis 87, 121, 158, 174, 193
Parley, Peter 43
Parts of a World 213
Passing 97, 164
'Passing' 164
Pat Hobby Stories 100
Paterson 74, 127, 241
Pathfinder, The 123
Patrimony 19, 191
Patten, William G. 64, 211
'Paul Revere's Ride' 188
Paulding, James Kirke 121
Penn, William 183
People of the Abyss, The 177
Percy, Walker 14, 76, 209
Perelman, Bob 122
Perelman, S. J. 104
Personae 172
Personal Narrative, A 19, 179
Personal Recollections of Joan of Arc 225
Peterkin Papers, The 43
Phillips, David Graham 146
'Philosophy of Composition, The' 170
Piano Lesson, The 242
Picano, Felice 231
Pictures from Brueghel 241
Pictures of Fidelman 131
Piercy, Marge 101, 194, 228
Pierre, or, The Ambiguities 135, 165, 246

Pike County Ballads 166
Pilot, The 188
Pinsky, Robert 127
Pioneers, The 123, 163
Pisan Cantos, The 31, 36, 172
Pistol, The 244
Pit, The 158
Planet News 91
Plath, Sylvia 14–15, 49, 100, **166–7**, 190, 191
Play it as it Lays 100
Playback 39
Players 59
Playing in the Dark 146
Pnin 156
Pocahontas: A Historical Drama 169
Pocahontas: Princess of Virginia 169
'Pocahontas' 169
Pocho 41
Poe, Edgar Allan 11, 14, 25, 34, 50, 61, 77, 91, 94,
    102, 107, 121, 136, 165–6, **169–70**, 174, 177,
    186, 189, 190, 193, 194, 200, 207, 219, 223, 226,
    228, 246
Poems (Eliot) 70
Poems (Emerson) 72
Poems on Various Subjects (Wheatley) 237–8
'Poet, The' 12, 86
'Poetic Principle, The' 170
Pollyana 43
Poodle Springs 39
Poor Richard's Almanac 85
Portable Faulkner, The 78
'Portent, The' 117
Porter, Cole 104, 222
Porter, Eleanor 43
Porter, Katherine Anne 192
Portillo-Trambley, Estela 42
Portnoy's Complaint 191
Portrait of a Lady, The 112
Possessing the Secret of Joy 232
Pound, Ezra 29, 31, 36–37, 70, 73, 86, 88, 98, 106,
    107, 126, 127, 128, 143, 144, 154, 171, **171–3**,
    181, 231, 234, 240, 243
Powell, Dawn 104
'Prague Orgy, The' 191
Prairie, The 123, 174
'Preacher and the Slave, The' 108
Precaution 52
Preface to a Twenty Volume Suicide Note 21
Price of the Ticket, The 20
Price, The 138
Princess Casamassima, The 112
Principles of Psychology 215
'Private History of a Campaign that Failed, The' 47

Professor's House, The 38
'Projective Verse' 29
Promised Land, The 115
Proulx, Annie 54, 126, 200, 211, 221
Prufrock and Other Observations 70
Public Burning, The 191
Pudd'nhead Wilson 3, 62, 153, 161, 164, 225
Purdy, James 93
'Purloined Letter, The' 170
Puzo, Mario 26
Pyle, Ernie 244
Pylon 78
Pynchon, Thomas 3, 14, 48, 77, 104, 136, 171,
    182–3, 195

'Quaker Graveyard in Nantucket, The' 69
Questions of Travel 28,
Quicksand 97
Quintasket, Christine/Mourning Dove/
    Humishuma 150

Rabe, David 229, 230
Ragged Dick 8
Ragtime 157, 184
Rain God, The 42
Raisin in the Sun, A 6
Rakosi, Carl 159
Ransom, John Crowe 7, 89, 118, 154
Ratner's Star 59
Ravelstein 24
'Raven, The' 170
Reality Sandwiches 91
Rebecca of Sunnybrook Farm 43
Rechy, John 42
Reckless Eyeballing 221
Recovery 8
Red Badge of Courage, The 47, 55, 56, 107
Red Record, A 130
'Red Wheelbarrow, The' 241
Redburn 135
Redding, J. Saunders 244
Reed, Ishmael 7, 105, 202, 221, 224
Rembrandt's Hat 131
Report from Part One 34
Report from Part Two 34
Representative Men 72
Requiem for a Nun 78
Reservation Blues 151
'Resistance to Civil Government' 137, 221
Revolt of the Cockroach People 42
'Revolutionary Romances' 188
Reznikoff, Charles 101, 115, 159
Rice, Allen Thorndike 158

Rice, Anne 26, 102
Rice, Elmer 77
Rich, Adrienne 81, 116, 171, **188–9**, 230
'Richard Wright's Blues' 31
Riders of the Purple Sage 145, 236
Ridge, John Rollin/Yellow Bird 150
Riding, Laura 89
'Rip Van Winkle' 109
Ripley, George 222
Rise of David Levinsky, The 107, 114
Rise of Silas Lapham, The 90
Rivera, Tomás 41
Rivers and Mountains 15
Road to Nirvana, The 100
Robber Bridegroom, The 21
Robbins, Harold 26
Robbins, Tom 104
Robe, The 26
Robinson, Edward Arlington 186
Roderick Hudson 111
Rodriguez, Richard 42
Roethke, Theodore 49
Roots 6
Rosen, Norma 100
Rosenbaum, Thane 101
Rosenfeld, Isaac 115
Rosten, Leo 105
Roth, Henry 115
Roth, Philip 19, 48, 100, 104, 115, 116, 134, 163,
    164, 165, **191**, 211
Roughing It 87, 92, 145, 225
Rowlandson, Mary 37, 119, 179
Rowson, Susanna 26
Rukeyser, Muriel 115, 197
Rumor of War, A 230
Running Dog 59
Runyon, Damon 104, 176, 210, 211
Russ, Joanna 77, 195, 228

Sabbath's Theater 191
Sacred Fount, The 112
Sacred Wood, The 70
'*Salem's Lot* 119
Salinger, J. D. 4, 26, 43, 116, 156, 244
Sanchez, Carol Lee 151
Sánchez, Ricardo 42
Sanchez, Sonia 6, 29
Sanctuary 37, 78
Sandburg, Carl 21, 86, 126, 169, 174, 186, 210
Sandoz, Marie 174
Sapphira and the Slave Girl 38–9
Saroyan, William 61
Sartoris 78

Save Me the Waltz 82
Scarborough, Dorothy 236
Scarlet Letter, The 98
Schaefer, Jack 236
School Days of an Indian Girl, The 19
Schulberg, Budd 99–100
Schuyler, James 16, 156
Schwartz, Delmore 24, 115, 163
Scottsboro Limited 197
Sea-Wolf, The 153
Second Hand Smoke 101
Secret Garden, The 43
Sedgwick, Catharine 91, 186
Seize the Day 24, 76
Selected Essays (Pound) 173
Selected Poems (Rich) 188
Selected Prose (Pound) 173
Self-Portrait in a Convex Mirror 15
'Self-Reliance' 12, 72, 198, 223
Sendak, Maurice 44
Sense of the Past, The 112
Sermon at the Execution of Moses Paul 149
Seven Guitars 242
*Several Poems Compiled with Great Variety of Wit
    and Learning* 32
Sewall, Samuel 1, 193
Sexton, Anne 49, 69
Sexual Perversity in Chicago 131
Sexual Politics 80
Shadow and Act 70
Shane 236
Shange, Ntozake 29, 76
Shapiro, Karl 115, 125, 244
Shaw, Irwin 26
Shawl, The (Mamet) 50,
Shawl, The (Ozick) 101
Sheldon, Charles 26
Shepard, Sam 100
Shining, The 119
'Significance of the Frontier in American History,
    The' 88
Sigourney, Lydia H. 169
Silko, Leslie Marmon 83, 151, 162, 171, 200, **201**,
    224, 229
Silliman, Ron 122
Simic, Charles 177
Simms, William Gilmore 47, 91, 166, 188, 204, 207,
    226, 246
'Simple Art of Murder, The' 39
Sinclair, Upton 13, 146, 153, 177, 192, 218
Singer, Isaac Bashevis 114, 157, 194
'Sinners in the Hands of an Angry God' 94
Sister Carrie 67

Sketch Book of Geoffrey Crayon, Gent, The 109
Slaughterhouse-Five 194, 244
Slave Songs of the United States 210
Slave, The 204
'Slavery in Massachusetts' 89–90, 221
Slow Learner 182
Small Boy and Others, A 19, 112
Smith, John 113, 168
Smith, Ormond G. 64
Smith, Rosamond 102
Smith, Seba 55, 246
Snapshots of a Daughter- Law 188
Snodgrass, W. D. 49
Snow White 156
'Snows of Kilimanjaro' 99
Snyder, Gary 23
Social Destiny of Man 84
Soldier's Pay 78, 229, 243
'Some Considerations on the Keeping of Negroes' 1
Some Fruits of Solitude 183
Some Imagist Poets 106
'Some Thoughts Concerning the Present Revival of
    Religion in New England' 94
Some Trees 15
Somebody in Boots 61
Son of the Forest, A 150
Sone, Monica 17, 107, 244
Song of Hiawatha, The 74
'Song of Myself' 74, 127
Song of Solomon 83, 146, 221
Song of the Lark 38
Song, Cathy 17
Songs from the Nursery 43
Songs of A Semite 114
Songs of the Cowboys 54
Sontag, Susan 163
Sophie's Choice 101
Sorensen, Virginia Eggertson 145
'Sot-Weed Factor, The' 103
Souls of Black Folk, The 65, 68, 210, 217
Sound and the Fury, The 78, **206–7**, 208, 215
Sovereignty and Goodness of God, The . . . see
    *Narrative of the Captivity of . . . Mary
    Rowlandson*
Spanish Prisoner, The 50, 132
Speak, Memory 19
Specimen Days 47
Speed-the-Plow 131
Spillane, Mickey 62, 178
Spires, Elizabeth 155
Sportswriter, The 212
Spring and All 240–1
Springsteen, Bruce 21, 163

Index of writers and works

Spy, The 52, 129
Stafford, Jean 8, 128
Stand, The 14, 119
Stanton, Elizabeth Cady 198, 216
Star Trek 87
Steel, Danielle 26
Steele, Timothy 155
Stein, Gertrude 19, 20, 98, 116, 126, 127–8, 143, 144, 177, **212–13**
Steinbeck, John 8, 26, 61, 73, 153, 157, 163, 177, 186, 243
Stephens, Ann 64
Stevens, Wallace 4, 12, 106, 126, 143, 144, 163, 165, 171, 174, 190, **213–14**
Stewart, Maria W. 205
Sticks and Bones 229
Stoic, The 67
Stone, John Augustus 53
Stories of Bernard Malamud, The 131
Story of a Bad Boy, The 43
Storyteller 151, 201
Stout, Rex 62
Stowe, Harriet Beecher 2, 11, 18, 26, 42, 53, 90, 91, 126, 148, 164, 166, 193, 202, 204, **214–15**, 226
Strachey, William 168
Strand, Mark 170
Strange Interlude 161
Stranger in a Strange Land 195
'Stranger in the Village' 21
Streamers 230
Street in Bronzeville, A 33
Streetcar Named Desire, A 240
Studs Lonigan Trilogy 61
Styron, William 101, 148, 163
Suddenly Last Summer 240
Sula 146
Sun Also Rises, The 8, 98–9, 128, 229
'Sunday Morning' 171
Surrounded, The 150
Susann, Jacqueline 26
Swallow Barn 166
Sweet Bird of Youth 240
System of Dante's Hell, The 22

'Talented Tenth, The' 217
Tan, Amy 17
Tar Baby 146
Tate, Allen 7, 47, 69, 89, 154, 199, 208
Tate, James 77, 171
Tattered Coat upon a Stick, A 192
Taylor, Bayard 166
Taylor, Edward 137, 179
Tell My Horse 105

Temple of My Familiar, The 232
Ten Nights in a Barroom and What I Saw There 8, 219
Tender Buttons 213
Tender is the Night 8, 82
Tennis Court Oath, The 15
Tenth Muse Lately Sprung Up in America, The 32
Terkel, Studs 61, 139
Terry, Lucy 5
'Thanatopsis' 93
'That Evening Sun' 207
Theater Essays 139
Theft, A 24
Their Eyes were Watching God 83, 97, 105
Thin Red Line, The 244
Things Change 132
Things They Carried, The 229, 230
Third Life of Grange Copeland, The 232
Thirteen Days 57
This Bridge Called my Back 42
This Side of Paradise 81, 128
Thompson, Jim 178
Thoreau, Henry David 4, 12, 63, 72, 89–90, 117, 125, 130, 137, 182, 186, 190, 205, **220–1**, 222, 223, 226, 227, 232, 246
Thorpe, Thomas B. 46, 103, 218
Three Lives 213
Three Poems 15, 177
Three Soldiers 243
Thrones Cantos 36
Through the Eye of the Needle 227
Thurber, James 104, 156, 200
Tiger-Lilies 47
Timebends 139
Timrod, Henry 47
Titan, The 67
Tom Sawyer, Detective 62
Tompson, Benjamin 69
Toomer, Jean 5, 56, 97, 183
Touching Evil 100
Tour on the Prairies, A 109, 174
Town, The 50, 78
Tracks 151
'Tradition and the Individual Talent' 70
Transport to Summer 213
Traveller from Altruria, A 227
Travels 165, 183
Trilling, Lionel 100
Tripmaster Monkey: His Fake Book 120
Troll Garden, The 38
Trumbull, John 50, 51
Truth, Sojourner 2
'Turn of the Screw, The' 112

Turner, Frederick 74
Turner, Frederick Jackson 87, 88
Twain Mark 3, 14, 18, 22, 26, 43, 47, 50, 53, 54, 62,
    87, 90, 92, 93–4, 97, 104, 126, 130, 145, 153, 158,
    161, 164, 166, 190, 205, 210, 218, **224–6**, 246
Twelve Million Black Voices 95
'Twentieth Century Fiction and the Black Mask of
    Humanity' 198
Twice-Told Tales 200
Two Trains Running 242
Tyler, Royall 103, 246
Typee 37, 134

U. S. A. 73
Uncle Remus stories 43
Uncle Tom's Cabin 2, 26, 53, 90, 164, 166, 202, 204,
    214, 215, 226
Uncle Tom's Children 42, 200, 245
Underworld 59
'United States of Lyncherdom, The' 130
Universal Baseball Association 212
Unvanquished, The 47, 78, 185, 200
Up from Slavery 19, 121, 185, 202
Updike, John 3, 57, 104, 118, 157, 211
Uris, Leon 100

V. 182
Valdez, Luis 41
Valley of the Dolls 26
Van Dine, S. S. 62
Van Vechten, Carl 96
Vandover and the Brute 153, 158
Vanishing American, The 236
Victim, The 24, 76
Victor, Frances Auretta Fuller 64
Victor, Metta Victoria Fuller 64
Vidal, Gore 100, 195
View from the Bridge, A 138
Village, The 132
Villareal, José Antonio 41
Vineland 182
Violent Bear It Away, The 160
Viramontes, Helena Maria 42
Virginian, The 54, 236
Vision of Columbus, The 50–1, 74
Vizenor, Gerald 149, 151, 224
V-Letter and Other Poems 244
Vocation and a Voice, A 44
Vollman, William T. 169
Vonnegut, Kurt 3, 14, 26, 77, 104, 136, 194, 229, 244

Wake Up, Stupid 75
Wakefulness 15

Walden, or Life in the Woods 221, 223, **232**
Waldron, William Watson 169
Walker, Alice 3, 6, 26, 31, 46, 75, 81, 105, 118, 141,
    164, 200, 209, 228, **232–3**
Walker, David 2, 204
Walker, Margaret 46, 79, 208
'Walking' 221
Wallace, Irving 26
Wallace, Lew 26, 47
Wanderground, The 228
War and Remembrance 244
War is Kind 55
Ward, Artemus 54, 104
Warner, Charles Dudley 90, 225
Warner, Susan 26, 43, 186
Warren, Robert Penn 7, 89, 154, 170, 208, 209
Wars I Have Seen 213, 244
Washington Square 111, 112
Washington, Booker T. 19, 68, 71, 109, 121, 185,
    202, 217, 224
Waste Land, The 63, 70, 77, 94, 172, **234**, 243
Wave, A 15
Way Forward is with a Broken Heart, The, 232
Way to Rainy Mountain, The 151, **235–6**
We Fed them Cactus 41
Weary's Blues 97
Wedge, The 241
Week on the Concord and Merrimack Rivers, A 221
Welch, James 151
Welcome to Hard Times 92, 237
Weld, Angelina Emily Grimké 2, 205
Wells-Barnett, Ida B. 130
Welty, Eudora 21, 157, 186, 200, 207, 208, 209
Wept of Wish-ton-Wish, The 119
West, Nathanael 3, 9, 14, 61, 104, 116
Whalen, Philip 23
Wharton, Edith 93, 102, 111, 131, 197, 200, 243
What I Lived For 218
*What is Found There: Notebooks on Poetry and
    Politics* 189
What Katy Did 43
What Maisie Knew 112
What Makes Sammy Run? 99
'What to the Slave is the Fourth of July?' 58, 204
What We Talk About When We Talk About Love 38
Wheatley, Phillis 5, 204, **237–8**
Wheeler, Edward L. 64
When Lilacs last in the Dooryard Bloom'd' 69
When She Was Good 191
Where I'm Calling From 38
Where White Men Fear to Tread 11
Whitcher, Frances 104
White Fang 92, 153

White Mule 241
'White Negro, The' 76
White Noise 59
White Shroud 91
White, E. B. 44, 104
White, Edmund 214, 231
White-Jacket 135
Whitfield, James M. 204
Whitlock, Brand 146
Whitman, Walt 4, 11, 12, 47, 49, 60, 69, 72, 73, 74, 75, 86, 90, 91, 102, 123–4, 127, 158, 165–6, 183, 186, 190, 219, 227, **238–40**, 241
Whitmore, George 231
Whitney, Phyllis Ayame 178
Whittier, John Greenleaf 2, 21, 47, 48, 81, 87, 117, 121, 125, 127, 183, 204, 220
Wide, Wide World, The 26, 43
Wideman, John Edgar 6, 200
Wieland 34
Wiggin, Kate Douglas 43
Wigglesworth, Michael 13, 26, 102, 127, 179
Wilbur, Richard 170
Wild Palms, The 78
Wilder, Laura Ingalls 43, 101
Wilder, Thornton 77
Will You Please Be Quiet, Please? 38
'William Wilson' 170
Williams, Sherley Anne 226
Williams, Tennessee 154, 186, 207, 209, **240**
Williams, William Carlos 4, 29, 69, 74, 77, 86, 91, 102, 106, 125, 126, 127, 139, 143, 144, 154, 159, 165, 171, 172, 174, 181, **240–1**
Wilson, August 6, 7, **241–2**
Wilson, Harriet E. 2, 202, 204
Wilson, Lanford 76
Wind, The 236
Winds of War, The 244
Winesburg, Ohio 200
Wings of the Dove, The 112
Winter in the Blood 151
Winter Trees 167
Winterset 192
Winthrop, John 132, 133
Wise Blood 160
Wister, Owen 54, 236
With His Pistol in His Hand 41

Wolf Whistle 221
Wolfe, George C. 139
Wolfe, Thomas 197, 209, 211
Wolfe, Tom 230, 233
Wolff, Tobias 65
Woman in the Nineteenth Century 80
Woman on the Edge of Time 194, 228
Woman Warrior, The 17, 19, 107, 120, **242**
Woman Who Owned the Shadows, The 151
Women and Economics 80
Women's Room, The 80
Wonderful Wizard of Oz, The 43
Wonders of the Invisible World, The 193
Wong, Jade Snow 17, 107
Woodcraft 166
Woods, The 131
Woodworth, Samuel 53
Woolman, John 1
Woolson, Constance Fenimore 47
World Doesn't End, The 177
World's Fair 19
Wouk, Herman 26, 244
Wounds in the Rain 55
Wright, James 201, 211
Wright, Richard 6, 19, 20, 26, 31, 61, 76, 79, 95, 116, 141, 151–2, 177, 199, 200, 202, 208, **245**
Wyandotté 129

X, Malcolm 19, 29, 118, 202

y no se lo tragó la tierra 41
Yamamoto, Hisange 17
Yamauchi, Wakako 17
Yellow Bird/ John Rollin Ridge 150
'Yellow Wallpaper, The' 93
Yellow Woman 201
Yerby, Frank 79
Yezierska, Anzia 19, 107, 114, 115
Yokohama, California 17
Your Name Here 15
Youth and the Bright Medusa 38

Zoot Suit 41
Zuckerman Bound 191
Zuckerman Unbound 191
Zukofsky, Louis 115, 127, 159